Contents

Publisher—Carl L. Weschcke; Managing Editor—Robert K. Anderson; Contributing Editor—Marylee Satren; Astrological computations and tables—Marylee Satren; Associate Editor—Jon Jackoway; Advertising—Pamela Teply; Typesetters—Larry Craig, Nancy Hamby, Arne Shulstad; Keyliner—Jackie Urbanovic; Cover art—design by Lynette Arndt Schmidt and photograph by Peter B. Weller. The Moon Sign Book is published annually by Llewellyn Publications, Box 3383, St. Paul, MN 55165. Opinions expressed by contributing authors are not necessarily those of the publisher. Advertisers take full responsibility for the content of their advertising. No claims of supernatural powers are made for any of the items, books, or articles in this publication. Descriptions of books are based on the author's claims.

1977 Calendar

January
```
                  1
 2  3  4  5  6  7  8
 9 10 11 12 13 14 15
16 17 18 19 20 21 22
23 24 25 26 27 28 29
30 31
```

February
```
       1  2  3  4  5
 6  7  8  9 10 11 12
13 14 15 16 17 18 19
20 21 22 23 24 25 26
27 28
```

March
```
    1  2  3  4  5
 6  7  8  9 10 11 12
13 14 15 16 17 18 19
20 21 22 23 24 25 26
27 28 29 30 31
```

April
```
                1  2
 3  4  5  6  7  8  9
10 11 12 13 14 15 16
17 18 19 20 21 22 23
24 25 26 27 28 29 30
```

May
```
 1  2  3  4  5  6  7
 8  9 10 11 12 13 14
15 16 17 18 19 20 21
22 23 24 25 26 27 28
29 30 31
```

June
```
          1  2  3  4
 5  6  7  8  9 10 11
12 13 14 15 16 17 18
19 20 21 22 23 24 25
26 27 28 29 30
```

July
```
                1  2
 3  4  5  6  7  8  9
10 11 12 13 14 15 16
17 18 19 20 21 22 23
24 25 26 27 28 29 30
31
```

August
```
    1  2  3  4  5  6
 7  8  9 10 11 12 13
14 15 16 17 18 19 20
21 22 23 24 25 26 27
28 29 30 31
```

September
```
             1  2  3
 4  5  6  7  8  9 10
11 12 13 14 15 16 17
18 19 20 21 22 23 24
25 26 27 28 29 30
```

October
```
                   1
 2  3  4  5  6  7  8
 9 10 11 12 13 14 15
16 17 18 19 20 21 22
23 24 25 26 27 28 29
30 31
```

November
```
       1  2  3  4  5
 6  7  8  9 10 11 12
13 14 15 16 17 18 19
20 21 22 23 24 25 26
27 28 29 30
```

December
```
             1  2  3
 4  5  6  7  8  9 10
11 12 13 14 15 16 17
18 19 20 21 22 23 24
25 26 27 28 29 30 31
```

Fill out this handy order blank to subscribe to the Moon Sign Book and Astrological Calendar!

Llewellyn Publications
Box 3383-MSB
St. Paul, Minn. 55165

I have enclosed a check or money order for $ _____
Please send me the following:

☐ Four-year subscription to the *Moon Sign Book*, $8.00
☐ Four-year subscription to the *Moon Sign Book* and the
                                        Astrological Calendar, $12.00
  Start my subscription with the _____ issue.

☐ One copy of the 1978 *Moon Sign Book*, $2.95
☐ One copy of the 1978 *Astrological Calendar*, $2.00

Name _____

Address _____

City _____

State _____ Zip _____

Minnesota residents please add 4%. All consumers please add 25 cents handling, plus 15 cents per item postage.

Introduction

Chats with the Publisher

Carl Weschcke

Novus Ordo Seclorum

A New Order
of the Ages

"Born again" is an expression that is suddenly very familiar, and that will probably become very *in* during the coming months of the presidential campaign and after the election.

"Born again" is an ideal—challenging to both individual and nation.

"Born again" has initiatory meaning: to see things from a new perspective and to act from a new recognition of one's place in the world. In many magical-mystery systems, the candidate for initiation is brought to the temple gates blindfolded to symbolize that his "old view" of the world is limited, and that the re-opening of the eyes will give an altered and expanded sight. The new initiate receives instructions that correspond with the expanded consciousness, and takes an oath to act accordingly—to accept a greater responsibility than he even knew of before.

"Born again" for America likewise means an initiation! We have gone through times of growth and change, and a time of troubles and depression. We have acted blindly and foolishly. We have seen cherished beliefs and ideals fail and even bring upon us ugliness, violence and disease.

A Vision
But we still have a *vision* of America that is unaltered.

This America was founded by men of vision, many of them initiates who had indeed been "born again" with an expanded consciousness and dedication of purpose. This vision guided the founding of the nation, its expansion westward and ultimate consolidation as a true nation during the first hundred years. A renewal of the vision guided the economic expansion and technological growth during the second hundred years, and the ultimate recognition of the failure of national politics on a world scale.

That same vision has brought increased freedom as it overthrew slavery, has brought increased personal growth and wealth, and has made technology an instrument of progress through which wealth is created rather than merely used or transferred.

National Symbols

There are many symbols common to this vision, symbols that are alive in the American soul, but I want to speak of just three of them here:

The Mother as Liberty: Mater Libertas—our statue of liberty, rising out of the waters, her torch held high. She shows the glory of the Person separating from the ocean of the collective unconscious in the achievement of individual freedom. Her torch is the Light of the World, consciousness, transforming the Earth—at the same time reaching high to the sky in recognition that this vision must be spiritually inspired. She should be seen in robes of the colors of the rainbow. She is the Earth Mother.

The Warrior Eagle: Aquila Bellatrix—The American Eagle that is also the Phoenix, born again and again from its own ashes. It is the cycle of renewal that we experience now. Our Eagle is strength, courage, and flies to the heights that it may see with the eagle-eye to the far horizons. The Eagle *is* the Born-Again Man.

The Winged Victory: Mater Stellarium—Mother of the Stars, seen again as the stars in our national flag, symbolizing the reach of our vision. But the Mother of Stars is also our *ultimate* material source, just as the Earth is our *immediate* material source. From dust we come, to dust we return—born of earth, our bodies return to earth at death—from the stars we came, to the stars we must return.

Three other symbols important to the American Soul, of which I will speak at a later time, are: the White Lady: *Alba Domina*—She who is Goddess, She who is Queen: crowned in every beauty contest in the land; Child of the Waters: *Puer Maris*—He who is born to fulfill the Divinity in each one of us; and the Great Spirit: *Magnus Spiritus,* the highest consciousness that we reach toward with every kind of magick, religion, and philosphy.

Each as Warrior Eagle

For each of us to be born again, we must become as the Eagle: and we must earn our eagle feather as initiates in the New Order of the Ages: *Novus Ordo Seclorum.* We must learn to see as does the eagle from the heights. We must learn to care for the young, the family, the home as does the eagle who builds and rebuilds the nest of his ancestors so that eagles have been seen to inhabit the same nest since the founding of this land. We must, each of us, have the courage and strength of the eagle, to defend the land and to rest upon our own resources.

To be born again, rise from the ashes of the past as does the Phoenix; become transformed into the American Eagle whose eye transcends the nation and sees to the far horizons of Earth; have vision, but never be blinded by the Sun to the needs of family and home. Fly as high as you can, but keep your feet on the Earth and let the Mother nourish you and give Her your love in return.

N.O.S.

N.O.S.—*Gnosis Aquarius:* Esoteric Knowledge in the

New Age. Yes, our great magickal order, America: A New Order of the Ages, is founded on Knowledge. No other nation was deliberately founded, out of the wilderness, to incorporate the best knowledge available, inspired by yet greater vision, so that a people could grow into freedom and stature.

N.O.S. The "silent *G*" of *Gnosis* stands for "GOD," for the silent prescence of the Creator is everywhere, and is the source of all Knowledge. But even more, it is the inner awareness of that fact, the ultimate great secret, that is the basis of the technology for the attainment of esoteric knowledge from which we derive mundane knowledge. When we turn within, to the "silent *G*," we are able to contact with needed sources of Knowledge.

Money to Buy Progress

In this day and age, many people turn from the idea that you "can buy progress," but it is exactly this ideal that perhaps best expresses the special purpose of America —that technology, under the inspiration and guidance of Esoteric Knowledge, can transform Man himself, can improve our way of life, and can make Man's home a garden of paradise. Man, as lover of the Earth Mother, can and must gain the needed knowledge to restore Nature from the injury he has wrought and yet enter into a closer relationship with Her so that he intelligently cooperates in the natural process as part of the family, and not as a parasite!

With The Moon Sign Book, we express this ideal. By working with Nature's cycles, we express Her energies and purposes. Doing this with Knowledge, we gain in stature and freedom. As the Warrior Eagle, Man defends his Mother, the Earth, and adds to her Beauty.

The "Silent" G

To be "born again" is to make God your "silent

partner": to realize that each of us is both a part of the great being that is Earth and also a vehicle of the Creative Force that brings evolution to each unit of consciousness. To be "born again" is to move within the Inner Silence in order to gain direct experience of Esoteric Knowledge. All of this is found in that formula of the "Silent *G*" that transforms *Gnosis* into N.O.S., the Novus Ordo Seclorum: America, the New Order of the Ages.

Now the challenge is to add the *is* to N.O.S., so that we can say that "the New Order of the Ages *is*." We must still realize the ideal of America, not as nation but as a people born again. As the Mother once opened Her arms to the poor of the old world, so now must America open Her heart to the world with courage and strength to fulfill the vision of the Warrior Eagle.

Each of us is invited to join this magical order, the N.O.S. Each of us is asked to win the eagle feather of higher initiation. Each of us, in every land, is called upon to become an American—a citizen of the ideal republic that is without borders.

Each of us has the obligation to become a "Nostic"—to add the "silent *G*" and be a *Gnostic*, one who experiences Knowledge from within, and who lives as a Warior Eagle.

The Lunar Connection

E.L. Abel

In the primitive world of our ancestors, historians have frequently pointed out that the importance of the Moon far outweighed that of its fiery rival, the Sun. The universal adoption of the month and its weekly divisions, which are based on the changes in appearance of the Moon, clearly indicates the reliance of mankind on the Moon for marking time.

As further witness to the place of the Moon in the thoughts of all the peoples of the ancient world, we have the adoration of the Moon as a god or goddess with powers to control events on our planet. Not only were the Greeks Moon-worshipers, but the Egyptians, the Assyrians, the Chaldeans, the Phoenecians and the Romans held the Moon in special veneration. Writing in the journal, *Numen* (1973), the biblical historian, Professor E. L. Abel, has recently shown that the god of the early Hebrews in the Bible was also none other than the venerable Moon.

Throughout man's long preoccupation with it, the Moon has stood as a symbol for the life-force, the reproductive energy that animates all living things—plants, animals, and even man. When the Moon is waxing, life-energy on earth increases; when it is waning, life-energy on earth decreases.

In the pages that follow, I will examine the origins

of the ancient belief that the Moon influences the conception, growth and development of plants and animals, and will present some of the modern scientific evidence proving that our ancestors were generally correct in attributing these special powers to the Moon. I will then examine some of the less beneficent ways in which the Moon affects life on Earth. By the end of this discussion, it should be quite apparent that, despite our voyages to the Moon, we have still a great deal to learn about the influence of our nearest celestial neighbor on our everyday lives.

Planting by the Moon

Many people still laugh when someone admits that he plants and harvests crops by the cycle of the Moon. To do so, they say, is nothing more than superstition. It is the folklore of a bygone era. It has no place in this modern age.

Yet the fact that such practices still continue and are defended vehemently by those who observe them suggests that they have proven themselves over the centuries and have stood the test of time. There is always room for improvement, but the mere fact that something is old does not make it obsolete.

Over 2,500 years ago, the Hebrews acknowledged the influence of the Moon in Ch. 33, vv. 13-14 of the *Book of Deuteronomy*: "Blessed of the Lord be this land...for the precious fruits brought forth by the Sun and for the precious things put forth by the Moon."

Throughout the ancient world of the Babylonians, the Moon goddess, Ishtar, was hailed by farmers as the "Green One" and the "All-Dewy One." It was to Ishtar that the Babylonians paid homage as the goddess who sent water so that plants would grow and thrive in the torrid dry desert lands of Mesopotamia. And it was her recurring movements in the sky that told them when to plant their seeds and when to harvest their crops.

Primitive ideas? Yes. But basically sound. We no longer believe that the Moon is divine, but we do know that there is a definite relationship between the cycle of the Moon and the weather.

Experiments that we shall cite momentarily have proven that there is more rainfall around the time of the Full Moon and that seeds absorb more moisture during this time than at any other time of the month. Therefore, if seeds are to receive the life-giving moisture they need to germinate, and plants are to survive in an arid land, what better time to sow than at a time when rain is most probable? It is as if the Moon has deliberately orchestrated the heavens and the earth into a concert of cosmic harmony.

People who use the Moon to guide them as to when it is best to sow and reap, believe that there is an intrinsic rhythm in nature. They believe that despite the vastness of our galaxy, the Sun, Moon, planets, stars and the Earth are all in tune. They believe that events in one part of the heavens influence events elsewhere, sometimes for the better, sometimes for the worse. By studying these events and the patterns that repeat themselves, people over the ages have become convinced that man can discover when it is favorable to undertake some tasks and when a particular job is best left undone for a time.

Those who garden by the Moon have found that there is a proper time to sow their seeds, set out their plants, weed their fields and harvest their crops. The proper time for all of these events, they have discovered, is dependent, to a very important extent, on the cycle of the Moon.

One of the earliest attempts to prove that the ancient practice of planting by the Moon was not superstition but good agriculture, was conducted by the famous English scientist of the sixteenth century, Francis Bacon.

Bacon had long been interested in the influence of the Moon on the germination of seeds and had conducted experiments in which he planted seeds during various phases of the Moon. His observations convinced him that those seeds that were sown immediately after the New Moon germinated and produced healthier plants than those that were sown during other phases of the Moon's cycle.

Although Bacon had reported details of the methods he had used and had included controls in his experiments, the scientific world preferred not to acknowledge his discovery, and it was not until almost five hundred years later that the relationship between the lunar cycle and plant growth was once again brought to the attention of the scientist.

This time the iconoclast was a Yale biology professor with impeccable credentials, Dr. Harold Burr. Dr. Burr had earlier discovered that there was a significant correlation between plant growth and the electrical potential or voltage emitted by plants. With this discovery in mind, he drilled holes in various trees around Hart-

ford, Connecticut, and filled these holes with pieces of
wire. These wires were then connected to a voltmeter
that indicated the electrical potential of the trees.

Dr. Burr took daily readings of the changes in the
voltage of these trees for several years and when he
finally analyzed these records, they indicated, as he
put it, that "of all the external factors examined, the
phase of the Moon seems to be the only one showing
any degree of correlation [with tree growth]."

Meanwhile in Stuttgart, Germany, a female biolo-
gist, Dr. Lilly Kolisko, was conducting studies of a different sort at the Biological Institute. For over ten
years, she planted a great many varieties of plants during different phases of the Moon, keeping exhaustive records not only of the growth of these plants, but also
of their taste when the leaves and fruit were picked!

The results of these detailed experiments demonstrated a significant and gratifying corroboration of the
ancient wisdom of the past regarding the Moon's influence on plant growth. During its first and second quarters, when the Moon is in its "increasing phase," Kolisko found that plants that produced their yield above
the ground grew especially fast. For example, leafy
vegetables such as cabbage, lettuce, celery, spinach, as
well as tomatoes, beans, peas, cereals, etc., all exhibited superior growth and were better tasting than when
sown during the waning phase of the Moon.

However, contradicting the folk wisdom that crops
producing their yield below the ground should be planted
during the waning or "decreasing phase" of the Moon,
Kolisko found that they too exhibited better growth
if planted during the increase.

Additional proof of the Moon's influence on plants
has been reported on a regular basis by Dr. Frank Brown
of Northwestern University. We will be mentioning
Dr. Brown's fascinating work with various animals short-

ly, but for now, let us consider his remarkable findings on the lowly bean and potato plants.

Dr. Brown is not a man who believes in purchasing costly and exotic specimens for his research when ordinary home-grown varieties of plants will do just as well. The supermarket has often been one of his favorite supply houses and it was there that he went to purchase sacks of garden beans for one of his experiments. When he got these beans back to his laboratory, he divided them into various piles of equal weight and then placed each pile in a separate basket. These baskets were immersed in water for twenty-four hours. The baskets were then allowed to drain and each was weighed. These weighings all took place at the same time and were repeated over and over again, careful records being kept of the weight of the baskets before and after they were submerged. The room in which all this was done was temperature and humidity controlled, so that no fluctuations in the weather could possibly have interfered with the weight of the beans from day to day.

In the controlled environmental conditions, the beans absorbed more water before the time of the Full Moon and, conversely, absorbed the least amount of water before the New Moon, than at any other times of the month.

In another experiment, Dr. Brown studied the respiration rate of potatoes to see if their breathing was influenced by the position of the Moon. The breathing rate is often used as an index of how much energy an organism is using in the manufacture of complex substances from simpler substances. This in turn reflects the growth of the plant.

Once again Brown visited the supermarket to obtain specimens for his studies and for ten long years he kept meticulous records of the amount of oxygen consumed by the potato plants in his environmentally controlled laboratory. At the end of the experiment, there was no doubt in his mind that the breathing rate of the plants increased shortly before the Full Moon and decreased shortly before the New Moon.

Here, then, was irrefutable proof that the Moon influenced the absorption of moisture and the breathing or metabolic rate, and the ultimate growth of plants. The work of scientists such as Drs. Burr, Kolisko, and Brown has thus corroborated much of the ancient folk wisdom concerning the influence of the Moon and has demonstrated rather conclusively that planting by the Moon is not superstition but good agricultural practice.

Weather
Every night, immediately after a summary of the latest news and sports on TV, a short portion of the news is given over to the prognostications of the much maligned weatherman. Standing in front of the cameras, a map of the United States behind him, the weatherman proceeds to tell us what the current temperature is, what the high and low for the day has been, what the barometric pressure is, and finally, what he predicts the weather will be like for the next twenty-four hours. This recap and prediction costs the TV producers thousands of dollars in terms of his salary, the salaries of cameramen, and those of countless numbers of other people whose faces are never seen or whose voices we never hear.

The irony of the whole thing is that, more often than not, the local almanacs for the regions serviced by these TV weather forecasts are generally as accurate and often are more so than these expensively staged productions. For as little as seventy-five cents, one can buy an almanac and read what the weather will be on a given day and be reasonably assured that this prediction will be as correct, if not more so, than the TV weather forecast on the night directly preceding the particular day in question.

How is it possible that the almanac is able to predict the weather as accurately as the scientifically trained meteorologist? The answer lies in the attention which the almanacs pay to certain regularly occurring cycles in the heavens which, through the long course of history, have been found to influence the weather.

The effect of the Moon on the weather is registered primarily in whether or not it will rain on a particular day. Appreciation of this fact has enabled farmers and city-dwellers alike to plan their activities, whether they be agricultural or recreational, far in advance of any given day. Although most meteorologists discount as superstition the ancient claim that the Moon affects rainfall patterns, some of the more open-minded professionals who are less dogmatic in their thinking are quite willing to entertain any ideas that may enable them to add to their knowledge of factors that affect weather.

One such group of professionals includes Drs. Donald A. Bradley and Max A. Woodbury of the University College of Engineering in New York and their colleague, Dr. Glenn W. Brier of the Massachusetts Insittute of Technology. Working as a team, these three scientists contacted the 1,544 weather stations across the United States that had been collecting data on the weather since 1909 and asked for copies of all their weather records. Next, they made a note of all those days on which it had rained throughout this long period and plotted these days against the position of the Moon. To the surprise of the scientists, the graphs clearly demonstrated that it had rained more often on days just after the New and Full Moon than at any other time of the month.

At about the same time that these American weathermen were studying this peculiar relationship between the Moon's orbit and rainfall in the northern hemisphere, two Australian meteorologists, Drs. E. E. Adderly and E. G. Bowen, of the Radiophysics Division in Sydney, were conducting similar inquiries in their part of the southern hemisphere. Like their American counterparts, they too found that it rained most often just after the New and Full Moon.

When the two groups of scientists found that they had been working on the same problem and had come up with the exact same findings, they agreed to publish their findings simultaneously. In 1962, their two studies documenting the Moon's influence on rainfall appeared in *Science*, one of the most prestigious journals in science.

Here, then, was unquestionable proof that the movements of the Moon influenced the weather. Yet, despite the evidence presented in this most reputable forum of scientific discussion, the meteorological profession has preferred to ignore the data from their own weather stations. Relying instead on information provided by weather satellites, forecasters confidently predict the weather for the next day and then sheepishly admit the following day that weather forecasters do make mistakes now and then. The sad thing about the entire business of weather forecasting is that they could do a lot better if only they supplemented the information they obtain from these weather satellites with information contained in their own scientific journals.

Farmers who have been planting by the Moon for countless ages were, of course, convinced of the Moon's influence on rainfall long before this relationship was proven to them scientifically. Nevertheless, it is gratifying to have a long-observed custom hold up under the scrutiny of the objective eye of the dispassionate scientist. Such gratification is made even greater when one considers that, as we noted earlier, the Moon also causes certain changes to take place in plants, enabling them to benefit maximally from this increase in rainfall.

Harvesting by the Moon

Just as farmers believe that crops planted during the increase of the Moon grow more rapidly because they absorb more moisture from the Earth at this time, so too do they believe that crops are best harvested during the waning Moon. The reason for this belief is the logical assumption that, with less water being absorbed, they will dry more readily.

In Roman times, Pliny the statesman wrote that "all kinds of cutting, picking, or shearing are accomplished with less damage during the waning Moon than when the Moon is on the increase." Another eminent Roman statesman, Cato, confined his remarks to chopping trees. "All timber should be cut and all stumps grubbed when the Moon is waning," he instructed his farmhands. Yet another Roman agriculturist, Columella, explained that "timber should be cut between the twentieth and the thirtieth day of the lunar month, when the Moon is waning; because all timber cut at this time is judged to be free from decay." Since one of the most important physical conditions affecting the extent to which wood decays is its moisture content, the Romans reasoned that the best time for felling trees was during the waning Moon when trees would be likely to absorb the least moisture and therefore would be much drier than if cut down during the waxing Moon.

In conformity with this practice, trees were routinely cut down in Europe during the Moon's waning phase. In fact, from 1669 until the Revolution, French authorities insisted that trees could be lawfully felled only under a waning Moon because experience had shown that the wood from these trees was more durable than that which came from trees felled under the waxing Moon.

There are some crops, however, that are better harvested when they are full of moisture. This is especially true of the grape if it is to be crushed into wine. "It helps greatly if one picks the grapes during the increasing Moon," advised Pliny. In this way they would retain their precious juice.

Animal Husbandry

The Romans not only experimented with the effects of the Moon on planting and harvesting crops, they also paid a great deal of attention to the influence of the Moon on animals.

For example, Columella instructed his workers "always to take care to set eggs under a hen when the Moon is waxing, from the tenth to the fifteenth day after the New Moon; for not only is the setting itself more likely to turn out well under these conditions, but one ought to manage thus in order that the hatch may take place when the Moon is again on the increase."

A thousand years later, Dr. L. J. Johnson reported an experiment that proved that the Moon could indeed influence the growth of chicks while they were still inside the shell. Taking his cue from Dr. Brown, Johnson used a specially designed apparatus to monitor the breathing rates of chick embryos. Analysis of these respiration patterns showed that, just as Brown's potatoes breathed faster or slower depending on the position of the Moon, so too did the breathing pattern of chick embryos vary in conjunction with the Moon's position.

Professor Johnson was not primarily concerned with proving or disproving the veracity of ancient husbandry practices, however. His interest lay in proving that even though secluded in its shell, deprived of changes in light, temperature, humidity, etc., the chick is responsive to cosmic forces operating hundreds of thousands of miles away. And this is exactly what he showed.

In general, agriculturists have long believed that animals born during the "increasing phase" of the Moon were stronger than those born during the "decreasing phase." In an ancient treatise, *On Animals*, Aelian stated quite adamantly that "young beasts of burden that are born when the Moon is on the wane are less capable and feebler than others, and what is more, knowledge of these matters recommends that animals born in this part of the month should not be reared on the grounds that they are not of good quality." Many centuries later, Francis Bacon expressed a similar basic view that "young cattle that are brought forth in the full of the Moon, are stronger and larger than those brought forth in the wane." However, thus far no studies have been able to prove or disprove the truth of these opinions.

The Inhabitants of the Sea

The intimate relationship between the cycle of the Moon and the rise and fall of the oceans was of special interest to our ancestors since it was one of the first clear examples of the Moon's influence on the Earth.

During the course of evolution, which we are told began in the seas, the Moon's influence on the tides must surely have affected the development of the various life-forms that came into being in the ocean. When it came time for some of these marine animals to leave the oceans and try to make a go of it on land, it is highly likely that they carried with them their sensitivity to the Moon and passed this sensitivity on to the more complex forms of life that were to evolve from them. We will soon see that land animals, including human beings, exhibit a responsiveness to the position of the Moon. At first, this responsiveness was assumed to derive from the oceanic origins of living matter and the tides which were thought to mediate the Moon's influence. Recently, however, scientists have been able to demonstrate that while the tides do indeed mediate the Moon's influence for some creatures, there are also many creatures upon which the Moon's influence is more direct.

Soon after the discovery that the movement of the tides was determined by the changing phases of the Moon, our ancestors discovered that certain marine animals such as the clam, the oyster and the sea urchin were "full" at the time of the Full Moon and were "empty" at the time of the New Moon.

These changes in the "fullness" of certain marine animals occur as a consequence of the stages of sexual readiness which they undergo. In the case of the sea urchin, *centrechinus cetosus*, which inhabits the Red Sea, genital material is released into the sea only during the Full Moon in the months of July through September. After this shedding of material, the size of the ovaries and testes in these animals decreases. Then the production of gonadic cells starts taking place once more, progressing through the New Moon and reaching its peak at the Full Moon when the eggs and spermatozoa are mature and ready to be released once more. This increase and decrease in the size of the sea urchin is thus directly related to its fertility cycle.

Although some scientists once speculated that the sexual changes in the sea urchin were brought about by the tides in the Red Sea, they had to do an about-face in their thinking when they visited that part of the world, for they found that there is virtually no tidal activity at all in the Red Sea!

In still other parts of the world, the coming of the Full Moon is a time of great excitement because of the ripening effects of the Moon on the sexual organs of some of the creatures that inhabit the sea. On the island of Samoa in the Pacific Ocean, for instance, the months of October and November are a time of eager anticipation and activity. By day, nets are mended, boats are caulked, and paddles are repaired or carved anew; by night, the natives chant festive songs and gaze up at the heavens waiting impatiently as the New Moon begins to fatten.

Then a few days before the Moon is full, the Samoans pour into their boats and head out to sea to fish for palolo. The nets are cast, buckets go into action, and soon their boats are teeming with this Samoan delicacy. Yet despite the enormous bounty reaped by these fishermen, millions upon millions of the palolo still remain in the sea searching for other palolos with which to mate.

The palolo is not really a fish but rather a worm known as *eunice viridis* to scientists. Of the countless creatures that inhabit the seas, this worm is perhaps the best known example of a marine animal whose breeding cycle is completely dependent on the phase of the Moon.

Palolo worms live in the rocks and coral of the South Pacific and during their breeding season, which occurs only in the months of October and November, their hind parts, which are filled with either sperm or eggs, break off from their front ends. While the front ends remain buried on the ocean bottom and subsequently die, the rear ends rise to the top and shed their genital matter.

So many palolos take part in this sexual rendezvous that the sea actually turns from blue to greenish brown. Were it not for the fact that this entire breaking apart ritual is so closely coordinated by the Moon, the vastness of the ocean would surely defeat the only purpose of this event, the mating and perpetuation of the palolo worm as a species. Without the Moon as a guide, or rather a stimulating force, the worms would probably come into their sexual maturity at different times and sperm and eggs would never find one another in the vast sea. And that would make a lot of Samoans very, very unhappy.

Back in the United States, laboratory experiments

by biologists such as Dr. Frank Brown and his colleagues at Northwestern University have shown beyond any doubt that many marine animals are indeed directly influenced by the Moon.

One of the animals that Dr. Brown has been working with for some time is the fiddler crab (*uca pugnax*), so called because one of its giant pincer claws resembles a violin. What first aroused Dr. Brown's interest in this animal was its peculiar characteristic of changing its color according to the position of the Moon even when it was confined in a closed room, completely cut off from the Moon's light and, needless to say, from the rise and fall of the ocean.

Intrigued by this mysterious force emanating from the Moon, Brown began to delve more deeply into this curious bond between the Moon and the creatures that inhabit the sea. In his next study, Brown shipped a number of oysters in hermetically sealed containers from their native habitats on Long Island Sound on the Atlantic Ocean, to his laboratory in Evanston, Illinois.

Once they arrived in Evanston, Brown began to watch the opening and closing of the valves of these animals to see if there was any pattern to this activity. At first, the oysters seemed to have retained some memory of the tide pattern on Long Island Sound since they opened their valves in time with the tides in the Atlantic.

However, after they had been in his laboratory for about two weeks, Brown found that the pattern of these openings was beginning to change. Eventually, an entirely new pattern emerged, one that would have been in synchrony with the tides at Evanston if that town had been located by an ocean. But there was no ocean at Evanston and the oysters were certainly not responding to any tidal movement in the laboratory. In fact, they were housed in rooms controlled for light, temperature and humidity. Nevertheless, deprived of all

regular sensory input, the oysters appeared to be responding directly to the movement of a heavenly sphere located
239,000 miles away from the Earth.

If some marine animals responded directly to the Moon
rather than indirectly to the tides, Brown wondered
whether land animals might also be sensitive to the
Moon's cycle. To find out, he confined some rats and
hamsters, two species of mammals, in his laboratory
under environmentally controlled conditions, and he
kept a record of their activity patterns.

Enclosed in these specially designed rooms, the animals
had no possible means of knowing where the Moon might
be relative to the Earth, or whether it was day or night
for that matter. Nevertheless, the record of their activity
patterns clearly showed that the movements of these
animals in their cages was related to the position of the
Moon.

If plants, marine animals, and mammals were responsive to the Moon, were human beings, the most complex
development in evolution's magnificent design, also
subject to the Moon's mysterious power? Popular superstition has always held that such an influence exists.
But superstition is one thing. Scientific fact is another.

The Female Fertility Cycle

Earlier we noted that nearly every ancient civilization
looked upon the Moon as a deity. In most cases, this
deity was considered to be female, and indeed the Moon
Goddess has been the patron of, and has been worshipped
chiefly by, women throughout history.

The rather close correspondence of the female menstrual cycle and the lunar cycle makes the link between
the Moon and women a phenomenon of great interest
and curiosity. A second reason that the Moon is associated so closely with the female psyche is, as we shall see,
its influence on childbirth.

Find The Road To A Healthier, Happier Life!

BOOKS THAT HELP YOU are our specialty. You can get any of these outstanding books quickly and easily. Our catalog contains the World's largest selection of important health related and self-help titles.

Nearly 2,000 different books are listed, described, pictured. Many are available at a special discount only from us. We will send you our Catalog with no obligation.

For a limited time you can receive this unique 24-page, illustrated Catalog just by sending your name and address with 15¢ in coin to:

AURORA
BOOK COMPANIONS
Dept. M/S

BOX 5852 • DENVER, CO 80216

ATTENTION Retailers and Organizations:
Write on your stationery for information on purchase of wholesale quantities.

The mysterious link between the female menstrual and lunar cycles in the minds of our ancestors can readily be seen in the etymology of the Greek and Latin words for menstruation. Our word, "catamenia," for example, is derived from the Greek words, *kata*, meaning "around," and *men*, meaning "Moon." Our word, "menses," is actually the Latin plural form of the word for "month," the time given to the cycle of the Moon. In France, a woman still speaks of her period as *le moment de la lune* ("the time of the Moon") and in Germany, she speaks of it simply as "the Moon."

Our sabbath, in fact, is actually a day given over to the female menses. Among the Babylonians, from whom we inherited the sabbath custom, Ishtar, the Moon Goddess, had her monthly bleeding when the Moon was full. This day was called *shabathu* ("sabbath"), the "evil day," and all work on that day was taboo. The origins of this custom reflect the belief that when a woman is menstruating, she is unclean and will contaminate anything that she touches. While this belief has long since faded, the sabbath custom based on it is still part of the culture of people all around the world.

The Greeks were completely convinced that the female menstrual cycle was governed by the course of the Moon. "The commencement of the menses in women occurs at a time when the Moon is waning," wrote Aristotle; "on this account, certain men who pretend to know assert that the Moon is feminine since the monthly period in women coincides with the waning of the Moon, and after the wane and discharge, both grow whole again."

Aristotle's explanation for the Moon's effect on women was that, as it approached its fullness, it caused the temperature of the female body to rise. But as it waned, its effect on body temperature decreased, and this caused the body to become colder. This in turn made women unable to retain their full reservoir of blood and as a result they lost some of this blood via the menses.

Today we know that the female menstrual cycle occurs as a result of changes that take place in the uterus as it prepares to receive a potential embryo. What happens is that the blood vessels in the uterus begin to increase in anticipation of the implantation of a fertilized egg. The egg, or ovum as it is sometimes called, is released from the ovary at the time of ovulation and lives for only about forty-eight hours unless it is fertilized by a sperm. If fertilization of the female ovum does not take place, there is no embryo and the unfertilized ovum is expelled, the blood vessels in the uterus rupture, and the menstrual bleeding period begins.

While scientists now comprehend the physiological processes involved in menstruation, they are still at a loss to explain the curious correlation that has often been observed between the female menstrual period in a great many women and the Moon's cycle as it passes around the Earth.

One of the first modern investigations of this relationship between the lunar and female cycles was conducted in 1898 by the Nobel prize-winning Danish scientist, Svante Arrhenius. Arrhenius carefully charted the cycles of over 12,000 women in a Stockholm maternity hospital and compared these with the position of the Moon. The close relationship in time between the two convinced him that the Moon did indeed have some special effect on the female menstrual cycle.

In 1936, two German physicians, Guthmann and Oswald, reported that of the 10,000 women they studied, more of them had their periods at the time of the Full or New Moon than at any other time in the Moon's cycle.

A quarter of a century later, in 1962, an eminent Czechoslovakian scientist, Dr. Jeri Malek, addressed a meeting of scientists at the New York Academy of Sciences on factors affecting the female menstrual cycle. One of these factors, he said, was the position of the Moon. Among the 7,420 women whose menstrual cycles he had closely followed over a long period of time, Malek reported that the female cycle began more often around the time of the Full Moon than during any other time of the month.

Although Dr. Malek was unable to explain just how the Moon influenced the female reproductive system, numerous authors have frequently pointed out the interesting observation that a large percentage of women exhibit the same reproductive responsiveness to the lunar cycle as do many of the marine animals we mentioned earlier. Is it possible that this similarity reflects some kind of evolutionary inheritance?

Charles Darwin, the originator of the theory of evolution, thought so. In the *Descent of Man* (1891), Darwin pointed to the coincidence between the reproductive cycles of the human female and those of marine animals as proof that man had evolved from the more primitive creatures of the sea. "Man is descended from fish," Darwin declared, and therefore, "why should not the 28-day feminine cycle be a vestige of the past when life depended on the tides, and therefore the Moon."

Although Darwin felt that the Moon brought on the reproductive cycle in marine animals via its influence on the tides, studies conducted after his death, many of which have been referred to above, have demonstrated that this effect on the reproductive cycle is not due to the tides but instead is a more direct result of the Moon's influence on living things.

One possibility that may account for the Moon's influence on reproductive cycles in animals and human females arises from an interesting discovery originally reported by Dr. Harold Burr, whom we previously met in connection with his work on electrical-potential changes in trees.

During the course of some related studies concerning similar changes in human beings, Dr. Burr found that a relatively large increase in electrical potential, lasting about twenty-four hours, occurred once a month in a group of female students he was studying. This increase appeared to occur between menstrual cycles and Dr. Burr thought it might in some way be connected with ovulation, the release of an egg from the ovary.

This idea was subsequently borne out during an operation on a female patient who agreed to participate in one of Dr. Burr's experiments. Dr. Burr had been testing the woman daily for several days while she was in the hospital waiting to undergo surgery. Since the operation was of a minor nature and did not necessitate immediate concern, Dr. Burr was able to continue watching for any changes in her electrical potential without any danger to her welfare. At last, on the day that Burr's instruments indicated that the woman's electrical potential had markedly increased, she was sent to surgery. During the operation, which involved examination of her ovaries, the doctors found that she had indeed just ovulated on that very day, just as Burr had predicted on the basis of the changes in her electrical potential.

The next clue to the Moon's influence on the female cycle comes from a report by Dr. Leonard Ravitz, a physician at Duke University in Durham, North Carolina. Dr. Ravitz was also interested in the changes in electrical potential that take place in the body, and during the course of his studies, he found that electrical potentials increase maximally in women during the Full Moon.

Here, then, was the basis for the cosmic connection between the Moon and the female reproductive cycle. When full, the Moon causes a dramatic increase in the electrical potential of the female body. This change, in turn, triggers the release of an ovum from the ovaries. If unfertilized, the ovum is expelled from the body, and menstrual bleeding occurs. The mystery yet to be solved is how the Moon alters the electrical potential of the body.

Childbirth

In view of the belief that the Moon affects the female menstrual cycle, it is not surprising that the Moon was also believed to influence the time of childbirth. The waxing Moon's increasing in size to a full-rounded orb and then growing smaller and smaller until nothing more than a sliver of light, was reminiscent of the growing stomach of the pregnant woman, and its decrease after the birth of the child. Furthermore, the veneration of the Moon as the fructifying energy force, the force that makes plants and animals grow and thrive, also gave it, in the primitive mind, a position of prime importance in conception and birth.

Recently I attended a series of lectures given by the head nurse of the obstetrical wing of a large hospital. One of these lectures was dedicated to the various superstitions associated with pregnancy and birth. The nurse covered all the old wives' tales about children in great detail. She mentioned the popular misguided idea that babies born with birthmarks that resemble animals or objects had these imprinted on their bodies when their mothers became frightened by these things during pregnancy. Another old myth was the one about expectant mothers not looking at deformed people because the sight of this deformity might cause their own children to become deformed.

After the lecture, the nurse invited questions from us and a soon-to-be mother raised her hand to ask why the superstition about more children being born during the Full and New Moons had not been mentioned.

"Because," replied the nurse, "that is not a superstition. It is a fact."

The room suddenly grew quiet again as the nurse explained that in the hospital she had been working in for quite some time now, experience had taught her and the other nurses in the obstetrics ward to expect a busy night in the delivery room when the Moon was full.

Although the belief in a lunar influence on birth rate has been considered just a bit of antiquated folklore by most doctors, the nurse explained that the doctors were only in the hospital for a few hours each day. They delivered one or two babies each, and then went back to their offices. The nurses, however, remained in the maternity ward sometimes as long as sixteen hours a day. They knew the days to look out for in terms of babies coming into the world because they spent more hours out of their long day in the ward helping mothers to deliver. And they worked with all the doctors. They saw more births than the doctors and their tired feet told them when they had had a particularly busy day.

Not all obstetricians, however, disagree with the observations of this head nurse. In fact, over the years a considerable body of literature has begun to accumulate from all over the world showing that the birth rate increases around the time of the New and Full Moon.

For example, in 1929, the prestigious French medical journal, *La Presse Medicale*, reported that just after the Full Moon, the birth rate was more than double that during any other phase of the lunar cycle.

In 1938, in the city of Cologne, Germany, Dr. H. Gunther reported a similar finding regarding the increase in the birth rate around the New and Full Moon.

The first study of the relationship between the lunar cycle and birth rates to appear in an American medical journal was reported by Dr. A. G. Schnurman, an obstetrician practicing in Roanoke, Virginia. Dr. Schnurman was convinced of the Moon's effect on the birth rate after analyzing birth frequencies over a five-year period at the Roanoke hospital. His analysis showed a lunar effect was evident in forty out of sixty months, or sixty-six percent of the births occurring in the hospital, with the greatest number of babies being born around the time of the Full Moon, or twenty-four hours before or after.

"Just what all this means I am incapable of stating," Schnurman confessed, but on the basis of an analogy with the tides, he ventured a guess. "One may theorize that there is a lunar effect, possibly electronic, on the amniotic fluid as a body of water, just as on the tides of water elsewhere."

In 1959, Dr. Walter Menaker caused a considerable stir in the medical profession when he reported his analysis of over a half-million births in the city of New York between January, 1948, and January, 1957. According to the results of his analysis, which he published in the *American Journal of Obstetrics and Gynecology*, the highest frequency of deliveries in New York City occurred around the time of the Full Moon.

In the same year, Dr. Edson J. Andrews likewise caused his medical colleagues to sit up and take notice when he reported his findings concerning the relationship between the lunar cycle and the birth rate to a meeting of physicians in Miami, Florida.

Dr. Andrews had plotted against the phases of the Moon the frequency of births at the Tallahassee Memorial Hospital in Tallahassee, Florida, for the years 1956, 1957 and 1958, and had been more than surprised at the pattern that emerged. Four hundred and one babies had been born within two days of the Full Moon, 375 had been born within two days of the New Moon, and only 320 had been born within two days of the Moon's first quarter.

In 1967, Dr. Menaker presented the scientific world

with an analysis of an additional half-million births from New York City covering the period from January, 1961, through December, 1963. Once again he discovered that more babies were born around the time of the Full Moon than at any other time of the month.

The influence of the Moon on the birth rate is only now beginning to be recognized by the medical profession, but, as with most phenomena connected with the Moon, such an effect has been recognized throughout the ages by the nonprofessionals. Now, at last, doctors are beginning to admit that this bit of folklore may have survived as long as it has because of its intrinsic truth. More babies do come into the world when there is a Full Moon. It is up to the scientists now to tell us why this is so.

Lunacy

In the field of mental health, the term lunacy has largely disappeared. Nevertheless, people still refer to lunatic asylums and lunatics when they talk about mental hospitals and the people who are confined therein.

The word, "lunatic," comes from the Latin word, *luna*, meaning "Moon," and signifies someone whose mind is affected by the Moon. Such an idea, we should not be surprised to acknowledge by now, dates back far into our past.

In the first century, A.D., Plutarch claimed that "everyone knows that those who sleep outside under the influence of the Moon are not easily awakened but seem stupid and senseless." In the same era, the Roman statesman, Pliny, whose interests seemed to have ranged the whole gamut of human curiosity, stated that the "Moon produces drowsiness and stupor in those who sleep under her beams." Apparently the Romans believed that moonlight had some kind of direct effect on the human brain. Similar to the way it acted on the oceans, it seemed to attract moisture into the brain and made it heavy and torpid. The accumulation of so much fluid in the brain made one unable to think clearly.

Allusions to the Moon's power to make men mad can be found throughout literature. In Shakespeare's *Anthony and Cleopatra*, for instance, Enobarbus refers to the Moon as "sovereign mistress of true melancholy." In *Othello*, the Moor, on hearing of the death of his friend Roderigo, remarks: "It is the very error of the Moon, she comes more near the earth than she was wont, and makes men mad." In *Paradise Lost*, John Milton, in alluding to the Moon's curious powers, talks of "demoniac frenzy, moping melancholy, and moon-struck madness."

The psychiatrists of by-gone centuries were fully convinced of the Moon's influence on the unstable mind, and their medical records testify frequently to instances of "moon-struck madness." In France, the eminent psychiatrist, Daquin, stated in no uncertain terms in 1791 that "it is a well-established fact that insanity is a disease of the mind upon which the Moon exercises an unquestionable influence." A half-century later, another eminent French psychiatrist, Guislain, described a patient who suffered from recurring fits of maniacal hysteria every time the Full Moon appeared.

During the 18th century, the conviction that the Moon produced insanity in some sensitive beings was legalized in England when the great jurist, Sir William Blackstone, legally defined a lunatic, or one who was *non compos mentis*, as "one who hath . . . lost the use of this reason and who hath lucid intervals, sometimes enjoying his senses and sometimes not, and that frequently depending upon the changes of the Moon."

During the course of legal debates involving this definition, a distinction was made between the "lunatic" and the "insane." The lunatic was deranged only during certain days connected with the appearance of the Full

Unitology; A breakthrough in applied Astrology

Marguerite Carter is a world famous astrologer who has spent a lifetime developing a method that makes astrological principles work for everyone, in every kind of situation. This method, called Unitology, can and will work for you whether your interest is love, money, career, or shedding burdens and worries.

Marguerite Carter has devoted her life to providing guidance for thousands of people from every walk of life. Early in her career, she became convinced that while astrology was an excellent tool for predicting trends, changes, dangers, and opportunities, a practical method was needed for helping people use astrological information in a beneficial way. After four decades the method has been perfected and proven over and over again by thousands of grateful users.

Let Miss Carter prove that you don't have to wait for luck to change the course of your life. You can begin immediately to fill it with the things you want most.

Send today for your own Unitology Forecast and a complete discussion of the Unitology system. Just ask for Miss Carter's Unitology Forecast with Special Notations for the year ahead. It will be compiled, based on your birthdate information. Print month, day, year, place, hour of birth (if known), and include $5.00 plus 50¢ for postage and handling. Please allow three weeks for receipt of your material. Address: Marguerite Carter, Box M7, 546 S. Meridian St., Indianapolis, Indiana 46225.

Moon. During the rest of the month he had control of himself and was responsible for his own actions. The insane man, on the other hand, suffered from a chronic condition. He was mentally disturbed every moment of his life and at no time was he in control of himself.

Although people who acted peculiarly were called lunatics without any distinction being made as to their particular psychopathology, many different kinds of lunacy were recorded by physicians. In addition to deep melancholy or maniacal frenzy, periodic drunkenness, called dipsomania, was attributed to the influence of the Moon in some alcoholics. Dr. T. Laycock reported one such case of periodical drunkenness associated with the appearance of the Full Moon in the prestigious medical journal, *Lancet*, which aroused a great deal of interest among his medical colleagues.

Pyromania, the uncontrollable urge to set fires, has also been found to be related to the cycle of the Moon. In many cities throughout the country, fire departments remain on special alert during the time of the Full Moon in anticipation of a rash of incendiary incidents. In the 1930's, there was a famous episode of Moon-related fires in a township not far from the city of New York. The authorities were said to be on the lookout for a firebug "whose madness apparently comes from the Moon."

Inspector William Faust of the Philadelphia Police Department is especially convinced that certain kinds of criminal acts are set off by the Full Moon. In a report entitled, "Effect of the Full Moon on Human Behavior," which was written for the American Institute of Medical Climatology, Faust declared that "the seventy-odd policemen who deal with telephone complaints have always reported that activity—especially crimes against persons—seemed to increase as the night of the Full Moon drew near. People whose antisocial behavior had psychotic roots—such as firebugs, kleptomaniacs, destructive drivers, and homicidal alcoholics—seemed to go on a rampage as the Moon rounded, calming down as the Moon waned."

Although they do not lose control of their senses, many people suffer from agonizing headaches during certain phases of the Moon. Berzelius, the famous Swedish scientist, is a particularly interesting example of an individual who suffered migraine headaches during the Full Moon. In his autobiography, Berzelius writes: "Since my 23rd year I had been tormented by a periodic headache, commonly called migraine. At first this occurred at long intervals, but soon showed itself twice a month, falling with greatest regularity on the day when the New or the Full Moon occurred, and lasting from 8 am to 8 pm."

Another particularly interesting example of a mental disorder in which the cycle of the Moon has been found to be a controlling factor is "Moon-walking." Moon-walking is a form of "sleep-walking" that has been frequently described in medical journals. Krafft-Ebing, the famous psychiatrist of the last century and a pioneer in studying sexual disorders, referred to "Moon-walking" as a "symtomatic manifestation of certain nervous diseases."

One of the most thorough studies of this disorder was conducted by a Viennese psychoanalyst, Dr. J. Sadger. Dr. Sadger found that Moon-walking occurs most often in adolescence and always takes place during the Full Moon, never occurring at any other time. "Under the influence of the [Full] Moon," explains Dr. Sadger, "the moonstruck individual is actually enticed from his bed, often gazes fixedly at the Moon, stands at the window or climbs out of it, and with the surefootedness of the sleep-walker climbs out upon the roof and walks about there, or, without stumbling, goes into the open. In short, he carries out all sorts of complex actions.

Only it would be dangerous to call the wanderer by name . . . He would awaken, collapse, and fall head-long with fright if he found himself on a height."

In view of what is now becoming a formidable body of evidence from scientific laboratories, police departments, and mental hospitals around the world, there can no longer be any doubt that the Moon does influence life on our planet. The cosmic connection between the Moon and Earth is as real as that which exists between the Sun and the Earth.

What is surprising is the grudging way in which the scientific world has admitted that any such cosmic link really exists. But scientists are conservative by nature. They must be certain beyond any shadow of a doubt that a phenomenon exists. Yet once they are convinced of the truth of some phenomenon, they tend to push the truth of that phenomenon to its limits. They probe, explore, tear apart, reconstruct, duplicate, and engage in a whole host of activities, trying to understand the principle or principles behind that phenomenon.

Now that the scientific wall of resistance to acknowledging the Moon's influence has been cracked, not only should we begin to see a rediscovery of ancient wisdoms concerning the Moon, but we should also be prepared for exciting new discoveries of the Moon's mysterious powers over our planet and its inhabitants.

Understanding Lunar Astrology

Marylee Satren

Astrology

The Study of Cycles and Coincidences. To define this ancient and venerable study of life in such a short phrase seems ludicrous, but let us examine these two ideas.

Cycles. Imagine the most primitive of human beings, fearful, vulnerable, gazing at the night sky. This is the first astrologer, aware of the basic cycles by which all life is timed: the daily rising and setting of the Sun and the annual seasons it controls; and the monthly waxing and waning of the Moon.

Coincidences. Almost simultaneously man recognized a connection between the solar and lunar cycles and nature's own rhythms. Everything on earth is affected by these cycles: the growth of plants, the fertility cycles of women, the tidal activity of the ocean, physical and psychological changes in human beings. The awareness of the correlation of these phenomena with the visible cycles of the Sun, Moon and planets is the essence of astrology.

From the beginning of civilization—and probably long before that—people lived by these planetary cycles. The Bible is full of accounts of astrologers advising ancient patriarchs and pharaohs. Famous scientists and visionaries throughout history—Pythagoras, Copernicus, Nostradamus, Kepler, Galileo, Newton—were accomplished astrologers.

It is only in modern times that man has divorced himself from nature to the extent of ridiculing our oldest and truest science. This is a direct consequence of the Industrial Revolution, and the conceit that people alone control nature. Astrology takes an integrated view of nature as a whole in which all parts affect and reflect all other parts. Not only is no man an island, but no thing: no animal, vegetable, or mineral.

Of course, centuries of study have made astrology an immensely complicated and comprehensive science, which is, in its totality, way beyond the range of one person's life study. However, there are many aspects of astrology that are not only within reach of the average man, but absolutely essential for a fulfilled life.

The Moon's cycles and their correlation with everyday life are the foundation of the *Moon Sign Book*. By providing explicit tables and articles on the Moon's influence, we hope to be able to bring a part of this valuable astrological knowledge within reach of everyone. First, let us look at some basic principles.

Astronomical Background

Look to the east where the Sun rises and trace with your eyes the path it follows through the sky to the western horizon where it sets in the evening. Imagine this path to be a circular belt around the earth. Along this path travel the Sun, Moon, and all the planets. This is the zodiac. It is no more than an imaginary circular ruler which forms a convenient measure of the planets' positions.

This zodiacal ruler is divided into 360 degrees of arc—twelve thirty-degree segments which are marked by the astrological signs. There are four major points on the ruler which divide the year into seasons. The zodiacal signs which begin at these four points, or angles, are the cardinal signs of Aries, Cancer, Libra, Capricorn.

The Vernal Equinox. The position of the Sun at 0 degrees Aries occurs around March 21, when day and night are equal in length. The Sun appears to cross the equator from south to north, when observed from the northern hemisphere. *The Summer Solstice*. Throughout the spring the days lengthen until the longest day of the year is reached, around June 21, when the Sun is at 0 degrees Cancer. The Sun's path reaches its most northern point, the Tropic of Cancer. *The Autumnal Equinox*. The Sun crosses the equator going south around September 21, when it is at 0 degrees Libra, and day and night are again equal. *The Winter Solstice*. The Sun's path is at its most southern point, the Tropic of Capricorn, around December 21, when the Sun is at 0 degrees Capricorn. This is the shortest day of the year.

The Zodiacal Signs

There are twelve signs of the zodiac. At one point in history, if one looked through the imaginary zodiac to the distant stars beyond, the zodiacal signs seemed to be on top of certain constellations. The signs and constellations with which they once corresponded have the same names. Today, due to the movement of our solar system around the galaxy of stars, each one with its own solar system, the signs and constellations no longer coincide. Except for a few fixed stars which do not concern us here, astrology does not deal with the stars or constellations at all. We are only concerned with the planets, including the Sun and Moon, and their positions in the signs of the zodiac. These signs are divided into different categories to help us better understand their natures.

Elements or Triplicities. Each of the signs is classified into fire, earth, air or water. These are the four basic elements of antiquity. *Fire-sign* personalities are outgoing, energetic, spontaneous, and impulsive. The fire signs are Aries, Leo and Sagittarius. *Earth-sign* personalities

(Taurus, Virgo, Capricorn) are more stable, conservative, practical and materialistic. Gemini, Libra, and Aquarius personalities—the *air-sign* types—are intellectual, critical, sociable, yet detached. *Water-sign* types (Cancer, Scorpio, Pisces) are emotional, receptive, intuitive, indecisive.

Qualities or Quadratures. Each sign is also classified as being cardinal, mutable, or fixed. There are four signs in each quadrature, one sign of each element. We have already discussed the *cardinal signs*—Aries, Cancer, Libra, and Capricorn. These most powerful signs occur on the four angles of the chart. Their keyword: action. Cardinal types are objective, impatient, creative. The *fixed-sign* types—Taurus, Leo, Scorpio, Aquarius—are persistent, organized, stubborn. Keyword: strength. *Mutable-sign* types are adaptable, impressionable, tolerant. They are Gemini, Virgo, Sagittarius, and Pisces; their keyword: flexibility.

Rulerships. Each planet has one or two signs in which its nature is particularly enhanced. The planets are said to "rule" these signs. Before the invention of powerful telescopes, only seven planets were recognized; the Sun (ruler of Leo), the Moon (ruler of Cancer), Mercury (ruler of Gemini and Virgo), Venus (ruler of Taurus and Libra), Mars (ruler of Aries, and traditionally Scorpio), Jupiter (ruler of Sagittarius, and traditionally Pisces), and Saturn (ruler of Capricorn and traditionally Aquarius). More recently Uranus (discovered in 1781), Neptune (1846), and Pluto (1930) were integrated into the astrological system and given rulership of signs previously ruled by other planets: Uranus of Aquarius, Neptune of Pisces, and Pluto of Scorpio.

Nature or Fertility. Based on the inherent nature of the signs and their ruling planets, each sign is classified as fruitful, semi-fruitful, or barren. This classification is the most important for *Moon Sign Book* readers, for most timing of events depends on the fertility of the sign occupied by the Moon. *Fruitful:* the water signs, Cancer, Scorpio, and Pisces. These are all moist, feminine signs. *Semi-fruitful:* the feminine earth signs, Taurus and Capricorn, and the masculine air sign, Libra, which is ruled by a fertile planet, Venus. *Barren:* the masculine fire signs, Aries, Leo, and Sagittarius, and the masculine air signs, Gemini and Aquarius, with the feminine earth sign, Virgo, which has a barren ruler, Mercury.

Aries. ♈ The ram. Ruled by Mars. Masculine, fire, cardinal, barren, hot, dry. Rules the head and face. Colors: red and scarlet. The Sun is in Aries March 21 to April 20. Energetic, original, impulsive.

Taurus. ♉ The bull. Ruled by Venus. Feminine, earth, fixed, semi-fruitful, cold, moist. Rules the throat and neck. Colors: pink and turquoise. The Sun is in Taurus April 20 to May 21. Peaceful, practical, stubborn.

Gemini. ♊ The twins. Ruled by Mercury. Masculine, air, mutable, barren, moist. Rules the hands, arms, lungs, and nerves. Color: silver. The Sun is in Gemini May 21 to June 21. Versatile, imaginative, superficial.

Cancer. ♋ The crab. Ruled by the Moon. Feminine, water, cardinal, fruitful, cold, moist. Rules the breasts and stomach. Colors: grey, silver, and brown. The Sun is in Cancer June 21 to July 23. Mothering, affectionate, possessive.

Leo. ♌ The lion. Ruled by the Sun. Masculine, fire, fixed, barren, hot, dry. Rules the heart and back. Colors: gold, scarlet. The Sun is in Leo July 23 to August 23. Confident, vital, domineering.

Virgo. ♍ The virgin. Ruled by Mercury. Feminine, earth, mutable, barren, cold, dry. Rules the bowels. Colors: navy and grey. The Sun is in Virgo August 23 to September 22. Efficient, analytical, critical.

Libra. ♎ The scales. Ruled by Venus. Masculine, air, cardinal, semi-fruitful, hot, moist. Rules the kidneys, ovaries. Color: blue-green. The Sun is in Libra September 22 to October 23. Friendly, diplomatic, weak-willed.

Scorpio. ♏ The scorpion. Ruled by Pluto. Feminine, water, fixed, fruitful, cold. Rules the sex organs. Color: blood red. The Sun is in Scorpio October 23 to November 22. Intense, forceful, proud.

Sagittarius. ♐ The archer. Ruled by Jupiter. Masculine, fire, mutable, barren, hot, dry. Rules the hips and thighs. Colors: purple and green. The Sun is in Sagittarius November 22 to December 22. Independent, sporting, undisciplined.

Capricorn. ♑ The goat. Ruled by Saturn. Feminine, earth, cardinal, semi-fruitful, cold, dry. Rules knees, bones, skin. Colors: black and dark brown. The Sun is in Capricorn December 22 to January 20. Patient, responsible, ambitious.

Aquarius. ♒ The water bearer. Ruled by Uranus. Masculine, air, fixed, barren, moist. Rules the calves and ankles. Colors: checks, stripes. The Sun is in Aquarius January 20 to February 18. Intellectual, humanitarian, impersonal.

Pisces. ♓ The fish. Ruled by Neptune, feminine, water, mutable, fruitful, cold, moist. Rules the feet. Colors: lavender and sea-green. The Sun is in Pisces February 18 to March 21. Sensitive, emotional, submissive.

The Moon's Phases

There are many different cycles of the Moon. The most familiar one is the *New-Moon cycle.* This cycle has a period of approximately 29½ days and is the interval between two successive phases of the Moon, that is, the period from one New Moon to the next, or from one Full Moon to the next. It results from a combination of the motions of the Moon about the Earth, and the Earth about the Sun. As the Moon makes a single journey among the stars, as seen from the Earth, the Earth advances

approximately one-thirteenth of its journey about the Sun. (There are usually thirteen lunar phases in a year.) Thus, the Sun appears to move toward the east with respect to the stars. And, after making its circle around the Earth, the Moon must travel a bit farther to overtake the Sun.

The Moon requires 27 1/3 days to make a cycle with respect to the stars, and this is called the *zodiacal cycle* of the Moon. The Moon makes one complete circle of the zodiac, passing through each of the twelve signs just once. Thus, the zodiacal cycle extends from when the Moon is in one sign until it returns to that sign.

The Four Phases. The astrological system of naming the lunar phases does not always correspond to those used in other almanacs and calendars. It is therefore important to follow only the *Moon Sign Book* or Llewellyn's *Astrological Calendar* for timing events. *The first quarter* begins when the Sun and Moon are in the same place, or conjunct. The Moon is not visible at first as it rises at the same time as the Sun, but during the end of this quarter the Moon's sliver can be seen just after sunset, as it follows the Sun over the western horizon. *The second quarter* begins approximately halfway between the New Moon and the Full Moon, when the Sun and Moon are at right angles, or square one another. Thus, the half-Moon rises around noon, and sets around midnight, so it can be seen in the west during the first half of the night. *The third quarter* begins with the Full Moon when the Sun and Moon are opposite one another. The entire round of the Moon can be seen rising in the east at sunset, and it rises a little later each day during the week. *The fourth quarter* begins approximately halfway between Full Moon and New Moon when the Sun and Moon are again square. This decreasing Moon rises at midnight at first, so it can be seen in the east during the last half of the night, and is about overhead when the Sun rises.

How To Use This Information

The purpose of the *Moon Sign Book* is to help you take advantage of the astrological wisdom handed down throughout thousands of years. We have divided some of this practical knowledge into six separate sections.

Part I: The Moon includes some general introductory material which should be read prior to the other sections of the book. It also contains "Moon Tables" listing the Moon's sign, element and phase for each day of every month, plus articles on how to apply this knowledge to understanding your shifting energies and interests and to knowing *when* they are likely to be most productive.

Part II: Daily Activities shows you how to time ordinary, everyday activities according to the lunar signs and phases. A complete introduction with specific examples explains two separate ways to put this information to work for you. You can take the data presented in the "Lunar Aspectarian" and the "Favorable and Unfavorable Dates" tables and correlate it with the information presented in the "Astrological Encyclopedia" to draw up your own personal schedule. Or you can simply use the precalculated "Astro-Almanac" as your guide.

Part III: Personal Forecasts consists of predictions for the coming year for each of the twelve signs. As the introduction to this section explains, the predictions are most accurate when read for the ascendant, or rising sign. A simplified method of estimating the ascendant is included. If your time of birth is unknown, the prediction for your sign will be more generally applicable.

Part IV: World Predictions includes forecasts of news events, weather, the economy and the commodities markets, written by experts in their fields.

Part V: Farm and Garden contains much valuable information on all aspects of gardening in accordance with the natural lunar cycles: planting, cultivating, fertilizing, irrigating, and harvesting. Tables include: "Planetary

Rulership of Planets," "Planting Guide," "Planting Dates," "Dates for Destroying Unwanted Plant and Animal Life," and "Dates for Breeding and for Setting Eggs."

Part VI: Sports and Recreation contains articles on using your lunar cycle to your advantage in all recreational activities. "Best Fishing and Hunting Dates" tables are found in this section, also.

There is much talk these days about the ideal of living in harmony with the rhythms of nature. But there is little in the way of practical advice on how to go about accomplishing this objective. This year's *Moon Sign Book* not only charts those rhythms for all to see, but lays out a program of living based on those rhythms. All the wealth of practical advice, however—from when to cut hair and plant perennials to using your talents most efficiently— will somehow seem flat if one cannot recapture something of primitive man's awe of the heavens and his sense of being one with them. One of the purposes of this introduction to lunar astrology and the preceding article, "The Lunar Connection," has been to try to restore to modern man that primitive sense of harmony with nature—to show him a basis for it and the practical application of it.

Time Changes

When the *Moon Sign Book* was first published in 1906 in Ventura, California, Pacific Standard Time was used in all the charts and tables. In the 1975 issue Greenwich Mean Time was used, because it is the standard time measurement used by astrologers the world over. However, this system seemed to create more problems than it alleviated, so it was decided to switch to Central Standard Time in this and all subsequent issues. Central Standard Time, being only two hours different from the time zones of the eastern and western seaboards in the continental United States, should be equally convenient for all our American readers. The handy conversion tables that follow show how the **Moon Tables** can be used anywhere.

When *Daylight Savings Time* is in use in your area, you must add one hour to the time used in the tables before making your correction.

Standard Time Zones
Greenwich Mean Time (GMT) 0° longitude, add six hours.

Atlantic Standard Time (AST) 60° W longitude, add two hours.

Eastern Standard Time (EST) 75° W longitude, add one hour.

Central Standard Time (CST) 90° W longitude, time used throughout the *Moon Sign Book.*

Mountain Standard Time (MST) 105° longitude, subtract one hour.

Pacific Standard Time (PST) 120° W longitude, subtract two hours.

Yukon Standard Time (YST) 135° W longitude, subtract three hours.

Central Alaskan Time (CAT) 150° W longitude, subtract four hours. *Note:* On November 25, 1967, this time zone was renamed Alaska-Hawaii Standard Time.

Hawaii Standard Time (HST) 150° W longitude, subtract four hours. Now called Alaska-Hawaii Standard Time.

Alaska-Hawaii Standard Time (AHST) 150° W longitude, subtract four hours.

Bering Time (BT) 165° W longitude, subtract five hours.

To find
the Other ...
Is to find
Oneself.
All nature is
expressed in one
loved face.

DIVINE UNION

The uniting of the Divinity within each partner in a sexual relationship—that's why marriage is known as a sacrament.

In perfecting sexual union there is a uniting of magnetic and electric currents to create a field of energy that extends both inward and outward to contact the Infinite Intelligence and the personal unconscious. In this lies *Magick*, for we gain insight into questions asked, or we may extend our personal power by becoming a channel to the powers of the Universe.

SEX MAGICK

To perfect that sexual union requires a knowledge that has been hidden away within the archives of esoteric orders and secret scoieties, and now is revealed in this *Manual of Sex Magick* by Louis Culling, past master of the Ordo Palladium Reformado through succession from Diana Vaughn and Wynn Westcott.

By means of this knowledge, sexual ecstasy is transmuted into the magickal fire that unites soul to soul and each to the "heavenly Bridedroom."

MANUAL OF SEX MAGICK, deluxe, hardcover edition, $5.00. If it's not available at your local bookstore, use the form on the last page and order by this number: 1-87542-106 from Gnostic-Aquarian Book Sales.

Time Zone Conversion Charts

GMT	EDT/ AST	CDT/ EST	MDT/ CST	PDT/ MST	YDT/ PST	AHDT/ YST	BDT/ AHST	BT
6 am	2 am	1 am	midnight	11 pm day before	10 pm	9 pm	8 pm	7 pm
7 am	3 am	2 am	1 am	midnight	11 pm day before	10 pm	9 pm	8 pm
8 am	4 am	3 am	2 am	1 am	midnight	11 pm day before	10 pm	9 pm
9 am	5 am	4 am	3 am	2 am	1 am	midnight	11 pm day before	10 pm
10 am	6 am	5 am	4 am	3 am	2 am	1 am	midnight	11 pm day before
11 am	7 am	6 am	5 am	4 am	3 am	2 am	1 am	midnight
noon	8 am	7 am	6 am	5 am	4 am	3 am	2 am	1 am
1 pm	9 am	8 am	7 am	6 am	5 am	4 am	3 am	2 am
2 pm	10 am	9 am	8 am	7 am	6 am	5 am	4 am	3 am
3 pm	11 am	10 am	9 am	8 am	7 am	6 am	5 am	4 am
4 pm	noon	11 am	10 am	9 am	8 am	7 am	6 am	5 am
5 pm	1 pm	noon	11 am	10 am	9 am	8 am	7 am	6 am
6 pm	2 pm	1 pm	noon	11 am	10 am	9 am	8 am	7 am
7 pm	3 pm	2 pm	1 pm	noon	11 am	10 am	9 am	8 am
8 pm	4 pm	3 pm	2 pm	1 pm	noon	11 am	10 am	9 am
9 pm	5 pm	4 pm	3 pm	2 pm	1 pm	noon	11 am	10 am
10 pm	6 pm	5 pm	4 pm	3 pm	2 pm	1 pm	noon	11 am

								noon
							1 pm	1 pm
						2 pm	2 pm	2 pm
					3 pm	3 pm	3 pm	3 pm
				4 pm	4 pm	4 pm	4 pm	4 pm
			5 pm	5 pm	5 pm	5 pm	5 pm	5 pm
		6 pm	6 pm	6 pm	6 pm	6 pm	6 pm	6 pm
	7 pm	7 pm	7 pm	7 pm	7 pm	7 pm	7 pm	7 pm
11 pm	8 pm	8 pm	8 pm	8 pm	8 pm	8 pm	8 pm	8 pm
midnight	9 pm	9 pm	9 pm	9 pm	9 pm	9 pm	9 pm	
1 am next day	10 pm	10 pm	10 pm	10 pm	10 pm	10 pm		
2 am	11 pm	11 pm	11 pm	11 pm	11 pm			
3 am	midnight	midnight	midnight	midnight				
4 am	1 am next day	1 am next day	1 am next day					
5 am	2 am	2 am						
6 am	3 am							
7 am								

Moon Tables

Sign	Dates	Ruler	Element	Quality	Nature
Aries	Mar 21 – Apr 20	Mars	Fire	Cardinal	Barren
Taurus	Apr 20 – May 21	Venus	Earth	Fixed	Semi-Fruitful
Gemini	May 21 – June 21	Mercury	Air	Mutable	Barren
Cancer	June 21 – July 23	Moon	Water	Cardinal	Fruitful
Leo	July 23 – Aug 23	Sun	Fire	Fixed	Barren
Virgo	Aug 23 – Sept 22	Mercury	Earth	Mutable	Barren
Libra	Sept 22 – Oct 23	Venus	Air	Cardinal	Semi-Fruitful
Scorpio	Oct 23 – Nov 22	Pluto	Water	Fixed	Fruitful
Sagittarius	Nov 22 – Dec 22	Jupiter	Fire	Mutable	Barren
Capricorn	Dec 22 – Jan 20	Saturn	Earth	Cardinal	Semi-Fruitful
Aquarius	Jan 20 – Feb 18	Uranus	Air	Fixed	Barren
Pisces	Feb 18 – Mar 21	Neptune	Water	Mutable	Fruitful

Using Your
Moon Tables
Section

This section gives you basic information on the sign the Moon is in and its phase. Later sections will give you more detailed information about the aspects it forms and how its position, phase and aspects apply to particular areas such as farming, gardening, sports and recreation. But knowing where it is, relative to the zodiac, and what phase it is in, is fundamental to living according to its cycles.

All subsequent sections of *The Moon Sign Book* will refer to the material in this section. The "Moon Tables" part of this section contains the daily chronicle of the Moon's movements in the coming year. When the "Farm and Garden" section says to irrigate when the Moon is in a water sign, to harvest mushrooms during the Full Moon, to gather root crops for food during the third and fourth quarters, to cultivate when the Moon is in a barren sign—it is in *this* section that you will find which signs are water signs and which are barren, and *when* the Moon will be in these signs, when it will be full, or when it will be in the fourth quarter.

The immediately preceding tables give the basic characteristics of the twelve zodiacal signs. The meanings of "Ruler," "Element," "Quality" and "Nature" are clarified in "Understanding Lunar Astrology" (pages 39-48). When the Moon enters Aries, for example, the attributes

associated with Mars—fire, cardinality and barrenness—
are accentuated.

What this means practically is elaborated in the following article, "Moon Signs." There we find that the Moon in
Aries signifies "a time of enthusiasm and beginnings," a
time when aggressiveness and egocentricity are emphasized, a time that favors skillful work with tools (which
are ruled by Mars). The meaning of the lunar transit of
each of the twelve signs is explained.

The key to *using* this information is contained in the
"Moon Tables" which follow it. These tables tell you exactly when the Moon transits each sign and what phase it
is in then, and they repeat the element and nature of each
sign. Thus by applying the "Moon Signs" information to
the 27th of April, for example, we find that we must
watch out for bad temper and selfishness, as Arian temper
blends with Taruean persistence. We learn that from the
10th through the 11th of April, when the Moon is in
Virgo, matters of hygiene and upkeep in the home are
favored, especially any activity requiring attention to detail, such as bargain-hunting. Inasmuch as Virgo is the harvest earth sign, this period might be good for planning a
garden.

The other bits of information in the "Moon Tables"—
element, nature and phase—qualify whatever we learn in
applying the "Moon Signs" article. For example, although
it is good to begin new projects when the Moon is in
Aries, as it is on April 26th, it might not be so good to
start a garden then, for Aries' nature is barren: furthermore, the Moon, in its fourth quarter, is waning on the
26th, suggesting that it is an inauspicious time to start a
new project, which is best begun when the Moon is waxing, so that its fruits can be enjoyed as the Moon wanes.
A better time to initiate a new project might be March
31st, when the Moon is not only in Aries but in the
first quarter.

Basic Moon-sign information is qualified yet further in the "Daily Activities" section that follows the "Moon Tables": lunar aspects, planetary rulerships as affected by these aspects, and lunar highs and lows further assist us in determining what to look for and when to begin.

In these two sections, "Moon Tables" and "Daily Activities," you can find most of the basic information necessary for guidance in your daily activities. "Your Personal Forecast" supplements this information with Sun-sign astrology, and "World Predictions" gives you some idea—through the techniques of mundane astrology—of the larger world in which you will be conducting your affairs. The last two sections, "Farm and Garden" and "Sports and Recreation," give specific applications of the material found in the primary "Moon Tables" and "Daily Activities" sections.

Throughout *The Moon Sign Book* there are tables based on these two primary sections—tables that provide specific day-to-day guidance on when to do an assortment of domestic chores, when to perform the various tasks associated with farming and gardening, and when to hunt and fish. But you can make your own judgments by coming back to these two primary sections. And all understanding *begins* here—in the "Moon Tables" section.

Moon Signs
Lee Duvlea

The Moon changes astrological signs every few days; the exact times the Moon will be in each sign are shown in the *Moon Tables*. The following is a brief description of the Moon's effects on people in general as it goes through its monthly cycle. We hope it will help you plan your daily activities to make the most of the Moon's influence.

Moon in Aries
A time of enthusiasm and beginnings. Tendencies to impulsiveness and snap decisions are accentuated. This is a favorable time for any kind of beginning, and for making changes (especially those that require bold or sudden moves). The cycle runs toward aggressiveness and egocentricity. This is also a good time for work that requires skillful (though not necessarily patient) work with tools, particularly sharp cutting instruments and the like. The first part of the Moon's transit through Aries, when it is closer to Pisces, is a more spiritual time; a sense of rebirth is evident and the mind is inclined to consider deeper subjects, usually from a new perspective, and to consider radical divergencies from previously held opinions.

Nearing the middle of the transit, the strongest Arian tendencies can be felt, which makes this an excellent time to indulge one's curiosity and to seek inspiration for a direction. Tendencies to bad temper and "selfishness" should be carefully watched, especially as the Moon approaches Taurus, as a combination of Arian temper and Taurian persistence could be very unpleasant indeed.

Moon in Taurus

The aggressiveness and verve of Aries "solidifies" into the placid patience of the Bull. People are inclined to be stodgy and cautious. The desire is to protect what one already has, rather than to strike out in search of something new. This is a poor time to seek change, especially in financial concerns. Bankers and others in charge of money are slow to make loans, demand the soundest of collateral, and then grant them only after thorough deliberation. Plan a barbecue for another time.

The first part of the Taurian Moon transit is the most cautious and reserved. Political power games become more earnest, the edge being with the established position. The middle area is more placid and calm, a time for rest, or for engaging in those things which require more patience than skill or nimbleness.

As the Moon moves toward Gemini, the Taurian solidity will gradually give way to the Geminian mode of quickness and change. Concern is directed more and more toward communication and thought, though still mostly in practical matters.

Moon in Gemini

Communication is the key drive of this time, senses of wit and intelligence becoming sharper. Practical concerns tend to be slighted in favor of intellectual pursuits and mental games. People are more changeable than usual. Statements should be taken with a grain of salt, particularly those from persons who have already shown signs of fickleness. This time is highly favorable for any activity concerning communication or the spreading of information, particularly toward the middle of the transit.

Toward the end, as the Moon blends into Cancer, more emotiveness becomes apparent, in contrast to the highly mental and abstract Geminian mode. Communication tends to be derived more and more from emotional needs. It is, for example, an excellent time to write letters or to make telephone calls about family matters.

As Gemini is a barren sign and primarily mental, it is not favorable for agricultural matters, though it is an excellent time to make preparatory arrangements.

Moon in Cancer

Sensitivity rises sharply in the sign of Cancer, and with it comes a strong drive toward self-indulgence, especially with food and drink. People with natural tendencies toward overindulgence should be on alert, for this is the time when dietary restrictions will face the strongest temptations. People with natural tendencies toward gullibility should be most prudent during the Moon's transit of Cancer, since appeals to their desire for security will have strong power to sway. A sharp tongue should be curbed during the Cancer Moon, when people are more inclined to have their feelings hurt, being more easily affected by personal criticism. By the same token, one should be more watchful of flattery or praise from suspicious sources; the desire to accept it increases with the strong Cancerian need for approval.

As Cancer is traditionally the most fertile of the signs and the Moon's natural home, it is friendly toward matters in which fertility is an important factor.

As the Moon moves toward Leo, Leonine pride blends with Cancerian sensitivity. This can be a time of great personal warmth and friendship, but it is important to be courteous during this phase, since a grudge created here will take a long time to pass.

Moon in Leo

Pride and circumstance come to the fore now, with matters of display and showmanship getting special priority. The noted Leonine generosity becomes evident, making it an excellent time for charitable activities. Overall vitality increases greatly, with the emphasis on entertainment and romantic pursuits. This is also a good time for dealing with persons in positions of power, especially if you appeal to their nobler motives. Conflicts over leadership are more likely to arise in the beginning of this transit, while those in an established position have the edge during the middle of the transit. The Moon in Leo is a favorable time for matters of entertainment, particularly the theater. One should be aware of tendencies to pomposity and overstated positions. As the Moon moves toward Virgo, the pride of Leo will blend with the exactness of Virgo, making it a good time for unassuming yet ultimately ambitious moves toward personal advancement.

Moon in Virgo

The early phase of Virgo is a good time to relate to matters of the home, as drives for hygiene and upkeep strengthen. An excellent time for dealing with health and dietary concerns. Attention to detail is the Virgo forte, so anything that requires painstaking attention is benefited. The Virgo Moon transit is a good time for intellectual matters, though better for those that require exactness rather than innovation. Editing a completed work would be better than attempts at spontaneous creativity. Virgo favors the careful, bargain-hunting shopper, especially when dealing with fruits of the earth.

As Virgo is the harvest Earth Sign, it is friendly toward agricultural matters, with greatest emphasis on vegetable raising. It is a favorable time for the care of animals, such as veterinarian work, but a poor time for the production of meat foods, such as slaughtering.

The Virgo capacity for objective (and at its worst, cold-blooded) calculation is strongest toward the middle of the transit, often being expressed as manipulation on a personal level as the Moon moves toward Libra.

Moon in Libra

In Libra, Venus shows her other side. Apart from her rulership of the stolid and earthy sign of Taurus, she rules Libra, the sign of balance and the harmonious interplay of forces. Naturally, it benefits anything that tends to beautify. Artistic work, especially involving color and color balance, is greatly enhanced. As Libra is also the sign of partnership and union, it is an auspicious time for forming partnerships, marriages, and agreements (if the aspects are otherwise favorable). The Moon in Libra accentuates teamwork, particularly teams of two, and tends to counter impulses to "go it alone." An Air Sign, the Moon in Libra favors the eloquent and the charming, though stronger overtones of sarcasm and satire will evolve as the Moon moves toward Scorpio.

Moon in Scorpio

In Scorpio, Mars shows its other side, from the splendid and fiery aggressiveness of Aries to the dark, brooding Scorpio. People tend to be suspicious in this phase of the lunar cycle, and will be wary and distrustful of anyone seeking information or money from them. As in Cancer, the Moon in Scorpio heightens sensitivity to insult and discourtesy, but the reaction common to Cancer changes to a malevolent reaction when the Moon is in Scorpio. During this time, people tend to give sharp and accurate criticism. People are most critical during the first and middle part of the Moon's passage through Scorpio, changing to a lighter, more philosophical mood as the Moon approaches Sagittarius. The middle part is the darkest, and it is advisable to walk past graveyards quickly, more so if the Moon is full or approaching fullness. The last part is the best for dealing with authority.

Moon in Sagittarius

The moody side of Mars gives way to the expansive optimism of Jupiter as the Moon moves into Sagittarius. This is the most philosophical of signs, inclining toward higher thinking in all respects. The suspicious reserve of Scorpio gives way to brisk candor. People who might have displayed suspicion in Scorpio now are honest and direct in their interchanges, and less reserved. Candor and honesty are enhanced at this time, and, as honest acceptance is reinforced, it is an excellent time to "get it off your chest." People tend to be generally more humane, and more interested in higher thinking (though more intellectual than mystical). It is a favorable time for dealing with institutions of higher learning, publishing companies and the like. The Moon in Sagittarius is a good time for sport and adventure, but this sobers quickly as the Moon moves toward Capricorn.

Moon in Capricorn

The expansive joviality of Sagittarius withers in the home of Saturn. Obstacles appear on an uphill path. Pessimism is rampant and the negative view becomes the accepted view. Spiritual and intellectual matters are nearly forgotten during this time, as they are dominated by the fretful concern of Capricorn with the material. This is probably the poorest possible time to seek a concession from one in authority or to depart from the accepted norms. It is also a guardedly acquisitive time, with ambition becoming the driving force. The secret plot conceived in Scorpio may be carried out in Capricorn, but the edge is strongly in favor of the established position. As Capricorn is the home of Saturn, insensitivity is pervasive, which can frequently lead to cruelties and malice justified on grounds of necessity (rather than enmity). These trends will mellow and be pacified as the Moon approaches Aquarius.

Moon in Aquarius

The mood changes dramatically in Aquarius, as this is the home of Uranus, the revolutionary and electric planet. The flow now is with the innovative, the new and the different. This transit reinforces the humane and rational in people, and favors social concerns. It promotes the gathering of social groups for friendly and convivial interchange. It is also strongly inclined to science and the scientific approach. People will tend to react and speak from rational rather than emotional view points. People are more apt to pay heed to suggestions for change, so long as the arguments are based on rational and clear evidence. As Uranus is traditionally connected to astrologers, it is an excellent time to consult an astrologer.

Moon in Pisces

Things tend to get a bit fuzzy in Pisces, as it is the home of Neptune, the planet of vagueness and deception. There is a strong undertone of spirituality, though it tends to be expressed in the early and middle part of the transit as a sense of martyrdom. Issues are clouded, there is difficulty in getting the cold facts of any situation. There is a pervasive sense of self-sacrifice. People are inclined to discuss their troubles, and are more easily manipulated. Things are, more than ever, not what they seem, and people tend to react with a sense of befuddlement or confusion. They will seek the counsel of persons they believe to be wiser, and as such, it is an excellent time for oracles and divinations. Entertainment, especially of an escapist or fantastic nature, is benefited by the Moon's transit of Pisces. This is an excellent time for retreat and contemplation. As the Moon moves toward Aries, the mood of Pisces lifts to a more cheerful level, and it appears that the last movement is ending and the dance is to be repeated once again.

January 1977
Central Standard Time

Date		Moon's Sign		Element	Nature	Moon's Phase	
1	Saturday	1:47 pm	Gemini	Air	Barren		2nd
2	Sunday		Gemini	Air	Barren		2nd
3	Monday		Gemini	Air	Barren		2nd
4	Tuesday	1:10 am	Cancer	Water	Fruitful		2nd
5	Wednesday		Cancer	Water	Fruitful	6:51 am	FM
6	Thursday	10:33 pm	Leo	Fire	Barren		3rd
7	Friday		Leo	Fire	Barren		3rd
8	Saturday	5:54 pm	Virgo	Earth	Barren		3rd
9	Sunday		Virgo	Earth	Barren		3rd
10	Monday	11:15 pm	Libra	Air	Semi-Fruitful		3rd
11	Tuesday		Libra	Air	Semi-Fruitful		3rd
12	Wednesday		Libra	Air	Semi-Fruitful	1:57 pm	4th
13	Thursday	2:47 am	Scorpio	Water	Fruitful		4th
14	Friday		Scorpio	Water	Fruitful		4th

15	Saturday	3:39 am	Sagittarius	Fire	Barren	4th
16	Sunday		Sagittarius	Fire	Barren	4th
17	Monday	6:40 am	Capricorn	Earth	Semi-Fruitful	4th
18	Tuesday		Capricorn	Earth	Semi-Fruitful	4th
19	Wednesday	9:18 am	Aquarius	Air	Barren	8:34 am NM
20	Thursday		Aquarius	Air	Barren	1st

Sun enters Aquarius 10:20 pm, January 20

21	Friday	1:47 pm	Pisces	Water	Fruitful	1st
22	Saturday		Pisces	Water	Fruitful	1st
23	Sunday	9:27 pm	Aries	Fire	Barren	1st
24	Monday		Aries	Fire	Barren	1st
25	Tuesday		Aries	Fire	Barren	1st
26	Wednesday	8:51 am	Taurus	Earth	Semi-Fruitful	11:12 pm 2nd
27	Thursday		Taurus	Earth	Semi-Fruitful	2nd
28	Friday	9:32 pm	Gemini	Air	Barren	2nd
29	Saturday		Gemini	Air	Barren	2nd
30	Sunday		Gemini	Air	Barren	2nd
31	Monday	9:18 am	Cancer	Water	Fruitful	2nd

February 1977
Central Standard Time

Date		Moon's Sign	Element	Nature	Moon's Phase	
1 Tuesday		Cancer	Water	Fruitful		2nd
2 Wednesday	6:23 pm	Leo	Fire	Barren		2nd
3 Thursday		Leo	Fire	Barren	10:35 pm	FM
4 Friday		Leo	Fire	Barren		3rd
5 Saturday	0:32 am	Virgo	Earth	Barren		3rd
6 Sunday		Virgo	Earth	Barren		3rd
7 Monday	5:10 am	Libra	Air	Semi-Fruitful		3rd
8 Tuesday		Libra	Air	Semi-Fruitful		3rd
9 Wednesday	9:03 am	Scorpio	Water	Fruitful		3rd
10 Thursday		Scorpio	Water	Fruitful	10:09 pm	4th
11 Friday	1:45 am	Sagittarius	Fire	Barren		4th
12 Saturday		Sagittarius	Fire	Barren		4th
13 Sunday	2:34 pm	Capricorn	Earth	Semi-Fruitful		4th
14 Monday		Capricorn	Earth	Semi-Fruitful		4th

15	Tuesday	5:59 pm	Aquarius	Air	Barren		4th
16	Wednesday		Aquarius	Air	Barren		4th
17	Thursday	10:52 pm	Pisces	Water	Fruitful	10:08 pm	NM
18	Friday		Pisces	Water	Fruitful		1st
19	Saturday		Pisces	Water	Fruitful		1st

Sun enters Pisces 1:29 pm, February 19

20	Sunday	6:35 am	Aries	Fire	Barren		1st
21	Monday		Aries	Fire	Barren		1st
22	Tuesday	5:00 pm	Taurus	Earth	Semi-Fruitful		1st
23	Wednesday		Taurus	Earth	Semi-Fruitful		1st
24	Thursday		Taurus	Earth	Semi-Fruitful		1st
25	Friday	5:36 am	Gemini	Air	Barren	8:51 pm	2nd
26	Saturday		Gemini	Air	Barren		2nd
27	Sunday	5:59 pm	Cancer	Water	Fruitful		2nd
28	Monday		Cancer	Water	Fruitful		2nd

March 1977
Central Standard Time

Date		Moon's Sign		Element	Nature	Moon's Phase	
1	Tuesday	Cancer		Water	Fruitful		2nd
2	Wednesday	3:23 am	Leo	Fire	Barren		2nd
3	Thursday		Leo	Fire	Barren		2nd
4	Friday	9:37 am	Virgo	Earth	Barren		2nd
5	Saturday		Virgo	Earth	Barren	11:33 am	FM
6	Sunday	12:48 pm	Libra	Air	Semi-Fruitful		1st
7	Monday		Libra	Air	Semi-Fruitful		1st
8	Tuesday	2:46 pm	Scorpio	Water	Fruitful		1st
9	Wednesday		Scorpio	Water	Fruitful		1st
10	Thursday	4:48 pm	Sagittarius	Fire	Barren		1st
11	Friday		Sagittarius	Fire	Barren		1st
12	Saturday	7:47 pm	Capricorn	Earth	Semi-Fruitful	5:37 am	4th
13	Sunday		Capricorn	Earth	Semi-Fruitful		4th
14	Monday		Capricorn	Earth	Semi-Fruitful		4th

15	Tuesday	0:26 am	Aquarius	Air	Barren		4th
16	Wednesday		Aquarius	Air	Barren		4th
17	Thursday	6:23 am	Pisces	Water	Fruitful		4th
18	Friday		Pisces	Water	Fruitful		4th
19	Saturday	2:42 pm	Aries	Fire	Barren	1:09 pm	NM
20	Sunday		Aries	Fire	Barren		1st
21	Monday		Aries	Fire	Barren		1st

Sun enters Aries 11:36 am, March 21, the Vernal Equinox

22	Tuesday	1:06 am	Taurus	Earth	Semi-Fruitful		1st
23	Wednesday		Taurus	Earth	Semi-Fruitful		1st
24	Thursday	1:30 pm	Gemini	Air	Barren		1st
25	Friday		Gemini	Air	Barren		1st
26	Saturday		Gemini	Air	Barren		1st
27	Sunday	2:00 am	Cancer	Water	Fruitful	4:27 pm	2nd
28	Monday		Cancer	Water	Fruitful		2nd
29	Tuesday	12:43 pm	Leo	Fire	Barren		2nd
30	Wednesday		Leo	Fire	Barren		2nd
31	Thursday	7:24 pm	Virgo	Earth	Barren		2nd

April 1977
Central Standard Time

Date		Moon's Sign	Element	Nature	Moon's Phase	
1	Friday			Barren		2nd
2	Saturday	10:37 pm	Virgo	Earth	Semi-Fruitful	2nd
3	Sunday		Libra	Air	Semi-Fruitful	10:19 pm FM
			Libra	Air		Lunar Eclipse
4	Monday	11:26 pm	Scorpio	Water	Fruitful	3rd
5	Tuesday		Scorpio	Water	Fruitful	3rd
6	Wednesday		Scorpio	Water	Fruitful	3rd
7	Thursday	0:20 am	Sagittarius	Fire	Barren	3rd
8	Friday		Sagittarius	Fire	Barren	3rd
9	Saturday	1:52 am	Capricorn	Earth	Semi-Fruitful	3rd
10	Sunday		Capricorn	Earth	Semi-Fruitful	4th 1:17 pm
11	Monday	5:49 am	Aquarius	Air	Barren	4th
12	Tuesday		Aquarius	Air	Barren	4th
13	Wednesday	12:25 pm	Pisces	Water	Fruitful	4th

14	Thursday		Pisces	Water	Fruitful		4th
15	Friday	9:33 pm	Aries	Fire	Barren		4th
16	Saturday		Aries	Fire	Barren		4th
17	Sunday		Aries	Fire	Barren		4th
18	Monday	8:23 am	Taurus	Earth	Semi-Fruitful	5:12 am	NM Solar Eclipse
19	Tuesday		Taurus	Earth	Semi-Fruitful		1st
20	Wednesday	8:39 pm	Gemini	Air	Barren		1st

Sun enters Taurus 11:58 pm, April 20

21	Thursday		Gemini	Air	Barren		1st
22	Friday		Gemini	Air	Barren		1st
23	Saturday	9:26 am	Cancer	Water	Fruitful		1st
24	Sunday		Cancer	Water	Fruitful		1st
25	Monday	8:59 pm	Leo	Fire	Barren		1st
26	Tuesday		Leo	Fire	Barren	8:43 am	2nd
27	Wednesday		Leo	Fire	Barren		2nd
28	Thursday	5:16 am	Virgo	Earth	Barren		2nd
29	Friday		Virgo	Earth	Barren		2nd
30	Saturday	9:09 am	Libra	Air	Semi-Fruitful		2nd

May 1977
Central Standard Time

Date		Moon's Sign	Element	Nature	Moon's Phase	
1	Sunday		Libra	Air	Semi-Fruitful		2nd
2	Monday	10:00 am	Scorpio	Water	Fruitful		2nd
3	Tuesday		Scorpio	Water	Fruitful	6:49 am	FM
4	Wednesday	9:46 am	Sagittarius	Fire	Barren		3rd
5	Thursday		Sagittarius	Fire	Barren		3rd
6	Friday	9:47 am	Capricorn	Earth	Semi-Fruitful		3rd
7	Saturday		Capricorn	Earth	Semi-Fruitful		3rd
8	Sunday	12:16 pm	Aquarius	Air	Barren		3rd
9	Monday		Aquarius	Air	Barren	10:10 pm	4th
10	Tuesday	5:48 pm	Pisces	Water	Fruitful		4th
11	Wednesday		Pisces	Water	Fruitful		4th
12	Thursday		Pisces	Water	Fruitful		4th
13	Friday	3:06 am	Aries	Fire	Barren		4th
14	Saturday		Aries	Fire	Barren		4th

15	Sunday	2:36 pm	Taurus	Earth	Semi-Fruitful		4th
16	Monday		Taurus	Earth	Semi-Fruitful		4th
17	Tuesday		Taurus	Earth	Semi-Fruitful	8:59 pm	NM
18	Wednesday	2:46 am	Gemini	Air	Barren		1st
19	Thursday		Gemini	Air	Barren		1st
20	Friday	3:29 pm	Cancer	Water	Fruitful		1st
21	Saturday		Cancer	Water	Fruitful		1st

Sun enters Gemini 10:08 pm, May 21

22	Sunday		Cancer	Water	Fruitful		1st
23	Monday	3:16 am	Leo	Fire	Barren		1st
24	Tuesday		Leo	Fire	Barren		1st
25	Wednesday	12:48 pm	Virgo	Earth	Barren	9:21 pm	2nd
26	Thursday		Virgo	Earth	Barren		2nd
27	Friday	6:31 pm	Libra	Air	Semi-Fruitful		2nd
28	Saturday		Libra	Air	Semi-Fruitful		2nd
29	Sunday	8:36 pm	Scorpio	Water	Fruitful		2nd
30	Monday		Scorpio	Water	Fruitful		2nd
31	Tuesday	8:32 pm	Sagittarius	Fire	Barren		2nd

June 1977
Central Standard Time

Date		Moon's Sign	Element	Nature	Moon's Phase	
1	Wednesday		Sagittarius	Fire	Barren	2:15 pm	FM
2	Thursday	7:57 pm	Capricorn	Earth	Semi-Fruitful		3rd
3	Friday		Capricorn	Earth	Semi-Fruitful		3rd
4	Saturday	8:56 pm	Aquarius	Air	Barren		3rd
5	Sunday		Aquarius	Air	Barren		3rd
6	Monday		Aquarius	Air	Barren		3rd
7	Tuesday	0:53 am	Pisces	Water	Fruitful		3rd
8	Wednesday		Pisces	Water	Fruitful	9:09 am	4th
9	Thursday	8:55 am	Aries	Fire	Barren		4th
10	Friday		Aries	Fire	Barren		4th
11	Saturday	8:21 pm	Taurus	Earth	Semi-Fruitful		4th
12	Sunday		Taurus	Earth	Semi-Fruitful		4th
13	Monday		Taurus	Earth	Semi-Fruitful		4th
14	Tuesday	9:02 am	Gemini	Air	Barren		4th

15	Wednesday		Gemini	Air	Barren		4th
16	Thursday	9:32 pm	Cancer	Water	Fruitful	12:38 pm	NM
17	Friday		Cancer	Water	Fruitful		1st
18	Saturday		Cancer	Water	Fruitful		1st
19	Sunday	8:57 am	Leo	Fire	Barren		1st
20	Monday		Leo	Fire	Barren		1st
21	Tuesday	6:46 pm	Virgo	Earth	Barren		1st
22	Wednesday		Virgo	Earth	Barren		1st

Sun enters Cancer 6:13 am, June 22, the Summer Solstice

23	Thursday		Virgo	Earth	Barren		1st
24	Friday	1:52 am	Libra	Air	Semi-Fruitful	6:44 am	2nd
25	Saturday		Libra	Air	Semi-Fruitful		2nd
26	Sunday	5:40 am	Scorpio	Water	Fruitful		2nd
27	Monday		Scorpio	Water	Fruitful		2nd
28	Tuesday	7:07 am	Sagittarius	Fire	Barren		2nd
29	Wednesday		Sagittarius	Fire	Barren		2nd
30	Thursday	6:48 am	Capricorn	Earth	Semi-Fruitful	9:33 pm	FM

July 1977
Central Standard Time

Date		Moon's Sign	Element	Nature	Moon's Phase	
1	Friday					3rd
2	Saturday	7:10 am	Capricorn	Earth	Semi-Fruitful	3rd
3	Sunday		Aquarius	Air	Barren	3rd
4	Monday	9:53 am	Aquarius	Air	Barren	3rd
5	Tuesday		Pisces	Water	Fruitful	3rd
6	Wednesday	4:19 pm	Pisces	Water	Fruitful	3rd
7	Thursday		Aries	Fire	Barren	4th
8	Friday		Aries	Fire	Barren	10:41 pm	4th
9	Saturday	2:40 am	Aries	Fire	Barren	4th
10	Sunday		Taurus	Earth	Semi-Fruitful	4th
11	Monday	3:34 pm	Taurus	Earth	Semi-Fruitful	4th
12	Tuesday		Gemini	Air	Barren	4th
13	Wednesday		Gemini	Air	Barren	4th
14	Thursday	4:00 am	Gemini	Air	Barren	4th
			Cancer	Water	Fruitful	4th

Date	Day	Time	Sign	Element		Time	Phase
15	Friday		Cancer	Water	Fruitful		4th
16	Saturday	2:55 pm	Leo	Fire	Barren	2:43 am	NM
17	Sunday		Leo	Fire	Barren		1st
18	Monday		Leo	Fire	Barren		1st
19	Tuesday	0:10 am	Virgo	Earth	Barren		1st
20	Wednesday		Virgo	Earth	Barren		1st
21	Thursday	7:05 am	Libra	Air	Semi-Fruitful		1st
22	Friday		Libra	Air	Semi-Fruitful		1st
23	Saturday	12:18 pm	Scorpio	Water	Fruitful	1:39 pm	2nd

Sun enters Leo 5:06 pm, July 23

Date	Day	Time	Sign	Element		Time	Phase
24	Sunday		Scorpio	Water	Fruitful		2nd
25	Monday	3:07 pm	Sagittarius	Fire	Barren		2nd
26	Tuesday		Sagittarius	Fire	Barren		2nd
27	Wednesday	4:17 pm	Capricorn	Earth	Semi-Fruitful		2nd
28	Thursday		Capricorn	Earth	Semi-Fruitful		2nd
29	Friday	5:36 pm	Aquarius	Air	Barren		2nd
30	Saturday		Aquarius	Air	Barren	5:32 am	FM
31	Sunday	7:53 pm	Pisces	Water	Fruitful		3rd

August 1977
Central Standard Time

Date		Moon's Sign	Element	Nature	Moon's Phase	
1	Monday		Pisces	Water	Fruitful	3rd
2	Tuesday		Pisces	Water	Fruitful	3rd
3	Wednesday	1:04 am	Aries	Fire	Barren	3rd
4	Thursday		Aries	Fire	Barren	3rd
5	Friday	10:21 am	Taurus	Earth	Semi-Fruitful	3rd
6	Saturday		Taurus	Earth	Semi-Fruitful	2:42 pm	4th
7	Sunday	10:32 pm	Gemini	Air	Barren	4th
8	Monday		Gemini	Air	Barren	4th
9	Tuesday		Gemini	Air	Barren	4th
10	Wednesday	11:15 am	Cancer	Water	Fruitful	4th
11	Thursday		Cancer	Water	Fruitful	4th
12	Friday	10:15 pm	Leo	Fire	Barren	4th
13	Saturday		Leo	Fire	Barren	4th
14	Sunday		Leo	Fire	Barren	3:46 pm	NM

15	Monday	6:44 am	Virgo	Earth	Barren	1st
16	Tuesday		Virgo	Earth	Barren	1st
17	Wednesday	12:38 pm	Libra	Air	Semi-Fruitful	1st
18	Thursday		Libra	Air	Semi-Fruitful	1st
19	Friday	5:25 pm	Scorpio	Water	Fruitful	1st
20	Saturday		Scorpio	Water	Fruitful	1st
21	Sunday	8:46 pm	Sagittarius	Fire	Barren	2nd 7:05 pm
22	Monday		Sagittarius	Fire	Barren	2nd
23	Tuesday	11:18 pm	Capricorn	Earth	Semi-Fruitful	2nd

Sun enters Virgo 11:54 pm, August 23

24	Wednesday		Capricorn	Earth	Semi-Fruitful	2nd
25	Thursday		Capricorn	Earth	Semi-Fruitful	2nd
26	Friday	1:59 am	Aquarius	Air	Barren	2nd
27	Saturday		Aquarius	Air	Barren	2nd
28	Sunday	5:20 am	Pisces	Water	Fruitful	FM 2:52 pm
29	Monday		Pisces	Water	Fruitful	3rd
30	Tuesday	10:35 am	Aries	Fire	Barren	3rd
31	Wednesday		Aries	Fire	Barren	3rd

Moon Tables

September 1977
Central Standard Time

Date		Moon's Sign		Element	Nature	Moon's Phase	
1	Thursday	6:47 pm	Taurus	Earth	Semi-Fruitful		3rd
2	Friday		Taurus	Earth	Semi-Fruitful		3rd
3	Saturday		Taurus	Earth	Semi-Fruitful		3rd
4	Sunday	6:24 am	Gemini	Air	Barren		3rd
5	Monday		Gemini	Air	Barren	8:35 am	4th
6	Tuesday	7:08 pm	Cancer	Water	Fruitful		4th
7	Wednesday		Cancer	Water	Fruitful		4th
8	Thursday		Cancer	Water	Fruitful		4th
9	Friday	6:35 am	Leo	Fire	Barren		4th
10	Saturday		Leo	Fire	Barren		4th
11	Sunday	2:55 pm	Virgo	Earth	Barren		4th
12	Monday		Virgo	Earth	Barren		4th
13	Tuesday	8:16 pm	Libra	Air	Semi-Fruitful	3:46 am	NM
14	Wednesday		Libra	Air	Semi-Fruitful		1st

15	Thursday	11:43 pm	Scorpio	Water	Fruitful		1st
16	Friday		Scorpio	Water	Fruitful		1st
17	Saturday		Scorpio	Water	Fruitful		1st
18	Sunday	2:11 am	Sagittarius	Fire	Barren		1st
19	Monday		Sagittarius	Fire	Barren		1st
20	Tuesday	5:00 am	Capricorn	Earth	Semi-Fruitful	0:19 am	2nd
21	Wednesday		Capricorn	Earth	Semi-Fruitful		2nd
22	Thursday	8:15 am	Aquarius	Air	Barren		2nd
23	Friday		Aquarius	Air	Barren		2nd

Sun enters Libra 9:40 pm, September 23, the Autumnal Equinox

24	Saturday	12:52 pm	Pisces	Water	Fruitful		2nd
25	Sunday		Pisces	Water	Fruitful		2nd
26	Monday	7:01 pm	Aries	Fire	Barren		2nd
27	Tuesday		Aries	Fire	Barren	2:53 am	FM
28	Wednesday		Aries	Fire	Barren		3rd
29	Thursday	3:23 am	Taurus	Earth	Semi-Fruitful		3rd
30	Friday		Taurus	Earth	Semi-Fruitful		3rd

October 1977
Central Standard Time

Date		Moon's Sign	Element	Nature	Moon's Phase
1	Saturday	2:20 pm Gemini	Air	Barren	3rd
2	Sunday	Gemini	Air	Barren	3rd
3	Monday	Gemini	Air	Barren	3rd
4	Tuesday	2:58 am Cancer	Water	Fruitful	3rd
5	Wednesday	Cancer	Water	Fruitful	4th 3:23 am
6	Thursday	3:07 pm Leo	Fire	Barren	4th
7	Friday	Leo	Fire	Barren	4th
8	Saturday	Leo	Fire	Barren	4th
9	Sunday	0:28 am Virgo	Earth	Barren	4th
10	Monday	Virgo	Earth	Barren	4th
11	Tuesday	6:00 am Libra	Air	Semi-Fruitful	4th
12	Wednesday	Libra	Air	Semi-Fruitful	NM 2:41 pm Solar Eclipse
13	Thursday	8:09 am Scorpio	Water	Fruitful	1st

14	Friday		Scorpio	Water	Fruitful		1st
15	Saturday	9:36 am	Sagittarius	Fire	Barren		1st
16	Sunday		Sagittarius	Fire	Barren		1st
17	Monday	10:50 am	Capricorn	Earth	Semi-Fruitful		1st
18	Tuesday		Capricorn	Earth	Semi-Fruitful		1st
19	Wednesday	1:35 pm	Aquarius	Air	Barren	6:46 am	2nd
20	Thursday		Aquarius	Air	Barren		2nd
21	Friday	6:43 pm	Pisces	Water	Fruitful		2nd
22	Saturday		Pisces	Water	Fruitful		2nd
23	Sunday		Pisces	Water	Fruitful		2nd
24	Monday	1:41 am	Aries	Fire	Barren		2nd

Sun enters Scorpio 6:48 am, October 24

25	Tuesday		Aries	Fire	Barren		2nd
26	Wednesday	10:44 am	Taurus	Earth	Semi-Fruitful	5:43 pm	FM
27	Thursday		Taurus	Earth	Semi-Fruitful		3rd
28	Friday	9:48 pm	Gemini	Air	Barren		3rd
29	Saturday		Gemini	Air	Barren		3rd
30	Sunday		Gemini	Air	Barren		3rd
31	Monday	10:19 am	Cancer	Water	Fruitful		3rd

November 1977
Central Standard Time

Date		Moon's Sign		Element	Nature	Moon's Phase	
1	Tuesday	Cancer		Water	Fruitful		3rd
2	Wednesday	11:12 pm	Leo	Fire	Barren		3rd
3	Thursday		Leo	Fire	Barren	10:00 pm	4th
4	Friday		Leo	Fire	Barren		4th
5	Saturday	9:30 am	Virgo	Earth	Barren		4th
6	Sunday		VIrgo	Earth	Barren		4th
7	Monday	4:06 pm	Libra	Air	Semi-Fruitful		4th
8	Tuesday		Libra	Air	Semi-Fruitful		4th
9	Wednesday	6:38 pm	Scorpio	Water	Fruitful		4th
10	Thursday		Scorpio	Water	Fruitful		4th
11	Friday	7:16 pm	Sagittarius	Fire	Barren	1:32 am	NM
12	Saturday		Sagittarius	Fire	Barren		1st
13	Sunday	7:02 pm	Capricorn	Earth	Semi-Fruitful		1st
14	Monday		Capricorn	Earth	Semi-Fruitful		1st

15	Tuesday	8:30 pm	Aquarius	Air	Barren		1st
16	Wednesday		Aquarius	Air	Barren		1st
17	Thursday		Aquarius	Air	Barren	3:53 pm	2nd
18	Friday	0:10 am	Pisces	Water	Fruitful		2nd
19	Saturday		Pisces	Water	Fruitful		2nd
20	Sunday	7:32 am	Aries	Fire	Barren		2nd
21	Monday		Aries	Fire	Barren		2nd
22	Tuesday	5:08 pm	Taurus	Earth	Semi-Fruitful		2nd

Sun enters Sagittarius 9:14 pm, November 22

23	Wednesday		Taurus	Earth	Semi-Fruitful		2nd
24	Thursday		Taurus	Earth	Semi-Fruitful		2nd
25	Friday	4:38 am	Gemini	Air	Barren	11:37 am	FM
26	Saturday		Gemini	Air	Barren		3rd
27	Sunday	5:05 pm	Cancer	Water	Fruitful		3rd
28	Monday		Cancer	Water	Fruitful		3rd
29	Tuesday		Cancer	Water	Fruitful		3rd
30	Wednesday	5:37 am	Leo	Fire	Barren		3rd

December 1977
Central Standard Time

Date		Moon's Sign	Element	Nature	Moon's Phase	
1	Thursday		Leo	Fire	Barren		3rd
2	Friday	5:14 pm	Virgo	Earth	Barren		3rd
3	Saturday		Virgo	Earth	Barren	3:18 pm	4th
4	Sunday		Virgo	Earth	Barren		4th
5	Monday	1:19 am	Libra	Air	Semi-Fruitful		4th
6	Tuesday		Libra	Air	Semi-Fruitful		4th
7	Wednesday	5:29 am	Scorpio	Water	Fruitful		4th
8	Thursday		Scorpio	Water	Fruitful		4th
9	Friday	6:10 am	Sagittarius	Fire	Barren		4th
10	Saturday		Sagittarius	Fire	Barren	12:01 pm	NM
11	Sunday	5:41 am	Capricorn	Earth	Semi-Fruitful		1st
12	Monday		Capricorn	Earth	Semi-Fruitful		1st
13	Tuesday	5:31 am	Aquarius	Air	Barren		1st
14	Wednesday		Aquarius	Air	Barren		1st

15	Thursday	7:55 am	Pisces	Water	Fruitful		1st
16	Friday		Pisces	Water	Fruitful		1st
17	Saturday	1:40 pm	Aries	Fire	Barren	4:38 am	2nd
18	Sunday		Aries	Fire	Barren		2nd
19	Monday	10:56 pm	Taurus	Earth	Semi-Fruitful		2nd
20	Tuesday		Taurus	Earth	Semi-Fruitful		2nd
21	Wednesday		Taurus	Earth	Semi-Fruitful		2nd
22	Thursday	10:53 am	Gemini	Air	Barren		2nd

Sun enters Capricorn 5:14 pm, December 22, the Winter Solstice

23	Friday		Gemini	Air	Barren		2nd
24	Saturday	11:33 pm	Cancer	Water	Fruitful		2nd
25	Sunday		Cancer	Water	Fruitful		2nd
26	Monday		Cancer	Water	Fruitful	7:13 am	FM
27	Tuesday	11:51 am	Leo	Fire	Barren		3rd
28	Wednesday		Leo	Fire	Barren		3rd
29	Thursday	11:25 pm	Virgo	Earth	Barren		3rd
30	Friday		Virgo	Earth	Barren		3rd
31	Saturday		Virgo	Earth	Barren		3rd

When the Marguis du Def-
fand was asked to explain
the miracle by which St.
Denis was able to walk six
miles, *after* his beheading—
with his head in his
hands—she replied:

**THE DISTANCE
DOESN'T MATTER:
IT'S ONLY THE
FIRST STEP THAT
COUNTS!**

That first step is Volume I
of our 12-volume series,

THE PRINCIPLES AND PRACTICE
OF ASTROLOGY by Noel Tyl

Twelve volumes might sound like a lot—but astrology is a *big* subject, and you should not expect to
master it without effort.

The important thing is that this series was designed by a master astrologer and psychologist to
teach astrology from step one to professional practice.

Volume I starts with the first step to learning astrology: learning to construct the horoscope itself, and understanding the meaning of what the student is learning to do. The volume is complete—with everything you need to learn.

Each successive volume moves forward in the same manner —complete with step-by-step procedures, many examples, fascinating case histories, all presented with the stimulating flow of communication that only a professional can maintain.

And each volume has won the same acceptance and achieved the same recognition that Volume I has. There are hundreds of testimonials from students and teachers, professionals and researchers, and even from people who had no real previous interest in astrology before coming into contact with these books.

ples and Practice of Astrology. These books meet all criteria, and those students who have purchased them on my recommendation have been as pleased as I. That test having been passed, it is now my intention to make student purchase of the entire Tyl series a requirement."

Valerie J. Young
Astrologer and School Director

Just as important as the progressive nature of each volume in the series is the fact that each can stand alone as a complete treatise on its speciality within the astrological framework. And that's why we sell each volume separately, or the series as an entirety.

And now there is a TEACHING AND STUDY GUIDE TO THE PRINCIPLES AND PRACTICE OF ASTROLOGY —a separate hardcover volume that guides teacher or student, in classroom or home-study setting, through the entire series—with exercises, problems, answers to questions, supplementary material and an overview of modern astrology that is monumental.

Volume I: Horoscope Construction
How to set up the horoscope in a clear and self-contained book with all needed tables and blank charts.
No. 1-87542-800   paper, $3.95

Volume II: The Houses: Their Signs and Planets
The rationale of house demarcation, the meanings of the signs and planets in the houses, and derivative house readings.
No. 1-87542-801   paper, $3.95

Volume III: The Planets: Their Signs and Aspects
The significance of every planet within every sign, the reading of aspects and dignities, and the meanings of all major aspects and Sun-Moon combinations.
No. 1-87542-802   paper, $3.95

Volume IV: Aspects and Houses in Analysis

Analytical synthesis with many examples, showing hemisphere emphasis, retrogradation patterns, the grand trine, grand square, T-square explained, the lunar nodal axis, parallels of declination, and the part of fortune. The "law of naturalness."

No. 1-87542-803   paper, $3.95

Volume V: Astrology and Personality

Never before presented: an explanation of psychological theories of personality translated into astrological terms and technique! All major schools of psychological thought.

No. 1-87542-804   paper, $3.95

Volume VI: The Expanded Present

Prediction: analysis of the time dimension in astrology—application and separation of aspects, "rapport" measurements, secondary progressions, primary directions, factor 7—with many examples that clarify the work of astrology toward understanding change and development in personality, within free will and fate.

No. 1-87542-805   paper, $3.95

Volume VII: Integrated Transits

The modern rationale, analysis, and application of transit theory within the needs and expectations of people today. Astrology is translated into behavior with real-life examples of every major transit. Also solar revolutions, rectification, eclipse theory, and accidents.

No. 1-87542-806   paper, $3.95

Volume VIII: Analysis and Prediction

The whole-view of astrological analysis: inspection of the past, expansion of the present, creation of the future. Each step of deduction, analysis, and projection is presented in the sharing of real-life horoscopes—*you become the astrologer!* Radix methods, progressions, and transits are fully interpreted. Includes an introduction to horary and electional astrology.

No. 1-87542-807   paper, $3.95

Volume IX: Special Horoscope Dimensions

Success: vocation, relocation, opportunity, elections. Sex: chart comparison, sex profile, love, homosexuality, abortion, creativity. Illness: health problems, surgery, vitality.

No. 1-87542-808   paper, $3.95

Volume X: Astrological Counsel

Never before presented: a full, detailed inspection of the psychodynamics of the astrologer-client relationship, with examples showing consideration of both the horoscope and the person, the difficulties encountered, techniques of communication.

No. 1-87542-809   paper, $3.95

Volume XI: Astrology: Mundane, Astral, Occult

The astrology of nations, the fixed stars, and beyond. International events, solar ingresses, great conjunctions. Astrology and the occult, sign subdivision and degree symbolism, karma and reincarnation.

No. 1-87542-810   paper, $3.95

Volume XII: Times to Come

A thorough introduction to new techniques of astrological practice—cosmobiology, sidereal astrology, the Uranian system—and their philosophical and behavior parallels involving the art of compromise, the remembrance of things past, and creative visualization. A complete index to all 12 volumes.

No. 1-87542-811   paper, $3.95

TEACHING AND STUDY GUIDE

Lesson plans, exercises and demonstrations to complement the entire series, and a wealth of supplementary material making this the most modern reference work of astrology ever written. Many illustrations. 744 pages.

No. 1-87542-812   cloth, $15.00

Order individual volumes at the price indicated, plus postage and handling charges (40¢ each), or the entire 12 volumes for $45.00 postpaid in U.S., or all 12 volumes and the Teaching Guide for $60.00 postpaid in the United States. Use the form on the last page to order.

Daily Activities

♈ **Aries:** head, face

Ⅱ **Gemini:** shoulders, arms,

♉ **Taurus:** throat, neck

♋ **Cancer:** breasts, stomach

♌ **Leo:** back, heart

♎ **Libra:** kidneys, ovaries, loins

♍ **Virgo:** intestines, bowels, solar plexus

♐ **Sagittarius:** hips,

♏ **Scorpio:** sex organs

♑ **Capricorn:** knees

♓ **Pisces:** feet

♒ **Aquarius:** ankles

Man of the Zodiac

Using Your Daily Activities Section

In this section the reader will find guides for choosing the best times to do a variety of different things, from advertising to weaning children. Timing is important to the success of every project and the tables in this section are designed to help you correctly time your everyday activities. There are two main ways in which you can use the information in this section: by availing yourself of the pre-calculated listings of the "Astro-Almanac," or by figuring your own individual schedule using the information listed in the tables and the "Astrological Encyclopedia."

The Astro-Almanac

This feature, new in the 1976 *Moon Sign Book*, is designed to simplify your project planning by listing the best times for a variety of generalized activities. Each different Moon sign and phase position is listed separately along with the activities best suited to that lunar position. The times are given in Central Standard Time.

Tables and Encyclopedia

For a more personalized schedule, or for planning activities not listed in the "Almanac," the "Encyclopedia" and the accompanying tables can be used. The "Encyclopedia" lists, alphabetically, approximately 150 different activities and the most advantageous time to perform each one. Most listings give the best lunar signs and phases, as well as the pertinent lunar aspects. Some listings mention your lunar cycle as well.

To use this information, first of all refer to the "Moon Tables" and note the dates of the correct lunar signs and phases. Then turn to the "Lunar Aspectarian" and record on which of these dates the correct aspects are in operation. The "Favorable and Unfavorable Dates" tables can also be consulted where relevant.

For example, in planning a major purchase, look under "Buying" in the "Encyclopedia." Note that the third quarter is recommended. Note the twelve or thirteen week-long periods during the year when the Moon is in the third quarter. Then turn to the "Lunar Aspectarian." During each of these third-quarter periods, look for days when Mercury is marked C (conjunction), T (trine), or Sx (sextile), for favorable aspects, and when Mars is either not aspected at all, or at least not marked with an O (opposition) or Sq (square), the adverse aspects. On the appropriate day Venus should also be in favorable aspect to the Moon, that is, marked C, T, or Sx. When these conditions have been met, look up your Sun sign in the "Favorable and Unfavorable Dates" tables, and, if possible, note when your lunar cycle is at its height (marked F) or is favorable (marked F).

When not all the most favorable conditions can be met on the same day, or when the best day is not practical, choose a day that fulfills the most conditions—the correct lunar sign and phase being the most important.

Favorable and Unfavorable Dates

These tables list your lunar-cycle highs and lows. You are at the peak of your lunar cycle when the Moon is in your Sun sign. This is marked with a bold F, under your sign. Your lunar cycle low occurs when the Moon is in the sign opposite your Sun sign, and this marked with a bold **U**. A mildly favorable time occurs when the Moon is trine or sextile your Sun sign, that is, two or four signs away, and these dates are marked with a light **F**. A mildly adverse time is when the Moon is square your Sun sign, or three signs away, and these dates are marked with a light **U**.

Days on which the Moon changes signs are marked according to the sign the Moon is in most of the day.

The Lunar Aspectarian

The new "Lunar Aspectarian" gives in tabular form the important aspects formed by the Moon every day of the year. Because the Moon makes one revolution of the zodiac in approximately 28 days, it forms every aspect to every planet during that period, each aspect lasting less than one day.

For example, when the Sun and Moon are conjunct, the Sun is marked C. This means that the Moon occupies the same position in the zodiac as the Sun, and this is, of course, the New Moon. The conjunction is often considered a good aspect, and was previously marked on the tables with a bold **G**.

The Moon quickly hurries ahead of the Sun, however, and in four to six days will have traveled through two signs, and be sixty degrees away. (The zodiac, being a circular ruler, is divided into 360 degrees, or twelve signs of thirty degrees each.) This is a sextile aspect, marked Sx, and is considered a mildly favorable aspect, and was previously marked with a light **G**.

The Sun moves about one degree a day, while the Moon moves about eleven to fifteen degrees a day, so in two to three days after the sextile the Moon is three signs or ninety degrees ahead of the Sun. This is a square aspect, marked Sq, and is considered an adverse aspect; it was previously marked with a light **A**.

Another two or three days pass, and the Moon is another sign ahead of the Sun, or 120 degrees from it, forming a trine aspect. This is marked T, and is considered a favorable aspect; it was formerly marked with a light G.

Four to six days after this trine, or about fourteen days after the conjunction, the Moon will be opposite the Sun (180 degrees from it); this is the position of the Full Moon, which is marked with an O. The opposition is usually considered an unfavorable aspect and was previously marked with a bold A.

The cycle then reverses itself, and the Moon forms another trine, then a square, a sextile, and once again a conjunction, completing its twenty-eight-day cycle with another New Moon.

The Moon forms these same aspects, in this order, with the other planets, but because of the variation in their orbital speed, and their apparent backward motion at times, the timing may be slightly different. With every planet, however, the Moon will conjunct, sextile, square, trine, oppose, trine, square, sextile, and again conjunct it within approximately twenty-eight days.

The Meaning of the Aspects

For those who want to pursue the subject more deeply the following is a general summary of the meaning of the aspects.

Conjunction. When two planets occupy the same position in the zodiac, as seen from the Earth, their vibrations are mingled, each one influencing the other. In this case one of the planets is the Moon, which is a fluid, reflecting body and easily takes on the characteristics of the planets it aspects. Therefore, the nature of the aspecting planet dominates and this must be taken into consideration when interpreting the conjunction of the Moon. Keyword: *strengthening*.

Sextile. This is usually considered a mildly favorable aspect, and is the least consequential of those listed. It often denotes opportunity, but it is up to the individual to take advantage of this opportunity. Keyword: *helpful*.

Square. When two planets are ninety degrees apart their influences are in conflict, for this is not a harmonious arrangement. The square often denotes a difficulty or challenge, making this an aspect which it is helpful to anticipate. Keyword: *obstructive*.

Trine. The trine is considered a favorable aspect, for the vibrations of two or three planets, 120 degrees apart, harmonize and blend with each other, forming a pleasing arrangement. Each planet will be in signs of the same element: fire, air, earth, or water. Some benefit is usually indicated. Keyword: *ease*.

Opposition. Two planets opposing each other (180 degrees apart) may be in conflict or may balance each other. The opposition was traditionally considered an adverse aspect, but the natures of the aspecting planets and their respective signs must be taken into consideration. Keyword: *competitive*.

Lunar Aspects

The Moon aspecting the Sun. The Moon and the Sun are considered the "luminaries," the most important planets in astrology. The Sun is the creative, positive force, while the Moon is the receptive, negative force. The conjunction of the two blends their natures into a balanced force, emphasizing the entire range of qualities of the sign in which they are posited. Keyword: *concentration*. The trine or sextile is a harmonious aspect in which the emotional nature of the Moon supports the direction of the Sun. Keyword: *confidence*. A square or opposition between the two indicates a conflict between desire and feelings. Keyword: *doubt*.

The Moon aspecting Mercury. Mercury rules the mind

and all intellectual functions, particularly communication. The conjunction of the Moon and Mercury enables us to explore the emotional consequences of our intellectual decisions. Keyword: *awareness*. The natures of the Moon and Mercury complement each other when the two are trine or sextile. Keyword: *perception*. A square or opposition indicates a conflict between the mind and the emotions. Keyword: *nervousness*.

The Moon aspecting Venus. Venus gives us a sense of beauty, balance and peace. It rules our relations with other people and our social interactions. A conjunction between the Moon and Venus emphasizes the feminine, receptive qualities of each. Keyword: *sensitivity*. The trine or sextile may be characterized by the keyword: *balance*. A square can indicate an over-sensitivity or lack of direction. Keyword: *vulnerability*.

The Moon aspecting Mars. In astrology Mars represents vitality, energy and physical force. It is an initiating force, while the Moon is a nurturing force. When the two are conjunct, the Moon can support the initial drive of Mars. Keyword: *intensity*. A trine or sextile can indicate a balance of sustenance and enthusiasm. Keyword: *strength*. When Mars and the Moon are in square or opposition, a conflict develops between their conservative and radical natures. Keyword: *competition*.

The Moon aspecting Jupiter. Jupiter is the "greater benefic," indicating its expansive, generous, successful nature. When Jupiter is in conjunction with the Moon, this nature is made more personal. Keyword: *fertility*. The trine or sextile is characterized by the keyword: *benefit*. Too much of a good thing is the result of the square or opposition between Jupiter and the Moon. Keyword: *carelessness*.

The Moon aspecting Saturn. Saturn is a defining or limiting force which often indicates a difficult lesson we are forced to learn. The conjunction between the

Moon and Saturn increases the cautious nature of both. Keyword: *moderation*. When the two are in favorable trine or sextile the keyword becomes: *conservation*. The square or opposition indicates a difficulty in personal expression or an emotional handicap. Keyword: *restriction*.

The Moon aspecting Uranus. The three trans-Saturnian planets are less personal in effect; nevertheless, they do affect individual actions. Uranus is the planet of rebellion, revolution, and cataclysmic change. When in conjunction with the Moon its dramatic genius is in evidence. Keyword: *magnetism*. The trine or sextile brings out the original qualities. Keyword: *inventiveness*. A square or opposition can mean self-will and rebelliousness. Keyword: *disruption*.

The Moon aspecting Neptune. Neptune rules our psychic nature, our dreams and inspiration. In some ways these are the higher manifestation of the lunar qualities of sensitivity and intuition. The Moon conjunct Neptune can lend mediumship. Keyword: *mysticism*. The trine or sextile can indicate meaningful visions. Keyword: *inspiration*. However, a square or opposition can bring out the negative, escapist nature of Neptune. Keyword: *delusion*.

The Moon aspecting Pluto. Pluto has associations with the underworld and symbolizes death and rebirth. The Moon conjunct Pluto can be summed up in the keyword: *power*. The Moon in trine or sextile to Pluto: *regeneration*. Squares or oppositions indicate the death of the old that necessarily precedes reincarnation. Keyword: *destruction*.

Things Ruled by the Planets

To check the planetary aspects for the activity you have in mind, first find the planet that rules it. For your convenience, the activities have been put into three categories. Look at all three listings to get the fullest guide to your activities.

Moon

Occupations
Caterer, domestic science, home economics, nursing, fisherman, navigator, sailor.

Hobbies
Collecting stamps, antique furniture, anything to do with the sea and sailing.

Activities
Any small change in routine, asking favors, borrowing or lending money, household activities such as baking, canning, cooking, freezing, washing and ironing, cleaning, taking care of small children.

Sun

Occupations
Advertising, all positions of authority, managerial and executive, chairmen, all positions related to organizational ability, acting, banking, finance, government, jewelry, law, public relations.

Hobbies
Community work, civic action, volunteer services, exercise and outdoor sports.

Activities
Advertising, buying, selling, speculating, short trips, meeting people, anything involving groups or showmanship, putting up exhibits, running fairs and raffles, growing crops

and taking care of health matters.

Mercury

Occupations

Accountant, ambassador, bookkeeper, brokerage, clerk, critic, craftsman, debater, disc jockey, doctor, editor, journalist, inspector, lecturer, librarian, linguist, medical technician, scientist, secretary, student, teacher, writer.

Hobbies

Writing stories, watching TV, anything dealing with communication and the mass media.

Activities

Bargaining, bookkeeping, dealing with lawyers or literary agents, publishing, filing, hiring employees, learning languages, literary work, placing ads, preparing accounts, studying, telephoning, visiting friends.

Venus

Occupations

Architect, artist, beautician, chiropractor, dancer, designer, domestic work, engineer, entertainer, fashion marketing, musician, painter, poet.

Hobbies

Embroidery, making clothes, music, painting, sculpture, sewing, landscape gardening.

Hobbies

Dealing with public matters, farming or working with the soil, papermaking, working with fertilizer or harnesses.

Activities

Anything involving family ties or legal matters such as wills and estates, taking care of debts, dealing with lawyers, financing, joint money matters, real estate, relations with older people.

Uranus

Occupations

Aeronautics advisor, aerospace technician, broadcaster,

electrician, government official, inventor, lecturer, radiologist.

Hobbies

Electronics, experimenting with ESP, novel ideas, the occult, studying.

Activities

Air travel, all partnerships, changes and adjustment, civil rights, new contacts, new ideas, new rules, patenting inventions, progress, social action, starting journeys.

Neptune

Occupations

Chain store manager, character actor, chemist, diplomat, photographer, psychiatrist, secret agent, wine merchant, working with religious institutions, the shipping business, and the sea.

Hobbies

Acting, pets, photography, music, movies.

Activities

Advertising, dealing with psychological upsets, health foods and resorts, large social affairs, night clubs, psychic healing, travel by water, restaurants, visits, welfare, working with institutions.

Activities

Amusement, beauty care, courtship, dating, decorating homes, designing, getting together with friends, household improvements, planning parties, shopping.

Mars

Occupations

Barber, butcher, carpenter, chemist, construction worker, dentist, metal worker, surgeon, soldier.

Hobbies

Anything that involves work with tools or machinery such as repairing cars, gardening, grafting, household improvements, wood carving.

Activities

Good for all business matters, mechanical affairs, buying or selling animals, dealing with contractors, hunting, undertaking study.

Jupiter

Occupations

Counselor, doctor, educator, guardian, horse trainer, hunter, jockey, judge, lawyer, legislator, merchant, minister, pharmacist, psychologist, public analyst.

Hobbies

Social clubs, travel.

Activities

Activities involving charity, education or science, correspondence courses and self-improvement, reading, researching, studying.

Saturn

Occupations

Agronomist, builder, civil servant, excavator, farm worker, magistrate and justice, mathematician, mine worker, osteopath, plumber, politician, real estate agent, repairman, shoemaker, printer.

Pluto

Occupations

Acrobatics, athletic manager, field of atomic energy, research breakthroughs, speculation, sports, stockbroker.

Hobbies

Any purely personal endeavor, working with children.

Activities

Anything dealing with energy and enthusiasm, skill and alertness, personal relationships, original thought, and pioneering.

Lunar Aspectarian

January 1977

	Sun	Mercury	Venus	Mars	Jupiter	Saturn	Uranus	Neptune	Pluto
1 Saturday			T	Sq	C				
2 Sunday									
3 Monday						Sx		O	T
4 Tuesday				T	O				
5 Wednesday	O	O					T		Sq
6 Thursday					Sx				
7 Friday					C	Sq	T	Sx	
8 Saturday					Sq				
9 Sunday		T	O	T			Sx		
10 Monday	T				T			Sq	
11 Tuesday			Sq	Sq					
12 Wednesday	Sq					Sx		Sx	C
13 Thursday		Sx							
14 Friday				T	Sx	O		Sq	C
15 Saturday	Sx								
16 Sunday			Sq			T		C	Sx
17 Monday									
18 Tuesday		C	Sx	C			Sx		Sq
19 Wednesday	C				T				
20 Thursday						O	Sq	Sx	T
21 Friday						Sq			
22 Saturday			Sx					T	Sq
23 Sunday		C	Sx	Sx					
24 Monday	Sx	Sq							
25 Tuesday						Sq	T	T	O
26 Wednesday									
27 Thursday	Sq	T				Sq	O		
28 Friday			Sx	T	C				
29 Saturday	T								
30 Sunday						Sx		O	T
31 Monday				Sq					

Favorable and Unfavorable Dates

January 1977		Aries	Taurus	Gemini	Cancer	Leo	Virgo	Libra	Scorpio	Sagittarius	Capricorn	Aquarius	Pisces
1	Saturday		F						U				
2	Sunday			F						U			
3	Monday	f		F		f	u	f		U		f	u
4	Tuesday				F						U		
5	Wednesday	u	f		F		f	u	f		U		f
6	Thursday				F						U		
7	Friday	f	u	f		F		f	u	f		U	
8	Saturday					F						U	
9	Sunday		f	u	f		F		f	u	f		U
10	Monday						F						U
11	Tuesday	U		f	u	f		F		f	u	f	
12	Wednesday	U						F					
13	Thursday		U						F				
14	Friday		U		f	u	f		F		f	u	f
15	Saturday			U						F			
16	Sunday	f		U		f	u	f		F		f	u
17	Monday				U						F		
18	Tuesday	u	f		U		f	u	f		F		f
19	Wednesday					U						F	
20	Thursday	f	u	f		U		f	u	f		F	
21	Friday					U						F	
22	Saturday		f	u	f		U		f	u	f		F
23	Sunday						U						F
24	Monday	F						U					
25	Tuesday	F		f	u	f		U		f	u	f	
26	Wednesday		F						U				
27	Thursday		F		f	u	f		U		f	u	f
28	Friday		F						U				
29	Saturday			F						U			
30	Sunday	f		F		f	u	f		U		f	u
31	Monday			F						U			

Lunar Aspectarian

February 1977

	Sun	Mercury	Venus	Mars	Jupiter	Saturn	Uranus	Neptune	Pluto
1 Tuesday								T	Sq
2 Wednesday		O		O	Sx				
3 Thursday			T			Sq			
4 Friday	O				Sq	C		T	Sx
5 Saturday									
6 Sunday					T	Sx	Sq		
7 Monday		T	O	T					
8 Tuesday	T					Sx	Sx	C	
9 Wednesday		Sq		Sq					
10 Thursday						Sq	C		
11 Friday	Sq	Sx		Sx	O				
12 Saturday			T			T	C	Sx	
13 Sunday	Sx								
14 Monday			Sq				Sx		Sq
15 Tuesday					T				
16 Wednesday		C	Sx	C		O	Sq		
17 Thursday						Sq		Sx	T
18 Friday	C								
19 Saturday							Sx	T	Sq
20 Sunday									
21 Monday		Sx	C	Sx		T		T	O
22 Tuesday									
23 Wednesday	Sx				Sq		Sq	O	
24 Thursday		Sq			C				
25 Friday									
26 Saturday	Sq			T			Sx	O	T
27 Sunday		T	Sx						
28 Monday	T							T	

Favorable and Unfavorable Dates

February 1977	Aries	Taurus	Gemini	Cancer	Leo	Virgo	Libra	Scorpio	Sagittarius	Capricorn	Aquarius	Pisces
1 Tuesday	u	f		F		f	u	f		U		f
2 Wednesday				F						U		
3 Thursday					F						U	
4 Friday	f	u	f		F		f	u	f		U	
5 Saturday						F						U
6 Sunday		f	u	f		F		f	u	f		U
7 Monday	U						F					
8 Tuesday	U		f	u	f		F		f	u	f	
9 Wednesday		U						F				
10 Thursday		U		f	u	f		F		f	u	f
11 Friday			U						F			
12 Saturday	f		U	U	f	u	f		F	F	f	u
13 Sunday				U						F		
14 Monday	u	f		U		f	u	f		F		f
15 Tuesday				U						F		
16 Wednesday	f	u	f		U		f	u	f		F	
17 Thursday					U						F	
18 Friday						U						F
19 Saturday		f	u	f		U		f	u	f		F
20 Sunday	F						U					
21 Monday	F		f	u	f		U		f	u	f	
22 Tuesday	F						U					
23 Wednesday		F						U				
24 Thursday		F		f	u	f		U		f	u	f
25 Friday			F						U			
26 Saturday	f		F	F	f	u	f		U		f	u
27 Sunday			F	F					U			
28 Monday				F						U		

Lunar Aspectarian

March
1977

	Sun	Mercury	Venus	Mars	Jupiter	Saturn	Uranus	Neptune	Pluto
1 Tuesday			Sq		Sx				Sq
2 Wednesday									
3 Thursday					O	C	Sq	T	Sx
4 Friday		O	T		Sq				
5 Saturday	O					Sx	Sq		
6 Sunday					T				
7 Monday						Sx		Sx	C
8 Tuesday		O	T						
9 Wednesday			T			Sq	C		
10 Thursday	T			Sq	O				
11 Friday						T			Sx
12 Saturday	Sq	Sq	T	Sx			C		
13 Sunday							Sx		
14 Monday	Sx	Sx	Sq		T				Sq
15 Tuesday									
16 Wednesday						O	Sq	Sx	T
17 Thursday				Sx	C	Sq			
18 Friday						T	Sq		
19 Saturday	C				Sx				
20 Sunday		C				T			O
21 Monday				C				T	
22 Tuesday				Sx					
23 Wednesday						Sq	O		
24 Thursday					C				
25 Friday	Sx			Sq	Sx			T	
26 Saturday		Sx	Sx					O	
27 Sunday	Sq			T					
28 Monday								T	Sq
29 Tuesday		Sq	Sq		Sx				
30 Wednesday	T					C	Sq		Sx
31 Thursday		T	T					T	

Favorable and Unfavorable Dates

March 1977

		Aries	Taurus	Gemini	Cancer	Leo	Virgo	Libra	Scorpio	Sagittarius	Capricorn	Aquarius	Pisces
1	Tuesday	u	f		F		f	u	f		U		f
2	Wednesday					F						U	
3	Thursday	f	u	f		F		f	u	f		U	
4	Friday						F						U
5	Saturday		f	u	f		F		f	u	f		U
6	Sunday						F						U
7	Monday	U		f	u	f		F		f	u	f	
8	Tuesday	U						F					
9	Wednesday		U		f	u	f		F		f	u	f
10	Thursday		U						F				
11	Friday	f		U		f	u	f		F		f	u
12	Saturday			U						F			
13	Sunday	u	f		U		f	u	f		F		f
14	Monday				U						F		
15	Tuesday					U						F	
16	Wednesday	f	u	f		U		f	u	f		F	
17	Thursday						U						F
18	Friday		f	u	f		U		f	u	f		F
19	Saturday						U						F
20	Sunday	F		f	u	f		U		f	u	f	
21	Monday	F						U					
22	Tuesday		F						U				
23	Wednesday		F		f	u	f		U		f	u	f
24	Thursday		F						U				
25	Friday			F						U			
26	Saturday	f		F		f	u	f		U		f	u
27	Sunday				F						U		
28	Monday	u	f		F		f	u	f		U		f
29	Tuesday				F						U		
30	Wednesday					F						U	
31	Thursday	f	u	f		F		f	u	f		U	

Lunar Aspectarian

April
1977

Date		Sun	Mercury	Venus	Mars	Jupiter	Saturn	Uranus	Neptune	Pluto
1	Friday				O	Sq	Sx			
2	Saturday								Sq	
3	Sunday					T	Sx			
4	Monday	O	O						Sx	C
5	Tuesday		O	O			Sq	C		
6	Wednesday					T				
7	Thursday					O	T			
8	Friday	T		T	Sq				C	Sx
9	Saturday		T							
10	Sunday	Sq		Sq	Sx			Sx		Sq
11	Monday					T				
12	Tuesday		Sq	Sx		O	Sq	Sx	T	
13	Wednesday	Sx					Sq			
14	Thursday			Sx				T	Sq	
15	Friday					C				
16	Saturday			C			Sx	T		
17	Sunday									O
18	Monday	C								
19	Tuesday		C				Sq	O		
20	Wednesday			Sx						
21	Thursday				Sx		C	Sx		
22	Friday							O	T	
23	Saturday	Sx			Sq					
24	Sunday			Sx	Sq		T			Sq
25	Monday									
26	Tuesday	Sq	T	T	Sx	C	Sq			
27	Wednesday			Sq					T	Sx
28	Thursday						Sq			
29	Friday	T	T					Sx	Sq	
30	Saturday			Sq						

Favorable and Unfavorable Dates

April 1977	Aries	Taurus	Gemini	Cancer	Leo	Virgo	Libra	Scorpio	Sagittarius	Capricorn	Aquarius	Pisces
1 Friday		f	u	f		F		f	u	f	U	U
2 Saturday						F						U
3 Sunday	U		f	u	f		F		f	u	f	
4 Monday	U						F					
5 Tuesday	f		U		f	u	f		F		f	u
6 Wednesday			U						F			
7 Thursday				U						F		
8 Friday	u	f		U		f	u	f		F		f
9 Saturday				U						F		
10 Sunday	u	f		U		f	u	f		F		f
11 Monday					U						F	
12 Tuesday	f	u	f	U	U		f	u	f	F	F	
13 Wednesday					U						F	
14 Thursday		f	u	f		U		f	u	f		F
15 Friday						U						F
16 Saturday	F		f	u	f		U		f	u	f	
17 Sunday	F						U					
18 Monday			F						U			
19 Tuesday	f		F		f	u	f		U		f	u
20 Wednesday			F						U			
21 Thursday	f		F		f	u	f		U		f	u
22 Friday			F						U			
23 Saturday				F						U		
24 Sunday	u	f		F		f	u	f		U		f
25 Monday				F						U		
26 Tuesday					F						U	
27 Wednesday	f	u	f		F		f	u	f		U	
28 Thursday					F						U	
29 Friday		f	u	f		F		f	u	f		U
30 Saturday	U						F					

Lunar Aspectarian

May 1977

Date	Day	Sun	Mercury	Venus	Mars	Jupiter	Saturn	Uranus	Neptune	Pluto
1	Sunday				O	T	Sx		Sx	
2	Monday									
3	Tuesday	O	O				Sq	C		
4	Wednesday									
5	Thursday			T	T	O	T		C	Sx
6	Friday									
7	Saturday	T	T	Sq	Sq			Sx		Sq
8	Sunday									
9	Monday		Sq	Sx	Sx	T	O	Sq	Sx	T
10	Tuesday	Sq								
11	Wednesday		Sx			Sq		T		
12	Thursday	Sx							Sq	
13	Friday									
14	Saturday			C	C	Sx	T		T	O
15	Sunday									
16	Monday		C				Sq	O		
17	Tuesday									
18	Wednesday	C								
19	Thursday			Sx	Sx	C	Sx		O	T
20	Friday									
21	Saturday		Sx					T		Sq
22	Sunday			Sq	Sq					
23	Monday	Sx								
24	Tuesday		Sq	T		Sx	C	Sq	T	Sx
25	Wednesday				T					
26	Thursday	Sq	T			Sq			Sx	Sq
27	Friday									
28	Saturday	T				T	Sx			C
29	Sunday			O	O				Sx	
30	Monday						Sq	C		
31	Tuesday		O							

Favorable and Unfavorable Dates

May 1977	Aries	Taurus	Gemini	Cancer	Leo	Virgo	Libra	Scorpio	Sagittarius	Capricorn	Aquarius	Pisces
1 Sunday	U		f	u	f		F		f	u	f	
2 Monday		U						F				
3 Tuesday		U		f	u	f		F		f	u	f
4 Wednesday			U						F			
5 Thursday	f		U		f	u	f		F		f	u
6 Friday				U						F		
7 Saturday	u	f		U		f	u	f		F		f
8 Sunday				U						F		
9 Monday	f	u	f		U		f	u	f		F	
10 Tuesday					U						F	
11 Wednesday		f	u	f		U		f	u	f		F
12 Thursday						U						F
13 Friday	F						U					
14 Saturday	F		f	u	f		U		f	u	f	
15 Sunday	F						U					
16 Monday		F		f	u	f		U		f	u	f
17 Tuesday		F						U				
18 Wednesday			F						U			
19 Thursday	f		F		f	u	f		U		f	u
20 Friday			F						U			
21 Saturday	u	f		F		f	u	f		U		f
22 Sunday				F						U		
23 Monday					F						U	
24 Tuesday	f	u	f		F		f	u	f		U	
25 Wednesday					F						U	
26 Thursday		f	u	f		F		f	u	f		U
27 Friday						F						U
28 Saturday	U		f	u	f		F		f	u	f	
29 Sunday	U						F					
30 Monday		U		f	u	f		F		f	u	f
31 Tuesday		U						F				

Lunar Aspectarian

June
1977

Date	Day	Sun	Mercury	Venus	Mars	Jupiter	Saturn	Uranus	Neptune	Pluto
1	Wednesday	O				O	T			Sx
2	Thursday			T	T					
3	Friday								Sx	Sq
4	Saturday		T							
5	Sunday					Sq	Sq	O	Sq	T
6	Monday	T	Sq			T			Sx	
7	Tuesday			Sx	Sx			T		
8	Wednesday	Sq				Sq			Sq	
9	Thursday		Sx							
10	Friday					Sx	T		T	O
11	Saturday	Sx								
12	Sunday			C	C		O			
13	Monday							Sq		
14	Tuesday									
15	Wednesday		C			C	Sx		O	T
16	Thursday	C								
17	Friday				Sx			T		
18	Saturday			Sx						Sq
19	Sunday									
20	Monday				Sq	Sq	C	Sq	T	Sx
21	Tuesday		Sx				Sx			
22	Wednesday	Sx		T			Sx			
23	Thursday		Sq	T		Sq		Sq		
24	Friday	Sq								
25	Saturday					T	Sx		Sx	C
26	Sunday	T	T							
27	Monday			O	O		Sq	C		
28	Tuesday									
29	Wednesday					O	T		C	Sx
30	Thursday									

Favorable and Unfavorable Dates

June 1977		Aries	Taurus	Gemini	Cancer	Leo	Virgo	Libra	Scorpio	Sagittarius	Capricorn	Aquarius	Pisces
1	Wednesday	f		U		f	u	f		F		f	u
2	Thursday			U						F			
3	Friday	u	f		U		f	u	f		F		f
4	Saturday				U						F		
5	Sunday	f	u	f		U		f	u	f		F	
6	Monday					U						F	
7	Tuesday						U						F
8	Wednesday		f	u	f		U		f	u	f		F
9	Thursday	F						U					
10	Friday	F		f	u	f		U		f	u	f	
11	Saturday		F						U				
12	Sunday		F		f	u	f		U		f	u	f
13	Monday			F						U			
14	Tuesday			F						U			
15	Wednesday	f		F		f	u	f		U		f	u
16	Thursday				F						U		
17	Friday	u	f		F		f	u	f		U		f
18	Saturday					F						U	
19	Sunday					F						U	
20	Monday	f	u	f		F		f	u	f		U	
21	Tuesday						F						U
22	Wednesday		f	u	f		F		f	u	f		U
23	Thursday	U						F					
24	Friday	U						F					
25	Saturday	U		f	u	f		F		f	u	f	
26	Sunday		U						F				
27	Monday		U		f	u	f		F		f	u	f
28	Tuesday			U						F			
29	Wednesday	f		U		f	u	f		F		f	u
30	Thursday				U						F		

Lunar Aspectarian

July 1977

Day		Sun	Mercury	Venus	Mars	Jupiter	Saturn	Uranus	Neptune	Pluto
1	Friday	O	O		T			Sx	Sq	
2	Saturday			T						
3	Sunday				Sq	T	O	Sq	Sx	T
4	Monday			Sq						
5	Tuesday	T						T	Sq	
6	Wednesday			T	Sx	Sx	Sq			
7	Thursday									O
8	Friday	Sq					Sx	T	T	
9	Saturday		Sq							
10	Sunday	Sx					Sq	O		
11	Monday					C				
12	Tuesday			Sx	C					T
13	Wednesday						C	Sx	O	
14	Thursday									
15	Friday							T	Sq	
16	Saturday	C				Sx				
17	Sunday		C	Sx				Sq	T	Sx
18	Monday						Sx	C		
19	Tuesday				Sq			Sx		
20	Wednesday			Sq					Sq	
21	Thursday	Sx				T	Sq			
22	Friday		T				Sx		Sx	C
23	Saturday	Sq	Sx			T				
24	Sunday						C			
25	Monday		Sq				Sq			
26	Tuesday	T			O				C	Sx
27	Wednesday		T	O			O	T		
28	Thursday							Sx	Sq	
29	Friday									
30	Saturday	O			T			Sq	Sx	T
31	Sunday				T		T	O		

Favorable and Unfavorable Dates

July 1977	Day	Aries	Taurus	Gemini	Cancer	Leo	Virgo	Libra	Scorpio	Sagittarius	Capricorn	Aquarius	Pisces
1	Friday	u	f		U		f	u	f		F		f
2	Saturday					U						F	
3	Sunday	f	u	f		U		f	u	f		F	
4	Monday						U						F
5	Tuesday		f	u	f		U		f	u	f		F
6	Wednesday						U						F
7	Thursday	F						U					
8	Friday	F		f	u	f		U		f	u	f	
9	Saturday		F						U				
10	Sunday		F		f	u	f		U		f	u	f
11	Monday		F						U				
12	Tuesday	f		F		f	u	f		U		f	u
13	Wednesday			F						U			
14	Thursday				F						U		
15	Friday	u	f		F		f	u	f		U		f
16	Saturday				F						U		
17	Sunday	f	u	f		F		f	u	f		U	
18	Monday					F						U	
19	Tuesday						F						U
20	Wednesday		f	u	f		F		f	u	f		U
21	Thursday	U						F					
22	Friday	U		f	u	f		F		f	u	f	
23	Saturday	U						F					
24	Sunday		U		f	u	f		F		f	u	f
25	Monday		U						F				
26	Tuesday	f		U		f	u	f		F		f	u
27	Wednesday			U						F			
28	Thursday	u	f		U		f	u	f		F		f
29	Friday				U						F		
30	Saturday	f	u	f		U		f	u	f		F	
31	Sunday					U						F	

Lunar Aspectarian

August 1977

	Sun	Mercury	Venus	Mars	Jupiter	Saturn	Uranus	Neptune	Pluto
1 Monday		O		Sq			T		
2 Tuesday								Sq	
3 Wednesday			Sq	Sq					
4 Thursday	T			Sx		T		T	O
5 Friday			Sx		Sx				
6 Saturday	Sq	T					O		
7 Sunday						Sq			
8 Monday									
9 Tuesday	Sx	Sq		C		Sx		O	T
10 Wednesday					C				
11 Thursday				C			T		Sq
12 Friday		Sx							
13 Saturday							Sq		
14 Sunday	C			Sx		C		T	Sx
15 Monday					Sx				
16 Tuesday				Sx				Sx	Sq
17 Wednesday				Sq	Sq				
18 Thursday								Sx	C
19 Friday	Sx			Sq	T	T	Sx		
20 Saturday								C	
21 Sunday		Sx		T		Sq			
22 Monday	Sq								
23 Tuesday		Sq		O		T		C	Sx
24 Wednesday	T				O		Sx		
25 Thursday		T							Sq
26 Friday				O			Sq		
27 Saturday						O		Sx	T
28 Sunday	O				T	T			
29 Monday		O						T	Sq
30 Tuesday				T	Sq	Sq			
31 Wednesday								T	O

Favorable and Unfavorable Dates

August 1977		Aries	Taurus	Gemini	Cancer	Leo	Virgo	Libra	Scorpio	Sagittarius	Capricorn	Aquarius	Pisces
1	Monday		f	u	f		U		f	u	f		F
2	Tuesday						U						F
3	Wednesday	F						U					
4	Thursday	F		f	u	f		U		f	u	f	
5	Friday		F					U	U				
6	Saturday		F		f	u	f	U	U		f	u	f
7	Sunday		F						U				
8	Monday	f		F		f	u	f		U		f	u
9	Tuesday			F					U	U			
10	Wednesday				F						U		
11	Thursday	u	f		F		f	u	f	U	U		f
12	Friday				F						U		
13	Saturday	f	u	f		F		f	u	f		U	
14	Sunday					F						U	
15	Monday						F						U
16	Tuesday		f	u	f	F	F		f	u	f	U	U
17	Wednesday					F	F						U
18	Thursday	U		f	u	f		F		f	u	f	
19	Friday	U						F					
20	Saturday		U		f	u	f		F		f	u	f
21	Sunday		U						F				
22	Monday	f		U		f	u	f		F		f	u
23	Tuesday			U						F			
24	Wednesday	u	f		U		f	u	f		F		f
25	Thursday				U						F		
26	Friday					U						F	
27	Saturday	f	u	f		U		f	u	f		F	
28	Sunday					U						F	
29	Monday		f	u	f	U	U		f	u	f		F
30	Tuesday	F						U					
31	Wednesday	F		f	u	f	U	U		f	u	f	

Lunar Aspectarian

September
1977

Date		Sun	Mercury	Venus	Mars	Jupiter	Saturn	Uranus	Neptune	Pluto
1	Thursday						T			
2	Friday	T		Sq	Sx	Sx		O		
3	Saturday		T				Sq			
4	Sunday									
5	Monday	Sq	Sq	Sx					O	T
6	Tuesday						Sx			
7	Wednesday		Sx			C	C	T		
8	Thursday	Sx								Sq
9	Friday									
10	Saturday					C		Sq	T	Sx
11	Sunday						C			
12	Monday		C		Sx	Sx		Sx	Sq	
13	Tuesday	C								
14	Wednesday					Sq	Sq			
15	Thursday		Sx				Sx		Sx	C
16	Friday		Sx		T	T		C		
17	Saturday		Sq				Sq			
18	Sunday	Sx	Sq							
19	Monday								C	Sx
20	Tuesday	Sq			T	O	T			
21	Wednesday		T		O			Sx	Sq	
22	Thursday	T								
23	Friday							Sq	Sx	T
24	Saturday		O			O				
25	Sunday		O		T	T		T	Sq	
26	Monday									
27	Tuesday	O					Sq			
28	Wednesday		Sq						T	O
29	Thursday						Sx	T		
30	Friday		T	Sx					O	

Favorable and Unfavorable Dates

September 1977

Date	Day	Aries	Taurus	Gemini	Cancer	Leo	Virgo	Libra	Scorpio	Sagittarius	Capricorn	Aquarius	Pisces
1	Thursday	F						U					
2	Friday		F		f	u	f		U		f	u	f
3	Saturday		F						U				
4	Sunday			F						U			
5	Monday	f		F		f	u	f		U		f	u
6	Tuesday			F						U			
7	Wednesday	u	f		F		f	u	f		U		f
8	Thursday				F						U		
9	Friday					F						U	
10	Saturday	f	u	f		F		f	u	f		U	
11	Sunday					F						U	
12	Monday		f	u	f		F		f	u	f		U
13	Tuesday						F						U
14	Wednesday	U		f	u	f		F		f	u	f	
15	Thursday	U						F					
16	Friday		U		f	u	f		F		f	u	f
17	Saturday		U						F				
18	Sunday			U						F			
19	Monday	f		U		f	u	f		F		f	u
20	Tuesday				U						F		
21	Wednesday	u	f		U		f	u	f		F		f
22	Thursday					U						F	
23	Friday	f	u	f		U		f	u	f		F	
24	Saturday					U						F	
25	Sunday		f	u	f		U		f	u	f		F
26	Monday						U						F
27	Tuesday	F		f	u	f		U		f	u	f	
28	Wednesday	F						U					
29	Thursday		F						U				
30	Friday		F		f	u	f		U		f	u	f

Lunar Aspectarian

October
1977

	Sun	Mercury	Venus	Mars	Jupiter	Saturn	Uranus	Neptune	Pluto
1 Saturday		T				Sq			
2 Sunday	T		Sq						
3 Monday								O	T
4 Tuesday		Sq			C	Sx			
5 Wednesday	Sq		Sx				T		Sq
6 Thursday				C					
7 Friday		Sx					Sq	T	
8 Saturday	Sx								Sx
9 Sunday					Sx	C			
10 Monday				C	Sx		Sx	Sq	
11 Tuesday						Sq			
12 Wednesday	C	C						Sx	C
13 Thursday									
14 Friday					Sq	T	C		
15 Saturday			Sx	T		Sq			
16 Sunday								C	Sx
17 Monday		Sx	Sx	Sq		T			
18 Tuesday					O		Sx		Sq
19 Wednesday	Sq	Sq		O					
20 Thursday			T				Sq	Sx	T
21 Friday	T					O			
22 Saturday		T			T		T		
23 Sunday								Sq	
24 Monday			T	Sq					
25 Tuesday		O						T	O
26 Wednesday	O			Sq	T				
27 Thursday		O			Sx		O		
28 Friday									
29 Saturday				Sx	Sq				
30 Sunday		T						O	T
31 Monday						Sx			

Favorable and Unfavorable Dates

October 1977		Aries	Taurus	Gemini	Cancer	Leo	Virgo	Libra	Scorpio	Sagittarius	Capricorn	Aquarius	Pisces
1	Saturday		F						U				
2	Sunday	f		F		f	u	f		U		f	u
3	Monday			F						U			
4	Tuesday				F						U		
5	Wednesday	u	f		F						U		f
6	Thursday				F						U		
7	Friday	f	u	f		F		f	u	f		U	
8	Saturday					F						U	
9	Sunday						F						U
10	Monday		f	u	f		F		f	u	f		U
11	Tuesday	U						F					
12	Wednesday	U		f	u	f		F		f	u	f	
13	Thursday		U						F				
14	Friday		U		f	u	f		F		f	u	f
15	Saturday			U						F			
16	Sunday	f		U		f	u	f		F		f	u
17	Monday				U						F		
18	Tuesday	u	f		U		f	u	f		F		f
19	Wednesday				U								
20	Thursday	f	u	f		U		f	u	f		F	
21	Friday					U						F	
22	Saturday		f	u	f		U		f	u	f		F
23	Sunday						U						F
24	Monday	F						U					
25	Tuesday	F		f	u	f		U		f	u	f	
26	Wednesday		F	F					U	U			
27	Thursday		F	F	f	u	f		U	U	f	u	f
28	Friday		F	F									
29	Saturday	f		F		f	u	f		U		f	u
30	Sunday			F						U			
31	Monday				F						U		

Lunar Aspectarian

November
1977

	Sun	Mercury	Venus	Mars	Jupiter	Saturn	Uranus	Neptune	Pluto
1 Tuesday	T				C		T		Sq
2 Wednesday		T	Sq						
3 Thursday				C					
4 Friday	Sq						Sq	T	Sx
5 Saturday		Sq	Sx			C			
6 Sunday	Sx					Sx		Sx	Sq
7 Monday		Sx							
8 Tuesday					Sx	Sq		Sx	
9 Wednesday									C
10 Thursday			C		Sq	T	Sx	C	
11 Friday	C								
12 Saturday		C		T		Sq			
13 Sunday								C	Sx
14 Monday				Sx	O	T	Sx		
15 Tuesday	Sx								Sq
16 Wednesday		Sx	Sq	O		Sq		Sx	
17 Thursday	Sq				T	O		Sx	T
18 Friday					T	O			
19 Saturday		Sq	T					T	Sq
20 Sunday	T					Sq			
21 Monday		T		T				T	O
22 Tuesday						T			
23 Wednesday				Sq	Sx				
24 Thursday				O				O	
25 Friday	O					Sq			
26 Saturday				Sx				O	T
27 Sunday		O							
28 Monday					C	Sx			
29 Tuesday								T	Sq
30 Wednesday			T						

Favorable and Unfavorable Dates

November 1977

Date	Day	Aries	Taurus	Gemini	Cancer	Leo	Virgo	Libra	Scorpio	Sagittarius	Capricorn	Aquarius	Pisces
1	Tuesday	u	f		F		f	u	f		U		f
2	Wednesday				F						U		
3	Thursday	f	u	f		F		f	u	f		U	
4	Friday					F						U	
5	Saturday						F						U
6	Sunday		f	u	f		F		f	u	f		U
7	Monday						F						U
8	Tuesday	U		f	u	f		F		f	u	f	
9	Wednesday	U						F					
10	Thursday		U		f	u	f		F		f	u	f
11	Friday		U						F				
12	Saturday	f		U		f	u	f		F		f	u
13	Sunday			U						F			
14	Monday	u	f		U		f	u	f		F		f
15	Tuesday				U						F		
16	Wednesday	f	u	f		U		f	u	f		F	
17	Thursday					U						F	
18	Friday						U						F
19	Saturday		f	u	f		U		f	u	f		F
20	Sunday	F						U					
21	Monday	F		f	u	f		U		f	u	f	
22	Tuesday	F						U					
23	Wednesday		F		f	u	f		U		f	u	f
24	Thursday		F						U				
25	Friday			F						U			
26	Saturday	f		F		f	u	f		U		f	u
27	Sunday			F						U			
28	Monday	u	f		F		f	u	f		U		f
29	Tuesday				F						U		
30	Wednesday					F						U	

Lunar Aspectarian

December 1977

Date	Day	Sun	Mercury	Venus	Mars	Jupiter	Saturn	Uranus	Neptune	Pluto
1	Thursday	T			C		Sq	T		Sx
2	Friday			Sq						
3	Saturday	Sq	T			Sx	C			
4	Sunday							Sx	Sq	
5	Monday		Sq	Sx		Sq				
6	Tuesday	Sx			Sx				Sx	C
7	Wednesday			Sx			T	Sx		
8	Thursday				Sq			C		
9	Friday							Sq		
10	Saturday	C		C	T	T			C	Sx
11	Sunday		C			O	T			
12	Monday							Sx		Sq
13	Tuesday									
14	Wednesday			Sx	O			Sq	Sx	T
15	Thursday	Sx	Sx			T	O			
16	Friday			Sq				T	Sq	
17	Saturday	Sq				Sq				
18	Sunday		Sq		T					
19	Monday				T				T	O
20	Tuesday	T	T				Sx	T		
21	Wednesday			Sq			O			
22	Thursday						Sq			
23	Friday				Sx					
24	Saturday		O	O					O	T
25	Sunday	O				C	Sx			
26	Monday							T		Sq
27	Tuesday									
28	Wednesday				C					
29	Thursday		T				Sq	T		Sx
30	Friday	T		T			Sx	C		
31	Saturday		Sq						Sx	Sq

Favorable and Unfavorable Dates

December 1977		Aries	Taurus	Gemini	Cancer	Leo	Virgo	Libra	Scorpio	Sagittarius	Capricorn	Aquarius	Pisces
1	Thursday	f	u	f		F		f	u	f		U	
2	Friday					F						U	
3	Saturday		f	u	f		F		f	u	f		U
4	Sunday						F						U
5	Monday	U						F					
6	Tuesday	U		f	u	f		F		f	u	f	
7	Wednesday		U						F				
8	Thursday		U		f	u	f		F		f	u	f
9	Friday			U						F			
10	Saturday	f		U		f	u	f		F		f	u
11	Sunday				U						F		
12	Monday	u	f		U		f	u	f		F		f
13	Tuesday					U						F	
14	Wednesday	f	u	f		U		f	u	f		F	
15	Thursday						U						F
16	Friday		f	u	f		U		f	u	f		F
17	Saturday						U						F
18	Sunday	F		f	u	f		U		f	u	f	
19	Monday	F						U					
20	Tuesday		F		f	u	f		U		f	u	f
21	Wednesday		F						U				
22	Thursday			F		f	u	f		U			
23	Friday	f		F		f	u	f		U		f	u
24	Saturday			F						U			
25	Sunday	u	f		F		f	u	f		U		f
26	Monday				F						U		
27	Tuesday					F						U	
28	Wednesday	f	u	f		F		f	u	f		U	
29	Thursday					F						U	
30	Friday		f	u	f		F		f	u	f		U
31	Saturday						F						U

Astrological Encyclopedia

Advertising

Write your advertisements on days when your lunar cycle is favorable, when Mercury is sextile, trine, or conjunct the Moon, avoiding days when Mars and Saturn are in square or opposition to the Moon. Your ad should reach the public on a day also within your lunar high cycle, for the people who read it and reply will be easier to deal with. The sale will be satisfactory and you will achieve better results all the way around.

Animals

For buying, choose the New Moon or First Quarter of the Moon, on a day marked favorable for your Sun Sign. For cows, select days when the Moon is not aspected with Saturn. Work horses may be bought or sold when Saturn is in aspect with the Moon, and race horses when Jupiter is in aspect with the Moon. Dogs may be bought when the Moon is not aspected with the Sun; cats when the Moon is not aspected with Venus.

In connection with breeding, it is important to arrange for the birth to occur during the *increase of the Moon*. The New Moon and First Quarter are best. Next, select the feminine signs at the time of the Moon's increase. The best times are when the Moon is in Cancer, Scorpio or Pisces, which are Water Signs. Second best are the Earth

It is more rewarding to read a book when Mercury is marked *good* on the Planetary and Lunar Aspects Tables.

It is also more rewarding when you can find a *good* book.

Signs Taurus and Capricorn. An example: *Rabbits* require a gestation period of thirty days. Therefore, arrange to have them mated on a day that will bring the litter when the Moon will be in the First Quarter and in a fruitful sign, either Cancer, Scorpio or Pisces.

Breeders of a stock find that the best stock is born in the Water Signs at the increase of the Moon. These animals become their best for future breeding.

A few words might prove helpful about the mating of birds. Since Taurus rules the throat, birds born in this sign could be good singers. Because Libra relates to form, color and grace, this sign is also a good one in which to mate the birds. Be sure too that the Moon is in a fruitful sign at the time of mating.

Automobiles

Choose a day in which your Sun Sign is favorable and Uranus is sextile, trine, or conjunct the Moon to buy or select an automobile. Mars and Saturn should not be aspected the same day, for they relate to accidents.

Baking

Baking should be done when the Moon is in the movable signs, Aries, Cancer, Libra or Capricorn. Bakers who have experimented with these rules say that dough rises higher and bread is lighter during the increase of the Moon.

Beauty Care

For beauty treatments, skin care and massage, the Moon should be in Taurus, Cancer, Leo, Libra, Scorpio or Aquarius and sextile, trine, or conjunct Venus and/or Jupiter. Plastic surgery should be done in the increase of the Moon, when the Moon is not in square or opposition to Mars. Nor should the Moon be in the sign ruling the area to be operated on. Avoid days when the Moon is square or opposite Saturn or the Sun.

Haircuts are best when the Moon is in a mutable or earthy sign, well-placed and aspected, but not in Virgo, which is barren. For faster growth, the Moon should be in a Water Sign. To make hair grow thicker, cut it when the Moon is in opposition to the Sun, the Full Moon, which is marked O. However, if you want your hair to grow more slowly, the Moon should be in Gemini or Leo, in the Third or Fourth Quarters with Saturn square or opposite the Moon.

Fingernails should be cut when the Moon is not in any aspect with Mercury or Jupiter. Saturn and Mars must not be square or opposite the Moon because this makes the nails grow slowly or thin and weak. The Moon should be in Aries, Taurus, Cancer, or Leo. For toenails, the Moon should not be in Gemini or Pisces. Corns are best cut when the Moon is in the Third or Fourth Quarter.

Permanent waves, straightening and hair coloring will take well if the Moon is in Aquarius and Venus is marked C, T, or Sx. You should avoid doing your hair if Mars is marked O or Sq, expecially if heat is to be used. For permanents, a trine to Jupiter is helpful. The Moon also should be in the First Quarter and at the same time check the lunar cycle for a favorable day in relation to your Sun Sign.

Medicinal baths will produce better results if the nature of the illness is taken into consideration. If it is of a cold or moist nature, take the bath when the Moon is in a Fire Sign and sextile, trine, or conjunct the Sun. If the illness involves fever, treatment should take place when the Moon is in a Water Sign and on days when Jupiter or Venus are marked C, T, or Sx.

For buying clothes, there are several astrological guidelines. First see that the Moon is sextile or trine to the Sun, and that the Moon is in the First or Second Quarters. When the Moon is in Taurus, buying clothes will bring pleasure and satisfaction. However, it should not be in any other fixed sign, especially Leo or Virgo. Different signs will be favorable for different articles of clothing. Aries is suitable for buying hats, Cancer for coats, shirts, blouses and vests, Scorpio for gloves, Libra for belts, Saigttarius for skirts, sports clothes, and Pisces for boots, stockings, shoes and socks. If possible, there should be a sextile, trine, or conjunction from the planet ruling the color of whatever is bought. Gold and yellow are ruled by the Sun, while the Moon rules silver, grey, green, brown and opaque colors. Venus rules pale blue, pink, turqoise and Mars rules red and scarlet. Jupiter is good for blue and purple and Saturn is good for black or very dark shades of any color. Uranus favors checks, stripes and color combinations, while Neptune rules lilac, lavender and mauve.

Dieting. Weight gain occurs more readily when the Moon is in a Water Sign, Cancer, Scorpio or Pisces. Experience has shown that weight may be lost though, if a diet is started when the Moon is decreasing in light (Third and Fourth Quarters), and when it is in Aries, Leo, Virgo, Sagittarius or Aquarius. The lunar cycle should be favorable on the day you wish to begin your diet.

Borrowing Money

To borrow money, see that the Moon is in its last quarters and in Leo, Scorpio, Sagittarius, Aquarius or Pisces. Jupiter and Venus should be sextile, trine, or conjunct the Moon.

Brewing

It is best to brew during the Full Moon and the Fourth Quarter. Plan to have the Moon in a Water Sign (Cancer, Scorpio, Pisces).

Building

Turning the first sod for the foundation of a home or laying the cornerstone for a public building marks the beginning of the building. Excavate, lay foundations, and pour cement when the Moon is full and in a fixed sign, Taurus, Leo or Aquarius. Saturn should be aspected but not Mars.

Bulbs

If you wish to develop bulbs for seed, choose a time when the Moon is waning, in Second or Third Quarters, to produce strong, healthy tubers. For blooms of fine quality, follow the rules for planting. Bulbs that are dug and rested for awhile before replanting should be dug during the decrease of the Moon while it is in a fruitful sign. See **Flowers** and **Harvesting.**

Business

As you begin training for any occupation, see that your lunar cycle is favorable that day and that the planet ruling your occupation is marked C, T, or Sx.

In starting a business of your own, see that the Moon is free of afflictions and that the planet ruling the business is marked C, T, or Sx.

When you take up a new job, Jupiter and Venus should be sextile, trine, or conjunct the Moon.

To make contracts, see that the Moon is in a fixed sign and sextile, trine, or conjunct Mercury, which should be marked Sx, T, or C.

Buying

When the Moon is passing from the full to the Last Quarter is the best time for buying. The Moon should be in conjunction, sextile or trine with Mercury. Mars should not be afflicted or in aspect with the Moon but Venus should be marked C, T, or Sx and your lunar cycle favorable.

Canning

Can fruits and vegetables when the Moon is in either the Third or Fourth Quarters, and when it is in one of the Water Signs, Cancer, Scorpio or Pisces. For preserves and jellies, use the same quarters, but see that the Moon is in one of the fixed signs; Taurus, Scorpio or Aquarius. See **Sauerkraut.**

Castration

Select a date when the Moon is not is Virgo, Libra, Scorpio or Sagittarius, and when it is within one week before or after the New Moon.

Cement and Concrete

Pour cement for foundations and concrete for walks and pavements during the Full Moon. It is best too for the Moon to be in one of the fixed signs, Taurus, Leo or Aquarius.

Cereals

Wheat, corn, barley, rye and oats are best planted when the Moon is increasing in light. Water Signs are the most productive, but planting may be done too when the Moon is in Libra. For corn, the First and Second Quarters are best along with the Moon in a fruitful sign. To seed hay, grain or cereals, use the First or Second Quarters in Cancer, Scorpio, Pisces or Libra.

Collections

Try to make collections on days marked favorable for your Sun Sign, when Venus or Jupiter are aspected. Avoid days in which Mars or Saturn are aspected. If possible, too, the Moon should be in a cardinal sign; Aries, Cancer, Libra or Capricorn.

Cultivation
Cultivate the ground when the Moon is in the Fourth Quarter and in a barren sign.

Dehorning Cattle
Select a date when the Moon is not in Aries, Taurus, or Pisces. One week before or after the New Moon is the best time.

Dehydration
The drying of fruits and vegetables should be done just after the Full Moon when it is in a Fire Sign; Aries, Leo or Sagittarius.

Dental Work
For this pick a day that is marked good for your planetary ruler. Mars should be marked Sx, T, or C and Saturn, Uranus and Jupiter should not be marked Sq, or O.

Teeth are best removed during the increase of the Moon in the First or Second Quarters. Avoid the signs of Aries, Cancer or Libra, also Taurus, Leo, Scorpio or Aquarius. The day should be favorable for your lunar cycle and Mars and Saturn should be marked C, T, or Sx.

Filling should be done when the Moon is in a fixed sign and decreasing in light. The same applies for having impressions made for plates.

Dressmaking
Design, cut, repair or make clothes during the First and Second Quarters on a day marked good for your Sun Sign. Venus, Jupiter and Mercury should be aspected, but avoid Mars or Saturn aspects.

Employment, Promotion or Favors
Choose a day when your Sun Sign is favorable and try

to have your lunar cycle during its high phase. Mercury should be marked C, T, or Sx.

Eye Glasses
Eyes should be tested and glasses fitted on a day marked good for your Sun Sign and on a day which falls during your favorable lunar cycle. Mars should not be in aspect with the Moon. The same applies for any treatment of the eyes which should also be started during the increase of the Moon.

Fence posts and Telegraph poles
Set the posts or poles when the Moon is in the Third or Fourth Quarters. The fixed signs, Taurus, Leo, or Aquarius, are best for this.

Fertilizing
This is best done when the Moon is in a fruitful sign. If chemical fertilizer is used, select a time when the Moon is increasing; for organic fertilizer, use the decreasing Moon.

Fishing
During the summer months the best time of the day for fishing is from sunrise to two or three hours after, and from about two hours before sunset until one hour after. In the cooler months, the fish are not actively biting until the air is warmed by the Sun. At this time the best hours are from noon to three o'clock. Warm and cloudy days are good for fishing. The most favorable winds are from the south and southwest while easterly winds are the most unfavorable. The best days of the month for fishing are those on which the Moon changes quarters and especially if the change occurs on a day when the Moon is in a watery sign, Cancer, Scorpio or Pisces. The best period in any month is the day after the Full Moon.

Flowers

Plant seeds during increase of the Moon, First Quarter preferred; in Libra for beauty and fragrance; in Cancer, Scorpio, and Pisces for abundance. Scorpio expresses the least beauty, but is very sturdy.

If you wish to develop choice blooms, plant in the First Quarter in Cancer for fruitfulness; second year, plant seeds from these plants in Libra for beauty; and third year plant second year seeds in Taurus to produce hardiness. Try this plan with various kinds of seed, keeping an exact record of times and results. This method develops fine stock. Let us hear of your results.

Friends

Friendship prospers when Venus is trine, sextile, or conjunct the Moon and your lunar cycle is favorable.

Grafting or Budding

By this process, new or better varieties of fruit are introduced on a less desirable tree or shrub. Use an increasing Moon in fruitful signs to produce a perfect union between parent tree and scion. The grafts from good bearing trees can be cut at any time while the trees are dormant, from December to March. Graft just before the sap starts to flow and while the Moon is going from new to full (First and Second Quarters), preferably while it is passing through the fruitful signs, Cancer, Scorpio or Pisces. The movable Earth Sign Capricorn is also good for this.

Groceries

Buy these in any quarter of the Moon, but try to choose a day marked good for your Sun Sign and a day when Mercury is trine, sextile, or conjunct the Moon. Avoid days when Neptune is square or opposite the Moon.

Habits

To begin to overcome any habit you wish to eliminate, start on a day when the Moon is in the Third or Fourth Quarters and in a barren sign. Gemini, Leo or Virgo are the best time while Aries and Capricorn are suitable too. Make sure your lunar cycle is favorable. These rules apply to smoking and will produce a good start. Every time you wish to overcome a habit watch for these positions of the Moon to help you.

Harvesting

Harvest root crops for food when the Moon is old, in the Third or Fourth Quarters. These crops keep better and longer. Dig potatoes in the Third and Fourth Quarters in dry signs; Aries, Leo, Sagittarius. Gemini and Aquarius are also good for harvesting the root crops. Never dig potatoes when the Moon is in a Water Sign for they will become soggy and sprout.

Pick apples and pears during the decrease of the Moon and bruised spots will dry. Fruit, too, should be harvested when the Moon is in a dry sign as above.

For seed, dig root crops in the Full Moon. They keep longer and are dryer. For flower seed, see **Flowers.**

Health Foods

When the Moon is in Virgo, it is favorable for buying vegetables and cereals. But if it is square or opposite Mars, Saturn, or Uranus, it is best not to eat herbs, vegetables and fruit, especially apricots and peaches. When the Moon is in Scorpio, it is a good time to buy medicines.

House

If you desire a permanent home, buy when the Moon is in one of the fixed signs, Taurus, Leo, Scorpio or Aquarius. If you're buying for speculation and a quick turnover, be certain that the Moon is not in a fixed sign, but in one of the movable signs, Aries, Cancer, Libra, or Capricorn.

House Furnishings

Follow the same rules for buying clothing, avoiding days when Mars is aspected. Days when Saturn is aspected make things wear longer and tends to a more conservative purchase. Saturn days are good for buying, and Jupiter days are good for selling.

Irrigation

Irrigate when the Moon is in a watery sign.

Lawn, When to Mow

Mow the lawn in the First or Second Quarters to increase the growth of grass. But if you wish to retard the growth, mow in the Third or Fourth Quarters.

Lost Articles

Search for lost articles during the First Quarter and when your Sun Sign is marked good. Also check to see that the planet ruling the lost item is also trine, sextile, or conjunct the Moon. The Moon governs household utensils, Mercury letters and books, and Venus clothing and jewelry.

Machinery

Tools, machinery and other implements should be bought on days when your lunar cycle is favorable and when Mars and Uranus are trine, sextile, or conjunct the Moon. Any quarter of the Moon is suitable.

Mailing

For best results, try to send mail as near to your lunar cycle high as possible. The Moon in Gemini is good, while Virgo, Sagittarius and Pisces are helpful, too.

Marriage

As a general rule, the best time for marriage to take place is during the increase of the Moon, just past the First Quarter. It is highly important for Venus to be trine, sextile, or conjunct the Moon. The Moon, Venus and Jupiter should be sextile or trine to each other if possible, and in a Water Sign.

However, the best date for both parties concerned needs more individual attention. Our *Personal Services Department* is available to you. You will need to know the time, place and date of birth of both parties for the astrologers to be of service.

Mining

Saturn rules drilling and mining. Begin this work on a day when Saturn is marked C, T, or Sx. If mining for gold, pick a day in which the Sun is also marked C, T, or Sx. Mercury rules quicksilver, Venus copper, Jupiter tin, Saturn lead and coal, Uranus radioactive elements, Neptune oil, and the Moon water. A venture started on a good day has the best chance of success.

Moving Into House or Office

Observe the rules for buying a house and check to see that your lunar cycle is favorable on the day chosen.

Mushrooms

Mushrooms are best and most plentiful at the Full Moon.

New Ventures

Things usually get off to a better start during the increase of the Moon, the First and Second Quarters. if there is impatience, anxiety or deadlock, it can often be broken at the Full Moon. Agreements can be reached then.

News

The handling of news is related to Uranus, Mercury, and to all of the Air Signs. When Uranus is aspected, there is always an increase in the spectacular side of the news. Collection of news is related to Saturn.

Painting

The best time to paint buildings is during the decrease of the Moon's light (Third and Fourth Quarters). For the needs of the artist, see that Venus, Jupiter, and Uranus are trine, sextile, or conjunct the Moon.

Partnership

Agreements and partnerships should be made on a day that is marked favorable for *both* parties. Mars, Neptune, and Saturn should not be square or opposite the Moon. It is best to make an agreement or partnership when the Moon is in a mutable sign, especially in Gemini or Virgo. The fixed and cardinal signs are not favorable with the possible exception of Leo or Capricorn. Begin partnerships when the Moon is increasing in light, as this is a favorable time for starting new ventures. Further questions of compatibility and optimum times for new partnerships can be answered for you by our *Personal Services Department*.

Photography, Radio, Television and Movies

For all of these activities, it is best to have Neptune, Venus, and Mercury well aspected, that is, trine, sextile, or conjunct the Moon. The act of photographing is not dependent on any particular phase of the Moon, but Neptune rules photography while Venus is related to beauty in line, form, and color.

Poultry

Eggs should best be hatched during the increase of the

Moon in a feminine Water Sign. If you use poultry hatched in this manner as breeders, you will find your flock improved.

Pruning

This operation checks limb growth, prevents too much spreading of the branches, and produces better fruit. Trees should be pruned during the decrease of the Moon while it is in a fruitful sign. The Third Quarter and the Sign of Scorpio is an ideal combination. See also **Planting** and **Trees.**

Public Relations

For this, Uranus, Mercury and Neptune should be marked C, T, or Sx, and your lunar cycle favorable.

Romance

Venus rules love, friendship, and the beauties of the nature while the Moon influences sexual inclination. The position of these two in a person's Natal Chart will indicate how transiting planets now affect these things. How the person is affected by the current position of the planets depends on the nature of his birth or Natal Chart. But in general, it is good to start a new relationship when Venus is marked C, T, or Sx, avoiding days when Saturn and Neptune are marked Sq, or O. Never accept a blind date when Neptune is aspected and more energetic activities are best on days when Mars is trine, sextile, or conjunct the Moon. For sexual activities, days on which the Moon occupies the same sign as that of the Sun Sign of either partner should be preferred. For better understanding of your romantic needs, write for our *Personal Services Brochure.*

Sauerkraut

The best tasting sauerkraut is made just after the Full

Moon, in one of the fruitful signs; Cancer, Scorpio or Pisces.

Selling or Canvassing

Contacts for this will be better near the top of your lunar cycle. Otherwise, make strong efforts to sell on days when Jupiter, Mercury, or Mars are trine, sextile, or conjunct the Moon. Avoid days when Saturn is square or opposite the Moon. For the selling of manuscripts, see **Advertising.**

Shingling

Shingling should be done in the decrease of the Moon when it is in a fixed sign. If shingles are laid during the New Moon, they have a tendency to curl at the edges.

Signing Important Papers

Sign contracts or agreements when the Moon is increasing (First and Second Quarters) in a fruitful sign, and on a day when Moon-Mercury aspects are operating. Avoid days when Mars, Saturn, or Neptune are square or opposite the Moon. Don't sign anything if you are at the bottom of your lunar cycle.

Slaughtering for Food

A man with experience in slaughtering animals for food in large numbers writes as follows: Kill the first three days after the Full Moon. Meat will keep better, be tender and have fine flavor. Avoid the sign Leo.

Spraying

Spraying to destroy pests is best done in the Fourth Quarter and when the Moon is in a barren sign, Gemini, Leo, or Virgo.

Sterilization

This shouldn't be done when the Moon is in Virgo, Libra, or Scorpio. If possible, operate within twenty-four hours before or after the New Moon.

Surgical Operations

The flow of blood, like the ocean tides, appears to be regulated by the Moon's phases. TIME magazine (page 74, June 6, 1960) reports on 1000 tonsilectomy case histories analyzed by Dr. Edson J. Andrews. Only eighteen percent of associated hemorrhaging occurred in the Fourth and First Quarters. Thus, a new astrological rule: To reduce the hazard of hemorrhage after a surgical operation, plan to have the surgery within one week before or after the New Moon. Avoid where possible surgery within one week before or after the Full Moon. Select, too, a date when the Moon is not in the sign governing the part of the body involved in the operation. The farther removed the Moon sign is from the afflicted part of the body, the better the healing.

Thoroughbred Seed

To develop thoroughbred seed, save seed for three successive years from plants grown by the correct sign and phase. Example: plant seed first year in Cancer, second year in Scorpio, third year in Pisces. Observe the rules for harvesting.

Timber

Timber cut in the last quarters of the Moon does season well and won't warp or decay. Try to avoid the Water Signs for cutting timber.

Travel

Start your journey on a day when the Moon is not in a fixed sign; Taurus, Scorpio, Leo, or Aquarius; and when your lunar cycle is favorable. Mercury, Uranus and Neptune should be marked C, T, or Sx. Uranus is good for air travel while Neptune is favorable for water travel.

Trees

Since trees are perennials, they should be planted at the decrease of the Moon. This promotes deep root growth, thicker bark and stronger branches. The slow top growth of the branches allows the tree a longer life. Trees planted in the increase of the Moon have a fast, showy top growth, but they don't stand up against weather hazards as well. See **Planting, Grafting or Budding,** and **Pruning.**

Unwanted Plant and Animal Life

Unwanted plant and animal life includes corns, calluses, warts, moles, superfluous hair, blemishes, stains, etc.; also weeds, thistles, poison ivy, devil grass, or any kind of vegetation, fungus growth, or undesirable insect, pests or animal life. Destroy such pests when both the Sun and Moon are in barren signs, and the Moon is decreasing, Fourth Quarter preferred. Barren signs are Leo, Aries, Virgo, Aquarius, Gemini and Sagittarius, listed according to the degree of nonproductive qualities.

Weaning Children

This should be done when the Moon is in Sagittarius, Capricorn, Aquarius, and Pisces. The mother should nurse the child in a fruitful period when it is the last time. Venus should then be trine, sextile or conjunct the Moon.

Weeds

Plowing and trimming to destroy weeds are best done when the Moon is in the Fourth Quarter, although the Third Quarter is also effective.

Mind your p's and q's!

. . . they can reveal an awful lot about you, as Ruth Gardner's *Graphology Student's Workbook* shows.

giggle

just

The way you end a word may tell a tale: a long, outward tending final stroke with a blunt end may suggest that you are a generous giver; an upward moving final stroke with a blunt end may indicate reluctance to give or the expectation of gain from giving.

An upward slanting bar across your "t" may suggest optimism; a downward directed last stroke may reveal that your initiative has not been followed through because of a pessimistic attitude.

t

f

Miss Gardner's book will introduce you to the mirror of personality that is in your handwriting. Everything about your handwriting—from its slant and heaviness to the very distinctive way you fill a page—is simply explained and clearly shown through several actual samples.

Amaze your friends, learn things about people that they would never be willing to tell you, and discover things about yourself you never were aware of before! Read:

A GRAPHOLOGY STUDENT'S WORKBOOK
No. 1-87542-250, $4.95 from GA Booksales. Use the order form on the last page to order.

Astro-Almanac
Central Standard Time

Dates	What to Do
Dec 30, 0:45 am - Jan 1, 1:47 pm Taurus 2nd quarter	Beauty treatments. Buy clothes. Buy house for permanent home. Sew clothes.
Jan 1, 1:47 pm - Jan 4, 1:10 am Gemini 2nd quarter	Write letters, send mail. Make agreements, form partnerships. Have teeth removed. Sew clothes.
Jan 4, 1:10 am - Jan 5, 6:51 am Cancer 2nd quarter	Beauty treatments. Bake. Cut hair to encourage growth. Start diet to gain weight. Buy property for speculation. Sign contracts.
Jan 5, 6:51 am Full Moon Cancer	Brew. Cut hair to increase thickness.
Jan 5, 6:51 am - Jan 6, 10:33 pm Cancer 3rd quarter	Beauty treatments. Can fruits, vegetables. Make sauerkraut. Buy property for speculation. Paint buildings.
Jan 6, 10:33 pm - Jan 8, 5:54 pm Leo 3rd quarter	Beauty treatments. Set fence posts. Cut hair to decrease growth. Start diet to lose weight. Borrow money. Dry fruits and vegetables. Have teeth filled. Put on shingles.
Jan 8, 5:54 pm - Jan 10, 11:15 pm Virgo 3rd quarter	Start diet to lose weight. Buy health foods. Write letters, send mail. Cut timber. Paint buildings.
Jan 10, 11:15 pm - Jan 13, 2:47 am	Beauty treatments. Cut timber. Buy property for

Libra 3rd and 4th quarters
Jan 13, 2:47 am - Jan 15, 3:39 am
Scorpio 4th quarter

speculation. Paint buildings.
Buy medicines. Put on shingles. Have teeth filled. Brew. Make jelly. Can fruits and vegetables. Borrow money. Buy house for permanent home. Beauty treatments.

Jan 15, 3:39 am - Jan 17, 6:40 am
Sagittarius 4th quarter

Start diet to lose weight. Borrow money. Cut timber. Write letters, send mail. Wean children. Paint buildings.

Jan 17, 6:40 am - Jan 19, 8:34 am
Capricorn 4th quarter

Cut timber. Buy property for speculation. Wean children. Paint buildings.

Jan 19, 8:34 am
New Moon Capricorn

Dock, castrate, and dehorn animals. Buy animals. Test and treat eyes. Fit glasses.

Jan 19, 9:18 am - Jan 21, 1:42 pm
Aquarius 1st quarter

Beauty treatments. Permanent waves, hair coloring. Buy house for permanent home. Wean children. Sew clothes.

Jan 21, 1:42 pm - Jan 23, 9:27 pm
Pisces 1st quarter

Cut hair to encourage growth. Wean children. Start diet to gain weight. Have teeth removed. Write letters, send mail. Sign contracts.

Jan 23, 9:27 pm - Jan 26, 8:51 am
Aries 1st quarter

Sew clothes. Bake. Buy property for speculation.

Jan 26, 8:51 am - Jan 28, 9:32 pm
Taurus 1st and 2nd quarters

Beauty treatments. Buy clothes. Buy house for permanent home. Sew clothes.

Jan 28, 8:51 am - Jan 28, 9:32 pm
Gemini 2nd quarter

Write letters, send mail. Make agreements, form partnerships. Have teeth removed. Sew clothes.

Jan 31, 9:18 am - Feb 2, 6:23 pm
Cancer 2nd quarter

Beauty treatments. Bake. Cut hair to encourage growth. Start diet to gain weight. Buy property for speculation. Sign contracts.

Feb 2, 6:23 pm - Feb 3, 10:35 pm
Leo 2nd quarter

Beauty treatments. Buy house for permanent home. Sew clothes.

Feb 3, 10:35 pm
Full Moon Leo

Lay foundations. Pour cement, excavate. Cut hair to increase thickness.

Feb 3, 10:35 pm - Feb 5, 0:32 am
Leo 3rd quarter

Beauty treatments. Set fence posts. Cut hair to decrease growth. Start diet to lose weight. Borrow money. Dry fruits and vegetables. Have teeth filled. Put on shingles.

Feb 5, 0:31 am - Feb 7, 5:10 am
Virgo 3rd quarter

Start diet to lose weight. Buy health foods. Write letters, send mail. Cut timber. Paint buildings.

Feb 7, 5:10 am - Feb 9, 9:03 am
Libra 3rd quarter

Beauty treatments. Cut timber. Buy property for speculation. Paint buildings.

Feb 9, 9:03 am - Feb 11, 11:45 am
Scorpio 3rd and 4th quarters

Buy medicines. Put on shingles. Have teeth filled. Make sauerkraut. Can fruits and vegetables. Borrow money. Buy house for permanent home. Beauty treatments.

Feb 11, 11:45 am - Feb 13, 2:34 pm
Sagittarius 4th quarter

Start diet to lose weight. Borrow money. Cut timber. Write letters, send mail. Wean children. Paint buildings.

Feb 13, 2:34 pm - Feb 15, 5:59 pm
Capricorn 4th quarter

Cut timber. Buy property for speculation. Wean children. Paint buildings.

Feb 15, 5:59 pm - Feb 17, 10:08 pm
Aquarius 4th quarter

Start diet to lose weight. Borrow money. Have teeth filled. Set fence posts. Wean children. Put on shingles. Paint buildings. Make jelly.

Feb 17, 10:08 pm
New Moon Aquarius

Feb 17, 10:52 pm - Feb 20, 6:35 am
Pisces 1st quarter

Dock, castrate, and dehorn animals. Buy animals. Test and treat eyes. Fit glasses.

Cut hair to encourage growth. Wean children. Start diet to gain weight. Have teeth removed. Write letters, send mail. Sign contracts.

Feb 20, 6:35 am - Feb 22, 5:00 pm
Aries 1st quarter

Sew clothes. Bake. Buy property for speculation.

Feb 22, 5:00 pm - Feb 25, 5:36 am
Taurus 1st quarter

Beauty treatments. Buy clothes. Buy house for permanent home. Sew clothes.

Feb 25, 5:36 am - Feb 27, 5:59 pm
Gemini 1st and 2nd quarters

Write letters, send mail. Have teeth removed. Make agreements, form partnerships. Sew clothes.

Feb 27, 5:59 pm - March 2, 3:23 am
Cancer 2nd quarter

Beauty treatments. Bake. Cut hair to encourage growth. Start diet to gain weight. Buy property for speculation. Sign contracts.

March 2, 3:23 am - March 4, 9:37 am
Leo 2nd quarter

Beauty treatments. Buy house for permanent home. Sew clothes.

March 4, 9:37 am - March 5, 11:33 am
Virgo 2nd quarter

Write letters, send mail. Have teeth removed. Make agreements, form partnerships. Sew clothes. Buy health foods.

March 5, 11:33 am
Full Moon Virgo

Cut hair to increase thickness.

March 5, 11:33 am - March 6, 12:48 pm
Virgo 3rd quarter

Start diet to lose weight. Buy health foods. Write letters, send mail. Cut timber. Paint buildings.

March 6, 12:48 pm - March 8, 2:46 pm
Libra 3rd quarter

Beauty treatments. Cut timber. Buy property for speculation. Paint buildings.

March 8, 2:46 pm - March 10, 4:48 pm
Scorpio 3rd quarter

Buy medicines. Put on shingles. Have teeth filled. Make sauerkraut. Make jelly. Can fruits and vegetables. Borrow money. Buy house for permanent home.

March 10, 4:48 pm - March 12, 7:47 pm
Sagittarius 3rd and 4th quarters

Start diet to lose weight. Borrow money. Cut timber. Write letters, send mail. Wean children. Paint buildings.

March 12, 7:47 pm - March 15, 0:26 am
Capricorn 4th quarter

Cut timber. Buy property for speculation. Wean children. Paint buildings.

March 15, 0:26 am - March 17, 6:23 am
Aquarius 4th quarter

Start diet to lose weight. Borrow money. Have teeth filled. Set fence posts. Wean children. Put on shingles. Paint buildings. Make jelly.

March 17, 6:23 am - March 19, 1:09 pm
Pisces 4th quarter

Brew. Borrow money. Can fruits and vegetables. Write letters, send mail. Wean children. Paint buildings.

March 19, 2:42 pm - March 22, 1:06 am
Aries 1st quarter

Sew clothes. Bake. Buy property for speculation.

March 22, 1:06 am - March 24, 1:30 pm
Taurus 1st quarter

Beauty treatments. Buy clothes. Buy house for permanent home. Sew clothes.

March 24, 1:30 pm - March 27, 2:00 am
Write letters, send mail. Have teeth removed. Make

Gemini 1st quarter	agreements, form partnerships. Sew clothes.
March 27, 2:00 am - March 29, 12:43 pm Cancer 1st and 2nd quarters	Beauty treatments. Bake. Cut hair to encourage growth. Start diet to gain weight. Buy property for speculation. Sign contracts.
March 29, 12:43 pm - March 31, 7:34 pm Leo 2nd quarter	Beauty treatments. Buy house for permanent home. Sew clothes.
March 31, 7:34 pm - April 2, 10:37 pm Virgo 2nd quarter	Write letters, send mail. Have teeth removed. Make agreements, form partnerships. Sew clothes. Buy health foods.
April 2, 10:37 pm - April 3, 10:19 pm Libra 2nd quarter	Sew clothes. Bake. Beauty treatments. Buy property for speculation.
April 3, 10:19 pm Full Moon Libra	Cut hair to increase thickness.
April 3, 10:19 pm - April 4, 11:26 pm Libra 3rd quarter	Beauty treatments. Cut timber. Buy property for speculation. Paint buildings.
April 4, 11:26 pm - April 7, 0:20 am Scorpio 3rd quarter	Buy medicines. Put on shingles. Have teeth filled. Make sauerkraut. Make jelly. Can fruits and vegetables. Borrow money. Buy house for permanent home.
April 7, 0:20 am - April 9, 1:52 am Sagittarius 3rd quarter	Start diet to lose weight. Borrow money. Dry fruits and vegetables. Cut timber. Write letters, send mail. Wean children. Paint buildings.
April 9, 1:52 am - April 11, 5:49 am Capricorn 3rd and 4th quarters	Cut timber. Buy property for speculation. Wean children. Paint buildings.

April 11, 5:49 am - April 13, 12:25 pm
Aquarius 4th quarter

Start diet to lose weight. Borrow money. Have teeth filled. Set fence posts. Wean children. Put on shingles. Paint buildings. Make jelly.

April 13, 12:25 pm - April 15, 9:33 pm
Pisces 4th quarter

Brew. Borrow money. Can fruits and vegetables. Write letters, send mail. Wean children. Paint buildings.

April 15, 9:33 pm - April 18, 5:12 am
Aries 4th quarter

Start diet to lose weight. Cut timber. Buy property for speculation. Paint buildings.

April 18, 8:23 am - April 20, 8:39 pm
Taurus 1st quarter

Beauty treatments. Buy clothes. Buy house for permanent home. Sew clothes.

April 20, 8:39 pm - April 23, 9:26 am
Gemini 1st quarter

Have teeth removed. Make agreements, form partnerships. Sew clothes. Write letters, send mail.

April 23, 9:26 am - April 25, 8:59 pm
Cancer 1st quarter

Bake. Beauty treatments. Buy property for speculation. Cut hair to encourage growth. Sign contracts. Start diet to gain weight.

April 25, 8:59 pm - April 28, 5:16 am
Leo 1st and 2nd quarters

Beauty treatments. Buy house for permanent home. Sew clothes.

April 28, 5:16 am - April 30, 9:09 am
Virgo 2nd quarter

Buy health foods. Have teeth removed. Make agreements, form partnerships. Sew clothes. Write letters, send mail.

April 30, 9:09 am - May 2, 10:00 am
Libra 2nd quarter

Bake. Beauty treatments. Buy property for speculation. Sew clothes.

May 2, 10:00 am - May 3, 6:49 am
Scorpio 2nd quarter

Beauty treatments. Buy house for permanent home. Buy medicines. Cut hair to encourage growth.

Sign contracts. Start diet to gain weight.
Brew. Cut hair to increase thickness.

Borrow money. Buy house for permanent home.
Buy medicines. Can fruits and vegetables. Have
teeth filled. Make jelly. Make sauerkraut. Put on
shingles.

Borrow money. Cut timber. Dry fruits and vegetables. Paint buildings. Start diet to lose weight.
Write letters, send mail.

Buy property for speculation. Cut timber. Paint
buildings. Wean children.

Borrow money. Have teeth filled. Put on shingles.
Set fence posts. Wean children.

Borrow money. Brew. Can fruits and vegetables.
Wean children. Write letters, send mail.

Buy property for speculation. Cut timber. Paint
buildings. Start diet to lose weight.

Beauty treatments. Buy house for permanent home.
Have teeth filled. Paint buildings. Put on shingles.
Put up preserves.

Buy animals. Dock and castrate animals. Fit
glasses. Test and treat eyes.
Have teeth removed. Make agreements, form part-

May 3, 6:49 am
Full Moon Scorpio
May 3, 6:49 am - May 4, 9:46 am
Scorpio 3rd quarter

May 4, 9:46 am - May 6, 9:47 am
Sagittarius 3rd quarter

May 6, 9:47 am - May 8, 12:16 pm
Capricorn 3rd quarter
May 8, 12:16 pm - May 10, 5:48 pm
Aquarius 3rd and 4th quarters
May 10, 5:48 pm - May 13, 3:06 am
Pisces 4th quarter
May 13, 3:06 am - May 15, 2:36 pm
Aries 4th quarter
May 15, 2:36 pm - May 17, 8:58 pm
Taurus 4th quarter

May 17, 8:58 pm
New Moon Taurus
May 18, 2:46 am - May 20, 3:29 pm

Gemini 1st quarter
May 20, 3:29 pm - May 23, 3:16 am
Cancer 1st quarter

nerships. Sew clothes. Write letters, send mail. Bake. Beauty treatments. Buy property for speculation. Cut hair to encourage growth. Sign contracts. Start diet to gain weight.

May 23, 3:16 am - May 25, 12:48 pm
Leo 1st quarter
May 25, 12:48 pm - May 27, 6:31 pm
Virgo 1st and 2nd quarters

Beauty treatments. Buy house for permanent home. Sew clothes.

Buy health foods. Have teeth removed. Make agreements, form partnerships. Sew clothes. Write letters, send mail.

May 27, 6:31 pm - May 29, 8:36 pm
Libra 2nd quarter
May 29, 8:36 pm - May 31, 8:32 pm
Scorpio 2nd quarter

Bake. Beauty treatments. Buy property for speculation. Sew clothes.

Beauty treatments. Buy house for permanent home. Buy medicines. Cut hair to encourage growth. Sign contracts. Start diet to gain weight.

May 31, 8:32 pm - June 1, 2:15 pm
Sagittarius 2nd quarter
June 1, 2:15 pm
Full Moon Sagittarius
June 1, 2:15 pm - June 2, 7:57 pm
Sagittarius 3rd quarter

Have teeth removed. Sew clothes. Wean children. Write letters, send mail.

Cut hair to increase thickness.

June 2, 7:57 pm - June 4, 8:56 pm
Capricorn 3rd quarter
June 4, 8:56 pm - June 7, 0:53 am

Borrow money. Cut timber. Dry fruits and vegetables. Paint buildings. Start diet to lose weight. Write letters, send mail.

Buy property for speculation. Cut timber. Paint buildings. Wean children.

Borrow money. Have teeth filled. Permanent

Aquarius 3rd quarter

waves, hair coloring. Put on shingles. Set fence posts. Wean children.

June 7, 0:53 am - June 9, 8:55 am
Pisces 3rd and 4th quarters

Borrow money. Can fruits and vegetables. Wean children. Write letters, send mail.

June 9, 8:55 am - June 11, 8:21 pm
Aries 4th quarter

Buy property for speculation. Cut timber. Paint buildings. Start diet to lose weight.

June 11, 8:21 pm - June 14, 9:02 am
Taurus 4th quarter

Beauty treatments. Buy house for permanent home. Have teeth filled. Paint buildings. Put on shingles. Put up preserves.

June 14, 9:02 am - June 16, 12:38 pm
Gemini 4th quarter

Cut hair to decrease growth. Cut timber. Paint buildings. Write letters, send mail.

June 16, 12:38 pm
New Moon Gemini

Buy animals. Dock, castrate and dehorn animals. Fit glasses. Test and treat eyes.

June 16, 9:32 pm - June 19, 8:57 am
Cancer 1st quarter

Bake. Beauty treatments. Buy property for speculation. Cut hair to encourage growth. Sign contracts. Start diet to gain weight.

June 19, 8:57 am - June 21, 6:46 pm
Leo 1st quarter

Beauty treatments. Buy house for permanent home. Sew clothes.

June 21, 6:46 pm - June 24, 1:52 am
Virgo 1st quarter

Buy health foods. Have teeth removed. Make agreements, form partnerships. Sew clothes. Write letters, send mail.

June 24, 1:52 am - June 26, 5:40 am
Libra 1st and 2nd quarters

Bake. Beauty treatments. Buy property for speculation. Sew clothes.

June 26, 5:40 am - June 28, 7:07 am

Beauty treatments. Buy house for permanent

Scorpio 2nd quarter	home. Buy medicines. Cut hair to encourage growth. Sign contracts. Start diet to gain weight. Have teeth removed. Sew clothes. Wean children. Write letters.
June 28, 7:07 am - June 30, 6:48 am Sagittarius 2nd quarter	Cut hair to increase thickness.
June 30, 9:33 pm Full Moon Capricorn	
June 30, 9:33 pm - July 2, 7:10 am Capricorn 3rd quarter	Buy property for speculation. Cut timber. Paint buildings. Wean children.
July 2, 7:10 am - July 4, 9:53 am Aquarius 3rd quarter	Borrow money. Have teeth filled. Permanent waves, hair coloring. Put on shingles. Set fence posts. Wean children.
July 4, 9:53 am - July 6, 4:19 pm Pisces 3rd quarter	Borrow money. Can fruits and vegetables. Make sauerkraut. Wean children. Write letters, send mail.
July 6, 4:19 pm - July 9, 2:40 am Aries 3rd and 4th quarters	Buy property for speculation. Cut timber. Paint buildings. Start diet to lose weight.
July 9, 2:40 am - July 11, 3:34 pm Taurus 4th quarter	Beauty treatments. Buy house for permanent home. Have teeth filled. Paint buildings. Put on shingles. Put up preserves.
July 11, 3:34 pm - July 14, 4:00 am Gemini 4th quarter	Cut hair to decrease growth. Cut timber. Paint buildings. Write letters, send mail.
July 14, 4:00 am - July 16, 2:43 am Cancer 4th quarter	Beauty treatments. Brew. Buy property for speculation. Can fruits and vegetables. Make sauerkraut. Paint buildings.

July 16, 2:43 am
New Moon Cancer

Buy animals. Dock, castrate and dehorn animals. Fit glasses. Test and treat eyes.

July 16, 2:55 pm - July 19, 0:10 am
Leo 1st quarter

Beauty treatments. Buy house for permanent home. Sew clothes.

July 19, 0:10 am - July 21, 7:05 am
Virgo 1st quarter

Buy health foods. Have teeth removed. Make agreements, form partnerships. Sew clothes. Write letters, send mail.

July 21, 7:05 am - July 23, 12:18 pm
Libra 1st quarter

Bake. Beauty treatments. Buy property for speculation. Sew clothes.

July 23, 12:18 pm - July 25, 3:07 pm
Scorpio 1st and 2nd quarters

Beauty treatments. Buy house for permanent home. Buy medicines. Cut hair to encourage growth. Sign contracts. Start diet to lose weight.

July 25, 3:07 pm - July 27, 4:17 pm
Sagittarius 2nd quarter

Have teeth removed. Sew clothes. Wean children. Write letters.

July 27, 4:17 pm - July 29, 5:36 pm
Capricorn 2nd quarter

Bake. Buy property for speculation. Sew clothes. Wean children.

July 29, 5:36 pm - July 30, 5:32 am
Aquarius 2nd quarter

Beauty treatments. Buy house for permanent home. Permanent waves, hair coloring. Sew clothes. Wean children.

July 30, 5:31 am
Full Moon Aquarius

Lay foundations, pour cement, excavate.

July 30, 5:31 am - July 31, 7:53 pm
Aquarius 3rd quarter

Borrow money. Have teeth filled. Permanent waves, hair coloring. Put on shingles. Set fence posts. Wean children.

Borrow money. Can fruits and vegetables. Make sauerkraut. Wean children. Write letters, send mail. Buy property for speculation. Cut timber. Dry fruits and vegetables. Paint buildings. Start diet to lose weight.

Beauty treatments. Buy house for permanent home. Have teeth filled. Paint buildings. Put on shingles. Put up preserves.

Cut hair to decrease growth. Cut timber. Paint buildings. Write letters, send mail.

Beauty treatments. Brew. Buy property for speculation. Can fruits and vegetables. Make sauerkraut. Paint buildings.

Beauty treatments. Borrow money. Cut hair to decrease growth. Have teeth filled. Set fence posts. Start diet to lose weight.

Buy animals. Dock, castrate and dehorn animals. Fit glasses. Test and treat eyes.

Beauty treatments. Buy house for permanent home. Sew clothes.

Buy health foods. Have teeth removed. Make agreements, form partnerships. Sew clothes. Write letters, send mail.

Bake. Beauty treatments. Buy property for specu-

July 31, 7:53 pm - Aug 3, 1:04 am
Pisces 3rd quarter

Aug 3, 1:04 am - Aug 5, 10:21 am
Aries 3rd quarter

Aug 5, 10:21 am - Aug 7, 10:32 pm
Taurus 3rd and 4th quarters

Aug 7, 10:32 pm - Aug 10, 11:15 am
Gemini 4th quarter

Aug 10, 11:15 am - Aug 12, 10:15 pm
Cancer 4th quarter

Aug 12, 10:15 pm - Aug 14, 3:46 pm
Leo 4th quarter

Aug 14, 3:46 pm
New Moon Leo

Aug 14, 3:46 pm - Aug 15, 6:44 am
Leo 1st quarter

Aug 15, 6:44 am - Aug 17, 12:38 pm
Virgo 1st quarter

Aug 17, 12:38 pm - Aug 19, 5:25 pm

lation. Sew clothes.

Beauty treatments. Buy house for permanent home. Buy medicines. Cut hair to encourage growth. Sign contracts. Start diet to gain weight. Have teeth removed. Sew clothes. Wean children. Write letters, send mail.

Bake. Buy property for speculation. Sew clothes. Wean children.

Beauty treatments. Buy house for permanent home. Permanent waves, hair coloring. Sew clothes. Wean children.

Brew.

Borrow money. Brew. Can fruits and vegetables. Wean children. Write letters, send mail.

Buy property for speculation. Cut timber. Dry fruits and vegetables. Paint buildings. Start diet to lose weight.

Beauty treatments. Buy house for permanent home. Have teeth filled. Paint buildings. Put on shingles. Put up preserves.

Cut hair to decrease growth. Cut timber. Paint buildings. Write letters, send mail.

Beauty treatments. Brew. Buy property for specu-

Libra 1st quarter
Aug 19, 5:25 pm - Aug 21, 8:46 pm
Scorpio 1st and 2nd quarters

Aug 21, 8:46 pm - Aug 23, 11:18 pm
Sagittarius 2nd quarter

Aug 23, 11:18 pm - Aug 26, 1:59 am
Capricorn 2nd quarter

Aug 26, 1:59 am - Aug 28, 5:20 am
Aquarius 2nd quarter

Aug 28, 2:52 pm
Full Moon Pisces

Aug 28, 2:52 pm - Aug 30, 10:35 am
Pisces 3rd quarter

Aug 30, 10:35 am - Sept 1, 6:47 pm
Aries 3rd quarter

Sept 1, 6:47 pm - Sept 4, 6:24 am
Taurus 3rd quarter

Sept 4, 6:24 am - Sept 6, 7:08 pm
Gemini 3rd and 4th quarter

Sept 6, 7:08 pm - Sept 9, 6:35 am

Cancer 4th quarter

lation. Can fruits and vegetables. Make sauerkraut. Paint buildings.

Sept 9, 6:35 am - Sept 11, 2:55 pm
Leo 4th quarter

Beauty treatments. Borrow money. Cut hair to decrease growth. Have teeth filled. Set fence posts. Start diet to lose weight.

Sept. 11, 2:55 pm - Sept 13, 3:46 am
Virgo 4th quarter

Sept 13, 3:46 am
New Moon Virgo

Buy health foods. Cut timber. Paint buildings. Start diet to lose weight. Write letters, send mail. Buy animals. Dehorn animals. Fit glasses. Test and treat eyes.

Sept 13, 8:16 pm - Sept 15, 11:43 pm
Libra 1st quarter

Bake. Beauty treatments. Buy property for speculation. Sew clothes.

Sept 15, 11:43 pm - Sept 18, 2:11 am
Scorpio 1st quarter

Beauty treatments. Buy house for permanent home. Buy medicines. Cut hair to encourage growth. Sign contracts. Start diet to gain weight. Have teeth removed. Sew clothes. Wean children. Write letters, send mail.

Sept 18, 2:11 am - Sept 20, 5:00 am
Sagittarius 1st and 2nd quarters

Bake. Buy property for speculation. Sew clothes. Wean children.

Sept 20, 5:00 am - Sept 22, 8:15 am
Capricorn 2nd quarter

Beauty treatments. Buy house for permanent home. Permanent waves, hair coloring. Sew clothes. Wean children.

Sept 22, 8:15 am - Sept 24, 12:52 pm
Aquarius 2nd quarter

Sept 24, 12:52 pm - Sept 26, 7:01 pm
Pisces 2nd quarter

Cut hair to encourage growth. Have teeth removed. Sign contracts. Start diet to gain weight. Wean children. Write letters, send mail.

Sept 26, 7:01 pm - Sept 27, 2:53 am Aries 2nd quarter	Bake. Buy property for speculation. Sew clothes.
Sept 27, 2:53 am Full Moon Aries	Cut hair to increase thickness.
Sept 27, 2:53 am - Sept 29, 3:23 am Aries 3rd quarter	Buy property for speculation. Cut timber. Dry fruits and vegetables. Paint buildings. Start diet to lose weight.
Sept 29, 3:23 am - Oct 1, 2:20 pm Taurus 3rd quarter	Beauty treatments. Buy house for permanent home. Have teeth filled. Paint buildings. Put on shingles. Put up preserves.
Oct 1, 2:20 pm - Oct 4, 2:58 am Gemini 3rd quarter	Cut hair to decrease growth. Cut timber. Paint buildings. Write letters, send mail.
Oct 4, 2:58 am - Oct 6, 3:07 pm Cancer 3rd and 4th quarter	Beauty treatments. Buy property for speculation. Can fruits and vegetables. Make sauerkraut. Paint buildings.
Oct 6, 3:07 pm - Oct 9, 0:28 am Leo 4th quarter	Beauty treatments. Borrow money. Cut hair to decrease growth. Have teeth filled. Set fence posts. Start diet to lose weight.
Oct 9, 0:28 am - Oct 11, 6:00 am Virgo 4th quarter	Buy health foods. Cut timber. Paint buildings. Start diet to lose weight. Write letters, send mail.
Oct 11, 6:00 am - Oct 12, 2:41 pm Libra 4th quarter	Beauty treatments. Buy property for speculation. Cut timber. Paint buildings.
Oct 12, 2:41 pm New Moon Libra	Buy animals. Dehorn animals. Fit glasses. Test and treat eyes.

Oct 12, 2:41 pm - Oct 13, 8:09 am
Libra 1st quarter

Oct 13, 8:09 am - Oct 15, 9:36 am
Scorpio 1st quarter

Bake. Beauty treatments. Buy property for speculation. Sew clothes.

Beauty treatments. Buy house for permanent home. Buy medicines. Cut hair to encourage growth. Sign contracts. Start diet to gain weight.

Oct 15, 9:36 am - Oct 17, 10:50 am
Sagittarius 1st quarter

Oct 17, 10:50 am - Oct 19, 1:35 pm
Capricorn 1st and 2nd quarter

Oct 19, 1:35 pm - Oct 21, 6:43 pm
Aquarius 2nd quarter

Have teeth removed. Sew slothes. Wean children. Write letters, send mail.

Bake. Buy property for speculation. Sew clothes. Wean children.

Beauty treatments. Buy house for permanent home. Permanent waves, hair coloring. Sew clothes. Wean children.

Oct 21, 6:43 pm - Oct 24, 1:41 am
Pisces 2nd quarter

Cut hair to encourage growth. Have teeth removed. Sign contracts. Start diet to gain weight. Wean children. Write letters, send mail.

Oct 24, 1:41 am - Oct 26, 10:44 am
Aries 2nd quarter

Bake. Buy property for speculation. Sew clothes.

Oct 26, 5:43 pm
Full Moon Taurus

Cut hair to increase thickness. Lay foundations, pour cement, excavate.

Oct 26, 5:43 pm - Oct 28, 9:48 pm
Taurus 3rd quarter

Beauty treatments. Buy house for permanent home. Have teeth filled. Paint buildings. Put on shingles. Put up preserves.

Oct 28, 9:48 pm - Oct 31, 10:19 am
Gemini 3rd quarter

Cut hair to decrease growth. Cut timber. Paint buildings. Write letters, send mail.

Oct 31, 10:19 am - Nov 2, 11:12 pm
Cancer 3rd quarter

Beauty treatments. Buy property for speculation. Can fruits and vegetables. Make sauerkraut.
Paint buildings.

Nov 2, 11:12 pm - Nov 5, 9:30 am
Leo 3rd and 4th quarters

Beauty treatments. Borrow money. Cut hair to decrease growth. Have teeth filled. Set fence posts.
Start diet to lose weight.

Nov 5, 9:30 am - Nov 7, 4:06 pm
Virgo 4th quarter

Buy health foods. Cut timber. Paint buildings.
Start diet to lose weight. Write letters, send mail.

Nov 7, 4:06 pm - Nov 9, 6:38 pm
Libra 4th quarter

Beauty treatments. Buy property for speculation.
Cut timber. Paint buildings.

Nov 9, 6:38 pm - Nov 11, 1:32 am
Scorpio 4th quarter

Borrow money. Buy house for permanent home.
Buy medicines. Can fruits and vegetables. Have
teeth filled. Make jelly and sauerkraut. Put on
shingles.

Nov 11, 1:32 am
New Moon Scorpio

Buy animals. Dehorn animals. Fit glasses. Test and
treat eyes.

Nov 11, 7:16 pm - Nov 13, 7:02 pm
Sagittarius 1st quarter

Have teeth removed. Sew clothes. Wean children.
Write letters, send mail.

Nov 13, 7:02 pm - Nov 15, 8:30 pm
Capricorn 1st quarter

Bake. Buy property for speculation. Sew clothes.
Wean children.

Nov 15, 8:30 pm - Nov 18, 0:10 am
Aquarius 1st and 2nd quarters

Beauty treatments. Buy house for permanent
home. Permanent waves, hair coloring. Sew clothes.
Wean children.

Nov 18, 0:10 am - Nov 20, 7:32 am

Cut hair to encourage growth. Have teeth removed.

Pisces 2nd quarter

Sign contracts. Start diet to gain weight. Wean children. Write letters, send mail. Bake. Buy property for speculation. Sew clothes.

Nov 20, 7:32 am - Nov 22, 5:08 pm
Aries 2nd quarter

Beauty treatments. Buy clothes. Buy house for permanent home. Sew clothes. Cut hair to increase thickness.

Nov 22, 5:08 pm - Nov 25, 4:38 am
Taurus 2nd quarter

Nov 25, 11:37 am
Full Moon Gemini

Cut hair to decrease growth. Cut timber. Paint buildings. Write letters, send mail.

Nov 25, 11:37 am - Nov 27, 5:05 pm
Gemini 3rd quarter

Beauty treatments. Buy property for speculation. Can fruits and vegetables. Make sauerkraut. Paint buildings.

Nov 27, 5:05 pm - Nov 30, 5:37 am
Cancer 3rd quarter

Beauty treatments. Borrow money. Cut hair to decrease growth. Dry fruits and vegetables. Have teeth filled. Set fence posts. Start diet to lose weight.

Nov 30, 5:37 am - Dec 2, 5:14 pm
Leo 3rd quarter

Buy health foods. Cut timber. Paint buildings. Start diet to lose weight. Write letters, send mail. Beauty treatments. Buy property for speculation. Cut timber. Paint buildings.

Dec 2, 5:14 pm - Dec 5, 1:19 am
Virgo 3rd and 4th quarter
Dec 5, 1:19 am - Dec 7, 5:29 am
Libra 4th quarter
Dec 7, 5:29 am - Dec 9, 6:10 am
Scorpio 4th quarter

Borrow money. Buy house for permanent home. Buy medicines. Can fruits and vegetables. Have teeth filled. Make jelly and sauerkraut. Put on shingles.

Borrow money. Cut timber. Paint buildings. Start diet to lose weight. Write letters, send mail. Buy animals. Dehorn animals. Fit glasses. Test and treat eyes.

Have teeth removed. Sew clothes. Wean children. Write letters, send mail.

Bake. Buy property for speculation. Sew clothes. Wean children.

Beauty treatments. Buy house for permanent home. Permanent waves, hair coloring. Sew clothes. Wean children.

Cut hair to encourage growth. Have teeth removed. Sign contracts. Start diet to gain weight. Wean children. Write letters, send mail.

Bake. Buy property for speculation. Sew clothes.

Beauty treatments. Buy clothes. Buy house for permanent home. Sew clothes.

Have teeth removed. Make agreements, form partnerships. Sew clothes. Write letters, send mail.

Bake. Beauty treatments. Buy property for speculation. Cut hair to encourage growth. Sign contracts. Start diet to gain weight.

Dec 9, 6:10 am - Dec 10, 12:01 pm
Sagittarius 4th quarter

Dec 10, 12:01 pm
New Moon Sagittarius

Dec 10, 12:01 pm - Dec 11, 5:41 am
Sagittarius 1st quarter

Dec 11, 5:41 am - Dec 13, 5:31 am
Capricorn 1st quarter

Dec 13, 5:31 am - Dec 15, 7:55 am
Aquarius 1st quarter

Dec 15, 7:55 am - Dec 17, 1:40 pm
Pisces 1st and 2nd quarters

Dec 17, 1:40 pm - Dec 19, 10:56 pm
Aries 2nd quarter

Dec 19, 10:56 pm - Dec 22, 10:53 am
Taurus 2nd quarter

Dec 22, 10:53 am - Dec 24, 11:33 pm
Gemini 2nd quarter

Dec 24, 11:33 pm - Dec 26, 7:13 am
Cancer 2nd quarter

Brew. Cut hair to increase thickness.

Beauty treatments. Buy property for speculation. Can fruits and vegetables. Make sauerkraut. Paint buildings.

Beauty treatments. Borrow money. Cut hair to decrease growth. Have teeth filled. Set fence posts. Start diet to lose weight.

Buy health foods. Cut timber. Paint buildings. Start diet to lose weight. Write letters, send mail.

Dec 26, 7:13 am
Full Moon Cancer

Dec 26, 7:13 am - Dec 27, 11:51 am
Cancer 3rd quarter

Dec 27, 11:51 am - Dec 29, 11:25 pm
Leo 3rd quarter

Dec 29, 11:25 pm - Jan 1, 8:43 am
Virgo 3rd quarter

Your Sun Sign

Sun-sign and Ascendant

Popular astrology—the sort encountered by most readers in newspapers and magazines—is Sun-sign astrology. Identity is complex—and the horoscope contains more than the Sun. It contains the Moon and all the planets; it contains their placement not only in the signs but in the houses; it contains the myriad aspects and relationships among all these elements. Only by viewing the horoscope as a *gestalt* can the elusive mystery of identity be glimpsed.

The forecasts in this section of the *Moon Sign Book* can be read for your Sun sign; they will tell you much about your coming year. But they can also—and more precisely—be read for your Ascendant. The Ascendant marks your first house, your horizon of life-awareness, your presentation of self to the world; your Sun reflects your basic nature, your essential energies and emotions. The Sun's energies and the Ascendant's projection blend, limit and qualify each other. In observing yourself or others in the light of the Sun-sign, any discrepancies you detect may be due, in part, to the Ascendant. As Noel Tyl states in *Horoscope Construction*, "The Aries energy of the Sun will register quite differently within a horoscope with a Capricorn or Pisces Ascendant. The identity will manifest *both*."

In the *Moon Sign Book* this year, therefore, we have

included Ascendant descriptions in addition to Sun-sign descriptions, descriptions of the Ascendant taken from Llewellyn George's classic, *A to Z Horoscope Maker and Delineator*. And we have included a method for estimating your Ascendant (Noel Tyl's "Beyond the *Moon Sign Book*," 1975 *MSB*). If you are mostly familiar with popular astrology, this additional information may give you greater insight into yourself and others. We hope also it will lead you to enquire more about astrology itself, for all capsule descriptions pale beside full analysis of the total pattern of the chart—the total pattern of identity.

Estimating the Ascendant

If you were born between 6 and 8 am Standard Time, note the sign after your birth sign (add one sign). If you were born between 8 and 10 am, add two signs; between 10 and noon, add three signs; between noon and 2 pm, add four; between 2 and 4 pm, add five signs; between 4 and 6 pm, add six; between 6 and 8 pm, add seven; between 8 and 10 pm, add eight; between 10 and midnight, add nine signs; between midnight and 2 am, add ten; between 2 and 4 am, add eleven signs; between 4 and 6 am, your Ascendant is probably the same as your Sun sign.

Nixon was born a Capricorn at 9:44 pm, between 8 and 10 pm. Adding eight signs in order after Capricorn (Aquarius, Pisces, Aries, Taurus, Gemini, Cancer, Leo, and Virgo), we get Virgo for the Ascendant. Immediately, we learn that the Sign Virgo will color Nixon's life horizon, his projection to others. We can read the Sun sign descriptions of both Capricorn *and* Virgo to get a better view of the man. Should you feel that there is a discrepancy—and there can be because of birth latitude and season of the year—look at the sign one behind or one ahead of the sign you come to through the approximation count. You'll know the right one right off the bat!

★★★★★★★★★★★ Famous Arians ★★★★★★★★★★★

3/20: Henrik Ibsen (1828), Sepharial (1864)   3/21: Otis
Spann (1930)   3/22: Marcel Marceau (1923)   3/23:
Dane Rudhyar (1895), Erich Fromm (1900), Joan Craw-
ford (1908)   3/24: Clyde Barrow (1909)   3/26: Tennessee
Williams (1914), Alan Arkin (1934)   3/27: Sarah Vaughan
(1924)   3/28: Raphael (1483)   3/30: Francisco Goya
(1746), Vincent Van Gogh (1853)   4/1: J.S. Bach (1685),
Lon Chaney (1883)   4/4: Muddy Waters (1915)   4/6:
Merle Haggard (1937)   4/7: Billie Holiday (1915)   4/9:
W.C. Fields (1879), Hugh Hefner (1926)   4/10: Omar
Sharif (1932)   4/14: Rod Steiger (1925)   4/15: Leonardo
da Vinci (1452), Bessie Smith (1898)   4/16: Charlie Chap-
lin (1889)   4/17: J.P. Morgan (1837)

Aries

Ruling Planet: Mars
Keyword: Action
Tendency: Impulsiveness
Lucky Day: Tuesday
Lucky Number: Nine
Friends: Gemini, Leo, Sagittarius, Aquarius

Aries is the spring sign—the *first*, pioneering, beginning, exploring, original and vital. Those of you born in this fiery, active sign are born leaders: dynamic, committed to causes, and full of enthusiastic, driving energy.

Your governing planet is Mars, ruling the head, and you are thus "headstrong," disliking to be disciplined by others, impatient, stubborn, and fearless. You are also very changeable and able to live by your wits.

Mentally, you are somewhat skeptical and inquiring. You enjoy logical, factual debates. You are also quick-tempered and fond of your own ideas! You are original, never following the other person's pattern.

Your love nature is passionate, dedicated and quite idealistic. You Aries men want to put your women on a pedestal, protecting, cherishing her, and keeping her as your own personal Love Goddess. You Aries women want a strong, dynamic, energetic mate, one fully capable of being a Rhett Butler, when necessary. You are ardent, demonstrative, responsive, proud, and—once you make your emotional decision—devoted, making a fine partner for a man who can fly at your own high level. Aries understands the necessity for a true partnership in marriage and are willing to give more than fifty percent, once convinced the relationship is truly what they want.

Arian energy has its negative side. You can be overbearing, headstrong, dictatorial and violent. At times, you can be overly adventurous, restless and brusque. Once committed, even to something lower than your ideals, you hold onto it with stubborn determination.

But that Aries-Mars energy, channeled positively, fuels reformers, soldiers, mechanics, journalists, artisans, teachers and enterprising businessmen. It makes you forward-looking, able to build today with tomorrow envisioned before your mind's eye. You are the true pioneer of the zodiac, with the gift of *leading* those less progressive than you.

First Decan Aries (March 20-March 31). You are an activist, a do-er and a go-er. Your nature is strong, full of integrity and energy. Watch your temper and a tendency toward dominating others. You need a cause toward which to devote your very strong energies.

Second Decan Aries (March 31-April 10). You have a sunny, bright, optimistic nature and are a born leader. You are also generous, intelligent and full of organizational, executive capacities. Harness these marvelous forces and you can be out in front in your areas of interest.

Third Decan Aries (April 10-April 20). You are slightly slower than the other two decans of Aries. You enjoy pleasure and luxury more. Your artistic side is strong, and anything connected with beauty and harmony appeals to you. Blend and balance your forceful nature with your artistic side, and you can be successful in your goals.

1977 Aries Forecast

Your financial situation is still benefiting from Jupiter's presence in your second solar house. As the year opens, Jupiter is retrograding back toward 21 Taurus where it will turn direct on January 16 to transit the remaining two decans by April 4. By increasing your resources you are able to insure your financial security for years to come. Use the first quarter of the year to buy land, learn a trade, start a business, etc. You can convince others of your reliability, so receive the financial backing you need.

Saturn spends the year in Leo, your fifth solar house. Since it entered this sign on June 6, 1976, you are by now used to its disruptive influence. You are in a lull in creativity, depressed by your inability to produce original creations. You simply cannot seem to express yourself to your satisfaction. Better spend this time in contemplation, study, and mechanical exercises: practice technique and wait for inspiration later.

Saturn forms two major long-lasting aspects this year: a trine to Neptune (July 8, 1976-September 3, 1977) and a square to Uranus (April 29, 1976-July 29, 1977).

Neptune is still in Sagittarius, your ninth solar house, causing you to question matters you previously took on faith. Your search for the meaning of life is based on intuition, not reason, and because of this you may easily be misled by religious quacks and occult con men. You are actually the one deceiving yourself, because you want to believe what others tell you, rather than figure it out for yourself.

Saturn's trine greatly improves the situation, enabling you to get a firmer grip on reality and to turn a more critical eye toward teachings you used to take for granted. Saturn balances Neptune's naive idealism with its own cynical pragmatism.

Uranus, meanwhile, is slowly vibrating between 8 and 15 Scorpio in your eighth solar house. This may be the cause of your sudden involvement with someone else's money: an inheritance, loan from a friend, financial backing, or the use of a partner's money. Be careful, though; an unexpected event could change the whole situation, leaving you holding the bag.

Uranus is also responsible for a sudden insight into the nature of life after death. You may receive a message from someone who has died, and it could contain some very startling news!

During Saturn's square to Neptune, the first half of the year, you may be haunted with the feeling that you are just on the verge of discovering an important truth, but cannot quite break through to it. This could be very disquieting, and discourage you from all other occult pursuits. To achieve your goal, work patiently and slowly, being careful not to neglect the slightest detail, following each hypothesis to its natural conclusion.

This aspect also has a distressing effect on your sex life. Uranus' position is involving you in some unusual sexual relationship, and Saturn's square may decrease your vitality, or cause a temporary period of dissatisfaction or enforced abstinence.

Mars, your personal planetary ruler, transits through half of the zodiac, this year, touching off a number of important aspects and conjunctions. Mars can be the vitalizing element needed to bring out the effects of some long-lasting aspect or planetary position.

On January 2, Mars enters Capricorn, your tenth solar house, and from here trines Jupiter (January 20-February 10). This is an excellent configuration, promoting your business or professional life, and bringing you recognition and reward for your career ambitions.

When Mars enters Aquarius on February 10, it becomes part of that distressing t-square, by opposing Saturn and squaring Uranus (February 15-March 6). During this period you may argue with the group or organization you belong to. You may leave this group in anger, or form a splinter group of which you are the leader. This schism is the cause of your social ostracism, and the social occasions you do attend are spoiled by arguments and anger.

You use someone else's money impulsively, or foolishly, and this may also be the cause of hard feelings among friends and associates. Be particularly careful in handling funds belonging to an organization: money is often the cause of lost friendships.

Mars' transit of Pisces (March 21-April 28) is a lot quieter, because it forms no major aspects during this period. Your sensitivity is increased and your thoughts are turned inward, focusing on your own feelings.

By this time Jupiter has begun its direct transit of Gemini (April 4-August 21). Here in your third solar house, Jupiter improves your communicative abilities, enabling you to get along better with others by charming them with your telling of humorous anecdotes.

You will excel in any dealings with the public now, especially in the advertising, broadcasting, or journalistic fields. Clerical work is also favored. A particularly beneficial period occurs between April 24 and August 21 when Jupiter is trine Pluto, thus giving you the ability to discard old, out-moded habits of communication and to devise new, more effective patterns of relating.

Mars in Aries (April 28-June 7), your ascendant-sign or

Sun-sign, is in its home sign and therefore strengthened. This position increases your self-confidence, assertiveness, and all-around vigor. Your enthusiasm and zest for life is increased, and you look forward to facing new situations and meeting new people.

The fact that Venus has been transiting here since **February 3** and now conjoins Mars (**April 28-July 7**) keeps your increased confidence from becoming arrogant and your assertiveness from becoming belligerent.

Here in Aries, Mars and Venus become the third leg of the grand fire trine, also involving Saturn in Leo and Neptune in Sagittarius—a great aspect under which to utilize your new-found vitality in practical, creative, and spiritually rewarding endeavors. Now is the time to put some of your imaginative ideas into concrete form, because for a short time your inspiration (Neptune), technical ability (Mars), critical judgment (Saturn), and sense of proportion (Venus) are all balanced. A real breakthrough can be expected.

On June 7, Mars and Venus together enter Taurus, Venus' home sign. Unfortunately, the two once again become part of the Saturn/Uranus square, this time opposing Uranus (Mars: **June 7-28**; Venus: **June 7-23**) and squaring Saturn (Mars: **June 13-July 7**; Venus: **June 12-30**).

This aspect has a depressing effect on your financial condition, which is particularly hard to take because of the recent economic success accompanying Jupiter's earlier transit of Taurus. Here again the problem probably involves someone else's money and you could be the victim of an economic accident.

When Mars enters Gemini, its sign position overlaps Jupiter's by a month: **July 18-August 21**. With both planets here, your biting wit and sense of irony are sharpened and you can be particularly direct with your sarcastic comments. At any other time this sharpness might annoy friends, but your charm and grace serve to captivate and flatter your audience. You can accomplish much in the way of errands, letter writing, and visits and calls on relatives and neighbors. You make many small trips and spend a lot of time taking care of diversified, unrelated tasks.

Jupiter enters Cancer on August 21, transiting to 6 Cancer by October 25 when it turns retrograde, re-entering Gemini on December 31. This is kind of a sneak preview of what Jupiter's longer transit will be like next year. This is your fourth solar house, ruling the mother and home. Jupiter's benevolent presence insures domestic tranquility, bringing peace and contentment into your home. You get along well with your family and enjoy reminiscing about your childhood. Your memories are all pleasant during this transit, regardless of what your growing years really held.

Mars follows Jupiter into Cancer on September 2, overtaking Jupiter and traveling alongside from August 21 through September 22. This is the time to make some concrete changes in your living environment; you may move into a new home now. You also spend some effort straightening out a family quarrel, an effort which results in improved relationships and happier feelings.

Mars makes one last transit this year, entering Leo on October 27, transiting 12 Leo by December 13, and turning retrograde to re-enter Cancer on January 27, 1978. Now, with Saturn's effects diffused due to its position just over the Leo/Virgo cusp (November 18-January 6, 1978), Mars can have a vitalizing effect on your social life, and creative endeavors. You are full of enthusiasm and enjoy getting out, going to the theatre, art shows, dinners, etc. Your gambling luck may pick up now, too. A holiday romance is likely.

★★★★★★★★★ Famous Taureans ★★★★★★★★★★

4/20: Adolph Hitler (1889), Miro (1893)   4/23: William
Shakespeare (1564), Vladimir Nabokov (1899)   4/26:
Marcus Aurelius (121 A.D.)   4/29: W. Randolph Hearst
(1863), Rod McKuen (1938)   5/1: Judy Collins (1939)
5/3: Henry Fielding (1707), Walter Slezak (1902), Pete
Seeger (1919)   5/5: Karl Marx (1818), Ho Chi Minh
(1890)   5/6: Victor Neuburg (1883), Orson Welles (1915)
5/7: Robert Browning (1812), Peter Ilyich Tschaikovsky
(1840), Gary Cooper (1901)   5/11: Margaret Rutherford
(1892), Salvador Dali (1904)   5/12: Jeddu Krishnamurti
(1895)   5/15: James Mason (1909) 5/16: Liberace (1919)
5/17: Eric Satie (1866), Dennis Hopper (1936)   5/18:
Bertrand Russell (1872)   5/20: Socrates (467 B.C.),
Honoré de Balzac (1799)

Taurus

Ruling Planet: Venus
Keyword: Stability
Tendency: Persistence
Lucky Day: Friday
Lucky Number: Six
Friends: Cancer, Virgo, Capricorn, Pisces

You, Taurus, are an earthy, stable person, fond of the arts, home, family, and comforts. You have a naturally easy-going temperament. You are loving, devoted and appreciative of all the "good things in life." You can be extravagant, materialistic, practical and full of common sense. You can also be sensual, stubborn, and fond of your own ideas.

You are a builder, a worker for a definite purpose, enjoying land, animals, children and the growing, protecting and nuturing of things. You are cautious, reserved and dislike change. Security, both emotional and financial, is extremely important to you.

Taurus is an artistic sign, governed by Venus (and also by the Earth). Most Taureans have a talent for music, singing, acting, and anything connected with beauty.

Taurus is the "slow but steady" sign, and in the long run, reaches its goal with a minimum of expended energy.

You can be very "bull-headed," rigid and overly conservative in your outlook and opinions. You can be loved into making a change, but never driven. You are deliberate, tenacious, trustworthy and practical.

Taurus types make excellent bankers, politicians, farmers, gardeners, teachers, doctors, chemists, nurses, builders and collectors. At times you may lack originality, adaptability and versatility, but you more than make up for these deficiencies through your persistence, perserverance and ability to endure and wait with patience.

You are very erotic and you need to love and be loved. You are intensely emotional, enjoy sex, and your heart generally rules your head! You need to discipline yourself, for you over-indulge in physical, sensual pleasures.

Your powers of concentration are wonderful, and you have a will that is formidable. Your mentality is not quick nor rapid-fire, but you seldom suffer from jumping to conclusions or from being overly impulsive intellectually. What you learn, you keep. Your mind is methodical. You are a cautious, step-by-step thinker and can accomplish excellent things.

You Taureans are the conservationists, the holders, the possessors, the constructionists of the zodiac. You are excellent at using your innate talents to protect, to keep, to invest, to develop all of your assets profitably.

First Decan Taurus (April 20-30). Your intellect combines well with a natural love of beauty. Your imaginative powers lend themselves toward decorating, sculpture, architecture, painting, any activity which applies your sense of beauty to the material world in the service of utility and practicality.

Second Decan Taurus (April 30-May 11). Your creativity, adaptability and imaginative fertility are high. You can become quite wealthy, enjoying financial comfort and even luxury with ease and a minimum of energy.

Third Decan Taurus (May 11-21). You have natural patience, determination and the ability to endure challenges which you convert into success through your ability to persevere.

1977 Taurus Forecast

In the middle of September of last year, Jupiter, the Greater Benefic, turned in its path and began a period of retrograde motion. It had only reached 1 Gemini, and was returning for a last loop through your ascendant- or Sun-sign, Taurus, before leaving it for twelve more years. This fortunate transit lasts from October 17, 1976, through January 16, 1977 (when it turns direct again at 21 Taurus) until April 4.

The first quarter of the year will be spent in establishing patterns of behavior and response which are most beneficial to you and your personal goals. Your confidence and self-assurance are high, and it seems that you can accomplish anything you set your mind to. You should be sure, during this favorable period, to probe the limits of self-knowledge to form a pool of personal security which can be drawn on for years to come.

Mars will be transiting your ninth and tenth solar houses during this first quarter, forming first a trine to Jupiter from its position in Capricorn (January 20-February 10), then a square from Aquarius (March 4-27).

The first aspect indicates a good time for an educational or publishing venture, especially if connected with foreign travel or the study of foreign cultures or religions.

The second period promotes an enthusiasm for business and professional matters, which may lead to rash or

improper actions. You are on the right track, but carry
things a little too far. Don't act superior when others do
not share your far-sighted visions.

Last year Saturn got as far as 17 Leo before turning
retrograde **on November 28, 1976.** It continues this
apparent backward motion **throughout the winter,** turning
direct **on April 12,** at 10 Leo, and progressing up to the
Virgo cusp before turning around again **on December 12.**
Saturn spends most of the year here in your fourth solar
house, just as it did during the second half of 1976. By
now you should be used to the family problems and
residential difficulties this involves. Saturn's lesson, here
as elsewhere, is one of acceptance and definition. You
must define your role in your family and learn to accept
your home life for what it is, instead of indulging yourself
in the fruitless frustration of comparing the real with the
ideal. Only then can real progress be made in accordance
with specific and realistic goals.

Your eighth solar house is once again the home of
Neptune as it continues its fourteen-year-long transit of
Sagittarius. Its two-steps-ahead-one-back pattern continues as it begins the year at 15 Sagittarius, retrogrades back
to 13 **(March 19-August 26)** and only manages to obtain
17 Sagittarius by year's end.

Under Neptune's influence you continue to feel the
mysterious pull of the supernatural. Your receptivity to
other-worldly communications remains high, but so does
your vulnerability and susceptibility to occult quacks. It is
hard to differentiate between meaningful messages and
the tricks of your own subconscious.

Saturn's long trine to Neptune **(July 8, 1976-Sep-
tember 3, 1977)** increases your discriminatory judgment
and allows you to evaluate more objectively your experiences. Your concentration, depth of feeling, and clearness
of thought are enhanced.

Uranus spends **this year** again transiting back and forth

through the middle of your seventh solar house in Scorpio. People with the Sun or ascendant between 8 and 15 Taurus will feel it most heavily, for Uranus will be directly opposite.

This whole long transit is one of conflict between your need for intimate relationships and your desire for freedom and independence, marked by abrupt dissolutions and explosive beginnings of partnerships. Your friendships are apt to be unconventional because you are drawn to unusual, exotic, and eccentric people.

A long, difficult period begins on February 24 when Saturn moves into an exact square to Uranus. Both planets retrograde slowly in their respective fixed signs until Saturn turns direct (10 Leo) on April 12; Uranus follows (8 Scorpio) on July 17. They move forward together, remaining square, until Saturn finally pulls ahead around July 29.

This whole period is marked with sudden imaginative ideas, eccentric impulses, and unusual cravings. This is a time of much genius and inspiration, but a lack of self-control or common sense can turn these tendencies toward violence and destruction.

From February 5 to March 7, Mars in Aquarius opposes Saturn and squares Uranus. In this position it forms the third point in a grand cross which is completed in your sign, Taurus. Mars tends to increase the likelihood of impulsive and foolhardy actions by increasing your energy without increasing your judgment. That is why you must draw heavily on your practical, down-to-earth Taurus qualities, now enhanced by Jupiter's transit. Reliance on habitual conservatism and thoughtfulness is essential.

The spring and summer months (April 4-August 21) mark Jupiter's rapid forward movement through Gemini, your second solar house. The keyword of this transit is *financial security*.

This is definitely the time to consolidate your financial holdings to insure an adequate income for the years ahead. Money will come easily, and you will be tempted to spend it carelessly. Friends and neighbors will be ready to share in your good fortune, but the practical Taurus will hold back. The idea here is to have a trade, land, or investment portfolio to fall back on when the easy times are over.

During this Gemini transit, Jupiter will come into opposition to Neptune, transiting through Sagittarius. Note these dates, **May 7-July 12,** for they define a period in which your susceptibility to medicines, liquor, hallucinogens and drugs is increased manifold. Be careful how you get high, because there is a point at which the up becomes a down.

Mars, meanwhile, is hurrying ahead at its normal rapid rate, averaging one sign every two months. **From March 21 to April 28** it is in Pisces, your eleventh solar house, and your sympathies are enlisted in the aid of an underdog—some social cause, charity, or political campaign.

Aries is transited next **(April 28-June 7).** It is during this time that Mars and Venus conjoin and travel together for over two months **(April 28-July 7).** This is a yin/yang type of union: the forceful, initiatory enthusiasm of Mars combining with the receptive, sensitive beauty of Venus. A perfect time for a love affair!

Both Mars and Venus, from their position in Aries, form the third point in the grand fire trine involving Saturn in Leo and Neptune in Sagittarius: your twelfth, fourth, and eighth solar houses.

This may be a time of immense spiritual growth balancing Neptune's inspiration and Saturn's self-discipline with the drive of Mars and Venus' sense of balance. The resulting insights may upset your family life even more—perhaps causing you to move away from your former home. These aspects never repeat themselves in exactly the same way, however. This is a sign to us to take advantage of their influence when we can, whether or not it is "convenient."

Mars and Venus both move into your own sign, Taurus, on June 7. As I wrote when this transit occurred in the summer of 1975: it makes you more aware of yourself and the image you project to other people. Since Venus is also here until July 7, you will radiate beauty and contentment as well as competence and drive.

However, Mars and Venus will also be reinforcing the Saturn-Uranus square by opposing Uranus (Mars: June 7-28; Venus: June 7-23) and squaring Saturn (Mars: June 13-July 7; Venus: June 12-30). So your good feelings may be abruptly deflated by the betrayal of a friend or a sudden accident.

From July 18 to September 2, Mars will be reinforcing Jupiter's second house transit. If you have laid your plans well and done adequate research, particularly in the area of what you want out of life, you can now proceed with some specific direct action designed to insure your future security. This is a good time to make a major purchase: real estate, a business, or apprenticeship training.

Jupiter spends the rest of the year (from August 21 on) making a shallow loop six degrees into Cancer. This is just a sampling of what the Cancer transit will be like next year. Your sensitivity to the needs of others is increased so that you can emotionally sympathize with those you interact with. This makes you a valued friend and confidante to many acquaintances, neighbors, and relatives. You are pleasant company, for your wit, humor, and story-telling talents are increased.

Mars follows Jupiter into your third solar house on September 2, and remains there until October 27. The two planets are conjunct from August 21 to September 22. Your humor can have a sharp edge to it during this time, and your sarcasm may inadvertently hurt someone's feelings. However, your charm quickly overcomes any ill feelings and the added zest of Mars only succeeds in enlarging your circle of friends.

Mars in your fourth solar house may not be so fortunate, for your family relations are already strained in the presence of Saturn. Arguments, temper tantrums, and even a fight may occur while Mars first transits direct (October 27-December 13), then retrograde (December 13-January 27, 1978) through Leo.

★★★★★★★★★★ Famous Geminis ★★★★★★★★★★

5/22: Richard Wagner (1813), Sir Arthur Conan Doyle (1859), Judith Crist (1922) 5/23: F.A. Mesmer (1733) Rennie Davis (1940) 5/24: Bob Dylan (1941) 5/25: Ralph Waldo Emerson (1803), Miles Davis (1926) 5/27: Isadora Duncan (1878) 5/28: Ian Fleming (1908) 5/29: John F. Kennedy (1917) 5/30: Benny Goodman (1909) 5/31: Walt Whitman (1819), Norman Vincent Peale (1898) 6/1: Marilyn Monroe (1926) 6/3: Allen Ginsberg (1926) 6/8: Frank Lloyd Wright (1869), Grant Lewi (1902) 6/9: Cole Porter (1893) 6/10: Judy Garland (1922) 6/13: Basil Rathbone (1892) 6/16: Stan Laurel (1890) 6/17: Igor Stravinski (1882), John Hersey (1914) 6/18: Paul McCartney (1942) 6/19: Guy Lombardo (1902)

Gemini

Ruling Planet: Mercury
Keyword: Versatility
Tendency: Diffusion
Lucky Day: Wednesday
Lucky Number: Five
Friends: Aries, Leo, Libra, Aquarius

"Duality" is the word that characterizes you, Gemini. You are volatile, at times irrational, full of conflicts and contradictions. Your ruler, Mercury, gives you extraordinary intelligence and skill with language, but a lack of self-discipline and constancy of purpose may make the fullest development of these wonderful talents difficult. You can become detached, analytical, non-emotional. Yet you can also be witty, charming, warm and fun.

Your restlessness and nervousness are due more to intellectual rather than emotional unrest. You have a hypercritical nature, desiring to understand the why's behind things. You are high-strung, irritable, changeable and undoubtedly the best and most interesting conversationalist in the zodiac!

You earn your way well in any line dealing with communications—writing, lecturing, teaching, TV, radio, acting, selling or politics. Since you chafe under rules and restrictions, Gemini, you should enter into careers giving you freedom and latitude of expression. You need intellectual challenge to do your best. Your manual dexterity is excellent and you also have linguistic talents. You are artful in trading, and in forming and manipulating opinion.

You get along well with others socially, particularly at first meeting and in casual relationships. You are an engaging and charming companion, delighting others with your wit and diversity of interests. You like having a wide variety of acquaintances, but tend not to have many close friendships. You avoid strong emotional commitments.

Developing your powers of concentration and directing your manifold talents toward the accomplishment of well-defined goals, plus nurturing a loving heart, will nicely balance your intellectual, verbal and social gifts.

First Decan Gemini (May 21-May 31). You deal well in abstractions, though there may be a tendency to be impractical in realizing your many ideas. You tend to be more conservative than those in the other two decans. Mastery of language is your forte.

Second Decan Gemini (May 31-June 11). You are more emotionally oriented than first or third decan Geminis, directing your intellectual efforts into emotional spheres. Exuberance is added to typical Geminian curiosity and restlessness.

Third Decan Gemini (June 11-June 21). Versatility, diversity, originality and experimentalism are accentuated in this decan. You need freedom and a variety of outlets and contacts to allow your complex interests full expression. Counter a tendency to become a jack-of-all-trades and master-of-none by applying your talents to a well-defined goal.

Struggling with a Career Choice?

1977 Gemini Forecast

As 1977 opens, Jupiter is just finishing its year-long transit of your twelfth solar house. It moves through the last two decans of Taurus by April 4. During this time you may receive help from a hidden friend: you have a secret admirer you didn't know about. You are also able to turn a former enemy into a devoted friend. Enduring your own secret sorrows, you keep your personal suffering to yourself, working things out in private. Some time spent in a retreat may prove helpful. A particularly favorable time for overcoming obstacles is **January 20 to February 10** when Mars is trine Jupiter. *Solitude* is the keyword here.

Mars at this time is in Capricorn (**January 2-February 10**). This position in your eighth solar house improves your romantic life and may entice you to initiate a new relationship. A message from someone who has died is likely now, too.

Saturn, this year, is transiting your third solar house with two retrograde periods: **November 28, 1976-April 12, 1977** from 17 to 10 Leo, and **December 12, 1977-January 6, 1978** from 1 Virgo to 29 Leo. As I described this position last year: this has a depressing influence on your ability to communicate with others. You are often misunderstood and cannot seem to get your point across. As a result, you become taciturn and withdrawn. Plans for short journeys may be disrupted, and your education may be cut short.

Uranus, meanwhile, is in the middle of your sixth solar house transiting between 8 and 15 Scorpio all year. This is the cause of your unstable health; periods of physical strength alternate with sudden debilitating illnesses and freak accidents. You may find the cure to your physical problems in some unusual remedy: acupuncture, yoga, or esoteric diet. Use whatever works for you, but guard against unscrupulous cranks and fakes.

The outlook is not good while Saturn squares Uranus, the aspect being exact on February 24, and again on April 23, due to Saturn's change in direction, then fading out around July 29. You may be involved in a hoax, or be the victim of a practical joke during this period; you take the whole thing very seriously and are not at all amused.

Another consequence of this long-lasting fixed square is an inability to get along with subordinates or supervisors. Employees are scheming to take over your job, and bosses, you suspect, are planning to fire you. It is better to work by yourself whenever possible. In any event, your job performance is very uneven, and you ary depressed by the way things are going.

This simple square becomes a t-square when Mars in Aquarius (February 10-March 21) squares Uranus and opposes Saturn (February 15-March 6). You have the desire to travel, attend advanced classes, or publish a book during this period, but your plans are frustrated after February 15. An accident is also possible, so watch yourself, particularly at work.

Mars enters Pisces, your tenth solar house, on the first day of spring, and things go better at work. Even though the details of working with others are giving you trouble, your overall career plans advance during this transit. You may achieve recognition for an inventive idea, or receive an award for a resourceful business innovation.

Throughout the year Neptune is transiting in Sagittarius opposite your ascendant or Sun-sign, in your seventh house. The long-term effect of this fourteen-year-long transit increases your idealism in relating to people. You have some very confused and impractical ideas about marriage and partnerships, and often find yourself disappointed in reality. You are looking for the perfect mate, and this you are not going to find.

Most of this year (until September 3) the effect of Neptune's position is modified by a trine from Saturn. This increases your skepticism and gives you a more sensible approach to dealing with other people.

When Mars enters Aries (April 28) to conjunct Venus (April 28-July 7), which has been transiting here in your eleventh solar house since February 3, the two tie into this grand fire trine by trining Saturn (Mars: May 1-23; Venus: April 1-May 24) and Neptune (Mars: May 7-28; Venus: February 10-May 29). This is a particularly nice configuration for dealing with other people, especially in groups. Mars and Venus lend the dual qualities of decisive leadership and sensitivity to the needs of others, while Saturn contributes serious, reliable communications, balanced by Neptune's trusting attitude.

By this time Jupiter has entered your ascendant or Sun-sign, Gemini, to transit the whole thirty degrees between April 4 and August 21. Jupiter made a brief, very shallow loop into Gemini last year: August 24-October 17, 1976, giving you a preview of what was to come. This is a transit which occurs only every twelve years, and is one we all look forward to.

Jupiter in your own sign bestows confidence, generosity, optimism, and graciousness to your personality. You seem to expand and mature under Jupiter's guidance. Others are attracted to you, as you present the world with a picture of a satisfied, attractive, capable person. During this time you can achieve anything which relies on your personality alone for success.

Jupiter's trine to Pluto (April 24-August 21) enables you to cast off old, stale habits, and to adopt new, more useful patterns of behavior. Be careful, though, when Jupiter opposes Neptune (May 7-July 12), for you may be betrayed by someone you trusted too much.

Mars and Venus, meanwhile, enter Taurus together on June 7, and from their position in your twelfth solar house once again tie into the fateful fixed t-square, this time opposing Uranus (Mars: June 7-28; Venus: June 7-23) and squaring Saturn (Mars: June 13-July 7; Venus: June 12-30).

During these periods, you may be jolted by the reappearance of a private problem which you thought you had solved. You made a considerable advancement during Jupiter's recent transit here, but now you are torn with doubt and disgust for your previous endeavors. The help of a friend now turns out to have had an ulterior motive, and you are embroiled in a messy situation based on understanding and mistrust. As part of this difficult midsummer situation, your health fails. An unusual solution may present itself if you have the foresight to grasp it.

When Mars enters your sign, Gemini, its sign position overlaps Jupiter by about a month: July 18-August 21. Your capacity for handling new situations increases and you welcome new experiences into your life. The previously troublesome Saturn-Uranus square is now dissolving, and your good spirits are restored.

Jupiter begins transiting Cancer on August 21, but achieves only 6 Cancer before turning retrograde on October 25, to re-enter Gemini on New Year's Eve. This shallow loop only serves to prepare you for the longer transit next year. Your financial condition improves considerably, for you are able to make some long-range plans for securing your future.

You are able to put some of these plans into practice when Mars enters Cancer on September 2, to conjunct Jupiter, August 21-September 22. Mars usually initiates some kind of physical action, and can provide the impetus to begin a program of sound economic investment. This is also a good time to make a major purchase, such as real estate or a business.

Mars makes one last transit this year, entering Leo on October 27, to reach 12 Leo by December 13 before heading back toward Cancer. The effect of Saturn's recent transit here is diffused, for it is presently just over the Virgo cusp (November 18-January 6, 1978). So Mars can bring a breath of fresh air to your dealings with others: you can reach a real understanding with your neighbors, relatives, and friends. Advertising, printing, electronic media, and clerical work are all favored now.

★★★★★★★★★ **Famous Cancers** ★★★★★★★★★★

6/21: Jean Paul Sartre (1905)   6/22: Gower Champion
(1921)   6/25: George Orwell (1903)   6/26: Colin Wilson
(1931)   6/29: Peter Paul Rubens (1577)   6/30: Buddy
Rich (1917)   7/1: Charles Laughton (1899), Olivia de
Havilland (1916)   7/2: Hermann Hesse (1877)   7/3: Franz
Kafka (1883)   7/4: Ann Landers (1918)   7/5: Jean Coc-
teau (1889)   7/7: Pierre Cardin (1922), Ringo Star (1940)
7/8: John D. Rockefeller (1839)   7/10: Marcel Proust
(1871)   7/12: Julius Caesar (102 B.C.)   7/14: Gerald
Ford (1913)   7/15: Rembrandt (1606)   7/18: John
Glenn (1921)   7/19: Degas (1834), George McGovern
(1922)   7/20: Natalie Wood (1938)   7/21: Ernest Heming-
way (1899)   7/22: Jason Robards (1922)

Cancer

Ruling Planet: Moon
Keyword: Tenacity
Tendency: Patriotism
Lucky Day: Monday
Lucky Number: Two
Friends: Virgo, Scorpio, Pisces, Taurus, Leo

You have a deep love of beauty, a capacity for idealism and vision, and a natural desire to help others. You are creative, imaginative and fertile. On the negative side, you tend at times to find fault, complain, nag and criticize. You can be envious, possessive, jealous and capable of revenge.

Your affections are generally centered on your family and home. You are protective, possessive and tend to be emotionally clinging. You give much appreciation, love, warmth and affection.

Unlike Gemini, you enjoy few but very deep relationships. In love, you are romantic, sentimental and cherishing. You are also highly sexed, but you may be somewhat repressed and inhibited. You cannot bear criticism from those you love, and you can be plunged into moody, brooding silence if this happens. In marriage, you are naturally happy in a conventional, formal marital tie, which gives you a sense of security and ownership.

You can be tenacious, not liking to give up the past. Your emotions are overly active; rather than only "feeling" your way toward decisions, think them through.

You also need to develop a more trusting attitude toward others. Shed any feelings of inferiority and grow a strong protective skin over your hypersensitive being.

You have a natural ability for business and financial

achievement. Cancer women make fine nurses, social workers, teachers, actresses and writers. Cancer men do beautifully in hotel management, catering, detail performance, antique shops, bookstores, and are also natural actors and performers.

You are a born counselor and a sympathetic listener. You could be very successful in psychiatric fields or in working with children, in healing and in directing the young. You are a naturally intuitive, psychic sign— "knowing" whether you can base it on fact or not.

First Decan Cancer (June 21-July 1). Keep your creativity on a high level of success. Your intellect is excellent and you use your fine mind to stay bright and optimistic, refusing self-pity or envy of others' good fortune. Stay constructively busy!

Second Decan Cancer (July 2-13). You can be very successful financially, for you are gifted with common sense in money matters. Watch a tendency toward being selfish or overly changeable. You are excellent with investments, holding onto and saving money, using it for intelligent building of assets.

Third Decan Cancer (July 14-23). You are imaginative, romantic and creative. Avoid being hypercritical or nagging in your close relationships. Make sure that the "end justifies the means" in gaining your goals. Keep your emotions harnessed in the service of positive objectives.

1977 Cancer Forecast

For the past couple of years Saturn has been moving in and out of your second solar house of monetary matters. This last transit began on June 6, 1976, and continues, uninterrupted, until November 18 of this year. Even then, the respite is brief because Saturn re-enters Leo on January 6, 1978, and remains until July 27, 1978.

So, regardless of the state of the general economy, your personal financial situation will not improve until the middle of next year. Real estate, stocks, or other securities you own may continue to drop in value, and opportunities to expand your income will be limited.

Mostly, though, it is not the amount of money you have, but your lack of financial security that bothers you. You never seem to have enough money to do what you want and you are always afraid of losing what you do have. This fear is not entirely unfounded, because there is a real possibility of losing money or property through theft or accident due to Saturn's influence.

You may get a spiritual insight about your economic situation—there is, of course, an important lesson here—during Saturn's trine to Neptune (July 8, 1976-September 3, 1977). During this aspect, which is exact on September 5, 1976, on January 6, 1977, and again on June 23, 1977, you should be able to detach yourself from the acquisitiveness and competitiveness innate in our economic

system, and better understand the role of money as only
one inefficient means to obtain your desires.

Neptune has been transiting your sixth solar house and
will fluctuate between 13 and 17 Sagittarius all year. This
is the cause of your sensitivity to medicines and food.
You must be very careful about your health and diet, and
above all, must avoid all unnecessary drugs.

Neptune's position might also promote a lazy indiffer-
ence to work, especially the dull, repetitive tasks that we
all dislike. But Saturn's beneficial trine improves your
self-discipline and work-efficiency, so that you are able to
perform disagreeable jobs quickly and competently. While
you do not like your chores any more, you have learned
that the best way to get rid of them is just to do them as
fast and efficiently as possible.

Uranus is another slow-moving planet: it is currently in
the middle of your fifth solar house, having entered
Scorpio for the first time in November, 1974. This whole
long transit is a time of creativity, originality, and personal expression. In fact, at times your ideas come so
chaotically that you cannot see any pattern to them at all.

If you are prone to gambling, you will experience wild
swings of "luck" this year, which no system seems to be
able to smooth out. Your children may be a problem to
you now, too. Your relationship with them will seem
strange in some way, and a separation is likely.

Unfortunately, Saturn will be squaring Uranus for over
a year: April 29, 1976-July 29, 1977, exact on July 2,
1976, February 24, 1977, and on April 23, 1977. There
are two consequences of this aspect: your financial status
is subject to unpredictable upsets, and your ability to
express your creative impulses is limited.

Two periods should be noted: February 15-March 7,
when Mars will oppose Saturn and square Uranus from
your eighth house in Aquarius; and around June 10-July
7, when both Venus and Mars, conjunct in Taurus, will

square Saturn and oppose Uranus. An inauspicious t-square is formed during both periods.

Mars takes two years to circle the zodiac, and as it does so it becomes involved in a series of important aspects, igniting into action one after another of the slower-moving planets. This year opens with Mars entering Capricorn, on the descendant of all those with Cancer rising. During its transit here (January 2-February 10) your attention is involved with your personal relationships, and you actively seek out those whose company you enjoy. Now is a good time to initiate a partnership.

From February 10 to March 21, Mars will be transiting Aquarius, where it touches off the above-mentioned fixed t-square. Your financial affairs could come to a head now and the important issue is someone else's money: an inheritance, a loan, or backing from another party. Beware, however, of invisibly attached strings, obligations, or restrictions. A sudden turn of events could change the picture entirely, and not to your benefit, unfortunately.

Mars' next transit is an uneventful one through Pisces (March 21-April 28), trine your ascendant or Sun-sign, Cancer. This transit should inspire you to begin a new traveling, learning, or publishing venture. Your enjoyment of organized sports is also enhanced.

On April 28, Mars enters Aries, following Venus, which has been transiting your tenth solar house since February 3. The two planets are conjunct from April 28 to July 7. Your whole work/money/property/career situation should improve as a result of Venus and Mars in your career house trining both Saturn in your money house and Neptune in your work house. You can gain a clearer picture of your economic prospects and your career benefits from a renewed ambition and dedication. You also get along better with those you work with, and a promotion may be forthcoming.

Mars and Venus together enter Taurus on June 7, and

it is there they again become part of the fixed t-square, squaring Saturn and opposing Uranus. The fifth/eleventh house axis indicates problems in social or group interaction and financial liability as a result of some political or organizational activity.

A group you belong to may be split apart along doctrinal lines or following leadership factions. This is a particularly hard blow to you, because until just recently you have gotten along so well with groups of people, due to Jupiter's transit here.

Jupiter first entered your eleventh solar house in March, 1976, though it retrograded back into Aries August 24-October 17, 1976. As 1977 opened Jupiter was retrograding back toward 21 Taurus, where it turned direct on January 16, to rapidly transit the remaining decan by April 4. These first months of the year were a time of smooth and rewarding group interaction and you seemed to be able to gauge naturally the direction of mass opinion and to use this intuitive knowledge to further your own aims. A humanitarian cause, favorite charity, political caucus, or ethnic association consumed a lot of your talents with great personal growth and ideological maturing.

From April 4 to August 21, Jupiter quickly transits Gemini, your twelfth solar house. This, too, can be a very rewarding period in terms of personal growth, especially when Jupiter is in opposition to Neptune May 7 to July 12. Gradually the whole world within you opens up under your patient probing. Psychoanalysis, Jungian dream interpretation, meditation, yoga, astrology, prayer—any of these may be the key you need to gain a deeper understanding of yourself. The questions you are asking: Who am I? What is my purpose here on Earth? What is my relationship to higher life forms?

Mars enters Gemini on July 18, while Jupiter is transiting the last decan. The presence of Mars, though the two are not yet conjunct, marks a concrete breakthrough in your quest for self-knowledge. Mars always signifies action of some kind, and it often lends the courage needed to initiate a new project. Take advantage of this added impetus to examine yourself objectively and thoroughly. You cannot discover anything you cannot handle.

Jupiter makes a shallow loop six degrees into Cancer between August 21 and New Year's Eve. This is only a preview of the real Cancer transit next year, but may furnish some important insights into what is in store for you. Every twelve years Jupiter will transit your own sign and it is a rewarding, fulfilling event. Your self-confidence and self-awareness are high and you feel capable of handling anything life has to offer.

Mars follows Jupiter into Cancer on September 2, and the two planets are conjunct August 21 to September 22. Your optimism and enthusiasm for living are increased by this fortuitous combination. Bounding good spirits, optimistic outlook, and zestful vitality are the results.

Though Jupiter turns retrograde on October 25, Mars continues through Cancer trining Uranus September 2-September 30. This may be just the aspect you need to order the jumble of ideas and inspiration that Uranus is sending you. Your creative impulses can find physical expression now.

Lastly, Mars makes a slow loop through the first decan of Leo, transiting direct until it reaches 12 Leo on December 13, then retrograding back into Cancer by January 27, 1978. Saturn is concurrently just over the Leo-Virgo cusp where its effects are diffused. So this could be a money-making time for you. You have the energy, ambition, and drive needed to go out and bring in some cash, though this may involve you in some hard physical labor (Mars represents the physical body). On this note the year ends, only to continue the whole cycle of light and dark next year.

★★★★★★★★★★ Famous Leos ★★★★★★★★★★

7/24: Amelia Earhart (1897)   7/25: Eric Hoffer (1902)
7/26: George Bernard Shaw (1856), Carl Jung (1875),
Aldous Huxley (1894), Stanley Kubrick (1928)   7/29:
Benito Mussolini (1883), Dag Hammarskjold (1905)
7/30: Emily Bronte (1818), Henry Ford (1863)   8/1:
Herman Melville (1819)   8/2: Myrna Loy (1905) 8/5:
Guy de Maupassant (1850)   8/6: Alfred Lord Tennyson
(1809)   8/7: Alan Leo (1860), Mata Hari (1876)   8/8:
Andy Warhol (1931)   8/12: Helena Blavatsky (1831), Cecil
B. deMille (1881)   8/13: Annie Oakley (1860), Alfred
Hitchcock (1899)   8/15: Napoleon Bonaparte (1769),
Ethyl Barrymore (1879), Julia Child (1912)   8/17: Llew-
ellyn George (1876), Mae West (1892)   8/19: Orville
Wright (1871), Ogden Nash (1902)

Leo

Ruling Planet: Sun
Keyword: Power
Tendency: Leadership
Lucky Day: Sunday
Lucky Number: One
Friends: Aries, Libra, Gemini, Sagittarius

Yours is the regal sign, Leo, governed by the Sun, endowing you with power, ambition, generosity, and a natural capacity for leadership. You are dominant, independent, and dramatic, with great will power and the determination to reach your own personal goals.

You have great magnetism, a sense of pride. You are generally optimistic and enthusiastic. You are well equipped for success, and you can reach your ideals fairly easily, backed by your natural energy and forcefulness.

You can gain power easily, but must take care not to be corrupted by it. You are vital, outgoing, impulsive and energetic. These traits negatively turn into bravado, irresponsibility and boastfulness.

You tend to be quite trusting and somewhat naive, reacting to flattery and approval. Watch your tendency to make promises you cannot keep. These can be baseless and impossible, but you will make them out of ego and self-pride, wanting to look well before others.

Mentally, Leos are geared to think in terms of doing things immediately and on a large scale. You are excellent at making instant decisions. Delays or extensive examination of a problem tends to slow or blunt your mentality, which thrives on the acceptance of challenge.

You can grasp the big picture, seeing the whole without paying too much attention to any of the minor details. At times, however, you encounter difficulties and obstacles just *because* you have failed to recognize flaws and faults which were fairly obvious.

You have a natural attraction toward wealth, banking, the sale of precious metals, military services, the entertainment fields, advertising, public relations and publishing. You could also do well in a business for yourself. You are a natural free-lancer and independent, a born organizer and executive.

First Decan Leo (July 23-August 1). You heart generally rules your head and your passions are strong and ardent, tending to govern your mind. You can be dramatic, temperamental. You need to learn patience and self-control, taking time to make intelligent decisions.

Second Decan Leo (August 1-12). Learn to look at life from the viewpoint of others, rather than from your own personal outlook. Your popularity will grow and you will become a more progressive, liberal person. Your determination and qualities of leadership can bring you toward your goals.

Third Decan Leo (August 12-23). You are well suited for partnerships and business ventures where cooperation is necessary. You are courageous, stubborn, and able to accept challenges victoriously. You are excellent at forming profitable relationships.

Do you know your Moon and Ascendant?

1977 Leo Forecast

On June 6, 1976, Saturn entered your ascendant or Sun-sign, beginning its difficult two-year-long transit of Leo. As 1977 opens Saturn has attained 16 Leo and is retrograding back to 10 Leo where it will turn direct on April 12. It takes from April 12 to November 18 to transit the last two decans, and people with their ascendant, Sun, or other major planet in this portion of the zodiac will experience the same personal restrictions that plagued first-decan Leos last year.

As I desribed it then: this is a depressing transit, for it robs you of your self-confidence. You feel very unsure of yourself and wonder if you can handle new situations. Others pick up on this, and start to think of you as a "down" person, causing you to withdraw further into yourself. You feel more conservative and resist changes in your personal life.

During the Leo transit, Saturn forms two major, long-lasting aspects: a trine to Neptune and a square to Uranus.

The Neptune trine is first exact on January 6, while Saturn and Neptune are both at fifteen degrees of their respective fire signs, Leo and Sagittarius. Neptune turns retrograde on March 19, and Saturn turns direct on April 12, while they both remain within orb of trine, coming exact again on June 23, and fading around September 3.

Neptune is in the middle of its long transit of your fifth solar house, Leo's natural house. The keywords here: *intuitive self-expression.* Your imagination is heightened so that your individual creations are more original and personally expressive. Along with this expressiveness comes a capacity for losing yourself in parties, amusements, fine art displays, romance, gambling, etc. Be careful lest your fantasy world becomes more desirable to you than the everyday world: you may be setting yourself up for a big letdown.

The trine between Saturn and Neptune is beneficial in that you visionary dreams are tempered with practical skepticism and realistic self-interest. Saturn provides a good common-sense counterbalance to Neptune's impractical genius.

During the Neptune trine, Saturn will also be square Uranus. This aspect is exact on February 24 when both planets are retrograding in fixed signs: Saturn at 12 Leo, and Uranus at 12 Scorpio. The aspect is again exact on April 12, after Saturn has turned direct and progressed to 10 Leo. Uranus turns direct itself on July 17, but Saturn has outdistanced it and moves out of orb around July 29.

Uranus, which first entered Scorpio in November, 1974, has been disrupting your family life for some time, causing sudden changes of residence and unexpected arrivals or departures of family members. Relationships with your mother, or a mother-figure, are particularly sporadic and unpredictable. You need a great deal of freedom and may find it in an unconventional living situation.

The Saturn square does not make matters easier, but serves instead to force you to redefine your personal family goals by imposing some new restriction or obligation on you. This may be an invalid relative, a prolonged visit from a family member, the necessity of sharing your room with a sibling, or something of this nature. Whatever it is, you face it with typical fixed-sign stubbornness, which increases the conflict until you learn to mellow out a bit.

On a more optimistic note, Jupiter will continue to transit your tenth solar house in Taurus for the first quarter of the year (the entire transit: March 27, 1976-April 4, 1977). This position is the high point of Jupiter's twelve-year cycle through your chart. Your business or career is going well; you are respected by those you work with; your standing in the community is high. You may be elected to a position of authority or given an honor or award of some kind. Except for a possible quarrel or jealous outbreak between March 16 and March 27 when Mars is square Jupiter, these first months of the year are full of prominence, respect, and reward in your profession.

Mars enters Capricorn, your sixth solar house, on January 2, and remains there until February 10. This month is marked by robust good health, and pleasurable work—a good time to start a new diet or physical-fitness program, particularly when Mars is trine Jupiter (January 20-February 10).

Mars transits Aquarius next, leaving on the vernal equinox, March 21. Because this is your seventh solar house, your dealings with others will be more intense; you are more outgoing and energetic than usual. You will be taking the initiative and beginning new relationships.

During this transit Mars will move into a position in the t-square formed by Saturn in Leo, Uranus in Scorpio, and Mars in Aquarius. (Mars will oppose Saturn and square Uranus February 15-March 6.) During this time all the frustrations, anger, and hurt engendered by the Saturn-Uranus square will burst out into the open in a violent explosion. While it is good to clear the air, indulging yourself in destructive displays of temper only makes matters worse.

Mars in Pisces (March 21-April 28) will turn some of this energy and enthusiasm inward, as spiritual matters absorb your interest. A message or legacy from someone who has died could come during this transit.

On April 4, Jupiter enters Gemini and makes a fast, direct transit through your eleventh solar house, leaving on August 21 for a shallow loop into Cancer, only to re-enter Gemini at the end of the year.

This period is characterized by political and social activity; group interaction is an area in which you can really shine now. You will be able to re-examine your personal ideals and you make your stand on a variety of issues known. You champion your favorite cause, and can work well with others to achieve your goals. Your idealism and optimism are high and serve to attract others to you.

The process of self-examination and redefinition of goals is aided by Jupiter's trine to Pluto (April 24-August 21). Pluto stands for regeneration, rebirth and constructive growth through the death of the old and unneeded. The keywords for this aspect: *creative renewal*.

About the time Jupiter enters Gemini, Mars enters Aries, your ninth solar house, trine your ascendant or Sun-sign, Leo. The faster-moving Venus comes up behind Mars and the two travel along together for a while (April 28-July 7). While in Aries, the two will be completing the fire trine also involving Saturn in Leo and Neptune in Sagittarius. (Mars trine Saturn May 1-23, and Neptune May 7-28; Venus trine Saturn April 1-May 24 and Neptune February 10-May 29.) This grand trine between your first, fifth, and ninth solar houses is very exciting. Romance, travel, and new friends can be expected. The imagination and vision of Neptune are combined with the practicality and prudence of Saturn, the enthusiasm and drive of Mars and the friendliness and grace of Venus.

When Venus and Mars enter Taurus, however, things

get heavier, for they will be squaring Saturn and opposing Uranus—part of the fixed t-square again. (Mars square Saturn **June 13-July 7**, and opposed Uranus **June 7-28**; Venus square Saturn **June 12-30**, and opposed Uranus **June 7-23.**)

Mars and Venus will be in your tenth solar house, so recently vacated by Jupiter. Your recent career success will begin to crack when you let your personal doubts and family problems affect your work. Try not to involve those you work with in your personal conflicts or you will soon find that they are really only interested in your work and not yourself.

From **July 18 to September 2**, Mars transits Gemini, your eleventh solar house, close on the heels of Jupiter. Your base of personal contacts and supportive backing will pay off now; you are ready for some direct action to fulfill your months of planning and organizing. You become chairman, enact legislation, open a settlement home, gain a committee appointment, or whatever.

This fall (**August 21-December 31**) Jupiter makes a shallow pass into Cancer, reaching only 6 Cancer before turning retrograde **on October 25**. This transit is really only a preview of what is in store next year, when Jupiter returns to stay for a while. Mars will also be here from **September 2 to October 27**, and the two are conjunct, **August 21-September 22**.

This is your twelfth house: the house of your unconscious, privacy, and hidden enemies. The presence of Jupiter and Mars here can open up the depths of your subconscious, depths suppressed for years. This is an excellent time to get to know yourself: your hidden motives, secret beliefs, unconscious longings. Mars here gives you the courage to face the unpleasant or difficult truths about yourself.

Mars makes one last transit this year. **On October 27** it enters your sign, Leo, progresses to 12 Leo before turning retrograde on December 13, to re-enter Cancer on January 27, 1978. This long three-month transit of your sign might be what you need to counteract the Saturn depression which has plagued you this year. It will increase your optimism, self-confidence, and enthusiasm for life. You will notice yourself and the impression you make on others, and take more interest in your appearance. This new zest for living is a welcome change.

THE JUPITER EXPERIMENT

By Margaret and Maurine Moon

Many have noted that humankind seems at a critical pass, having advanced its technology faster than its ability to use it wisely. What is needed, they say, is a quantum leap in human evolution. But how is this to come about? Some say that only intervention by extraterrestrial intelligences can save us from ourselves.

The Jupiter Experiment details such a plan of intervention, *now* being conducted by the Planning Group on the Astral Plane. Received in automatic writing from a Being intimately involved in that plan, it vividly depicts life on the Astral Plane and tells the story of a mortal and her spirit-lover caught in the demands of the Experiment.

The Jupiter Experiment shows, in technical detail, how immortals communicate through auras, "flashing," "psychic burns," privacy screens; how they recharge their energies by invoking the Source of All; how they materialize and dematerialize according to their desire, everything from hamburgers to villas.

It depicts the Astral World in all its layers based on varying levels of spiritual development, with its institutes and a whole new school of psychotherapy directed at getting the newly dead to accept their bodily death, their loss of earthly ties, and their new-found immortality.

The Jupiter Experiment is a journey through the Afterlife, realized with all the impact of sophisticated Science fiction—but all the more startling because it tells the simple truth.

No. 1-87542-498   paper, $1.95

Use the order form on the last page to order.

★★★★★★★★★★ Famous Virgos ★★★★★★★★★★

8/23: Edgar Lee Masters (1869)   8/25: George C. Wallace (1919)   8/27: Martha Raye (1914)   8/28: Donald O'Connor (1925)   8/29: Oliver Wendell Holmes (1809), Elliott Gould (1938)   8/30: Jean-Claude Killy (1943), Mary Shelley (1797)   9/1: Yvonne de Carlo (1924)   9/3: Alan Ladd (1913), Memphis Slim (1915)   9/9: Leo Tolstoy (1828)   9/13: Claudette Colbert (1907)   9/15: Jackie Cooper (1922)   9/16: Lauren Bacall (1925), B.B. King (1925), Peter Falk (1927)   9/17: Ken Kesey (1935)   9/19: Twiggy (1949)   9/20: Upton Sinclair (1878), Sophia Loren (1934)   9/21: H.G. Wells (1866)

Virgo

Ruling Planet: Mercury
Keyword: Discrimination
Tendency: Chastity
Lucky Day: Wednesday
Lucky Number: Five
Friends: Taurus, Capricorn, Scorpio, Cancer

You Virgos are excellent at using your fine intellect to communicate and to deal with others. You have a natural tendency for gossip, financial gain, mathematics and literature. Your positive qualities of reason, caution, practicality and analysis can point you toward success in life.

Your personality can be deceptively reserved, cool and reticent, hiding deep and ardent passions. You have a very definite need to be of service, and to do work where healing, couseling, research, teaching and communicating knowledge through writing or lecturing are important. You are very good at passing on information in concise, precise ways.

Your Virgo "caution," which is so highly advertised, is generally one of reason, and through calm, intellectual analysis you come to decisions which are sensible and workable. You are not irrationally restrained, and this sense of native caution merely protects you from unnecessary dangers and risks.

Your mentality is subtle, capable of building defenses and making schemes for attack and counter-attack, when necessary. Your literary talent is a natural Virgo ability, and you could do well not only in writing books, but in newspaper reporting or compiling textbooks in specialized fields of interest.

Achieving financial success is also important to you,

Virgo. Your mentality is well suited to making money, and you have the capacity for recognizing values and analyzing situations, arriving at moves and solutions way ahead of others. This gives you a distinct advantage in the marketplace.

With your fine ability for detail, research and analysis, you are naturally attracted to laboratory work, nursing, editing, office work, hospital or welfare administration, government and politics. You also do well as designers, architects, draftsmen, or in any line where communications is important.

First Decan Virgo (August 23-September 3). Your temperament is naturally reticent, but once you decide to make friends, you are loyal, devoted and delightful. You are talented in a creative way, with good dexterity, and are able to bring your love of the arts into material form.

Second Decan Virgo (September 3-13). You can be quite materialistic, making money overly important in your life. You have a need for harmony, beauty and peaceful surroundings, and you should try to find a balance between this side of your nature and your desire for financial security.

Third Decan Virgo (September 13-23). Once you learn to direct your highly skilled intellectual abilities, you can reach your goals. You need to learn discipline and self-control, not procastinating nor being lazy about taking action which will bring you success.

1977 Virgo Forecast

Beginning in June last year and continuing throughout most of 1977 Saturn will be transiting your twelfth solar house with a retrograde period November 28, 1976, to April 12, 1977, from 17 to 10 Leo. This whole Saturn transit is characterized by your desire to be left alone, to work out your problems in private. You are suspicious of letting others become too intimate. Your enemies and problems do not confront you directly and it is likely that a friend will secretly betray or hurt you.

Neptune is still in the middle of its fourteen-year-long transit of Sagittarius, occupying your fourth solar house. You may be confused or misled about some situation at home; things are not what they seem. Sentimentality clouds your judgment in matters pertaining to your family and it is difficult to make rational decisions. Your memory is poor and it is better to rely on written records when dealing with emotionally sensitive subjects. This is a poor time to speculate in real estate for sentimental considerations often outweigh financial practicality.

Your objectivity is increased when Saturn trines Neptune: the aspect is exact on January 6 and again on June 23, due to Saturn's change of direction, and fades out around September 3. You may clear up a mystery or discover a secret concerning your background, ancestry, or family history now.

Saturn also makes a long-lasting square to Uranus, which is in effect **April 29, 1976 to July 29, 1977.** Uranus is fluctuating between 8 and 15 Scorpio in your third solar house all year. As I wrote about this transit last year: you will do a lot of moving around—short trips will be required on a moment's notice. This stems from your intense desire to experience new things and to expose your mind to a wide range of ideas and stimulations. You are particularly attracted to avant-garde literature, unusual writings, the latest slang, and modern television and radio programs. And you may try your hand at writing for publication or the stage. You mind is sharp, as is your tongue, and you may offend your less intimate friends with your sarcasm and bitter wit.

The less favorable aspects of this transit are evident during Saturn's square. You alienate people with your brusque, abrupt manner and your taste for intellectual stimulation becomes so bizarre that others have difficulty relating to you. You have trouble communicating with people and are constantly misunderstood; this causes you to withdraw and stop trying to get along with others at all.

Jupiter's transits are always more pleasant, and as the year opens Jupiter is situated in your ninth solar house retrograding toward 21 Taurus where it will turn direct on **January 16** to transit quickly the remaining decan by **April 4.** *Travel* and *study* are the keywords of this position. Foreign languages, cultures and religions fascinate you and you make many a tour of far-away exotic lands—through the pages of *National Geographic*, anyway, if not in person.

Mars transits your fifth solar house first this year—traveling through Capricorn from **January 2 to February 10.** Romance, parties, artistic expression, and gambling are featured. A particularly lucky streak occurs between **January 20 and February 10** when Mars is trine Jupiter.

When Mars next moves into Aquarius (February 10) it becomes part of the fixed square also involving Saturn in Leo and Uranus in Scorpio. Mars will oppose Saturn and square Uranus February 15-March 6. Your health may suffer from your brooding about your problems. Your depressed mental state may cause lack of physical energy or an unconsciously self-inflicted accident. Be particularly careful about what you eat and avoid all drugs and medicines.

Mars in your seventh solar house (March 21-April 28) improves your relationships with others, as you are more cheerful and enthusiastic in your dealings. You may initiate a new friendship or form a partnership during this time.

Jupiter, by now, has entered Gemini, which it will transit with steady direct motion (April 4-August 21). This is the height of its twelve-year cycle, and you should see a noticeable improvement in your professional position. Your work is recognized and you may receive a promotion or award for superior achievement during this time. Others respect your opinions and you are looked up to by the community as a whole. Your difficulties in getting along with individuals this year (Uranus in your third house) do not affect your professional status and you are regarded as an authority in your field.

Mars, meanwhile, enters Aries, where Venus has been transiting since February 3. The two are conjunct April 28-July 7. You experience a marked increase in your sexual vitality, and your intimate relations are more satisfying to both you and your partner.

Venus and Mars here tie into the long-lasting fire trine by trining both Saturn (Mars: May 1-23; Venus: April 1-May 24) and Neptune (Mars: May 7-28; Venus: February 10-29). This serves to improve your home situation by making you more aware of the behind-the-scenes forces that affect your family. Your intuition and sensitivity are increased and you may very well receive a psychic communication now.

Next, Mars and Venus enter Taurus together on June 7, and they once again become part of the fixed t-square, this time opposing Uranus (Mars: June 7-28; Venus: June 7-23) and squaring Saturn (Mars: June 13-July 7; Venus: June 12-30). Now all the carefully laid travel and educational plans you worked on while Jupiter was in your ninth solar house earlier this year are suddenly disrupted. Unexpected problems could cancel your study program or delay publication of a book.

These delays, while frustrating, do not last long, for Mars continues forward and enters Gemini on July 18. Here its sign position overlaps Jupiter's by about a month, though the two are not yet conjunct. Your recent business success will culminate in some concrete action now, as you enter a new phase in your career. On the job you are decisive, confident, and capable of handling new situations. An excellent period in terms of career achievement.

On August 21, Jupiter entered your eleventh solar house, for a shallow loop into Cancer: on October 25 it turns retrograde at 6 Cancer to re-enter Gemini on New Year's Eve. This is just a preview of next year's longer transit of this sign, but it gives you a taste of what is in store for you. Your interest is caught by some social-welfare cause, ecological crusade, or political platform. You join a group of like-minded people and set out to change the world. It is the sentimental, emotional side of the question that attracts you at first, but after Mars enters Cancer (September 2) and conjuncts Jupiter (August 21-September 22) you are incited into direct action. You assume more and more of the leadership role during September, and may be paving the way for an election when Jupiter re-enters this sign next year.

Mars quickly passes the slower-moving Jupiter and trines Uranus on September 2. This month brings a remarkable increase in your ability to communicate with others, and people respond by seeking your opinion on many diverse subjects. Whereas earlier in the year your ideas were considered too advanced and put off others, these same people have now come around to your position and see you as the far-sighted Aquarian-Age representative that you are.

Mars makes one more transit this year, a three-month (October 27-January 27, 1978) leisurely swing into Leo: it achieves 12 Leo by December 13, when it turns retrograde. With Saturn out of the way, on the cusp of Virgo, your sign, you can expect a real breakthrough in some personal problem that has been bothering you this year. You are able to understand some of your subconscious motives and hang-ups, and can take positive action to deal with them now.

Saturn reached the end of Leo on November 18, but only progressed one degree into Virgo before turning retrograde on December 12, to re-enter Leo on January 6, 1978. What you experience now is just a taste of what the longer transit will be like later. Saturn's position in your first solar house has a maturing effect, serving to tone down your personality and increase your conservatism. More on that next year!

Astrological Birth Control!

★★★★★★★★★★★ Famous Libras ★★★★★★★★★★★

9/23: Walter Pidgeon (1898), Ray Charles (1930)   9/24:
F. Scott Fitzgerald (1896)   9/25: Sarah Bernhardt (1844),
William Faulkner (1897)   9/26: George Gershwin (1898)
9/28: Al Capp (1909) 9/29: Gene Autry (1907), Anita
Ekberg (1931)   9/30: Truman Capote (1924)   10/1:
Marc Edmund Jones (1888)   10/2: Mohandas Gandhi
(1869), John Sinclair (1941)   10/3: Thomas Wolfe (1900),
Gore Vidal (1925)   10/7: James Whitcomb Riley (1849)
10/9: Cervantes (1547)   10/10: Giuseppe Verdi (1813)
10/12: Aleister Crowley (1875)   10/13: Paul Simon (1941)
10/15: Oscar Wilde (1856)   10/16: Eugene O'Neill (1888)
10/17: Montgomery Clift (1920)   10/18: Nicholas Cul-
peper (1616)   10/21: Dizzy Gillespie (1917)   10/22:
Franz Liszt (1811)

Libra

Ruling Planet: Venus
Keyword: Balance
Tendency: Justice
Lucky Day: Friday
Lucky Number: Six
Friends: Aquarius, Leo, Gemini, Sagittarius

Yours is a highly intellectual sign with a deeply emotional nature. You much prefer doing everything with another person; marriage, partnerships, and relationships are all areas of life which come under your sign.

You are continually seeking balance. You do not as a rule already have this equilibrium, but spend most of your life looking for it. Seeing both sides of a question can be a very fine attribute, or negatively, it can cause you to procrastinate and to lose valuable opportunities.

Your mentality and your strong emotional temperament are at odds. These emotions are strongly sexual, but you also have a desire for wealth and the possession of luxuries. Your nature is naturally indolent, and you can easily escape from realism into idealism. Because of this imbalance, Libra has a deep need for balance and equilibrium.

This seeking for balance is not the same as actually creating it, and stirring the surface of situations can cause disruptions and disharmony among your relationships. At times, your concept of living harmoniously means living *your* way. You need to become more tolerant of circumstances and less demanding that everyone adhere to your own concepts.

Your personality is fascinating, magnetic, full of old-fashioned "sex appeal." You are a fine companion and devoted friend, often living for your family and loved ones. You crave approval, attention and flattery, and you will even play games to receive it.

Your feelings are sensitive and delicate, and should someone fall short of your rules, you become terribly "hurt," resentful and despondent. You need to learn to be more objective, realistic and logical. These traits generally lie hidden beneath your delightful, charming surface personality, and they are often quite a surprise.

Areas where your personality is an important factor and where your charm and magnetism come before the public promise success for you. Sales work, executive positions, design or high-fashion areas, arts, either acting or music, performance or composing, and writing and politics are naturally attractive fields. Once you learn to keep your emotional nature in hand, you can be an excellent counselor, teacher, and mediator.

First Decan Libra (September 23-October 3). Your feelings are intense, restless, and changeable. You tend to find the opposite sex very appealing and you could have more than one affair and/or marriage. You are supportive, understanding, and sympathetic in your emotional relationships.

Second Decan Libra (October 3-October 13). You need to learn persistence, patience, and endurance to balance out a natural tendency toward procrastination and self-indulgence. Keep your energies pointed toward your goals. Concentration and direction are necessary keywords if you are to find success.

Third Decan Libra (October 13-October 23). You are an "all or nothing at all" type, finding over-indulgence in many areas of your life. You can drain your energies through excesses. Moderation is a path which can lead you toward your Libra goal of balance and equilibrium.

1977 Libra Forecast

Uranus continues its slow transit of your second solar house, as it fluctuates between 8 and 15 Scorpio all year. This planet is responsible for the sudden changes of fortune you have experienced during the last few years. Your financial situation can change dramatically overnight, and these unpredictable upsets are very disconcerting. Your main concern is to insure your financial independence: you do not want to be under obligation to anyone and resent monetary assistance in the form of welfare payments, family gifts, or loans of any kind. You come up with one outlandish money-making scheme after another, and though some of them might prove lucrative, you never stick to any economic plan long enough to find out.

Neptune is another slow-moving planet: it spends about fourteen years in a sign. Neptune entered Sagittarius, your third solar house in 1970 and will remain there until 1984. This year opens with Neptune at 15 Sagittarius. From March 19 to August 26 it retrogrades back from 16 to 13 Sagittarius, then turns direct and has reached 17 Sagittarius by year's end. Net gain: two degrees.

As I wrote of this transit last year: this whole period will be characterized by mental confusion and the inability to concentrate, but compensated for by increased psychic awareness and sharpened intuitive powers. Feelings and emotions replace reasoning and logic.

It is important during this whole third house transit to be very precise and specific when communicating with others, for you are easily misunderstood. One helpful aspect occurs between July 8, 1976, and September 3, 1977, when Saturn will be trining Neptune from its position in Leo. This should increase your powers of concentration and your ability to reason logically.

Saturn is a faster moving planet than Uranus or Neptune. It spends an average of two-and-a-half years in each sign. Entering Leo in June, 1976, it will remain there this year, except for a brief period just over the Leo/Virgo cusp (November 18-January 6, 1978).

During this time you will be taking a close look at group memberships—social circles, civic associations, service clubs, religious or political organizations. You may have had an unfortunate, embarrassing-to-insulting experience in relation to some group you belong to, and you now repudiate membership. You are willing to work hard, especially with clerical, bookkeeping, or administrative duties, but your work does not seem to be appreciated. It is easier to go your own way, you decide.

Friends, too, disappoint you. People, when acting as a group, never seem to meet your high standards of behavior and you are quick to put off friends who do not make the grade.

Saturn forms two major long-lasting aspects this year: the Saturn-Neptune fire trine, mentioned above, and a fixed sqare to Uranus. This aspect is exact on February 24, remains within orb when Saturn turns direct on April 12, is exact again on April 23, continues when Uranus, too, turns direct on July 17, and fades out around July 29.

The effects can be very exciting. Your thoughts and opinions are original, imaginative, peculiar. Your ideas of correct behavior can be so unusual that others shy away from associating with you. Though you have the power to fascinate other people, you do not form close relationships during this aspect. Your eccentricity may also be a financial liability. You are apt now to lose money or property through theft, fire, or accident. Whether you are ready or not, this period may be the beginning of financial independence.

Mars' first transit of the year is through Capricorn (January 2-February 10). During this transit you spend a lot of time and energy at home; you want to straighten out your relationship with your family and determinedly set about doing so. An occasional argument does not dampen your spirits and your initiative does bring to the surface any concealed problems, which are resolved during Mars' trine to Jupiter, January 20 to February 10.

When Mars transits Aquarius (February 10-March 21), it becomes part of the fixed t-square by opposing Saturn (February 15-March 6) and squaring Uranus (February 15-March 7). This could signify an interruption in your social life. Your strange ideas may put off a lover, and others are embarrassed by your forthright defense of unpopular ideas.

Mars' transit through Pisces (March 21-April 18) is a quiet one: no major aspects are formed. This should be a period of robust good health and enjoyable work. Gardening and taking care of pets bring you many hours of soothing contentment.

Aries is transited next, April 28-June 7. Venus has been transiting here since February 3, and Mars now conjoins Venus, April 28-July 7. This is your seventh solar house: Libra's natural house, and Venus is your personal ruler. Your relationships, so recently strained because of ideological differences, are now improved. You initiate the rebuilding process, for good friends are so important to you. Venus here helps smooth the way. You can be so charming and graceful that old quarrels are easily forgotten.

Mars and Venus become part of grand fire trine involving also Saturn in Leo and Neptune in Sagittarius. (Mars trine Saturn, May 1-23; Mars trine Neptune, May 7-28; Venus trine Saturn, April 1-May 24; Venus trine Neptune, February 10-May 29.) This helps tremendously by increasing your sensitivity toward others' feelings. You seem intuitively to know just the right thing to do or say to please others.

Mars and Venus together enter Taurus on June 7, a sign recently vacated by Jupiter. Jupiter transited the last decan of Taurus, your eighth solar house, from the beginning of the year until April 4.

During this first quarter of the year, your interest in the occult grew. You are slowly and patiently building a solid foundation of occult knowledge reflecting a growing curiosity about the forces controlling the physical world. As your knowledge increases, you discard early theories for more complex ideas, and through this process of casting off and replacing theorems, your knowledge grows and matures.

There is also the possibility of an inheritance, or benefit from some kind of legacy during these first few months, though problems arise in this area later from Mars' transit, June 7-July 18.

This is because Mars, and now Venus, too, once again become part of that bothersome t-square, opposing Uranus and squaring Saturn. (Venus opposed Uranus, June 7-23; Venus square Saturn, June 12-30; Mars opposed Uranus, June 7-28; Mars square Saturn, June 13-July 7.) During these periods, particularly the oppositions, you may find that involvement with others' money causes more problems than it solves. This should serve to renew your decision to maintain financial independence.

You may also be startled, now, by a psychic manifestation of some sort. This is more scary than enlightening, and may shy you away from this area for some time. In any event, your occult investigations were faltering since Jupiter has now entered your ninth solar house.

Jupiter's Gemini transit is a fast and direct one: **April 4-August 21.** This is an excellent time to pursue philosophical or religious studies, to take up a foreign language, and to prepare plans for traveling abroad.

Mars enters this sign **on July 18,** and the two planets' sign positions overlap by about a month, though they are not yet conjunct. The presence of Mars may inspire you to some concrete action: an excellent time to travel or publish. Your earlier planning now proves its worth.

Mars is catching up with Jupiter, and when Jupiter enters your tenth solar house for a shallow loop six degrees into Cancer (**August 21-December 31**), Mars follows (**September 2-October 27**) and the two are conjunct for a time (**August 1-September 22**). This is excellent news for your career or profession.

Jupiter is now at the height of its twelve-year cycle, and this is really only a preview of the longer transit next year. Your business acumen is good; your professional competency, the highest; your judgment on the job, the best. You earn a promotion, official recognition, a raise, etc. Others respect your opinions, and your standing in the community is high. You have become an established authority in your chosen field.

Though Jupiter does not progress very far into Cancer, Mars continues and will trine Uranus **September 2-30.** This may be just the aspect you need to break free of the financial impasse you are in, especially now that Saturn is no longer square Uranus. Uranus is the planet of the unexpected, and with Mars in favorable aspect, the unexpected could be a financial windfall. Your luck is high, and you can afford to speculate now. Seize whatever business opportunity comes your way.

Mars now slows down and makes an almost leisurely swing into Leo, taking three months to transit twelve degrees and back (October 27-January 27, 1978). With Saturn's effects diffused due to its position just over the Leo-Virgo cusp (November 18-January 6, 1978), your interest in group activities is revived. You even attract something of a following with your progressive social ideas, the same ideas which alienated others just a short time ago. You have always been proud of your futuristic Aquarian-Age ideas, and sure that you were right and all others, wrong. Now other people seem to think so, too.

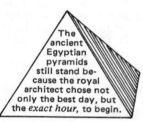

Scorpio

Ruling Planet: Pluto (Mars)
Keyword: Emotional Drive
Tendency: Investigation
Lucky Day: Tuesday
Lucky Number: Nine
Friends: Cancer, Virgo, Capricorn, Pisces

Scorpio is the sign of the occult, subterranean forces, the mysterious and hidden. This is also the sign of leadership, of the explorer, the person with the courage and drive to go first into unknown areas. As a Scorpio, you are ambitious, enterprising, possessing great pride and sensitivity. You dislike criticism in any form directed at you, but you can dish it out to others!

You are a law unto yourself, Scorpio. You are not really concerned about what others may think of your actions and decisions. You rarely seek advice or counsel, but you make your own personal choices and then with force and energy—*go*!

You are a combination of practicality, awareness and desire for material success, as well as being introspective and deeply philosophical. You have a volcanic temper, you bear grudges and resentments when hurt or crossed, and your passions are strong.

Negatively, you should watch being intolerant, vindictive, jealous, envious and dishonest. Positively, you have a high, penetrating intelligence, strong will power, leadership qualities and devotion to causes and ideals. More than any other zodiacal sign, you Scorpios need a *goal*—something to which you can harness your marvelous strengths.

You have a natural need for solitude, and you do not need numerous friends. A few proven, selected and care-

fully tried friendships keep your social life full enough for
your needs. However, you need to watch being domineering and possessive with those you love, expecting others
to follow your rules or orders and demands.

You are a very sexy sign, and your basic, underlying
drive is sexual—the elemental life-force of your astrological sign. You have enormous erotic appetites. Putting too
much emphasis upon the physical can drain and enervate
other areas of your personality.

Professionally, you can do well in the arts, the military,
particularly in surgery, chemistry, banking, investment,
psychiatry, and acting.

First Decan Scorpio (October 23-November 2). You
need to learn to cooperate with others, to see things with
their eyes. Your energy, force, leadership qualities and
magnetism are high. Use your native patience and persistence to harness your force and then go toward your
goals.

Second Decan Scorpio (November 2-November 12).
You have a natural drive toward achievements and attain-
ment which is positive and can propel you toward success.
You are generally optimistic, eager to teach and to lead.

Third Decan Scorpio (November 12-November 22).
The arts appeal to you. You have a love of beauty combined with initial creative drive which can bring you
success in this area. Learn to balance your love of the
sensual with the enjoyment of true creativity.

1977 Scorpio Forecast

Uranus continues to transit your ascendant or Sun-sign, Scorpio, all year. On July 11, 1976, it began a period of direct motion at three degrees which ends on February 15, 1977, at 12 Scorpio. Uranus retrogrades back four degrees till it turns direct again on July 16, ending the year at 15 Scorpio. Thus people with their ascendant or Sun between eight and fifteen degrees will be most affected this year.

Uranus, as you know by now, is causing something of a sustained identity crisis. You fluctuate between one extreme and another and seem determined to try every life-style that you can think of. In your manner of dress and personal appearance, too, you alternate periods of immaculate stylishness with times of sloppy carelessness. When Uranus finally leaves your first solar house, these opposing facets will have melded into a composite personality that is uniquely *you*.

A difficult aspect this year is Saturn's square to Uranus, which is exact on February 24, and again on April 23, due to Saturn's change of direction, and then fades out around July 29. Saturn has been having a depressing effect on your business or professional career since it first entered your tenth solar house in July, 1976, and will continue to do so until it leaves in July, 1978. Promotions and pay raises are delayed, and you are just not able to achieve your goals. On the plus side, however, you are developing more mature business judgment, and are able to make an in-depth study of the subjects needed for further career advancement.

The Saturn-Uranus square may result in an unexpected setback at work, which has a depressing effect on your personality. Your dour countenance, in turn, further discourages career opportunities, and the cycle is not broken until this fall.

Jupiter, meanwhile, is brightening up your seventh solar house as it transits the last two decans of Taurus until April 4. This position increases your popularity, optimism, and charm, making it easier for you to get along with others socially. Good friends cheer you up and an enjoyable time is had by all this first quarter.

Mars trines Jupiter, **January 20 to February 10**, from its position in Capricorn. This adds sexual overtones to an intimate relationship—an exciting aspect!

On February 10, Mars enters Aquarius, your fourth solar house. Here it ties into the Saturn-Uranus square by opposing Saturn and squaring Uranus, **February 15 to March 6.** You find yourself brooding at home on your business problems, which causes you to be rude and irritable with family members. Arguments and anger may provoke you suddenly to move out now.

Mars' transit of Pisces, in your fifth solar house (**March 21-April 28**), gives you a breather in which to reconsider any rash actions. You relax a little and enjoy attending a party, the theatre, an art show, etc. You feel particularly creative and may try your own hand at some form of artistic expression.

Neptune again spends **the year** in your money house, transiting between 13 and 17 Sagittarius, in three broad swaths. Neptune is the cause of your naive, confused attitude toward money. You somehow expect the physical plane to take care of itself, and it somehow does.

Saturn's long-lasting trine to Neptune (**July 8, 1976-**

September 3, 1977) helps matters by enabling you to take a more realistic approach toward budgeting. Money still seems to come and go of its own accord, but you are a little more practical in your financial dealings. For a while you are not quite so gullible about get-rich-quick schemes; you may have learned something from past experience.

When Mars enters Aries on April 28, it meets Venus which has been transiting here since February 3. The two are conjunct April 28 to July 7. This should serve to improve your health, and you will find that a lot of pleasure can be derived from your body: hard work and physical exercise feel good!

When Venus and Mars tie into the Saturn-Neptune fire trine (approximately May 5-25), your whole money/work /career situation improves. You now combine the qualities of shrewd business judgment (Saturn, tenth house) with imaginative money handling (Neptune, second house) and the capacity for hard work with a pleasant, cheerful attitude toward your job (Mars and Venus, sixth house)—a winning combination!

By now Jupiter has moved into Gemini, which it transits direct from April 4 to August 21. You got a brief taste of this eighth house transit when Jupiter was here last year (August 24-October 17, 1976). The effects of this position can be divided into three categories: sex, death, and the occult.

Sexually you are more sensitive to the needs of yourself and your partner, and are kind and considerate in finding ways to fulfill these needs. The result is a maturing of the relationship, providing a more rewarding experience.

In the realm of death, you gradually achieve a greater understanding of the meaning of death as a transition between this life and a better one. The death of a close friend may serve as an object lesson, and a legacy left you points the way to a more evolved attitude.

Your interest in the occult is heightened by this transit, and you are eager to learn more about the forces behind the physical world.

Meanwhile, Mars and Venus together move into Taurus **(June 7)**. Normally this would benefit your dealings with others by making you simultaneously more decisive and assertive, and more sensitive and gracious.

Now, however, Mars and Venus once again become part of the distressing t-square, opposing Uranus **(Mars: June 7-28; Venus: June 7-23)** and squaring Saturn **(Mars: June 13-July 7; Venus: June 12-30)**. Whenever you seem to be getting along well with others, your old self-doubt comes back to disrupt things. You may be forced suddenly to break off an enjoyable relationship as an increased work load prevents you from fulfilling some social obligations. This is the last of the problems in this area for already the Saturn-Uranus square is fading.

When Mars next enters Gemini, its sign position overlaps Jupiter's by about a month **(July 18-August 21)**. Your physical and sexual capacities are increased. You may desire to test an idea concerning the nature of life after death, and may take part in a ritual or seance now.

Jupiter itself moves into Cancer **on August 21**, but only achieves six degrees before turning retrograde **on October 25** to re-enter Gemini **at year's end**. This is an excellent time to plan for a long voyage, graduate studies, or the publication of a manuscript to take place next year when Jupiter again enters this sign for a longer, more important transit.

Mars follows Jupiter **on September 2**, and the two are conjunct **August 21-September 22**. Mars greatly increases your enthusiasm and drive in the areas of travel, education, publishing, and philosophy or religion. Now is a good time to finalize your plans.

Mars makes one last transit, a twelve-degree loop into Leo which takes three months to execute: **October 27 to**

January 27, 1978. Saturn at this time is just over the Leo-Virgo cusp (November 18-January 6, 1978). Mars' position here, then, does much to alleviate the recent depressing influence of Saturn. Be prepared for a sudden dramatic upsurge of ambition and work capacity. You have the drive, courage, and energy to make a bold move which brings you to the attention of your superiors. A promotion is likely.

SEX

A three-letter word!   Like the words God and joy and *you*!

Creative Power

Everyone knows that Sex and procreation go together "like a horse and carriage"—but the important part of that fact of life is *Sex and Creation.* In a very true sense, Sex is everything (which isn't quite the same as saying "everything is sex").

Sex is not an *act*; it's not a body organ! It is an intrinsic part of our being as humans. It's the fullness of life, beauty, the body as a whole. It's the power to create!

Worship

In Tantra, the sex "act" is one of worship: to "make love" is to worship the Divinity within your partner, and to be a channel for the expression of that Divinity within your lives. To "love God" with all your might is to see all Sex as sacred and to awaken the God-person in each of you.

Magick and Yoga

SEXUAL OCCULTISM teaches you how to release and direct the Creative Power that is the foundation of your body and being for magical accomplishment and yogic achievement.

Each of us is a cup of overflowing Creative Power that makes life possible. To awaken ourselves to the channeling of that power is to experience joy and to open ourselves to the ecstasy of complete union: that's Yoga! And to use that Creative Power to awaken your psi and ESP abilities, to win success in everyday life: that's magick!

Art of Love
SEXUAL OCCULTISM teaches you the art of making love and the "secrets" for going beyond the *joy of Sex* to ecstatic union with the Divinity behind all existence.

Psychic Ability
Sex is also the awakening of the various Centres of the body that brings about various psychic abilities: clairvoyance, psychokinesis, astral travel, etc. And it is the direction of these awakened energies under will and desire that causes things to happen. Yes, even money, power, success; influencing others; and even contacts with other intelligences—all these are possible through the knowledge given in this book.

Sexual Love becomes a partnership between Man and Woman: Marriage becomes an entry into the Heaven World. You and your partner *together* can truly work miracles.

In giving and receiving are the forces of life multiplied!

SEXUAL OCCULTISM, deluxe, hard-cover edition with color illustration, $10.00. Use the form on the last page and order No. 1-87542-491 from Gnostic-Aquarian Book Sales, if it is not available through your regular bookstore.

✶✶✶✶✶✶✶✶✶ Famous Sagittarians ✶✶✶✶✶✶✶✶✶

11/23: Boris Karloff (1887), Harpo Marx (1893)   11/24:
Baruch Spinoza (1632), Toulouse-Lautrec (1864), William
F. Buckley (1925)   11/26: Charles Schulz (1922)   11/27:
Jimi Hendrix (1942)   11/28: William Blake (1757)   11/29:
John Mayall (1933)   11/30: Jonathan Swift (1667),
Brownie McGhee (1915)   12/1: Lou Rawls (1935)   12/5:
Walt Disney (1901)   12/6: Dave Brubeck (1920)   12/8:
James Thurber (1894)   12/9: John Milton (1608), Douglas
Fairbanks, Jr. (1909)   12/10: Emily Dickinson (1830)
12/14: Nostradamus (1503), Margaret Chase Smith (1897)
12/16: Ludwig Beethoven (1770), Margaret Mead (1901)
12/17: Paracelsus (1493), Arthur Fiedler (1894)

Horoscope Blanks

1. NATAL CHART BLANKS
Circle with numbered houses, space for name and birth data
No. 1-87542-476

2. MECHANICAL ASPECTARIAN
For natal and progressed charts, two wheels, 360 degrees
No. 1-87542-477

4. NATAL, PROGRESSED TRANSIT (Combination)
Three wheels with numbered houses, aspect grid
No. 1-87542-479

5. TRANSPARENCY OF NATAL, PROGRESSED TRANSIT
For use in chart comparisons, progressions
No. 1-87542-456

9. NOEL TYL HOROSCOPE BLANK
Maximum-size wheel divided into twelve houses, aspect grid
No. 1-87542-457

Pads of 100, $3.00 each. Please order by number from GA Book-
sales by using the form on the last page.

Sagittarius

Ruling Planet: Jupiter
Keyword: Foresight
Tendency: Honesty
Lucky Day: Thursday
Lucky Number: Three
Friends: Aries, Leo, Libra, Aquarius

You are the teacher and the student of the zodiac, always willing to learn and then pass on the knowledge and information to others. Your powers of communication are excellent, whether verbal or written. You have a native love of independence, liberty, and freedom, and you insist upon having them in your personal life.

This is a very youthful astrological sign. Most of you keep your young outlook far into middle and old age. You are enthusiastic, sunny-natured, optimistic, interested, and have a deep love of travel, whether physical or mental. You are idealistic, constructive, friendly, and warm.

You have a need for being outdoors and should you find it necessary to live in cities, you prefer spending your spare time near lakes, mountains, woods and seashore—anyplace where you can smell fresh air and feel the sun on your body.

You are companionable and tolerant, feeling you can learn from almost anyone. You are usually open to suggestion, are forthright, direct, and your word is your bond. You need to learn to be more tactful and diplomatic in expressing yourself, for most people don't understand your honest way of saying just what you mean.

You are fearless when you have a goal, never counting the odds—in fact, these can exhilerate and challenge you.

You can achieve rapport with a wide variety of people. You are good at maintaining harmonious relationships both socially and professionally. Your sense of honesty, fair play, and integrity draw others to you. This is a Royal Sign, conferring a quality of nobility, command, and ability to lead and direct others.

Jupiter, your planetary ruler, gives you a natural feeling for abundance, wealth and luxury. You can be successful in numerous and varied professions and occupations. With your charm, magnetism, bright and friendly personality, work dealing with the public is naturally successful for you. Sales, travel, advertising, public relations, teaching, acting, writing, finance and investment are all potentially successful areas for your talents.

First Decan Sagittarius (November 22-December 2). Your initiative, drive, and independence are exceptional. Your powers of communicating with others are strong, but you tend to skim the surface of things, leaving them half-done. Keep concentrated and pointed toward goals.

Second Decan Sagittarius (December 2-December 11). Your intelligence and creativity can bring you success. However, watch inconstancy which could lead to disillusionments and disappointments if you don't face facts and reality. The arts, acting, literature and dealing with the public are natural outlets for your talents.

Third Decan Sagittarius (December 11-December 22). Keep your reliability rating high and learn to keep to your choices and decisions. Your inner voice and intuitive qualities should show you the positive, constructive ways to your desires and goals.

1977 Sagittarius Forecast

As the year opens, Jupiter, your personal ruling planet, is retrograding toward 21 Taurus, where it will turn direct on January 16 and rapidly transit the remaining decan by April 4. This is an excellent position for robust health; you feel good and enjoy physical activity. There is also pleasure in taking care of those dependent on you: pets and other small animals, invalids you are nursing, even house plants and crops. You enjoy watching things grow; in feeding them you are also nourishing yourself.

A particularly energetic period is January 20 to February 10 when Mars trines Jupiter from its position in Capricorn. You might enjoy participating in some sports contest or exercise program now. Walking, jogging, and hiking are recommended.

Mars entered Capricorn on January 2, and remains in your second solar house until February 10, causing a boost in your fortunes. Now is good time to initiate a money-making scheme: take advantage of whatever sound economic venture presents itself.

Saturn, this year, is occupying your ninth solar house. It has two retrograde periods: from November 28, 1976, to April 12, 1977, when it retrogrades from 17 to 10 Leo, and from December 12 to April 26, 1978, when it retrogrades from 1 Virgo to 24 Leo. Throughout the year your mind takes a philosophical turn, examining religious or ethical questions with systematic, logical reasoning. You are essentially a skeptic, but once convinced of a spiritual truth, you are dogmatic and stubborn in defending it.

Saturn's position in your ninth house discourages traveling, for plans will be delayed or interrupted, and journeys taken will end unhappily.

Uranus is in the middle of its long, slow transit of your twelfth solar house this year. If there is a guilty secret in your past, it could suddenly come out; a slanderous rumor could be spread about you by a secret enemy.

Your interest in spiritual evolution and psychic phenomena may take sudden turns, now advancing by leaps and bounds, now suffering an unexpected setback. One problem is that you desire to pursue this interest in private, and have no one to discuss it with. You do not want to be influenced by others' opinions, and are convinced that you can uncover the secrets of the universe by yourself. You may be surprised by what you discover!

A difficult time of doubt and disbelief occurs during Saturn's long square to Uranus, which is first exact on February 24, becomes exact again on April 23, due to Saturn's change of direction, and then fades out around July 29. You may contact other-worldly forces you are not prepared to deal with now, and this results in a severe testing of your faith.

Shortly after Mars enters Aquarius on February 10, it moves into position as the third leg of the fixed t-square, involving Saturn and Uranus. This aspect lasts from February 15 to March 7, while Mars is opposite Saturn and square Uranus. It is a trying time, for you have trouble communicating with others, particularly about spiritual, philosophic, or religious ideas. You are constantly misunderstood, and this could result in quarrels with friends.

When Mars enters your fourth solar house, in Pisces, on

the first day of spring, **March 21,** your attention is directed to your home situation and your relationships with other family members. You are more out in the open with your feelings about close family, and in turn more sensitive to their emotions.

On **April 28,** Mars enters Aries, its own sign, where Venus has been situated **since February 3.** The "Lesser Malefic" and the "Lesser Benefic" are conjunct **April 28-July 7.** This yin/yang mixture of the masculine and feminine principles promotes greater personal harmony because the anima (female element) in men and the animus (male element) in women are emphasized.

While in Aries, the two planets become part of a grand fire trine also involving Saturn in Leo and Neptune in your ascendant or Sun-sign, Sagittarius.

Neptune in almost half-way through its fourteen-year-long transit of your sign, Sagittarius (1970-1984). **As the year opens** it is at fifteen degrees; when it reaches sixteen degrees **on March 19** it turns direct, moving back three degrees before turning direct **on August 26,** and advancing to seventeen degrees **by year's end.** People with their Sun or ascendant in these degrees are therefore particularly vulnerable to its influence **this year.**

Neptune's position increases your sensitivity toward yourself, though your feelings are often vague and confused. You have a general idea of how you would like to be, but reality does not often conform to this self-image. One problem is that you do not view yourself as others do. You have spells of dreaminess or moodiness and your receptivity to outside influence is increased. It is, in fact, difficult at times to distinguish between your own feelings and opinions and those which others impress upon you.

Neptune's trine to Saturn **(July 8, 1976, to September 3, 1977)** helps matters considerably this year. Saturn gives you more personal stability, and the ability to make a more realistic self-appraisal. It promotes critical and skeptical qualities, which you need to apply to yourself this year.

When Mars and Venus also trine Neptune (Mars: **May 7-28**; Venus: **February 10-May 29**) and Saturn (Mars: **May 1-23**; Venus: **April 1-May 24**), the situation improves even more. You are able to express your feelings creatively and originally. Socially you are more relaxed and at ease, while maintaining the ability to discriminate between situations which will bring you enjoyment and those which will be boring, embarrassing, or uncomfortable. A romance is highly likely at this time—just what you need to bolster your flagging self-image! You are, after all, an attractive, desirable individual.

Mars and Venus move together into Taurus **on June 7** where they again tie into the unfortunate t-square, this time opposing Uranus (Mars: **June 7-28**; Venus: **June 7-23**) and squaring Saturn (Mars: **June 13-July 7**; Venus: **June 12-30**). This period could be hard on your health, particularly during the oppositions. An illness or accident is doubly depressing because, **until April 4** when Jupiter left your sixth solar house, your health was so good. The loss of a friendly pet or favored plant may also occur. All in all, your spirits are low during this aspect.

Jupiter entered Gemini, opposite your sign, **on April 4**, to the benefit of your relations with others. Jupiter in this position bestows charm and popularity, graceful and pleasing relationships with others, and the ability to get along with a variety of different people in many different situations. You are tolerant and generous, two qualities which earn you many friends. You are by nature sociable and attractive, and your circle of friends widens even more during this transit.

On July 18, Mars also enters your seventh solar house, and while the two are not yet conjunct, their house positions overlap by about a month (Jupiter leaves Gemini **on August 21**). The presence of Mars here steps up the pace somewhat, and you are even more eager to go out and meet new people and initiate a number of new relationships. You may form a partnership now.

Jupiter makes only a shallow loop six degrees into Cancer this year, giving you a preview of what its longer transit will be like next year. It remains in your eighth solar house **from August 21 to December 31.**

Here Mars overtakes and quickly passes Jupiter: the two are conjunct **August 21-September 22.** Jupiter's position may awaken a new interest in the supernatural, and when Mars trines Uranus (**September 2-30**), a definite breakthrough is likely. Watch out for communications from other planes—a departed person may speak to you now, you may have a precognition of the future, or a flash about your former lives. Jupiter promotes a general philosophic interest in such matters; Mars forces you to do something about this interest. You want some definite action, and active participation in a ritual or seance may be what you are looking for.

Mars makes one more transit this year: **from October 27 to January 27, 1978,** it slowly swings through the first decan of Leo and back. Saturn at this time is just over the Virgo cusp (**November 18-January 6, 1978**) so its influence is diminished. This would be a good time to take that long-postponed trip you have been planning, or publish that delayed book, or begin work on the graduate thesis which you have been putting off. Take advantage of this opportunity now, for Saturn re-enters this house **on January 6, 1978,** and things bog down again.

FREE OCCULT BOOK CATALOG

★★★★★★★★★ Famous Capricorns ★★★★★★★★★

12/24: Howard Hughes (1905) 12/25: Rod Serling (1924),
Little Richard (1935) 12/26: Mao Tse Tung (1893),
Richard Widmark (1914) 12/27: Louis Pasteur (1822)
12/30: Rudyard Kipling (1865), Bo Diddley (1928) 12/31:
Henri Matisse (1869) 1/1: Barry Goldwater (1909), J.D.
Salinger (1919) 1/3: Zazu Pitts (1900) 1/5: Yogananda
(1893) 1/9: Richard M. Nixon (1913) 1/12: Jack Lon-
don (1876) 1/14: Albert Schweitzer (1875) 1/15:
Aristotle Onassis (1906), Gene Krupa (1909), Martin Luther
King, Jr. (1929) 1/17: Anton Chekhov (1860), James
Earl Jones (1931), Al Capone (1899) 1/18: Daniel Web-
ster (1782), Oliver Hardy (1892) 1/19: Robert E. Lee
(1807), Edgar Allan Poe (1809), Paul Cezanne (1839)

Capricorn

Ruling Planet: Saturn
Keyword: Ambition
Tendency: Caution
Lucky Day: Saturday
Lucky Number: Eight
Friends: Taurus, Virgo, Pisces

You Capricorns are governed by that old cause-and-effect planet, Saturn, which gives you ambition and all the time in the world to reach your goals. Saturn rules Eternity, and your patience and persistence have the same flavor, for you can always wait, knowing your dreams will come true.

Although you are a traditionalist, you are practical, methodical, realistic and logical. You have the beautiful ability to bring your dreams into material form. Your common sense pervades all areas of your life. You are seldom blinded by rosy lights, generally seeing facts and reality.

You are a very complex sign, Capricorn. Just when people think they have you figured out, another colorful facet of your personality surfaces, puzzling them. Much goes on beneath your rather conventional exterior. Sophistication, fun, wit, a cosmopolitan outlook comprise the hidden iceberg section of your temperament.

Capricorn is a mysterious, occult and deeply intuitive sign. Your "hunches" are strong. You would do well to follow them, rather than always insisting that things make sense in a practical, material fashion. Your ultra-conservativism can turn into intolerance, rigidity and narrow-mindedness. You insist that rules and regulations for others are necessary—from your viewpoint, not theirs.

You are quite concerned with your prestige, honor and esteem in your community and occupation. Similar to your Virgo relatives, you can be a snob, oriented to family traditions which possibly are outmoded.

You have a strong drive for the accumulation of wealth and for getting public regard, power and influence. You persevere where others would give up. Your ambition never dies, nor does your patience. You track your desire and goals steadily and with unflagging energy. Many of you seek ego-fulfillment through finance and positions of authority.

Occupations needing unemotional, cool and practical attributes appeal to your nature. Iron nerves and objectivity are your stock in trade. You can be successful in investing, real estate, manufacturing, research, FBI or detective work, accounting, and administration. You are investors, not speculators. You cannot relate easily to bizarre, novel or unusual ventures. You need the proven, the established and the conventional.

First Decan Capricorn (December 22-Decermber 31). Your intelligent and hopeful outlook help you form relationships of mutual value. You work well with expansive, progressive and large concerns for the betterment of all.

Second Decan Capricorn (December 31-January 10). Use your enormous patience and persistence to take you toward your goals and desires. Your inner drive and creativity are high, and can be used in the artistic or business field, according to your taste.

Third Decan Capricorn (January 10-January 20). You can be a leader in your field, using your energies and determination to carry you toward success. Watch your tendency toward temper and bluntness, however. Be more tactful and diplomatic in achieving your goals.

Death could not part them!

Judy Boss is a remarkable woman who would not accept the fact of her husband's death. Through automatic writing she reestablished contact with him, and now, in her two books, she shares with you the joy and peace she found in once again communicating with the man she thought she'd lost forever.

IN SILENCE THEY RETURN gives the first-person facts behind her premonitions of the deaths of her mother and husband, her first astonishing contacts with the spirit world and explanations of how it all works.

A GARDEN OF JOY describes the strengthening of her clairvoyant powers, her recollection of past lives and the advice she's received from her spirit-guides. It will challenge you to explore the unknown regions of *your* psyche, to find the divine spark within, to learn to live and love more fully.

If you've ever wondered about life beyond this world or worried over the loved ones you've lost, you'll find comfort in Judy's truly amazing story.

IN SILENCE THEY RETURN
No. 1-87542-080, $2.95

A GARDEN OF JOY
No. 1-87542-082, $3.95

Both from GA Booksales. Order form on the last page.

1977 Capricorn Forecast

Last year closed with Mars approaching the ascendant of all those with Capricorn rising. **On January 2** it enters Capricorn and remains there **until February 10.** This transit increases your self-confidence and awareness and adds an element of vitality and zest to your personality.

While in Capricorn, Mars will be trining Jupiter **(January 20-February 10)**, which entered Taurus **in March, 1976.** This increases your optimistic outlook and gives you a positive approach to new situations.

Jupiter transits the last decan of Taurus **during the first quarter of the year**, entering Gemini **on April 4.** Its fifth house position, trine to your ascendant or Sun-sign, is a happy one. Parties, theatres, art shows, romance, gambling, and all manner of amusements occupy your time and talents. You abound with creativity, generosity, and popularity. Children are also featured, and they bring you pleasure, enriching your life now.

Saturn will be transiting Leo, your eighth solar house, **until November 18.** Inasmuch as Saturn began this transit **in June, 1976,** you should be used to its effects in the areas of sex, death, and the supernatural.

Sexual problems could include enforced abstinence, loss of vitality, or unsatisfying relations. There may be the death of a friend or relative, or the death of a cherished idea or life style. Problems may rise when new ideas or experiences which contradict your firmly held beliefs are thrust upon you. In each case, the necessary solution is to re-evalute your position and redefine your expectations and goals along more realistic lines.

Uranus remains in the middle of your eleventh solar house, swinging back and forth between 8 and 15 Scorpio all year. Uranus is in its natural house for those with Capricorn rising. This is the kind of transit which can touch off a dramatic revolutionary conversion, à la Patty Hearst. Some violent action can change your politics overnight. You involve yourself with a group of like-minded people and actively work for social reform on some level. The intensity of your feelings, combined with your personal magnetism, attract others to your position. They may be perplexed, however, when the ideals you so fervently subscribed to yesterday, directly oppose those you are passionately advocating today. In either case, it is groups of people and their effects on social change that fascinate you.

Unfortunately Saturn will be squaring Uranus from its position in your eighth house for over a year (April 29, 1976-July 29, 1977). Under such an aspect you could be involuntarily drawn into a violent or destructive situation. Things get out of hand and you are pulled under in the rush of events. In the end the cause you were so sincerely promoting may be set back because of the very actions you initiated to advance it.

Mars enters Aquarius on February 10, and on February 25 moves into position as the third leg of the fixed t-square. It will oppose Saturn and square Uranus from February 15 to March 7. Physical violence is particularly likely during this period, and it could be very costly, too. A lot of your time and energy will be taken up in raising money, though you will not benefit personally from your efforts.

On March 21, the vernal equinox, Mars moves into

Pisces, your third solar house, and things calm down a bit. Friends, relatives and neighbors lend their support, and your rhetoric mellows out into persuasive argument. Your ability to influence others through speaking, writing, and the electronic broadcast media is at its height.

Neptune is transiting its natural house, the twelfth, for those with Capricorn rising. **Last August** Neptune began a period of direct motion at 11 Sagittarius, and **by March 19, 1977**, had progressed to sixteen degrees. Retrograding backward three degrees, it turns direct once more **on August 26.** The following **March (1978)** Neptune has attained 18 Sagittarius and begins another retrograde period. At this rate it is no wonder Neptune takes 165 years to circle the zodiac!

This is a highly psychic position: your sensitivity and receptivity are increased, and you often find you know what people are going to say or do before the fact. You are also emotionally more vulnerable, and become unwillingly drawn into others' problems. You easily absorb the moods of others and find it difficult to sort out your own feelings, though you resent this intrusion. A period of seclusion is needed at such times to regain your inner independence.

For over a year Neptune will be trine Saturn **(July 8, 1976-September 3, 1977)** and this helps matters tremendously. Saturn adds just the realistic skepticism and common-sense outlook you need to offset Neptune's vagueness.

Throughout May the grand fire trine is completed by Venus and Mars in Aries. This trine involves your fourth, eighth and twelfth houses. Now Neptune's illusive inspiration is balanced not only by Saturn's stubborn practicality, but also by the energy of Mars combined with Venus' sense of balance. This period of heightened awareness should lead to some useful insights, directly applicable to your life, into the mysteries of the universe and your place in the scheme of things.

Mars first entered Aries on April 28, following Venus, which began its own Aries transit on February 3. The two are conjunct April 28-July 7 as they move through Aries and Taurus together.

In Taurus, which they enter together on June 7, they move into position as part of the t-square formed by Saturn in Leo, Uranus in Scorpio, and Venus and Mars in Taurus. (Venus square Saturn June 12-30, Venus opposed Uranus June 7-23; Mars square Saturn June 13-July 7, Mars opposed Uranus June 7-28.)

This is not as violent an aspect as the previous t-square, but it could affect your social life. You may lose friends because of an unpopular political or social stand, or see a romance break up over a political argument. Whatever happens, it will definitely affect other people.

Jupiter has by now entered Gemini, which it transits quickly from April 4 to August 21. This period is marked by excellent health, increased vigor, and a capacity for enjoying good, old-fashioned hard work. Your life is rewarded by your newly found ability to help others find better health, and your interest in nutrition, diet and physical fitness. Taking care of pets and plants nourishes your soul as much as you nourish them. You also find it easier to organize your life, and self-discipline comes naturally. Now is the time to expand into healthy new directions.

One caution: be careful between May 7 and July 12 not to go overboard on some new drug cure or weird diet. You are unusually susceptible to medicines, drugs, liquor, trances and other consciousness-changing elements during Jupiter's opposition to Neptune.

Mars quickly runs through the next two signs. From July 18 to September 2 it is in Gemini, right on the heels of Jupiter. This reinforces Jupiter's influence and gives you a little more energy and enthusiasm for your new hobbies. This is a good time to start a new diet.

From September 2 to October 27 Mars transits Cancer conjunct Jupiter (August 21-September 22). Jupiter entered Cancer on August 21; on October 25 it turns retrograde at 6 Cancer, and re-enters Gemini on New Year's Eve. This is just a pre-season exhibition of what the longer Cancer-transit will be like next year.

Jupiter, in your seventh solar house—opposite your ascendant or Sun-sign—increases your popularity; you find getting along with others comes naturally. Your friendships are enriched by new understandings and you cultivate the ability to see both sides of any question. Your reputation for fairness prompts others to seek your opinions on controversial questions. A rewarding partnership may be started at this time.

On October 27 Mars begins a three-month-long loop into Leo, turning around half-way through, on December 13. This is your eighth house, which Saturn occupies until November 18. Mars here will increase your sexual vitality, and you may initiate a new relationship.

Saturn also gives us a preview of a future transit by making a very shallow loop one degree into Virgo from November 18 to January 6, 1978. Since this is still the Leo-Virgo cusp, Saturn's influence will not be much different than when it was entirely in Leo. It may, however, cause a delay in some travel, educational, or publishing plans. A foreigner may enter your life now.

★★★★★★★★★ Famous Aquarians ★★★★★★★★★

1/21: Jack Nicklaus (1940)   1/22: Francis Bacon (1561)
1/23: Edouard Manet (1832)   1/25: W. Somerset Maugham
(1874), Virginia Woolf (1882)   1/26: Hanz Holzer (1920)
1/27: Wolfgang Mozart (1756), Lewis Carroll (1832)   1/30:
Tammy Grimes (1936), Boris Spassky (1937)   1/31: Franz
Schubert (1797)   2/1: Clark Gable (1901)   2/2: Ayn Rand
(1905)   2/3: Felix Mendelssohn (1809), Gertrude Stein
(1874), Norman Rockwell (1894)   2/4: Charles Lindbergh
(1902)   2/5: William Burroughs (1914)   2/6: Ronald
Reagan (1911)   2/7: Sinclair Lewis (1885)   2/8: Dame
Edith Evans (1888)   2/12: Charles Darwin (1809)   2/14:
Galileo (1564), James Hoffa (1913), Magic Sam (1937)
2/17: Hal Holbrook (1925)

Aquarius

Ruling Planet: Uranus
Keyword: Forward
Tendency: Progress
Lucky Day: Sunday
Lucky Number: Four
Friends: Aries, Sagittarius, Libra, Gemini

You are the most original and unusual of all of the astrological signs. You are capable of deep wisdom, a desire for truth and great imagination, combined with a penetrating intelligence and introspection. You are a combination of social charm, excellent intellect, business acumen and intuitiveness.

Aquarians are very productive, well-balanced and practical, despite delineations making you the "absent-minded professor" type. Only when you are mentally engrossed in your latest brain storm is this true. You are easy to know, friendly and gregarious, with a deep inner need to help and assist.

You are a "group" person. You enjoy dealing with a wide variety of people. In this, you are similar to your Gemini friends, since you have much of their versatility, duality, adaptability and flexibility, particularly of intellect. You need all kinds of people, circumstances, ideas and concepts to keep that active mind acutely alive.

Aquarians also have the marvelous talent for bringing down dreams and ideals to the material plane. With organizational and executive capacities, you can formulate and construct stable foundations.

You are courageous in your convictions, a good sport when things go wrong. You have the ability to continue your enthusiasm, even in the face of apparent failure. You can lead others through inspiration and example. You are completely unafraid to follow through an undertaking merely because it is uncharted, unknown or dangerous. You are highly intellectual, often verging on brilliant, and are independent, with a natural need for liberty.

In forming relationships on any level, you want to have intellectual companionship. Any long-lasting, enduring alliance made with you must never bog down or become boring. You need to be constantly refreshed and regenerated through your relationships.

Teaching, politics, acting, writing, medicine, law, philosophy, and science are all areas which are naturally attractive to you Aquarians. Your inventive ability indicates success in business. You are excellent in discovering new products and original methods of doing things. Welfare, humanitarian, and healing occupations also appeal to you.

First Decan Aquarius (January 20-January 30). You are fun, gay, and delightful, with creative, artistic talents which can bring you rewards. You need to learn patience, however, and perseverence before you can reach your goals.

Second Decan Aquarius (January 30-February 8). You are a born money-maker and financial wizard. You know how to get your ideas across to others and can fulfill your very ambitious nature through communicating your desires and needs to others.

Third Decan Aquarius (February 8-February 18). You can be restless, needing more stability and reliability in your nature. However, your fertile imagination and creative abilities can bring you quickly toward your goals.

1977 Aquarius Forecast

Mars begins the year entering your twelfth solar house. If you have been working toward a specific goal in the fields of spiritual evolution or development of psychic talents, you may achieve your goals during this transit. Time is especially ripe for initiation between January 20 and February 10 when Mars is trine Jupiter.

Jupiter transits the last decan of Taurus, your fourth solar house, during the first three months of the year. As you have already learned from its position here (March 17-August 24, 1976, and October 17, 1976-April 4, 1977) Jupiter favors you with domestic tranquility. Now is the time to enjoy the peace and harmony you have at home, and to improve your relationship with your intimate family so that you will have the memory of these happy times to sustain you through the difficult periods to come.

When Mars crosses your ascendant, or enters your Sun-sign, Aquarius, on February 10, things unfortunately take a turn for the worse. Mars here does give you more self-confidence and you become more assertive and aggressive. Mars also ties into an important t-square, opposing Saturn in Leo and squaring Uranus in Scorpio, February 15-March 6.

Saturn spends the year troubling your seventh solar house as it vibrates, beginning at 16 Leo on January 1,

reaching a low of 10 Leo **on April 12**, and a high of 1
Virgo **on December 12**, then ending the year at 29 Leo.
Saturn is the reason you have been so serious and
conscientious about personal relations. It is difficult now
for you to relax and enjoy frivolous social occasions. It is
more in your nature, during this transit, to combine
business with pleasure. You are highly critical of hedonis-
tic party-goers, and turn a disdainful eye toward some of
your more lighthearted companions. You generally enjoy
the company of older, more sedate friends, and may form
a partnership with an older person.

Uranus, meanwhile, is still transiting your tenth solar
house, where it fluctuates between 8 and 15 Scorpio **all
year**. Uranus, as your ruling planet, is important in your
chart. Its position in your house of business has been
causing some disruption of your career: things are simply
not working out as planned. On the other hand, you have
always valued spontaneity and independence and are able
to cope with these sudden setbacks or opportunities.

Uranus' position also makes it difficult to work for
others or to follow a rigid schedule. You do better
working when you feel like it, and, given a free rein, will
prove inventive, imaginative, and resourceful. Other
people view you either as unstable, impulsive and unreli-
able, or as inspired, decisive, and visionary.

A difficult time is in store **between April 29, 1976, and
July 29, 1977**, while Saturn and Uranus are square one
another. This aspect seems to bring out the worst in both
planets: in relationships you are alternately agreeable and
stand-offish, thus confusing and alienating your friends; at
work you tend to be critical and resentful of others'
authority.

When Mars appears on the scene strengthening this
difficult aspect **(February 15-March 6)**, you can expect
the situation to erupt into open quarreling which could
lose you your professional position or a valued friend.

Take solace in the fact that this, like everything else, will soon pass.

Mars' quieter transit of Pisces (March 21-April 28), your second solar house, should help your financial situation. You are unusually perceptive about money matters, and may experience a windfall now.

While Mars is in Pisces, Jupiter moves into your fifth solar house (April 4) to transit quickly Gemini, by August 21. *Creativity* is the keyword here. You are able to express yourself in some artistic way, and have a better appreciation of other people's creations in the fields of art, literature, theatre, dance, etc. Your life is enriched through these creative pursuits, and a previously neglected talent emerges. A romance is also likely during this transit.

Mars enters Aries on April 28, where Venus has been transiting since February 3. Mars overtakes Venus and the two are conjunct April 28-July 7. Their position here in your third solar house improves your powers of communication by enabling you to express yourself forthrightly with conviction, tempered with enough charm and wit that, instead of offending others with your belligerence, you are able to convince others of almost anything—at least while you are talking to them.

Mars and Venus also become part of a grand fire trine while here in Aries. Saturn and Neptune have been trine since January 6, and remain within orb until September 3. Neptune is in the middle of its fourteen-year-long transit of your eleventh solar house, Aquarius' natural house.

This transit has served to increase your idealism and vulnerability, for you tend to view the world more as you would like to see it than as it really is. You may join a group of some kind—a social circle, service club, political caucus, religious organization—that is not what it appears to be. You will be disillusioned by the actions of this organization, and are disappointed in the way people act in groups. Crowds always respond to the lowest common denominator—and this is something you do not want to accept.

The Saturn trine (**July 8, 1976-September 3, 1977**) is helpful in that it forces you to take a more skeptical look at your associates; it tempers Neptune's impractical visions with some of Saturn's no-nonsense pragmatism.

With Venus and Mars both trine Saturn (Mars: **May 1-23**; Venus: **April 1-May 24**) and Neptune (Mars: **May 7-28**; Venus: **February 10-May 29**), you are able to understand the meaning behind the rhetoric, analyzing the practical consequences of political actions. The merciful blinders are taken away for a moment and you can see what is really going on, in the world: what forces are in control of your life and how these forces manipulate you for others' benefit.

Mars and Venus enter Taurus together **on June 7**, and the domestic harmony you so recently enjoyed is threatened. Arguments and hard feelings replace consideration and good will. Mars and Venus here are once more part of a difficult t-square, this time opposing Uranus (Mars: **June 7-28**; Venus: **June 7-25**) and squaring Saturn (Mars: **June 13-July 7**; Venus: **June 12-30**). Your family problems could affect your business performance now, and you may aggravate friends by talking about your troubles. Others simply are not interested, and it is best to keep to yourself.

On July 18 Mars enters Gemini where Jupiter is still transiting. The two overlap sign positions by about a month. Whereas earlier you were content to enjoy others' creative efforts, you now feel the need to produce something of your own. Now is an excellent time to take art or crafts lessons. You have the ability to put your ideas into some concrete form now. Instead of being entertained, you would now like to do some entertaining of your own. By all means throw a party or organize an outing. The romance that has been growing since Jupiter's entrance into this sign on April 4 may now blossom into a more intimate relationship.

On August 21 Jupiter moves into your sixth solar house for a shallow loop six degrees into Cancer, and on September 2 Mars follows. The two are conjunct August 21 to September 22. This is a great configuration for your health. You feel wonderful! Robust and strong, you enjoy all manner of physical activities. You particularly enjoy working in your garden, growing house plants, or playing with and caring for your pets.

You work well with others and may be promoted to a supervisory position at work (especially September 2-30 when Mars is trine Uranus). This is because you display sympathy and compassion for your subordinates, yet are assertive and decisive at the same time. You expect no more of others than you are willing to do yourself and your self-discipline and efficiency are uncommonly high.

Jupiter turns retrograde on October 25, and re-enters Gemini on New Year's Eve, but Mars continues to make a slow, three-month-long transit twelve degrees into Leo and back (October 27-January 27, 1978). With Saturn now out of square with Uranus, and just over the Leo-Virgo cusp, Mars brings a welcome new interest in other people. You are far less critical and can let go and enjoy yourself a little more. You also seek out new people and tend to be the one to initiate new relationships during this holiday season.

★★★★★★★★★★ **Famous Pisceans** ★★★★★★★★★★

2/19: Copernicus (1473)   2/20: Ramakrishna (1833),
John Daly (1914)   2/21: W.H. Auden (1907), Nina
Simone (1933)   2/22: Fredric Chopin (1810), Edna St.
Vincent Millay (1892), Sybil Leek (1922)   2/24: Winslow
Homer (1836)   2/25: Pierre Renoir (1841)   2/26: Victor
Hugo (1802), Johnny Cash (1932)   2/27: Elizabeth
Taylor (1932), Ralph Nader (1934)   3/2: Dr. Seuss
(1904), Tom Wolfe (1931)   3/6: Elizabeth B. Browning
(1806)   3/9: Bobby Fischer (1943)   3/12: Vaslav Nijinsky
(1890), Edward Albee (1928)   3/17: Rudolph Nureyev
(1938)   3/18: Edgar Cayce (1877), Manly P. Hall (1901),
John Updike (1932)   3/19: Philip Roth (1933)

 # Pisces

Ruling Planet: Neptune
Keyword: Sympathy
Tendency: Idealism
Lucky Day: Monday
Lucky Number: Seven
Friends: Cancer, Scorpio, Taurus, Capricorn

You are an intuitive, psychic sign, sensitive and subtle. Although you may not appear strong physically, your endurance and "lasting" power are magnificent. You are quite ambitious, with a deep inner need for approval and love from others. You are considerate, generous, kind, full of sympathy, and could do beautifully in counseling or training the slower-than-average child.

Your emotions are warm, loving, affectionate and demonstrative. You are a "patter" and a "kisser" and enjoy a good hug! You are a devoted friend, full of empathy when things go wrong; happy and joining in lovingly, when things are going well.

Negatively, you can be full of self-pity, vacillation, and procrastination. You dislike hurting others and will avoid an unpleasant truth or encounter as long as possible.

You have strong character, will power and determination, not always apparent on the surface. When the chips are down, you come out victoriously. Sometimes you are more courageous during a crisis than in your daily life. You have a natural understanding of how to bend, how to flow, and thus, you do not break in difficult situations.

Following your intuition is the best method to reach your goals. Your mentality is shrewd. You can see through sham and farce, often to the discomfort of others bent on using you.

You tend to drain your energies through your sympathetic empathy with others. You need to recharge your emotional batteries quite often.

You are a natural healer, and how you use this gift can be your own personal choice. Hospitals, nursing homes or psychiatry are outlets which can harness your need to be needed and also give you good money.

Social-service occupations, teaching, psychology, counseling, restaurant work, both ownership and management, are also natural fields for your talents.

The arts are favorable for you also. Music, either performing or composing, is naturally attractive to your temperament. Acting, writing, painting, sculpting, decorating; working in libraries, art shops, flower stores, and antique shops or museums are also areas where your talents can be usefully employed.

First Decan Pisces (February 18-February 28). Your sex drive is high, and you can channel some of this force into creative fields of interest for success. After working with restlessness and indecisiveness in youth, during maturity you can achieve stability.

Second Decan Pisces (February 28-March 10). You make financial successes quickly and easily. Money sticks to your fingers! You can realize your ambitions and reach your goals by following your intuition.

Third Decan Pisces (March 10-March 20). Don't let your heart rule your head. Keep your emotional nature in harness. Learn balance and equilibrium, avoid moodiness and self-indulgence. With self-discipline, you can find successful rewards.

1977 Pisces Forecast

As the year begins Jupiter is retrograding through your third solar house, its position since March, 1976. On January 16, Jupiter turns direct at 21 Taurus and rapidly transits the remaining two decans. As you found out last year, this position increases your intellectual understanding, making it easier to assimilate and interpret a variety of stimuli. You can wade through a mass of details and come up with an overview of the situation. Your communicative abilities are increased, too, and you enjoy debating theoretical subjects because your persuasive arguments can convince others of almost anything. You will be successful in dealing with the public, particularly in the advertising field.

Your sense of humor and biting wit come out during Mars' trine to Jupiter January 20 to February 10. Mars is then transiting Capricorn, your eleventh solar house (January 2-February 10). Take advantage of this position to try for the leadership of your service club, social circle, political party, etc. You have the enthusiasm and drive to lead others now.

When Mars enters Aquarius (February 10), it becomes part of a fixed t-square also involving Saturn in Leo and Uranus in Scorpio, which are square one another for over a year (April 29, 1976-July 19, 1977).

Saturn entered Leo on June 6, 1976, and will remain

there most of the time until July 27, 1978. This year it will be transiting back and forth between 10 Leo (on April 12) and 1 Virgo (on December 12). This long period is marked by hard work, discipline and attention to details. The most unpleasant, unproductive work seems always to fall on you and it is difficult to feel a sense of real accomplishment. On the other hand, your ability to organize details and work efficiently is increased. You may have trouble getting along with fellow employees, but that is because you try to assume a supervisory position that is resented by others.

Saturn is the cause of your poor health during these two years. You are bothered by dull, aching feelings which seem to elude treatment. Though your appetite may be dulled, pay particular attention to your diet; good exercise is also essential.

Uranus, meanwhile, is squaring Saturn from its position in Scorpio, your ninth solar house. Uranus is causing a sporadic disruption of your religious or ethical beliefs. An intense religious experience may cause you to question your basic philosophy of life and your doubts will not be resolved as long as Uranus is in this position. When you do latch onto a defined religious or philosophical creed, you become a fanatical advocate—until something else comes along to disturb your peace of mind.

Educational, travel, and publishing plans are apt to be suddenly interrupted or drastically changed. Traveling in foreign countries is not recommended this year.

The Saturn-Uranus square does not improve matters. Your health may be suddenly altered through an accident or severe illness. Your religious beliefs become more rigid and illogical. This aspect does evoke a certain amount of original, though sometimes perverse, thinking, as well as promoting impulsive, violent behavior.

When Mars opposes Saturn and squares Uranus (February 15-March 6), these destructive tendencies are inverted and your psychological health may be unstable for a time.

Luckily, Mars does not linger long in Aquarius, but enters your sign, Pisces, on March 21, the first day of spring. Here your self-confidence is bolstered, and you eagerly await new situations, enjoying meeting new people. You present the world with a picture of a competent, self-assured, vital person.

From April 28 to June 7, Mars transits Aries, the sign which has held Venus since February 3. The two are conjunct between April 28 and July 7. This is particularly good for improving your immediate environment; you have the energy and taste to redecorate skillfully and economically. Now is a good time to make a major purchase.

While in Aries, Mars and Venus tie into a grand fire trine which has developed between Saturn in Leo and Neptune in Sagittarius. The two are trine one another for over a year (July 8, 1976-September 3, 1977).

Neptune, your personal ruler, is in the middle of your tenth solar house, this year, as it travels back and forth between 13 and 17 Sagittarius, including a retrograde period between March 19 and August 26. As I explained this transit in the *1975 Moon Sign Book:* this is excellent if your lifework lies in a field dealing with mysticism, spiritualism, the occult, the sea, chemicals, drugs, oil, or other Neptune-ruled areas. However, as always with Neptune, there is a tendency to be too idealistic about your business or professional status. Don't deceive yourself about the real state of your career.

Saturn's trine lends just the right amount of objective skepticism to Neptune's impractical genius. It adds an element of self-protective realism which can give quite a boost to your career.

With Mars and Venus both trine Saturn (Mars: May 7-28; Venus: April 1-May 24) and Neptune (Mars: May 7-28; Venus: February 10-May 29), matters look even better. Your judgment is improved and your feeling for economically sound moves may earn you a promotion. Your financial situation will advance.

Mars and Venus enter Taurus together **on June 7**, and once more become part of the fixed t-square that has been so disruptive to your peace of mind this year. (Mars square Saturn **June 13-July 7**, Mars opposed Uranus **June 7-28**; Venus square Saturn **June 12-30**, Venus opposed Uranus **June 7-23**.)

In contrast to the beginning of the year when Jupiter's position here caused communications to come so easily, you now experience difficulty expressing yourself and find that you are often misunderstood. This causes some of your friends or relatives to be alienated from you despite the presence of the usually soothing Venus. It is best just to keep your mouth closed and wait until matters improve.

Jupiter, by this time, has left Taurus, and entered Gemini for a relatively quick transit **(April 4-August 21)**. Pisces was traditionally ruled by Jupiter, before the discovery of Neptune in 1846. Jupiter can be considered a sub-ruler, or co-ruler, of Pisces, and is particularly important to your sign.

Jupiter in the fourth house will greatly benefit your home situation by increasing the feeling of warmth, security, and good cheer. You enjoy spending time at home and find the support and encouragement you need from your family members.

Jupiter's trine to Pluto **(April 24-August 21)** gives you the courage to let go of old, unhelpful patterns of behavior and to replace them with more constructive habits of relating to other family members.

The good feelings intensify when Mars enters this sign **on July 18**, following close behind Jupiter; though the two planets are not yet conjunct, their sign positions overlap by about a month, **July 18-August 21**.

The presence of Mars may indicate a split in your family—opinions differ and some arguments may develop. However, you find that you have a lot of energy to put into the situation, and these differences can be easily resolved, especially when Jupiter returns around the end of the year.

Jupiter entered Cancer on August 21, to be quickly followed by Mars on September 2. Mars now catches up with Jupiter and the two travel together from August 21 to September 22. This transit couldn't be more favorable, with no adverse aspects to diffuse it.

Your creativity is high and you might enjoy taking art or craft lessons of some kind—as much for the enjoyment of the company as for the instruction. Your zest for living and sense of amusement are increased so that parties, theatre, movies, dinners, and other social events occupy a lot of your time and energy. You might find that a love affair awaits you now.

Jupiter reaches only 6 Cancer before turning retrograde on October 21, but Mars continues on to trine Uranus September 2-30. Uranus has, of course, been wreaking havoc with your educational, religious, or philosophical pursuits. Now with Mars in favorable aspect, Uranus' assets of originality, resourcefulness, independence, ambition, and inventiveness are brought out. Your thinking may still take sudden turns but a new courage of conviction and enterprising spirit is added.

Mars next spends three months (October 27-January 27) looping through the first decan of Leo, your sixth solar house. This should improve your health, and give you the determination and strength you need to begin a better diet and physical fitness program. You may also take the initiative to resolve some conflict among your co-workers.

Back to Nature

There's more to tuning into Nature than herb teas and organic foods. Man must once again become *part* of Nature; he must once again know that the Earth is Mother to us all.

Back in the beginnings of known history, Man achieved a oneness with the Earth through rituals celebrated at the time of the Full Moon and the points of the four seasons. The Cycle of the Year became identified with the cycle of Man's life, and these seasonal celebrations took on a psychological function through which men and women found special meanings.

The Old Religion

These rites and this inner awareness and integration with the Earth Mother were the foundation of Man's oldest religion—a religion that lives now, as always—not as the antithesis of any other religion, but as simple personal spiritual experience.

You can learn about this religion and practice its ways—the seasonal rituals, the initiations, the techniques of growth and attainment. You can learn the meaning of various symbols and words, the lore and craft, the songs and dances. This religion is called *WitchCraft*, or Wicca. And it is entirely different from the image given it by Hollywood and people who believe in the Devil. It's also called "white magic."

It's all in **THE GRIMOIRE OF LADY SHEBA.** Deluxe, hardcover edition, illustrated, $10.00. If it isn't at your local bookstore, order No. 1-87542-076 from *Gnostic-Aquarian Booksales* by using the form on the last page.

Astrological Birth Control
Glenn Blakesley

"There is nothing new under the sun," the old saying goes. One wonders whether some astrologer in ancient Chaldea turned to his brother and uttered the same thing thousands of years ago; what does it mean—that history repeats itself? That it's all been done before? That the files are full in the Akashic records, in which are stored the astral memories of gods and men alike?

Whatever it means, the topic of discussion here, astrological birth control, is as old as the proverbial hills. Although ABC has been brought to public attention only relatively recently, the concept has existed for millennia.

Astrology has always been concerned with the birth process. As we turn our attention to astrological birth control, we tap the very sources of astrological tradition. Hasn't astrology always taken the birth chart as a symbol of the potentials in an individual's entire life-process—the soul's journey from past lives through the present and on to future incarnations? Hasn't astrology always been used to decipher the character and destiny of our ancestors, ourselves and our offspring? Yes, it has.

The potentials for modern usage of astrological birth control are absolutely profound in their implications for every level of human life. At the idealistic extreme, the universal use of ABC could possibly facilitate mankind as a whole taking a conscious leap into the new Age of

Aquarius, and thus a giant step forward in its contribution to planetary evolution. These high aspirations are mentioned in the writings of Alice A. Bailey and Dane Rudhyar. While they may represent the long-range objectives of ABC, the more immediate and practical implications will be shown to be just as cosmic, but relevant in a more experimental and personal sense.

Birth, life, death and rebirth—this is the basic cycle of life. The substantive link in this cyclic chain is sex. The sexual process generates and regenerates life on this planet. Sex is at the root of the evolutionary process. It is the fuel, the driving force, the lubricant of life.

In dealing with astrological birth control, then, we shall be synthesizing an occult blend of the concepts of astrology, sexuality and evolution with the underlying spiritual disciplines of synastry, Tantra, alchemy, and Yoga.

The Work of Dr. Jonas

The publication of *Psychic Discoveries Behind the Iron Curtain* by Lynn Schroeder and Sheila Ostrander a few years ago was responsible for the popularization of astrological birth control. In that book, the authors included a chapter on the work of a Czechoslovakian gynecologist-psychiatrist, Dr. Eugen Jonas, who had been carrying out studies and experiments with ABC for over a decade—with goverment support and the use of computer facilities. During his research period, and before he ran into some political trouble, Jonas tested certain astrological hypotheses on hundreds of women and came up with an astonishing accuracy of 98 percent!

Since this publication, there have been a number of recent expansions on the ABC theme. Widespread general interest in the Czechoslovakian techniques prompted Schroeder and Ostrander to co-author a separate volume called *Astrological Birth Control* in 1972. This book laid out the methods in detail and included a history of the

research and tables of reference for plotting ABC charts.
(A bibliography of related works accompanies this article.)

The methods of Dr. Jonas were based on two major
hypotheses whose sources, interestingly enough, were
some ancient Indian texts on astrology. What Jonas was
doing, then, was turning over new sod in an old field and
planting some fresh seeds. The two principles were as
follows: 1) that conception takes place when the Sun and
the Moon return every month to the same angular relationship that they held in the mother's birth chart; and
2) that the sex of the offspring depends on the position
of the Moon at the time of conception, i.e., whether it is
in a positive or negative field of the ecliptic.

To illustrate: if a woman were born three days after a
New Moon, then each month the time when the Moon is
three days old would be her astrologically fertile period.
Or, if she were born at the Full Moon, then it is during
this phase of the lunar cycle that she is most fertile, and
therefore most likely to conceive, throughout her pro-
creative years.

Also, sex-determination depends on whether the Moon
at conception is passing through a positive (traditionally
masculine) or a negative (feminine) sign. The zodiac, of
course, is divided into twelve equal and alternating positive and negative fields of thirty degrees each. If the Moon
is in one of the six positive fields, the resulting child will
be male; if it is in one of the negative (even-numbered
according to natural distribution) signs the child will be
female.

This seems as simple as ABC, theoretically, but on a
practical level, the situation is somewhat more complex.
Many women have irregular menstrual cycles. Many have
been taking that pernicious drug known as "the pill"
for years, and their metabolisms are out of tune with
natural rhythms. Add to this the various kinds of mental,
emotional and physical diseases so prevalent in modern

times, and the apparent simplicity becomes very complex indeed. Nevertheless, the practice of ABC can be splendid therapy for the individual, as well as a panacea for many of humanity's problems.

Biology and Astrology

The scientifically accepted theory of sex-determination is based on the type of chromosome carried by the spermatozoon. If the ovum is fertilized by a sperm carrying XX chromosomes, the child will be female; if it is fertilized by a sperm carrying XY chromosomes, the child will be male. The factor that determines which type of sperm will fertilize the ovum is unknown. Russian experiments have achieved separation of the two sperm types by a process called *electrophoresis.*

It has become increasingly evident from scientific studies of plant and animal life that all organisms living in the biosphere are affected by regular cyclic variations from the influence of the Moon and its phases, by circadian rhythms due to the earth's rotation and by energies passing through the fields of the ecliptic.

Recent discoveries and writings along these lines have been to the mutual benefit of both the scientific and the astrological communities. Why should the Sun and, especially, the Moon have an effect on the fertility cycles of women? The answers may be results of the various research projects currently being conducted by scientists who are testing empirically the claims of modern astrology. Finally, scientists and astrologers are working together in fields which could properly be termed Biocosmology, Chronobiology or Cosmo-ecology.

The Moon has always demonstrated clearly some of its effects upon the earth. Its gravitation pulls entire oceans this way and that, creating the tides. It becomes logical to assume that it has the same effects upon human organisms, who are some 75 percent water. The effects of

New and Full Moons and eclipses are particularly potent in influencing our own tides of feeling in everyday experience.

The menstrual cycle in women is the most lucid example of the effects of rhythmic celestial influences on the human organism. The basic premise of astrology is that through it, we learn to live in harmony with the cosmic cycles. Mother Nature herself is the archetype of ordered cyclic change, as is reflected in the seasons.

"To everything there is a season" is a familiar Biblical quote, and unto man and woman there is a season—for sex, conception and procreation, as well as a season for continence and meditation.

ABC Charts

The Jonas method of astrological birth control is to be used in conjunction with the regular menstrual cycle commonly known as the rhythm method, which postulates that ovulation occurs midway during the feminine monthly cycle. This implies that there may be two fertile periods during the month.

Here's what an astrologer will do for a female client. On a calendar for an entire year, her astrologically fertile periods will be marked. From the birth chart, based on the exact time and place of birth, the natal Moon phase is noted. Then, the astrologer will consult the ephemeris for the year in question to determine the dates each month when this phase of the Moon recurs. This day, and three days prior to it, are marked in red. These are the astrological days on which she is most likely to conceive.

Then, the astrologer asks the client to superimpose her rhythm days onto the ABC chart. She marks the actual day menstruation commences, then counts 15 days after that and circles the thus-derived day in green. Six days before and after this green day are also marked off. This period serves to indicate the ovulation stage of the client, according to the rhythm method.

These two periods, which sometimes overlap and some-times do not, are the days to consider fertile—thus, the days to use for birth prevention or promotion. Further-more, in each month the moon is in either a positive or negative polarity, indicating the sex of the potential off-spring.

The ABC's of Family Planning

Jonas' work in Czechoslovakia attracted a great deal of criticism. It was accused of "bringing back" astrology, among other things, like tampering with sexual freedom and privacy. However, studies by established authorities have consistently supported his findings. The results of his experiments have enormous practical implications.

In the first place, they give a natural and practical way of determining a woman's fertility cycle, and thus a method of contraception that is independent of mechani-cal or chemical means (subject to both medical and religious objections). Secondly, parents knowledgeable in astrology can choose not only the sex of their offspring, but also a Sun sign and various planetary placements that are harmonious with their own. This implies intelligent family planning and foresight, and thus a more conscious and practical control of character and destiny—through a judicious timing of sexual intercourse in accordance with the positions of the cosmic bodies.

Synastry is the special branch of astrology dealing with the potentials of human relationship. Many modern couples are considering the meaning and value of their relationships in astrological terms. The potentials for com-patibility or incompatibility, and for service or disservice on many different levels of relationship, are explicitly revealed through a competent comparison of horoscopes. Some also employ electional astrology to choose the most auspicious time to marry or consummate a union.

By the same token, when mature consenting adults make a mutal decision to have children, they are practicing an unconscious form of astrological birth control. I suggest, however, that parties to a union take this a few steps further. God willing, parents may select the sex and approximate birth date of their children in such a way that these children are compatible with them, and can take their place within the family unit. "The family is society in embryo"—the *I Ching*.

Astrological birth control therefore presupposes a basic knowledge of astrology—the signs, planets and houses of the horoscope. It warrants a fundamental awareness of our solar environment and the planetary motions within it. These are necessary parts of the intelligent ordering of life and the conscious adjustment to its cycles and natural rhythms.

Thus, family planning evolves into a realized and mature sense of one's individual and relational place in the grand scheme of things. This involves the Plutonian concept of the manipulation of poetntiality. The potential horoscope of the child, as measured in relation to the existing birth charts of the parents, represents the epitome of astrological free will. Conception can thus take place at the most appropriate season in the life-cycles of the parents, and the offspring will be a result of their combined self-expression and the consciously controlled use of divine laws. This is true cosmic alchemy.

ABC and Tantra Yoga

Tantra, a Hindu-Buddhist doctrine centuries old, might commonly be called the Yoga of sex; it literally means "weaving," or "continuity." It is a means whereby union of the individual self with the absolute infinite may be achieved. Tantra implicitly assumes that the body is a temple, the abode of truth, and the epitome of the universe. "He who realizes the truth of the body can then come to know the truth of the universe."

Tantra has become increasingly popular among Western students of occultism in the past decade. This represents an indication of the underlying (unconscious) need for union, liberation and self-control through the occult use of sex. Many people are beginning to practice Tantra Yoga in lieu of having ordinary sexual relations. These practices entail the use of *pranayama* and the study of the science of *chakras*—the whirling centers of energy in the subtle body. (The reader is referred to Jonn Mumford's *Sexual Occultism*, Llewellyn Publications, 1975.)

There has been a corresponding transcendental planetary emphasis in the reproductive trinity of zodiacal signs over the latter half of the twentieth century. Neptune, the planet of mystery and idealism, entered Libra, the sign that balances opposites, in the early forties; then it was in Scorpio, the sign of sex, death and regeneration, in the mid-fifties, until 1970. Now Neptune is about halfway through Sagittarius, the sign of spiritual aspiration. Meanwhile, Uranus, the awakener, also transited Libra from 1968 to 1975, and is currently beginning its seven-year passage through Scorpio, only to pave the way for Pluto, the redeemer, now a third of the way through Libra on its way to Scorpio in 1932-4, by which time Uranus will have entered Sagittarius.

To make a long story short, these transcendental planets are together placing tremendous cosmic stress on relationship—its power and meaning; its expansion, enlightenment and perfection. The emphasis is on the exalted use of sexuality as a means of transforming and regenerating matter—matter that is not only the substance of physical human bodies, but also the subtler substances of the astral (emotional), mental and spiritual bodies of souls coming into incarnation.

In the Scorpio phase of the cosmic cycle there is a straining out of quality from the quantity of matter provided by the opposite Earth sign, Taurus. Scorpio eliminates non-essentials, concentrates life-force (as in a seed) and regenerates this concentrated essence of life into new and improved forms, i.e., human beings of the future.

Scorpio, ruled by Mars (and, some feel, Pluto), is associated with the substance of relationship (the potentials of Libra). Thus it is concerned with the meaning and worth of the coming together of opposites. Here is a clue to the true meaning of sex: the propagation and transmutation of life-forms as means of perpetuating the race and refining its quality.

The meaning of Scorpio has long fascinated astrologers. It is the sign of death—the death of old forms, the ground for rebirth of new ones. Scorpio rules the occult forces in nature—those perennially profound mysteries: the great transition, the Serpent Power and the release of the seed.

But with the nebulous Neptune having already transited Scorpio during the current cycle, and with electric Uranus having really just begun its Scorpio phase, we are now able to penetrate, intuitively, unexpectedly, independently, the veil of these mysteries; and we can re-emerge with startling new discoveries (under the "old" Sun!) regarding the true meaning and function of sex in the present-day world. Many initiations and expansions of consciousness will take place during this time. The mysteries and secrets of sex, death and regeneration, of after-death states of being and consciousness, and of Tantric disciplines will be uncovered and put into intelligent practice.

When Pluto enters Scorpio in 1984 (it will remain there until the mid-nineties), the collective purge will have begun. The planet representing cultural self-realization will embark on the most intense and significant phase of its journey since its discovery in 1930. Pluto is the planet of the twentieth century. During its passage through Scorpio, its own astrological domain, Pluto will reach its perihelion (closest to the Sun) point in 1988, as well as its fastest orbital speed (faster because it will be closer to the Sun than Neptune will), plus its changeover from northern to southern declination. All this portends a cultural do-or-die situation for humanity as a whole.

In any case, to return to astrological birth control and its creative relation to the growing practice of Tantra Yoga: obviously these two concepts fit very well together. The union of sperm and ovum, at the proper time, in the appropriate place, and under the ideal conditions, is the flowering consummation of Tantric ABC. Tantra by itself is concerned with the union of Atman with Brahman, lingam and yoni—the mystical union of opposites, male and female, as a means of transcending the illusion of duality and separateness. ABC by itself is concerned with the enlightened and creative selection of progeny. The two together (the ABC of Tantric synastry) result in the truly purposeful bliss of sexual union.

Semen (Scorpio, Pluto) is the quintessential secretion produced by the human body. Sexual energy is the finest, most subtle and most powerful force circulating through the physical vehicle. The proper use of this exquisite energy is the purpose of life.

Sexual intercourse of parents planning to consummate their otherwise purely Tantric Yoga may be accompanied by any desired Tantric ritual or magickal ceremony. This serves to heighten, exalt and enhance the conjugal consciousness, and it consecrates the sexual act to the highest purposes. In such consecration is the divine blessing of the most sacred of human acts, Tantric sexual union—the rainbow bridge by which the discarnate soul may cross over from the unmanifest realms into the world of spirit-made-manifest in flesh.

The Problems

It may not be surprising to astrologers that the Jonas

method of ABC works with such a high degree of efficiency. All astrologers are idealists at heart. They recognize the basic order and rhythm inherent in the orbital motions of the planets and celestial bodies. They have had a glimpse of the zodiacal light, heard a few strains of the music of the spheres, sensed the wonder of cosmic harmony. Yet, living on the earth, they also realize the necessity and the responsibility of bringing these heavenly rhythms to bear upon practical living. Theirs is the task of understanding and interpreting life-cycles for themselves and others.

As in any consideration of the education and evolution of humanity, the problems lie within people themselves. At present, some of these problems seem enormous, possibly overwhelming. In this age of materialistic thinking and technological jungles, most of us have our noses in the mud, and cannot see the forest for the trees. We are blinded by a proliferation and confusion of petty and materialistic concerns of the daily rounds in which we get so caught up.

Nevertheless, one initiates the regenerative process within oneself; slowly, ever so slowly, does the evolutionary progress of the race reveal itself. Change seems so painfully slow at times, yet a gradual and complete mutation takes place. "The greatness of man is that he can always be greater."—Rudhyar.

The immediate problems with astrological birth control center around the scientific and empirical verification of the methods. The ingrained effect of collective habits and general cultural inertia are the greatest enemies to progress. Understandably, men and women will be reluctant to experiment unwittingly with ABC, due to their lack of ABC education and their uncertainty as to its reliability. Many people do not even acknowledge astrology. Thus, problems exist on customary moral, ethical and religious levels, as well as on physical, mental and spiritual ones.

It has been said that humans differ from animals in two respects: 1) they have conscious intelligence by which they can control their lives; and 2) they have financial worries! The latter reason is not as facetious as it seems at first glance. The long-range problems of humanity in the last quarter of this century will be economy and ecology— very serious problems indeed. We must be continually more concerned about the global population problem, and the proportionate energy reserves and natural resources of the planet.

The problems are indeed far-reaching. However, it may be stated that some of the objective solutions are education, research and the promotion of human rights and the status of women, along with new methods of medical training concerned with contraception, sterilization and abortion. Any way one looks at it, birth control is an urgent necessity for the positive progress of the human race.

Spiritual Aspects of the Problem

While our problems seem to hurt us at the economic level, they do not originate there. Besides looking at the effects of overpopulation, whether in the Western Hemisphere, the Orient or the Third World, we must analyze its causes. The spiritual aspects of these probelms are discussed in Alice Bailey's *Education in the New Age* and *Esoteric Psychology* and in Dane Rudhyar's *Occult Preparations for a New Age*. Both indicate that poverty, insecurity and the lack of education are the causes of overpopulation. Motives for having children must receive global attention. Far too many unwanted children are the result of uncontrolled sexual relations. It should be better realized that the act of copulation ought to be the result of a loving desire to provide a new vehicle for a soul.

Most astrologers and occultists believe in the twin doctrines of karma and reincarnation, which postulate the immortality of the soul throughout successive incarnations on its journey toward perfect enlightenment and ultimate fulfillment. In each incarnation the soul takes up mortal residence in a new body—a potential vehicle of enlightenment or temple of God. Each incarnation is a unique opportunity for the soul to express its inherent divine nature through the medium of the human body.

The sexual act is the means of providing for a reincarnating soul. Thus, birth is a means of evolution—and birth control implies controlled evolution. Obviously, as we develop, more and more souls will pass on to higher realms, and will not require physical vehicles. This is the esoteric truth of human evolution. "As the intelligence of the race is developed, as the Laws of Rhythm and Approach are grasped, it will then be found that certain innate reactions will negate conception, and mechanical means will no longer be required."—Bailey.

The reference here is undoubtedly to Tantric sex (which in its highest aspects forbids male ejaculation) and natural birth control, i.e., ABC. The plea is for more sexual self-control on the part of all men and women. Too many souls have come into incarnation over the last century or so—souls that have not been ready. This is solely the result of the abuse of the sexual principal.

Many mechanical and chemical means of contraception have been researched and introduced, from diaphragms and condoms to IUDs and pills. All are artificial; they preclude human control and will power. None are too recommendable or reliable, and some of them are actually quite dangerous to physical well-being. There must instead be a compelling motive to control sexual impulses from within, or to explore other natural methods.

No successful lead is at present given by any religion. Indeed, many of them are stymied by the moral issues. The answer will eventually issue from the field of education. It must eventually be fully understood and taught that sexual energy and strong physical desires can be sublimated and used by the mind in any creative activity. Children and adults alike must be taught how these energies may be misdirected on the one hand, or directed properly and successfully contolled on the other. Then we can all be encouraged to develop the creative side of our natures.

"The inculcation of the desire to share, of right motive and greater sense of responsibility and self-control are the inner means of dealing with this population problem, and will eventually cause its disappearance. Family planning is essential at the moment, but the sharing of resources generating a freer life, the opening of doors to women releasing them from a sequestered life, greater knowledge of energy control—these will eventuate in the population problem disappearing without mechanical aids. Through growth in consciousness leading to realization of total interdependence, humanity now faces the urgent necessity for a complete reorientation from materially valued living, towards the radiant vision of a golden age of mankind—guided by the Light of Spirtual Love-Wisdom and Divine Purpose."—Bailey.

Conclusions

I acknowledge the tendency to wax poetic with idealistic visions of an evolved and consecrated humanity despite the gulf that exists between these aspirations and the actual state of affairs in the world today in which sex, has been the source of much of the suffering. The abuse, misuse and disuse of the sexual principle has caused humanity much grief, misery, poverty and insecurity, and has given rise to an entirely negative host of human weaknesses—jealousy, greed, arrogance, lust, power-hunger, possessiveness, and so on.

It is the task of humanity to transform itself and transmute these weaknesses into sources of strength, grace and knowledge, that we may demonstrate our highest attributes on the seven rays. Truly we must cultivate calm, passion, self-control, purpose of endeavor, vision, trust, faith, truth and love, along with patience, the will to good, and hope. What else are we here for?

Astrology will be one of the major sciences of the future. Yet, it takes time . . . first to realize, acknowledge and accept our many faults as human beings; then, to uproot and eliminate our ignorance, folly and blind, conditioned prejudices. This must be done before we can return, revise and regenerate the current human condition.

Humanity must pass the tests of Scorpio before it re-emerges into the light promised by the coming Aquarian Age of knowledge, truth and brotherhood. Truly, we must use sex as a cosmic priciple, a conscious tool in the propagation of the ideal man (Aquarius). There are more than enough people inhabiting the earth presently. We must reduce the quantity and refine the quality of human beings that are born. We must give consciously controlled birth to leaders, to seed-men and seed-women; to a Christ or a Buddha. It is a matter of life and death, or birth and rebirth.

Recent statistics for the U.S.A. reveal a sharp decline in the birth rate over the last few years. This is an indication of a beginning, and it will continue. One way we can help it to continue is by practicing astrological birth control. Every birth must henceforth be significant to the evolution of the race as a whole. Every being must be born in harmony with the cosmos. How can we achieve an ideal state without first controlling the wild herd of passions, instincts and selfish desires that motivate sex? Can we continue to attempt to do so with drugs and devices, with external and artifical means—at the expense of our self-control and inner, spiritual development, which are the very requirements of enlightened evolution?

LLEWELLYN'S

Personal Services

Astrology can give a personal touch to daily living, giving you a deeper understanding of who you are and what your purpose in life is. *Llewellyn Personal Services* was designed around your needs and desire to know more about yourself and the world around you. We offer a full spectrum of services to allow you to choose the service that best fits your needs at any particular moment.

The personal touch of astrology is carried over into the work we do for you. Our astrologers want to find the direction in life which will lead you to a greater fulfillment of your potentials and to greater happiness. Let us help you understand yourself better through our knowledge of astrology. All orders are kept in the strictest confidence and, although we process orders as promptly as possible, please allow us sufficient time to do an accurate and thorough job.

Carol Kent

Carol Kent, Director
Llewellyn Personal Services

Locate an Element

Specific planetary position or ascendant will be computed from your birth date—day, month, year, time and place.   **$4.00**

Natal Chart Without Interpretation

If you want to interpret your own horoscope, but prefer to avoid the mathematical computations, a Llewellyn astrologer will accurately cast and aspect your chart.   **$15.00**

Natal Chart With Reference

Your choice of Noel Tyl's *The Principles and Practice of Astrology* (Vol. 1-3) or Llewellyn George's *A to Z Horoscope Maker and Delineator* accompanies your natal chart, cast and aspected especially for you. For those who want to interpret their own horoscope.   **$25.00**

Abbreviated Natal Horoscope

This service is designed to meet the needs of those who are not interested in a highly detailed analysis, but would like to know the major influences in their lives. The major planetary configurations are outlined and interpreted.   **$35.00**

Natal Horoscope

The analysis is more detailed, focusing on the specific area of your life you specify when ordering—love life, financial situation, etc. (does not apply to vocational).   **$50.00**

Complete Natal Package

This analysis is a complete guide to the universal forces at work in your life. The potentials of every area in your life are analyzed, as well as the tensions or problems. Included in this package are the general trends for the coming year.   **$100.00**

Progressed Horoscope

The Progressed Natal Horoscope is for those who are already familiar with their natal chart, but feel they need to know in what direction their development will progress during the coming year. This service includes the use of the major transits.

$35.00

Natal/Progressed Horoscope
A combination of the Abbreviated Natal Horoscope and the Progressed Horoscope, which will enable you to see how the potential of your natal horoscope will develop during the coming year. $60.00

Five-Year Progressed Horoscope
The cycles and trends of the coming five years are analyzed for you so you can make long-range plans. $150.00

Astrological Fertility Cycle
Your personal Astrological Fertility Cycle is computerized for maximum accuracy and comes with an easily understood chart.
$20.00

Compatibility Analysis
Compatibility Analysis consists of the comparison of any two charts to determine areas of strengths and weaknesses and to provide the means for a deeper understanding of interpersonal relations. $60.00

Compatibility and Composite Charts
The Compatibility Analysis along with a Composite Chart of the relationship itself. $100.00

Monthly Trends
Projected for a single month or as many months as requested, this service indicates specific trends of the transits of the personal planets during the specified periods and details how you can take advantage of them. per month, $20.00
per year, $225.00

Electional Chart
If you are about to take an important step in your life, whether it be starting a business, getting married, beginning a project, or whatever, we will tell you the most favorable time to begin your venture. Be as specific as possible about the upcoming event, including the time limits for making your decision.
$50.00

Vocational Guidance
Through your natal horoscope, we will tell you the type of work or range of activities you are best suited for and in which field you are most likely to discover success and happiness. **$30.00**

Birth Pattern Analysis Package
This service includes a complete Natal Horoscope, Progressed Horoscope, Vocational Guidance and Monthly Trends for one year. This package provides the most in-depth study of your horoscope available. **$450.00**

Rectification of Birth Time
Working backward through your life, a Llewellyn astrologer will attempt to locate your exact time of birth by adjusting a hypothetical chart to fit the events significant to your development. We will continue to correspond with you until we have arrived at the most probable time of birth. **$100.00**

Student Forum
This service is designed for the student of astrology to assist in finding answers to astrological questions. For each question submitted, we will provide the student with a well-researched answer plus additional information for further study. **$20.00**

Horary Chart
This service is developed from the concept that the moment a question is asked, that moment contains the answer. Include the date and the *exact* time of writing, phrasing your question as precisely as possible. Your chart will then be analyzed and you will be given a prompt reply. **$40.00**

Esoteric Horoscope
This Esoteric Horoscope provides a complete analysis of your spiritual and astral capabilities from your natal chart and specific direction for development of psychic abilities, understanding of past and future lives, and personal analysis of your experiences within the framework of karma. Describe your occult interests and experiences when ordering. **$150.00**

Child Guidance

This service will help you gain an "inside" point of view on your child and your relationship with him. By understanding his potentials and his problems, you can guide your child so his future will be happy and productive. **$60.00**

Business Analysis

This analysis includes the cycles you are in and how they affect your business, as well as an analysis of the coming year indicating when you should act and when you should double-check your work. If you are in business, includesthe date you first signed the papers. **$100.00**

Relocation Chart

Environmental changes can produce astonishing results. Let a Llewellyn astrologer locate an environment where you will flourish and where your talents will be appreciated. **$40.00**

This list is not exhaustive. If you require any service that is not listed above, please write to us, describing exactly what you need, and we will do whatever we can to help.

When ordering, be sure to include your name and address, the title of the service requested, a check or money order for the correct amount, and all pertinent information: month, day, year, time and place of birth. For services involving more than one person (such as the Compatibility Analysis), be sure to include the complete birth data for each. Any additional information which you would like to include will be appreciated. Send to:

LLEWELLYN PERSONAL SERVICES
Box 3383-MSB
St. Paul, Minnesota 55165

World Predictions

IS THE END OF THE WORLD COMING?

Will there be war, famine, plague, enslavement?
Will there be spiritual renewal, salvation, peace, plenty,
health, progress?

NOSTRADAMUS PREDICTS

The most famous astrologer-seer of all time gave us these answers.

Are his prophecies reliable?

Nostradamus' record of success is without equal. In *The Fate of the Nations*, Nostradamus scholar Arthur Prieditis not only gives us the most accurate translation of his famous prophecies, but shows how they have been fulfilled, and interprets those still remaining to be fulfilled along with the predictions of other great seers of today concerning the events of tomorrow.

The Fate of the Nations is not a book for amusement! It will astound you, frighten you, challenge you, and give you answers to many questions. It is not for persons with a weak stomach or those who fear to know what the future may bring. It will help the reader who wants to play an active role in his personal survival and success and in the survival of his family and the successful triumph of humanity over the coming crisis.

The Fate of the Nations, over 400 pages, hardcover, deluxe edition, $12.95. If it's not available at your local bookstore, use the form on the last page and order No. 1-87542-624.

The News Ahead
Frank McCarthy

Peace or war? Prosperity or depression? Rising or decreasing unemployment? These are the primary questions usually asked of astrologers as a new calendar year begins, and they well might make good subtitles for this analysis of national and international conditions during 1977.

The year begins with Saturn just beyond the nadir of the U.S. national horoscope (July 4, 1776; 2:17 am), and as a result Saturn can be something of the taskmaster in national matters, restricting the Administration's interests at times because domestic conditions may not permit wide spending overseas or too much absorption in the problems of other nations.

Saturn will be transiting the U.S. fourth house throughout 1977, even after November 17th, when it makes its Virgo ingress. Throughout 1977 it will be moving away from those adverse squares it formed with Uranus during 1975 and 1976, which wrought havoc in the economy. Moving in the fire sign Leo, Saturn indicates respect for the domestic status quo and a slowing down in liberal experimentation. Home-grown theories will be on the decline, particularly in the late spring and early summer of 1977. A sense of resentment can rise sharply among the American people, perhaps aimed at Washington and the Administration around late July when Saturn at 18 Leo will be in exact opposition to the U.S. natal Moon in Aquarius. Because the Moon always represents the mood of the people, over the summer months the public may feel that there is too much foreign spending and insufficient attention to domestic problems.

As the year ends, Saturn will be moving toward favorable sextiles with the U.S. natal Venus and Jupiter, so an era of improved feelings can be forecast for December, a time when the accent is on positive economic thinking and the near conviction that this current round of recession is indeed petering out. Even so, it would be foolhardy to grant early 1977 a clean bill of economic health.

Inflation will be in the news in February and March. Saturn will prove a damper on home construction during these months. There can be another round of inflation in late March and early April that picks up on the heels of the one that possibly extended into early March. You will have to keep a close check on supermarket prices early in the year, for some of them can change from day to day.

The first six months of 1977 bring considerable conflict and confusion to the national scene. It is increasingly recognized that government must stop its heavy spending programs if inflation is to be controlled and people put back to work. But about eighty percent of government spending is mandated by law and Congress isn't going to be in any mood for wiping out legislation that any democratic society tends to be proud of, legislation that treats the ailments of its people, that feeds, houses, clothes and educates them.

Tax increases will be in the news during 1977. Increased taxation will be necessary but unpopular. Taxation in the United States never can be popular, for the eighth house of the national chart contains the part of fortune at 13 Capricorn. To escape unfair taxation, millions emigrated to this land; to escape unfair taxation, the American people declared their independence of Great Britain. The spectre of a tax revolt always has harried the U.S. government and 1977 will be no exception. With states and cities contributing to the heavy burden of taxation, the federal government has some reason to worry, for it is one thing for taxpayers to pay federal income taxes, which have some ring of legitimacy, but paying increasingly higher city taxes, for instance, to corrupt city governments with poor fiscal records is quite another thing. What goes on at the metropolitan and state levels can irk citizens with all types of taxes at a time when government spending isn't being kept in line.

But how can government spending be kept in line? The people of Alabama and Kansas didn't give a darn about the plight of New York City, nor do they care if the military closes its bases *outside* their states. But Alabama citizens react strongly to any rumor that military bases are going to be closed *in* their state, and even more strongly when told by Washington to clean up their jails and to feed and house their prisoners better. There is great selfishness at the basis of many of these conflicts, and much of the confusion marking the United States charts during 1977 corresponds with financial Jupiter in intellectual Gemini opposing an insidious Neptune of chicanery, illusion, and subterfuge in spirited Sagittarius.

The Neptune Story

Throughout 1977 Neptune will be in Sagittarius, sometimes fluctuating there, favorably aspecting Saturn and to a lesser extent Pluto and Uranus, but taking oppositions not only from Jupiter but also from a particularly warlike Mars early in August.

Neptune is now out of the U.S. 6th house, which rules trade unions and national health programs. No longer will there be so much illusion in these matters. Americans may stop sitting around and waiting for that expert who is going to fix up every labor and health matter, bring some instantaneous cure for cancer and some new heart surgery that will guarantee life on this planet forever. With the illusion gone, the more corrupt labor unions, such as the Teamsters, will have less of a hold on the rank and file. Union members will be less apt to vote as their bosses tell them to vote and to look the other way when their bosses tell them to look the other way. Situations where individual union members, who have been paying into retirement funds all during their working years, find themselves denied retirement income when they are old, will be corrected by investigation and new legislation. One of the unions that refused to pay retirement pensions to its members actually loaned millions from the retirement funds to underworld organizations. You can mark 1977 as the year when government takes giant steps to clean up these corrupt practices in labor unions.

Medical and health legislation may not be as grandiose as that talked about the past several years, but it will be solid legislation that will guarantee good medicine to all Americans who require it, without permitting the corruption that attached itself to Medicare and Medicaid programs. The illusion, the subterfuge, the kickbacks, the under-the-table payments, the doctors who carried too many patients on their books in order to claim big medicaid payments, the filthy rest homes, the so-called havens where the aged were denied adequate food, the crooks who got in on the government's efforts to provide for the very old and infirm—all these will decline during 1977.

Also on the decline will be malpractice suits, the legitimate claims and the vast number of illegitimate claims, and the enormous record-keeping demanded of hospital administrations and station nurses, often at the expense of their legitimate medical functions. These are the areas where the Administration and Congress will do some of their best work during 1977.

The Jupiter Story

At the beginning of 1977, mighty Jupiter will be retrograding in Taurus, resuming direct movement on January 16th. It will make its Gemini ingress on April 4th and its Cancer ingress on August 22nd. It will be retrograding in Cancer at the close of the year.

While in Taurus, Jupiter benefits the United States by permitting us to extract from our past and to call into full play basic national strengths. In Gemini, Jupiter promises new economic programs and, conjoining with natal Uranus and Mars in Gemini, it can go a long way toward curing the ills of the nation. The Jupiter transit of Gemini will call forth national inventiveness, positive solutions, and enthusiastic approaches so that the recession of the middle 1970's can be brought under genuine control.

In Cancer, Jupiter buttresses all wealth production in the United States. More Americans will be working than ever before in 1977, but this doesn't mean that the chronically unemployed and underemployed will be working. The chasm between the employed and unemployed in this country actually can widen over the summer months of 1977. As it has often been said, "The rich get richer, the poor, poorer."

Despite higher levels of employment, in-depth analysis of the U.S. horoscope against the backdrop of 1977's planetary trends shows that Americans are going to have to work harder for less. Americans are going to have to re-examine their history, and find anew their sacred purposes in life; there's no better year in this decade for doing so than 1977.

The Uranus Story

Throughout 1977, Uranus will be in Scorpio. In the U.S. national chart, it will be in the 6th house and will, through its semi-sextiles to Neptune and Pluto, produce an enormous change in the way Americans work, earn their livelihood, view their luxuries, and modify their lifestyles. It will change existing health plans, health-insurance matters, social-security arrangements, and the way Americans take care of their mental and physical well-being, select doctors and hospitals, and move to correct and improve their jails, orphanages, adoption programs, prisoner-rehabilitation projects, and the way they take care of their older citizens.

Uranus is unpredictable and from time to time it will fluctuate in Scorpio, so there will be a lot of discussion, planning, reorganizing, and investigative effort before the real gains brought by this Great Awakener are realized.

In many ways, Uranus is going to revamp the lifestyles of the American people. Older people will cohabitate together, without benefit of clergy, for economic reasons. Marriage, on the decline since the Uranus transit of Libra, will now revive as an institution under the increasing power of Pluto in Libra. More and more Americans will face up to the fact that divorce tears up the fabric of society. The United States is now chalking up forty-five divorces out of every 100 marriages. True, the rate of divorce is even higher in Sweden and the United Kingdom, but those two nations make a far smaller pretense at being Christian than the United States. Although both Sweden and England have state churches, very few citizens of those countries bother to attend religious services any more and there is evidence that marriage is going the same way as divorce in large cities like London, Liverpool, and Manchester. People just don't bother to get married legally any more than they bother to get divorced legally. In France, the divorce rate is only twelve out of every 100 marriages.

Younger Americans are going to want to set up their own establishments at increasingly earlier ages, and, not being able to afford high rents or down-payments for suburban dwellings, they will increasingly favor mobile homes or igloo-type apartments which can be built at the present time for less than $3,000. Fewer Americans, under the stringent aspects that Uranus will be forming with Saturn, Jupiter, and the personal planets from time to time this year, will be opting for college; more will prefer technical training schools, where basic skills increasing earning power can be learned.

While Uranus is moving in Scorpio during 1977, it favorably trines the Sun-sign of the United States. It can induce changes in fashion, the world of entertainment, and the way in which land beneath sea level is viewed, explored and mined. Interest will increase in new sources of food from beneath the sea. Off-shore oil discoveries will increase also, but not in the proportion expected a few years ago.

Uranus rules the Holy Land itself, even though Sagittarius rules the Arab nations and Israel is considered a Taurus-ruled nation. Uranus can bring about changes in the way Jerusalem is administered, and the move to make the Holy City international can be a strong force this year.

Foreign Affairs

Throughout 1977, it will be difficult for the U.S. Administration to avoid entanglements in foreign affairs, although it is still too early (after the debacle in Viet Name) for any chief executive to feel free to commit American troops even where and when they may be needed—Lebanon, elsewhere in the Middle East, Rhodesia, and elsewhere in Africa and Asia. March can be a particularly tense month in the Middle East and in Spain and Portugal. Britons can seem to reverse themselves in Nato, the Middle East, Northern Ireland, Africa, and in their relationships with Washington and Moscow. April can give Great Britain some kind of a breather—perhaps a royal romance may get off the ground—but talks in matters involving Israel and Ireland, also Greece, can bog down during April.

Expect much forthright thinking in British life over May. Can the present government force the British to bite the bullet, to face up to the fact that it now takes two Englishmen to do the work of one American, one German, and half a Frenchman? Unfortunately, 1977 is a year when the British Cabinet can attempt to do too much in Northern Ireland, which has been death to British governments. New elections called in 1977 will produce gains for the off-shoot parties, such as the Liberals and the Welsh and Scottish nationalists.

The United States is bolder in international affairs once we are into July, with Mars moving toward a powerful conjunction with Jupiter in Gemini, the national ascendant; and generally any confrontation with enemies or would-be enemies over July and even August will go our way in the end.

Relations among the Superpowers

Not only can there be a series of confrontations with Soviet Russia during 1977, but with Uranus now moving over the natal Sun of the Kremlin, anything is possible. Russia can reverse itself again and again, supporting detente one month and criticizing it the next. Soviet Russia undoubtedly will have learned during the 1976 elections that detente is being questioned across the United States. Russia has gained huge successes, for at Helsinki in 1976, Soviet influence across Eastern Europe was pretty much accepted by Washington, while our sphere of influence in Cuba and elsewhere in Latin America has not been accepted by the Kremlin.

The Soviet role in Cuba will become as economically expensive to the Kremlin this year as did her role in

Egypt, and when all was said and done, Sadat kicked her out and canceled the old Moscow-Cairo treaty of friendship and alliance. During 1977, the Kremlin will be buying a greater sphere of interest in Syria and will be engineering coups in Morocco, Tunis, Algeria, Libya, Saudi Arabia, Jordan and elsewhere in the Middle East. They will continue their fishing expeditions in the internal politics of dozens of nations.

The appalling spectre of Kremlin-Peking confrontations looms throughout 1977. These two supergiants will show signs of behaving themselves in their relationships with Washington only when we show any friendship for one of them that might be at the expense of the other. They can clash in Mongolia this year and in North Korea, Viet Nam, Cambodia, Laos and Africa. Both sides will be doing their best to upset established authority in Thailand and Burma, and throughout Africa and Asia.

There can be some critical days associated with the increasing rise of nationalism among Soviet satellite nations and also in Yugoslavia. The Croats, Ruthenians, Slovenians, and Slovaks, to name a few peoples, want increasing autonomy, and this is only part of the general resurgence of nationalism that also shows up in the West—the desire of the Irish, the Bretons, and the Basques to rule themselves. Any change of government in Yugoslavia, Eastern Germany, and Portugal this year is likely to attract interference by the Kremlin.

Soviet maneuvering in the Mediterranean, the Persian Gulf, and the waters off Latin America can keep the midnight oil burning in Washington. Tense naval confrontations may occur in these areas. Soviet activity on Malta, Cyprus, and in the rich Persian Gulf sheikdoms may increase.

There isn't much relief from Soviet aggression during 1977, and in late December, when Mars is erratic, the men in the Kremlin can pull off something special.

The Testing of British and Italian Democracies

With Saturn in Leo, which rules France and Italy, you can expect much tampering with existing order. Cabinets can fall, money be be devaluated, and the Communists will make increasing inroads into local administrations and trade unions. Some purely national solution may be required for Italy, because the situation isn't very different from that when Mussolini took over; and "people facing anarchy will accept the strong man."

Forms of anarchy are evident in the 1977 charts of both Italy and Great Britain. No democracy ever has been able to withstand the inflation rate now prevalent in those two allies. While the Kremlin would like to see this near-bankruptcy continue in order to neutralize two of our allies in NATO, the truth is that the yearning on the part of the common workers in British and Italian factories to take over and run things has little to do with the plans of Moscow. In fact, this idea of people running things is as frightening to the men in the Kremlin as it is to British and Italian capitalists. If workers are to rise to board positions in plants and factories any place in the West, this will happen in Great Britain and Italy; mistakes will be made, with many of the industries going bankrupt, even as the Soviet Army went bankrupt and failed in its attack on Finland because orders were debated by the common soldiers rather than merely issued by the officers.

In-depth analysis of pertinent seasonal charts shows that spring and fall are the crucial testing periods for London and Rome, and what transpires in those magnificent cities during 1977 will hit the headlines of your newspapers on several occasions.

Monthly Briefs

January: Mars in Capricorn gives much clout to the new Washington Administration; the usual honeymoon is on. Jupiter resumes direct movement in Taurus on the 16th and Mercury goes direct in Capricorn again on the 18th. Snowfalls, avalanches, sleety disasters can be in the news. Starvation roams Asia and Africa, and some of these pitiable stories won't be released until later in the year. Growth rates in soft goods can slow down but military hardware can enjoy gains.

February: Work stoppages, transportation problems, nautical disasters, strikes, real-estate financing problems can all be in the news. Mars gives greater self-confidence to Congress and the honeymoon with the Administration can show signs of an early disillusionment. Much legislation is being discussed. Weather remains dreadful. Utilities are pressured. There can be great dissatisfaction about economic cutbacks in the larger cities. Cities are going to have to be seeking federal handouts again—seriously, this time.

March: Trouble brews in the Middle East. Oil talks won't register progress. There can be some street uprisings in Spain, Portugal, and across the Middle East. Things come to some kind of standstill in London; the old traditions can be shaken and the British Cabinet can waver—either because of some activity in Northern Ireland or because the IRA, denied bombing privileges in Northern Ireland through increased British-United States cooperation on the matter of importation of weapons, might build up military activity within England itself. The Greek government seems to be less entrenched, with monarchism no more dead in Greece than it is in Bavaria, France, Italy, and Austria. Foreign nations tamper with United States currency and there can be some rumors of devaluation. Expect a lot of talk about civil service reform, but any move to cancel legislation by which civil servants benefit will reap a fierce backlash.

April: The French and Italian governments can show greater clout for the time being. Royal romance can surface in Europe and give Great Britain some kind of national breather—resulting in a resurgence of the old "Buy British" code. Change hits high gear in Washington and elsewhere in the world. Adverse Uranus-Saturn aspects can hit the United States economy hard and suggest that the calm in England, France, and Italy is that before the storm. The world seems to be sitting on its usual powder keg. Troop movements can be in the news. There can be confrontations between Washington and Moscow, Moscow and Peking; people are doing what nobody said they would or could do. There are the stirrings of revolt where people are subjugated. New Delhi, North Africa, Cambodia, Laos, Viet Nam, even China itself can know street uprisings, the desire of the people for change, improvement, correction.

The entire March-April period has to be considered a time of mounting tension. Is Moscow out to test the clout of Washington? This isn't a good time for any summit conferences but one may have to be called. At home, there can be some surprising changes in the Cabinet. Wall street may have to turn increasingly to astrology as a result of its own poor economic forecasts.

May: Wealth production can step up in the United States. Israel and Ireland, also Greece and Cyprus, can feel the impact as Mercury resumes direct movement in Taurus on the 14th. The Kremlin vacillates and prevaricates. Great Britain is spurred by new leadership to attempt improvement and correction of her many economic woes. France and Italy are showing unusual imagination in the way they are approaching some local disturbances. Uranus retrogrades in Scorpio, away from that awful point of combust with Saturn in Leo. In Washington, Congress can prove innovative, inventive. The Supreme Court seems to be reversing itself again.

Also during May, airlines can report that they are in trouble again, in need of more national subsidies. New currency scandals can hit the fan in large financial centers of the world. There can be new revelations about industrial payoffs abroad and much talk of legislation to stop this practice. The old talk about tax relief is a thing of the past. Government moves to take more of the taxpayer's dollar.

June: Wealth production is stepped up in the United States. Management takes better charge; citizen responsibility is evoked. The United States can take stronger stands in its relationships with the rest of the world, including Soviet Russia. Employment figures can be better this month. New fashions are popular. Young women, who have been letting their hair hang free as though they were on the sunny side of puberty, will now begin putting it up again as their grandmothers did when they were fifteen. Braiding was a mark of maturity; today's long hair marks the prolongation of childhood—another indication of the youth-orientation of the American people. Travel increases, with a strong accent on seeing America first again this year; the government's reluctance to have Americans take cold cash out of the country will result in many having trouble getting passports. There can be new scandals about the heavy waves of illegal immigration into the United States and about the black market in passports; greater caution will be required on the part of those who issue passports. News may surface about the black market in adoptions, the easy issuance of diplomas which lack credibility, and the possibility that people across the country are practicing professions without being truly qualified to practice them. It can be a month of weird stories and scandals.

July: Legislation held up earlier in the year can now be passed. Jupiter, Mars, and Venus, all moving in the national ascendant, favor the United States economy and can foster a period of good feelings across the country. But some residue of the earlier Saturn-Uranus combust can still be dominating where disaffected types gather in large numbers. Scandals about the increasing use of hard drugs can be in the news this month. Real estate can be doing much better than earlier in the year. Air and transportation stocks look good. The early harvest is promising.

August: Jupiter moves into the wealth-production house of the U.S. national chart and the year can really begin to show an upswing in the economy and employment. The retrogression of Mercury in Virgo can present unanticipated problems with the harvest and new wheat deals with Eastern Europe can be in the news. Starvation is reported again in Asia and Africa. There can be some domestic and agricultural crises in the United States this month. Weather can be freakish. New oil discoveries can be in the news now. The economy of Western Europe is pressured. Nations report bankruptcies again—Italy and Great Britain in the lead. Insidious, hard-to-pinpoint taxation irks the American people. The new fiscal year hasn't brought the promotions and increases in salaries that many Americans anticipated.

September. The Administration shows a hard nose in its relationship with Congress and troublemaking third-world nations. Production rates in factories tend to be slow. The need for replacement equipment and parts can be stringent. There can be some food shortages in the supermarkets. Inflation is a problem again. Work goes forward at mid-month, and the Jupiter-Mars conjunction in Cancer buttresses the U.S. economy for the remainder of the year, these transiting planets passing over the position of natal Venus, Jupiter, and the Sun in the national horoscope. Some markets that were lost or almost lost overseas can be regained by American business. There can be evidence of greater rapproachement with Communist China. Income can rise slightly this month for many Americans; there can be much talk of more progressive legislation than this Administration wants to supervise. Workers want more periodic increases to match the stepped-up rate of inflation, which nobody admitted was growing last year when national elections were in the offing.

October: Supreme Court decisions can capture the headlines; they are marked by conservatism. There can be rebellion where people are held under restraint this month. Jupiter goes retrograde in Cancer; Venus and Mercury make their Libra ingress, Mercury rushes through Libra and reaches Scorpio on the 22nd. The month has an unusually fast pace to it. The entertainment world can show its more romantic face this month. Royal marriages are in the news. France and Italy show clout in the way they face up to disturbing internal matters: demonstrations, people in the streets shouting demands. Marriage as an institution is more popular than it has been for a long time. Colleges can report falling enrollments; private schools will be seeking federal assistance. Currency and investment scandals can hit the headlines.

November: Saturn makes its Virgo ingress, and national crises get primary attention. Transportation disasters and teamster-union scandals are to the fore. There can be another round of hijacking. Relationships with South American countries can be improved this month. Many innovations mark the celebration of Thanksgiving. There can be a great burst of unexpected, spontaneous travel. New treaties can be in the making. There may be a break in old deadlocks in the Middle East. Old revolutionary theories from the 1930's in Spain, Portugal, and even parts of Africa will resurface. King Juan Carlos can and must show a strong face now. His grandfather always called himself the cork in the explosive Spanish bottle of beer; Juan Carlos can prove a good national cork now and in the immediate future.

December: Everything slows down this month. The

stock market can do some major wavering. Saturn assumes apparent retrograde movement on the 12th. So does Mercury in Capricorn, and Mars goes erratic on the 13th. Fires, arson, explosions, natural and unnatural disasters can hit the headlines. Earthquakes and freakish weather are possibilities. There are many unexpected events now, some of them possibly quite violent. Fortunately, Mars goes retrograde before it becomes combust with Uranus, but the adversity here casts a shadow over the close of 1977 and the beginning of 1978. Markets fluctuate widely over December, a month of uncertainty with many ill-founded rumors in the national capital and indeed in the world. There can be a lot of grumbling now about inflated prices in department stores. There can be special sales later on in December in order to lure back reluctant shoppers and buyers. Talk of war can surface as the year closes and many Americans will want to see their beloved country flex its military muscles more. Still, nobody anyplace wants war, and the confrontations of 1977 can make everybody edgy, particularly as the Prince of Peace arrives again.

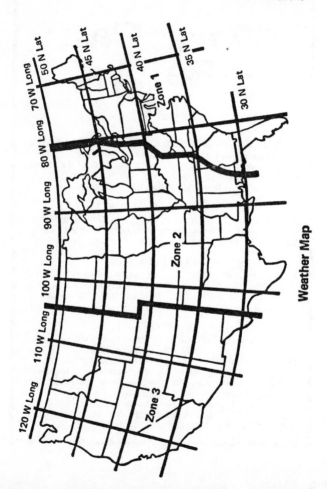

Weather Map

Weather
Forecast
Francis J. Socey

The 1977 weather forecast focuses on the areas of the United States within the boundaries shown on the map on page 328. The sparse information for areas outside these boundaries makes forecasting for them much less accurate. For each month there is a brief description of the general weather around the world according to the position of the various planets.

Zone 1. Eastern Canada, New England, Middle Atlantic and South Atlantic States and Florida.

January. New Moon on January 19th at 8:11 am CST (14:11 GMT). Generally speaking, there will be much activity with Venus square to both the nadir and azimuth and within 2 degrees of Pluto. These positions bring maximum moisture near Honolulu, Hawaii; maximum mildness and winds—or extremes of temperature changes—near Peiping, China. There are Neptunian influences in western China, while the severest weather is in west central Siberia.

Cold periods will be prevalent near the 10th through the 12th, followed by sharply rising temperatures with cloudiness and rain or snow from the southern Great Plains to the Middle Atlantic States. Again, sharp temperature changes will follow during the cold period from near the 23rd through the 26th with dangerous gales and heavy rain or snow over New England into the Middle Atlantic region. In general, the period from the 23rd through the 26th will be memorable for the severity of the weather.

February. The New Moon occurs on February 17th at 9:37 pm CST (3:37 GMT). With Mars, Mercury and the Sun so very close to nadir position, the maximum influence of these volatile planets will be felt in the zone.

The usual build of high pressure in Bermuda will be of greater strength during the period after the 17th to insure a severe contrast of weather. This will be especially true in eastern North America.

Uranus' maximum influence is near 5W, on Hawaii; Saturn's is in eastern China—the cold Siberian winds dominate to make all Aleutian low-pressure systems more active.

Watch for the influence of milder Jupiter over western Russia. The moist Venus in the dry atmosphere of Aries will influence spring prospects for the large grain and vegetable crops of the region. Jupiter in Taurus gives indications of extremes in mildness and rainfall west of Moscow.

Weather systems will be very active along the Atlantic zone after the 17th through the 21st under the influence of aspects between Mercury, Neptune and Saturn. The remainder of the month will be nearly normal except for a few cold days near the 2nd under the influence of Saturn.

Storm centers will be more northerly because of the high-pressure area in Bermuda that will have a major influence over the east coast south of Cape Hatteras, North Carolina.

March. The New Moon occurs on March 19th at 12:33 pm CST (18:33 GMT), with the unpredictable Pluto at nadir position. Pluto indicates weather that is difficult to forecast accurately. Strange precipitation conditions and temperature ranges are always expected. This is true during the days after the 19th.

Cold periods near the 6th, 8th and 11th will be followed by milder weather after the 12th through the 15th and typical March weather during the remainder of the month. Variety and extremes will be the theme.

Planetary patterns will be very localized; for example, Uranus will be near 53W, indicating storm centers and places where systems become stationary because of blocking action; Neptune, near 18W, so that England will experience cool, light rains and snows and a measure of fog; Venus over western China will bring rains that insure a good crop, in contrast to Jupiter over Tokyo, indicating that mildness and a lighter amount of precipitation could bring trouble to the southern islands.

The weather of North America will be very difficult to forecast because of the variety of departures from normality in rainfall and temperatures—quite a mixed picture.

April. New Moon on April 18th at 4:33 am CST (10:35 am GMT). This is the month when the air becomes warmer, the days grow longer and the prospects of having less snow are greater. Such prospects this month are not that promising. This month will be an average April in all respects.

April is the month when rain and snow are generally deposited in shower activity. Over North America the maximum precipitation will be over the South Atlantic States, while precipitation of a showery nature will be found over northern areas, in contrast to the milder and lighter amounts over the Rockies and Pacific Coast.

Temperatures will be nearly normal everywhere except in the region west of the Rockies.

Contrasting weather will be noticed over Europe, especially in areas under the influence of Uranus, such as the area just east of Moscow. There will also be a fickle and unpredictable pattern over central Europe. Damage to grain and fruit crops will be expected in Eurasia.

May. The New Moon occurs on May 17th, at 8:51 pm CST (2:51 GMT). This month there will

be excessive rains and severe storms in the Ohio
Valley that will bring the rivers to above flood stage.
When Venus' conjunction with Mars on the 17th is followed on the 17th by the trine of each to Neptune there
will be a disastrous period. The same strong rain and
storm period will occur near the latitude of the western
Aleutians. Earth tremors will be felt in Japanese islands at
this time.

Again, western Russia will be dominated by stormy
periods with cold winds that will be a hindrance to crops
in much of its western lands. Saturn will be the dominant
influence.

Uranus over the China seas will be very rough on
shipping because of the increased vigor of the storms of
the season.

June. The New Moon occurs on **June 16th** at 12:23
CST (18:23 GMT). The position of Venus and Mars
within 8 degrees of nadir at Washington on **May 17th**
is too close for comfort for the heavily populated eastern
United States. But to the industrial Ohio Valley and
lower Great Lakes regions, there should be very interesting weather during this period. The rain and resulting
high water, in addition to severe storms and likely
danger of tornados, will be real and frightening. All
of this precipitation will move east during the following days.

Usually, during June there are periods of real heat and
dryness. This is not so this month because there are just
too many aspects between colder planets. Again, though,
the mildness from the southwest will sweep east near the
6th through the **9th**; near the **19th** through the **21st** and
near the **29th** of the month.

July. The New Moon occurs on **July 16th** at 2:37
CST (8:37 GMT). Midsummer season is usually a
warm period such as it was in 1918. This will be
an interesting month after the **16th** because of the action

of Mercury conjunct Saturn over the corn and wheat belt in North America. A sharp, cold high-pressure system should move across the northern Great Plains through the Great Lakes and into New England through the Middle Atlantic region, preceded by sharp lines of thunderstorms and somewhat lower temperatures. It will be cold enough for frost in the northern climes.

Milder periods will be near the 2nd through the 4th; the 6th through the 8th; the 11th through the 14th and again near the 28th. Cool periods near the 17th through the 22nd and the 25th through the 27th will be real chillers.

Eastern Europe and western Russia will again be under the influence of Neptune, which insures cloudiness, light rain and fog.

August. The end of the summer season is near but the weather over this zone will be close to the seasonal average in both precipitation and temperature. The New Moon occurs at 3:31 pm CST (21:31 GMT) on the 14th.

In general, the wildest of the weather will be over eastern Europe, from eastern Germany to the Ural Mountains; all of the elements will have maximum effect. Western Europe will be hot and, for the most part, rather dry for the season. Some real heat records will be broken near August 13th and again near the 19th, when Mercury has moderate to strong aspect to Mars and Jupiter.

Hurricanes will come very close to the Atlantic Coast under the influence of Uranus at the azimuth, but their direction will be difficult to predict.

September. This is the month of the hurricanes that strike eastern North America. The number of such storms will be increased this year by just a few more. The assumption of the influence of sunspots and solar radiation on the number of hurricanes will be established as true. The most severe hurricanes this year will be in the southeast, rather than near New England waters.

Uranus, making severe storms, will have a concentrated effect to the west of Chicago, near 97W near the 15th, 20th, and 30th.

The Venus and Saturn conjunction near 166W always brings colder weather with rain and storminess. Watch the Aleutian low-pressure center action.

European weather now will at last settle so that the fruits of the harvest may be gathered after all of the fluctuation of the elements during the past months.

October. The New Moon occurs on October 12th at 2:31 pm CST (20:31 GMT). Once again the time is near when colder weather increases in frequency. This October will be milder in the southeastern states and Florida, near normal in the Middle Atlantic area and progressively cooler in Canada (except Newfoundland and Nova Scotia; they will have temperatures a bit above normal).

All of eastern Canada into the Middle Atlantic States will have light to moderate precipitation this month.

Major aspects will be infrequent this month; an important one, though, is Mercury square Sun followed by Mercury square Mars. The first brings a rapid rise in temperatures and, when followed by the second within a few days—by the 21st—indicates a surge of colder air from central Canada bringing frost to northern portions. Another period of colder weather with rain or snow will be the 27th, when Mercury is parallel to Uranus and Venus is sextile to Neptune. These aspects will be most effective in northern areas but some relief can be expected from the mildness over the southeast.

November. The New Moon occurs on November 11th at 1:09 am CST (7:09 GMT). This will be a very interesting month after the 11th across the United States and Canada because of the positions of Neptune, Mercury and the Sun. The aspects formed to and between these planets will move vigorously over the Ohio Valley east to the Atlantic Coast.

Temperatures will be mild over the Atlantic Coast but colder over New England and eastern Canada.

Precipitation will be light except near southern Georgia and Florida.

A reversal of the usual wet Asian weather will be noticed over China. Jupiter over China will bring mild temperatures and a tendency toward dryness (at least compared to the usual monsoon season). Many of the typhoons will move over southern Viet Nam and Japan rather than China.

December. The New Moon occurs on **December 10th** at 11:33 am CST (17:33 GMT). Jupiter is at nadir position near 81W for maximum effect, producing a milder trend in temperature, lighter precipitation and slower pressure movements.

Mercury, Saturn and Mars will become stationary in their movements on the 12th and the 13th so that they in turn will influence the changes of the movements and degree of intensity of the elements for the coming month(s). Good references to past Decembers for a study of the elements are: December 6, 1934; November 23rd, 1946; and December 10th, 1958—when the New Moon occurred very close to the time it does during the present month. The definite difference is the position of Jupiter at the nadir in the present chart.

December is always a colder month, with the sweeping of high-pressure systems south from western Canada and the increase of the snow line toward the Middle Atlantic States.

Saturn over western Europe designates a cold region and, with Uranus to the east over eastern Russia, there may be reports of severe weather in Siberia.

Mars near Great Britain will bring many days of fog, and misty, low wind flow that will hamper air travel except in Scotland.

Mercury at exact nadir over Peiping will bring substantial movement of cold air from the interior against the tropical air to the south, so watch for heavy rain and storms over the interior. The same will be true for Japan.

Christmas season does not promise snow for the western European countries but it will bring surprise packages for North America.

Zone 2. Central Canada, Great Lakes, Ohio Valley, Gulf States and all Great Plains.

January. For the most part, the weather this month will be typical winter weather, with rain and snow. The bending of the aspects will be influential in the increase in intensity of cold weather. High-pressure systems this month will be very intense, and their contrast with the deeper low-pressure systems moving east and northeast from the Gulf of Mexico promises real records as to the amount of precipitation that will follow. Such periods will be near the 2nd, during the 10th through the 11th, near the 24th and again near the 29th. Each of these periods of maximum strength will be most severe near dates of perigee.

The storms from the Pacific Northwest and the Gulf of Mexico will contain phenomenal precipitation, bearing qualities in the Gulf States and lower Tennessee Valley that compare with the cold winds from central Canada, primarily in the last period of the month. The contrast, to the warming qualities of Mercury, by Mars will be made manifest near the 11th by an ice storm near the Ohio Valley region.

February. Cloudiness will be above normal this month, resulting in many periods of light precipitation except during days near the 16th through the 21st, when maximum storminess will be noted. Waves of southern mildness with seasonal rain and snow will cover the region from the Ohio Valley to the Gulf of Mexico early in the month.

From near the 4th through the 9th there will be a period of changeableness when cloudiness, light precipitation and fog will be quite normal before a period of mildness and contrasting conditions gains sway near the 12th through the 14th. A deep storm will form in the southwest at this time. Watch for tornado danger in the deep south.

March. March is the month when tornado danger increases. This is especially so in the Southern Plains States —Texas, Oklahoma and nearby states. This year will see another season (possibly an abnormally large number) of them occur after the 16th through the 19th and again near the 25th. These periods will be especially dangerous because of the many aspects of Mercury to the colder planets. Wind storms will stir the dust, and the contrast of the cold winds from the north with the warmer winds from the south will be dangerous. Many low-pressure systems will sweep from the central Rockies to the deep south before their normal swing to the north and northeast. Precipitation in all respects will be sporadic, but it will be heavier in eastern portions of this zone.

Western Canada will be wet with greater amounts of rain and snow just ahead of all sweeping cold spells in the south. Such cold spells will occur near the 1st, 8th and the 23rd.

April. Cold as well as warm days will continue this month but such days will become more infrequent in the south. Snow will continue to be seasonal in the northern plains. The weather will become drier; only the immediate Gulf of Mexico coast and Louisiana will have excessive moisture, and the immediate Mississippi River valley will be near average in precipitation. There is a danger of dryness and growing mildness near the end of the month in western areas. Local severe storms will move north and east into the Southern Plains but such storms will not be so concentrated as they were during March. In all respects, this month will be a bit drier and milder, especially in the south and west.

May. This zone will contain the most noteworthy weather during May. Venus and Mars and their relation to Neptune will make the news after the 17th. There will be an unusual possibility of major flooding east of Chicago, Illinois during the latter part of the month. Heavy snow in eastern Canada and the previous rains in the United States within the Ohio Valley and Tennessee will make news because of the amount of precipitation and the duration of the storms.

Consequently there will be a great range of temperatures within this zone because of the conflict of heat and cold expected now. Temperatures will be very sharp, and the changes pronounced. Western areas are expected to be drier and colder, except near Nebraska, where the warm air from the south will meet the colder air from western Canada.

June. The influence of Venus on Mars will remain until after the June 7th conjunction, when Venus continues to move faster than Mars. During this time the rain and heat will become less excessive.

Temperature and precipitation will be above normal over the Hudson Bay through the Ohio Valley and below normal over the eastern Gulf States and the lower Great Plains (except Texas).

After the 22nd of June temperature and windfall will become tropical and more normal. The growth of grain crops will stop in western regions because of the moisture, though it will be normal in the east.

July. This is one of the most critical crop-growing months of the year within this region. Mercury and Saturn will be the major influences this month after the 16th.

Mercury's influence on weather, with that of Saturn, always brings heavy storms with hail, local tornado danger and frequently heavy rains. Somewhat colder weather follows so that heat waves are broken and more pleasant weather follows. Watch for very severe storms near the

20th over many portions of this zone. Damage to grain and fruit crops will be heavy locally.

Weather this month will be similar to that of July, 1918, and will continue well into August. Temperatures will be seasonal, but sudden changes in the north will keep them lower than over the Southern Plains. The precipitation will be spotty and lighter than normal except on the coast of the Gulf of Mexico. Canadian areas will be windy and unseasonably cold.

August. This month will not receive maximum heat until near the 12th, when Mercury makes a favorable aspect to Mars, and then again near the 19th through the 21st to continue until near the 25th. Only short and weak cooler interludes will interrupt the continued northern movement of heat from a very warm Southern Plains.

Precipitation levels will be slightly below normal over most of the zone with only some readings slightly above normal in the northern Great Lakes and portions of the deep Southeast. Temperatures will be above normal in western areas and slightly below normal in Canada and the Great Lakes.

September. The first surge of colder air comes south from central Canada. Each thrust will be stronger and will move farther south near the 1st, 8th, 14th, 18th and the 30th since Uranus will be at nadir near 97W.

The harvest will be close to completion at an early date this year because of the frequent storms and cold snaps that move south and east during the above dates. Precipitation will be very unusual in its distribution but temperatures will be below normal in the Northern Plains to the Ohio Valley and milder from Texas to Alabama.

True, this is the month of maximum hurricane intensity; all coastal areas will be under the threat of heavy rains and high winds.

Frost and early freeze will reach the Great Lakes and lower Northern Great Plains near the 20th and there will be subsequent cooling farther south.

October. All planetary aspects will again be at a wide angle to this region. The constant movement of low-pressure systems from the lower Great Plains moving northeast will insure milder-than-normal temperatures over the lower Ohio Valley to the Gulf of Mexico and the Central Plains States through Texas, while the prospects of rainfall are somewhat different.

Texas and the Mississippi Valley will be close to normal in rains; much of the Southeast and western Plains will be very close to normal to a bit below. This is usually the case because of the slow change in seasonal trends.

The warmest period of the month will be near the 16th through the 20th.

November. With Mercury and Neptune exerting maximum influence over the Prairie states, there is a possibility of considerable light moisture and winds. Watch for severe storminess east of the Rockies and western Gulf of Mexico.

Precipitation may be excessive from the eastern Gulf of Mexico and along the mountains into western New York, while deficient in the northwestern Plains into central Canada.

November is usually a quiet month given to considerably cool nights and unsettled days. During this month there are no concentrated stormy periods but near the 13th through the 16th a mild session will take place that could be labeled as Indian Summer. There will be a cold period near the 21st through the 25th.

December. With Jupiter very close to the nadir position at New York and the remainder of the planetary influence over Europe and western Asia, much of the significant weather activity will be concentrated in those regions. Eastern Russia and western Siberian areas will have good prospects for snow but southern areas will suffer from a freeze that will damage crops. Heavy rains and snowstorms will visit China and Japan this month.

The central United States will have nearly normal rain and snow but the southern Great Plains and Gulf of Mexico will be deficient in both, since many of the high-pressure systems will sweep far to the south but modify quickly the weather changes so that mildness and considerable cloudiness will result. This will be an unhealthy month in many respects because of the changeable weather.

Zone 3. Western Canada, Rocky Mountain States, Southwest and Pacific Coast.

January. Jupiter, stationed near 105W for maximum strength, should insure a milder and drier region, especially over southern regions for most of the month after the 19th. Fortunately, the greater portion of the earlier days will have seasonal amounts of rain and snow. The storms from the waters of southern Alaska will be very heavy in rain and snow and will move from western Canada into the deep Rockies rather frequently this month. The cold winds over the central states and states east of the continental divide will keep those areas drier than expected. Watch for record cold weather being modified by these storms so that the eastern Rockies and the western Great Plains will have alternating stormy and cold weather within a short period of time. The regions will be narrow but their records will be long standing. The severe period will occur a day or so earlier than the corresponding one in the east.

Again, this month will be quite different from the last month of the present winter in the severity of the weather and the length of such severity.

February. A variety of weather will be noted, with much fog and storminess and heavy periods of rain and snow that may cause much flooding and many mud-slides in southern portions near the Pacific Coast. Inland there will be above-normal rain and snow west of the continental divide.

Severe weather near the 12th will be noted in the form of a strong storm system within this zone, indicating a danger of very cold air moving south over the northern portion of this zone. The period from the 16th through the 23rd will be the coldest part of the winter for much of North America.

Under the influence of Uranus the storms over Alaskan waters will insure the maximum flow of moist air over western North America.

March. Saturn between Hawaii and the Pacific Coast brings cooler and damp air into the Rockies, especially near the 16th and again near the 26th through the 30th for active periods.

March is always a month of unusual weather, with more than the usual amounts of rain and snow over western Canada into Oregon. The above-mentioned periods are critical because excess precipitation may be expected over large areas; continued movements of both low- and high-pressure systems should be rapid. Before the 16th, the weather will be very unsettled and difficult to forecast since the pressure systems will be weaker when they enter the western United States so that cloudiness and fog will be maximum.

April. Spring always brings mildness, but it does not always bring dryness as it promises this year within this zone. Still, a little of both will be welcome after the months of so much rain and snow. Coastal fog and cloudiness will be frequent, and the Southwest will be rather warm with temperature readings over 90°. Moisture will be above the seasonal norm in the northern Rockies and deficient in southern portions, where the moisture of the Pacific coast will be sufficient.

Coastal storms will be less severe but will be good providers of rain and snow over Washington and Oregon and into northern California. The cold period near **the 15th** will generate the danger of frost in Nevada and Utah, and also northern California.

Mercury and Jupiter will be dominant factors in the influence of weather over this zone.

May. Again, this is the month when pressure systems move more to the north across Washington to the Great Lakes and the southern areas become warmer and drier in nature.

After May 17th, with the influence of Mars and Venus, the warm winds from the Southwest will move more to the north than usual for a few days and conflict with the cooler air to the north. Watch for substantial rain and storms near Oregon through southern Wyoming.

Neptune square to nadir at San Francisco indicates that cloudiness, fog and very light drizzle will be covering that area for much of the month. The fog may be a very serious detriment to shipping in all waters south of Alaska.

June. This month is always expected to be a very warm period, since by now summer has begun and a range of maximum influences should be felt. This month will be no exception. More than the normal number of southern hurricanes will come close to Hawaiian waters and there will be an unusual southern dip of storms south of Alaska. Coastal waters will be unsettled, but cloudiness and fog will be above normal. Inland, the Rockies will be cool and wet over Montana but dry to the south. Range lands will be in need of moisture; there is a serious possibility of a critical water shortage in the Southwest and California.

July. Both Mercury and Saturn are so close to Denver, Colorado that maximum cold and windy weather with preceding storms, many with hail and heavy rains, will be frequent after July 16th.

Montana and the northern Rockies will be very cool with many areas of heavy precipitation. Snow will fall in high elevations and temperatures may reach unusually low readings deep into Wyoming and Colorado in contrast to the drier and very warm southern states.

Concentration of heat inland from the coast and coastal dryness is promised by the actions of the Sun, at nadir near San Francisco, and Mars, square to this zone. These contrasting elements of weather will make news this month.

August. Once again there will be a general concentration of mildness from western Canada well into the Pacific coast states to the Southwest. Only the area from east of the Rockies to the eastern Plateau will continue to be cool and wet. Summer thunderstorms will only bring local relief. Widespread relief will precede the southern movements of expected cold air on very few occasions near the 3rd, 8th and the 27th.

Typhoon activity will be very strong and destructive in Chinese waters this month. The Philippines will be visited by very bad storms. A major earthquake will visit both central China and the region just west of Japan. A volcano will become violent also within the Aleutians and northern Japan. Rainfall will be heavy and the summer heat unbearable in China.

September. As they usually do during a change from a warm to a cooler season, the pressure systems alter their course to a more northerly direction. This will be a very changeable month, especially after the 13th, in all respects.

All aspects between the Sun and the planets at this time will be of primary importance over western Canada into the central Rockies so that the temperature range until October 10th will be above normal for most of the Rockies and west central Canada, with only coastal areas being cooler.

The precipitation will be extremely variable in nature in the United States but above normal in southern Alaska and western Canada.

October. West to southwest winds will be the chief factor behind this zone's mildness for the remainder of the month, but a different story is expected over Canada and much of Alaska. A deep freeze over Alaska will do harm to southern crops and farming activity.

Rainfall will be light within this zone except for a bit in the Northwest Pacific states and Alaskan and Canadian waters. No rain will fall in the Southwest or southern California.

All of the planets over this zone are above the horizon so that their effect on the weather is to the southwest, over the ocean areas.

November. November is usually a quiet month, in terms of the weather. This year many of the major planets are within the region of the Sun; thus their elements are forceful. Venus, Uranus and Mercury will add their various elements to make this one of the most interesting months of 1977. Heavy rain and snow may be expected, and storminess may be anticipated near the 9th, 22nd and, to a lesser extent, near the 30th.

The major aspect that will have the greatest effect within this region will be Venus conjunct Uranus over the eastern Pacific coast states and Mercury conjunct Neptune over the western Plains states. These two aspects on the same day will bring severe weather within those regions for a few days. There will be an early heavy rain and snowstorm, and tornado danger in the plains below Nebraska.

December. With no major planets within this zone, December will be a very unusual month because of the unusual weather expected over large areas of western North America and Alaska.

Temperature and rainfall patterns will be very varied in many portions of this zone. Heavy rain will fall along all coasts; above normal, in western Canada; below normal, in the Southwest; and near normal, elsewhere.

The temperatures will be cool, for the most part, with

the greatest departures from this trend over eastern portions and the Plateau states with the temperatures in the Southwest states and southern Alaska being milder than normal.

Seasonal Forecasts
Spring
Zone 1. March 20, 1977 at 11:43 am CST (17:43 GMT). This promises to be an unusual spring season in that variety will be a major portion of it. Uranus, the storm breeder, is found over the Atlantic near 41W so that those storms that reach western Europe will spread cool, misty and foggy weather for a number of days. Western Europe will have a generally cool season because of the colder winds from the ocean.

One of the most vital areas on Earth for vital crop growth is indicated by the position of Mars east of Moscow near 66E. The weather here will be terrible, with extremes in temperature that will do much damage to grain cover.

The most interesting locale will be China, where the Sun, Mercury, Moon and Venus will bless the land with the best of everything. Still, there may be too much moisture in the southern monsoon lands for proper growth.

All of the eastern United States will be feeling the results of a blockage of weather systems because of the storms over the ocean.

Zone 2. The strong movements of high pressure from northwestern Canada will bring cold and a high probability of heavy rains to the eastern Great Lakes down through Alabama and the western Gulf of Mexico, while cold will also be prevalent in most of the northern Great Plains and west central Canada.

Zone 3. Again Saturn will influence Alaska and western

Canada and, to a lesser degree, the western portions of the United States from 130W, with very nasty weather. Only the deep Southwest will be warm and dry.

Summer

Zone 1. June 21st, 6:14 am CST (12:14 GMT). This promises to be a season of events very much like the spring. The stormy portions will be a bit more to the west (near 55W) with subsequent movement of blocking action westward.

This will be a strange season in that the planets have their major influence in very definite localities on the Earth, none of which are of a disastrous nature. Even Mercury and Jupiter cover no land areas with their dryness—except near the northwestern Canadian coast. But Venus and Mars, near Tokyo, Japan, in a position indicating heat and moisture, will actually be disastrous, since the faster planets are moving away from major positions.

Actually, the eastern portions of North America will have a variety of weather that will make it difficult to do accurate forecasting for any long periods during this season.

Zone 2. The summer is usually hot and dry, and the coastal areas are usually moist. This is true for this season, and it will be much like the summer of 1915, with adjustments for the difference in time.

No major planets are present this summer. The intensity of the elements will be so close to typical seasonal values that no extremes will be expected except the heat.

Zone 3. The influence of Saturn and the Moon within the western portions of this zone will be keen. Saturn always brings storms and cold weather; the Moon, slow, easy rains, light winds and cool conditions to reinforce the actions of Saturn. Watch it and weep, along coasts and inland northern waters.

Autumn

Zone 1. Autumn begins on September 22 at 9:20 pm CST (3:22 GMT). Mercury, Venus and Saturn, within 10 degrees of the nadir position (80-85W), will indicate areas of maximum action just four days after they are in conjunction. Watch the area near Miami and 5 degrees westward for weather news of major importance during the following days, when Mercury moves into a conjunction with the Sun for the building of a strong high-pressure system in Bermuda. This will be a very interesting season for eastern North America since contrasting weather for a wet autumn is almost guaranteed.

Such a contrast to the position of Uranus, west of Moscow, again, at the end of the harvest and the important time of planting grains for the winter, will be vital. Press reports will tell the story of the weather in full. Neptunian rains will be heavy over eastern Poland and areas to the north and south.

Zone 2. Saturn and Venus are very close to the nadir position at Chicago so that colder winds and low-pressure trends may be expected, from west central Canada down through the Alabama area, feeding very serious weather over the east coast. At least the serious weather will be to the east of all grain-producing areas so that the harvest, though smaller than usual, may be completed.

Zone 3. All areas near 116W will be very warm and dry with the actions of Jupiter and Mars at maximum strength. This will be a record season for heat to the west of the Rockies; the heat will be somewhat tempered to the east. Storm centers will be shunted far to the north so that most of the precipitation will appear over Alaska and northwestern Canada and weather will be more nearly normal elsewhere.

Winter

Zone 1. Winter begins on December 21st at 5:24 pm

CST (23:24 GMT), with a repeat of the weather of this spring and summer over this region.

Once again the individual planets are well spaced for activity within certain boundaries. The same type of weather may be expected over the eastern portions of North America as those areas experienced during the past spring and summer. There will be a confusion in the forecasting of the elements.

Western Europe and the British Isles will be very wet with Venus, Mercury and the Sun at nadir position. Record-breaking rain, snow and sleet will be very common there. Generally speaking, all of Europe will be wet with snow in colder climes and rains to the south. Polar air will bring freezing temperatures and winds to make blizzards galore.

Sweeping cold air from polar North America will sweep south to bring constant high pressure over the Southeast and Florida. There is a danger of fruit and vegetable freeze.

Zone 2. The spilling of cold air into the Rockies will be less severe than the colder air to the east. Saturn over the western Plains will bring little rain and snow to the south but normal weather to the north. There will be little chance to protect grain crops to keep them from freezing.

Zone 3. Near 128W Mars will be centered so that tropical air will be dominant along the coast; temperatures will be definitely mild to the east but maximum along the coast. Weather in Alaska will be milder; storms will occur more northerly than usual, accompanied by heavy precipitation. Cold waves will be shunted to the east before moving south through Canada.

What the Economy Holds in Store

Charles M. Bradlaw

Economically, the year 1977 will be one of slow recovery, inflationary spirals inherent in the system, fitful rises and declines in the stock market, and increased spending for military preparedness—mostly in the area of unuseable and quickly obsolete hardware. Increasingly, it will be a year when the technology for making money will be available but blocked by one or more factors, such as nature-loving antipollutionists or a lack of investment capital. It will be a year when the power pendulum swings even more from the Northeast to the Sunbelt States. More Americans than ever will be employed, because more and more Americans will be entering the job market, but, by the same token, the unemployment rate will be disastrously high.

The Winter Season

As early as February 24, 1977, the economy will be assaulted by the severe squares between Uranus in Scorpio and Saturn in Leo. These will hit local transportation, hard-core unemployment, labor unions, the home construction business, school-building programs and the cost of maintaining public as well as private schools exceptionally hard. Rising over late February and throughout March is the Uranus-Saturn conflict that will result in increased medical and hospital costs. In the US national horoscope (July 4, 1776; 2:17 am, Philadelphia), this

Uranus-Saturn explosion involves the third and sixth houses.

Saturn has been a damper on the US national economy for over four years as it moved across the ascendant of the national horoscope and through the second house of wealth production. Its squares to Uranus during 1975 and 1976 harried the stock market, driving it down from its 1,000 points almost as soon as it attained that average. It devastated the real estate and home construction markets, eroded the savings of the elderly, who are so strongly ruled by Saturn, and it fed the fires of inflation, which have been a fact of life ever since Neptune entered Sagittarius. Moving in Leo, Saturn invited drought and crop destruction; again, during late February and throughout March, 1977, it will block those Uranus-ruled cure-alls that the administration will advance from time to time.

The year opens with the lunar north node at 29 Libra, the exact degree of Libra where the destructive solar eclipse of October 23, 1976 took place, with its nefarious consequences for the election processes and the weak administration that will be inaugurated in January, 1977. The New Moon of January 19th rises in Capricorn, the sign that rules the incoming chief of state and the role that he will be called upon to play. So, he will commence his term of office with much good will. Mars in Capricorn gives him plenty of clout at the outset, but the Saturn-Uranus squares of late February signify a short honeymoon with the other two branches of government. The fierce solar eclipse of October 23rd, 1976 in 29 Libra and the resumption of that thread on January 1, 1977 by the dragon's head of the zodiac warn against the ultimately costly decisions that the Supreme Court will be making during 1976, 1977 and subsequent years until 1982.

Congress has that charismatic Venus reigning over it as it picks up its cudgels with the executive branch of government—and with the judicial branch, for that matter. A somewhat spiritual renaissance can make prayer-in-the-public-schools and abortion issues explosive between Congress and the judicial branch. Throughout the year, Congress will be whittling away at the executive branch, attempting to get back some of those powers it lost during the past forty-five years.

These matters will be strongly felt in the economic trends holding sway over the winter months of 1977.

There can be labor troubles, a new wave of unemployment, and much slowing down in genuine labor circles and trades around February 18th, when Uranus assumes apparent retrograde movement of the US sixth house. Viral ailments can be prominent at that time and hospital construction can be dragging its feet. Saturn has been retrograde since the beginning of the year, and it is retrograde when these two giants (Saturn and Uranus) enter into mortal conflict.

The Spring Quarter

Hardly has spring arrived when a lunar eclipse takes place midway in Libra. Disenchantment with some new Supreme Court decisions can touch the stock market. This eclipse hits all security markets and since it conjoins natal Saturn in the US national horoscope, it can have a severe impact upon traditional methods of investing, on the way Americans spend their leisure time and on the type of entertainments they seek. The world of entertainment, motels, hotels, expensive restaurants and the fashion industry can all be hit hard by this eclipse's conjunction with natal Saturn.

Fewer Americans will be getting married; fewer babies will be born. These statistics will reflect themselves in the industries associated with weddings, home buying, and all the baby-feeding, -clothing, and -entertaining trades, such as the manufacture of nursery furniture and toys. Ethnic foods, such as pizza, sweet and sour pork, and soul food

will be helped along, however; and with expensive restaurants hard hit over the spring, those hurry-up, simple
chains like Colonel Sanders' and Church's fried chicken
and McDonald's hamburgers will be doing a crash business.

The 1977 picture for oil was largely set by the exact sextiles between Universal Neptune, whose orb is associated
with oil, in Sagittarius, which rules the Arab world, and Pluto
on the cosmic bridge between the East and West at the close
of 1976. Government restrictions are anathema to oil-
seekers this year. Far from getting on to the high road of
lesser dependency upon foreign imports, United States
consumers will be more dependent during 1977 on continued good relationships with Saudi Arabia and Iran.

The oil picture is assaulted by the Jupiter-Neptune
oppositions of early June. Otherwise, the year is rather
uneventful, Uranus helping with the construction of the
Alaskan pipeline over late spring and early summer, and
good news emanating from coastal Scotland, Borneo and
other oil quests in Asia and the United States.

Jupiter makes its Gemini ingress on April 4th but remains in the US twelfth house until the second week of
May, when it crosses the ascendant at 7 Gemini to give
the American people a better picture of themselves and
greater optimism in coping with their economic problems.
Surely, the administration will make some positive and
optimistic declarations in May as transiting Jupiter conjoins natal Uranus in the US national horoscope. Over
the rest of spring, the administration can experience
greater success in its handling of domestic problems than
in its handling of foreign affairs.

Legislation for higher employment rates can get off
the drafting boards during late spring. The government
will be helping the bankrupt cities and picking up many
state tabs. There will be greater spending to teach American youngsters how to read in elementary and high schools

so that they don't show up at college, as they have been doing, without these basic skills. Jupiter's transit of Gemini will help elementary schools and their questionable curricula enormously. It will swing the pendulum back from all the child labor that has been going on in this country during the affluent 1950's and early 1960's to greater leisure time for kids. Jupiter will send teachers back to school and to their textbooks to the end that they will become better teachers.

You can expect the publishers of children's books, of textbooks, and of visual aid materials for teachers to do well. Jupiter will conjoin natal Mars in the US national horoscope early in July and greater amounts of money will be earmarked for elementary schools in the new fiscal year. Private schools can depend on more friendly financial decisions from the Supreme Court during 1977.

There will be an annular eclipse of the Sun in the last decan of Aries on April 18th. Forming in the dungeon of the US horoscope, this eclipse can bring considerable disenchantment and mentally depressing ecomonic trends in military matters. The emphasis can be on the building of unuseable hardware—unuseable in a nuclear age that doesn't dare use this sort of power—and on the building of planes and ships that will be obsolete almost from birth. This eclipse can be difficult on our NATO allies and their economies. Great Britain, a nation ruled by Aries, can be hardest hit of all. The eclipse hits industries using fire and furnaces, manufacturing steel, iron, bronze and copper products. Steel plants, which have had a good 1976, can be hit over the spring of 1977 with many layoffs and cutbacks. The automotive industry, which got off to a good start in 1977, can know declines during late April and then recover toward the close of summer.

Stock market performance during the second half of April can be called lackluster.

In-depth analysis of the spring charts reveals that Washington is strongly bent on maintaining reasonable price stability. Price-setting by the superindustries won't be viewed as the unforgivable sin it was back in the 1960's. Exceptionally moderate financial policies will be prevalent throughout 1977.

The Summer Quarter

Recovery is the word for summer. Jupiter moving away from its opposition to Neptune can revitalize the US economy over summer. The administration is liberated from bureaucratic blockage to a certain degree. Much optimism enters economic thinking and government and big business enjoy a honeymoon. More and more wealth is produced. The employment picture is better than it was earlier in the year.

The Washington administration has a good grip of financial matters as the new fiscal year begins, since the Full Moon of the 1st forms in Capricorn, the sign of chief executives and their national programs. A rather logical budgeting comes to the fore in the nation's capital and in great metropolitan areas like New York. For the first time in years, members of government bureaus are seeing that the money they spend has value, the same value it has when it's in their personal wallets. And with the various bureaus at the federal, state and city levels learning this lesson, citizens will stop thinking that the eagle lays dollar bills for every misbegotten cause that comes along. There are good housekeeping trends seeping down from Washington into state and city administrations.

Although most economic forecasters will be hesitant by early July, mostly because they've been proved so wrong in the past, you can believe that recovery is more and more a fact of life. But you aren't getting back the halcyon economy of the early 1960's. Those days, in a sense, like all of the past, are gone forever. This is a new

world, full of economically alive and ambitous new nations, and the pie that is to be shared is no larger.

Never was the ascendant of the US national chart bus-
ier than it will be at the outset of the new fiscal year. Venus joins Jupiter in Gemini on July 7th, Mars enters this
part of the US national chart on July 18th, and all of these
orbs are in favorable aspect to the Sun, Mercury and
Saturn.

Many new federal programs are going forward. They
are designed to protect economic matters, to keep more
and more employees employed, and to cushion any occasional times of economic stress. A new pioneering spirit
is in the land. The stock market can do pretty well over
July. Stocks associated with defense, Navy and Air Force
materials are recommended. The picture for oil is somewhat improved beneath the surface, but, visibly, there can
be problems and worries since the Gemini orbs are moving
toward opposition aspects with Neptune's orb (associated
with oil) in Sagittarius, the sign that rules most of the oil-
producing nations.

New oil can surface after July 15th, when Uranus resumes direct movement in Scorpio.

Jupiter will make its momentous Cancer ingress in mid-
August. Here is the real guarantee that the economy has
come a long way since the beginning of the year. Fabulous
economic, industrial and stock market gains can be anticipated now, for mighty Jupiter will conjoin our natal Venus by September 2nd and the US national Sun by early
1978. More importantly, before it commences an interval
of fluctuations in Cancer, Jupiter will momentously conjoin the US natal Jupiter on September 18th, making
the period between early September and late November
one of the best for the economy in a long, long time.

Sheer good luck plays a part now. Cooperation between the Washington administration and big business will
be at its best. The administration will have the confidence

of stock market investors. There's a bit of gambling in all of this, for Jupiter's is the orb of chance-taking, of belief in one's self, of enthusiastic and jovial approaches toward earning one's living and investing in the products of the country. Still, the antipollution budgets of many giant industries will be rising. There's plenty of citizen watch-dogging indicated for the July-September interval. There can be some grumbling because many of the products that you use which bear an American brand name will actually have been produced in American plants based abroad, where their production costs are lower because of cheaper labor. This new trend can become something of a very unpopular whipping boy in American thinking. The summer quarter and the second half of 1977 will see many gains in industries related to cosmetics, perfumes, motels, hotels, restaurants, food chain stores and chain restaurants serving ethnic foods. The picture for steel, coal and iron is so-so, but there can be some labor problems forming in steel industries. Furniture manufacturing will do well over the summer. Automotive industries will be registering gains during July and again during late October and early November.

Increases in the price of gasoline will be less than anticipated as this is being written. Iron ores, publishing, home construction, travel industries and agriculture will have a good July, and an even better September-October.

Behind the News Headlines

There are some economic facts of life to be faced. Neptune in Sagittarius is a force indicating continued inflation. In the US sixth house it is a depressant on labor ingenuity and it can continue to promote the increasing elite (and nondemocratic) status of physicians, surgeons, dentists and scientists in general, pushing up the prices of anything that this group is associated with, such as casual medicine, hospitalization and the costs of any long illness. American history is full of incidents where a certain group aspired to elite status and had to be knocked from its ridiculous perch by new legislation. Trusts were busted by Teddy Roosevelt; along came the internal revenue and a dozen other legislative bits to curb the power of the robber baron billionaires. The Security Exchange Commission was passed by FDR to curb the nefarious practices of the big investors, who could practically push the stock market up or down to suit their own whims. Not only economic groups, but certain organizations attempted to be superelite, superpatriotic and super-important; one after the other, they were knocked from their perch, including the white race, which attempted to uphold a million forms of white supremacy. Men had to be knocked from their male chauvinist perches also. Much earlier in our history, we had trouble with the landed gentry; later, with radical farmers in the South and West who attempted a radical form of unity, aimed mostly at the robber baron railroads. First aggressive capitalists and then equally aggressive unions, such as the teamsters, attempted to claim an elite status. Now attention will be given to medical and legal upstarts and their organizations, which have been aiming at forms of extreme domination of our lives, not only by outlandish prices, but by fear tactics and questionable links between their prescriptions and the amount of stock they seem to have in certain pharmaceuticals and medicines.

Watergate went a long way to expose the chicanery built into the US legal mind and systems. The domination of both Houses of Congress by this dubious system is about to be called into greater questioning by the citizens of the United States. These trends are prominent over the second half of 1977. Laws that prevented doctors, lawyers, dentists and even drugstores from advertising and thereby letting the rest of us in on their prices will be off the books and out of the realm of so-called "ethics."

This trend, so strongly seen in the United States throughout its history, by which one group attempts to suborn
democracy and gain some lordly elite status, is related to
the presence of the nefarious dragon's tail in Aquarius in
our national horoscope. When we face up to these matters, the cost of medicine will begin to come down in this
country. Also, the cost of legal services and something of
the mystical chicanery that has entered legal matters in
the US over the past 200 years will become a thing of
the past. These trends can't be underestimated, for they
eventually will give you safer streets and lower security-
protection costs; death from assault on the street will
be less likely when the assaulters are behind bars and some
of their clever lawyers are with them. You will be less and
less at the mercy of questionable medicine when the medical profession is forced to police its own ranks and to
get the malpractitioners out of business. In knocking
medicine and law down to size, you will be permitting
a wider latitude for true democracy in this land and opening up the way for fabulous gains through improved, dedicated science and legislation. These trends will have a
greater impact upon the economies of the future than any
other trends in the US national horoscope.

The Autumn Quarter

Hardly does autumn begin when the Moon is eclipsed
on September 27th. This is a depressant for steel, coal,
iron and most of the heavy industries for the time being.
It can bring some citizen disenchantment (the Moon rules
the people) with the unveiling of past secrets.

It brings home the truth of Henry Ford's once-ques-
tioned statement, "History is bunk." History, of course,
is the distorted picture of what happened, based on prop-
aganda, myths and prejudices of those who made the
history—that is, whatever monarch, dynasty or political
party happened to be in power when many truths were

hidden and tossed away, and facts arranged and rear-
ranged to give you a good picture of what really happened.
From evidence, for example, we know today that while
schools go on teaching that Richard III murdered his ne-
phews in the tower, the murders were actually carried out
by Henry VII, their brother-in-law. Now, by the same
token, the true history of many past American administrations is coming into view. Just as the truth was unpopular
when it was unveiled in England over the past century, so
the truth is somewhat unpopular when it is unveiled in
the United States. But Neptune is unveiling it in the wake
of its exact sextile to Pluto in Libra.

These trends are mentioned here because they have due
impact upon the economy, upon investors. After the middle of 1977, Americans will have to live with certain truths
that run counter to gradeschool history and fairy tales.
The nefarious practices of unions, which accomplished
much good as a kind of byproduct of their weird and evil
links with the underworld, will be exposed. There is here
the beginning of the nadir of labor in this country. Nefarious practices of the federal government, the true story of
the sensational assassinations of the past, the tampering
that has gone on in economic matters, the extent of corruption in high places—all are rather hard to take, in a
sense, over the last four months of 1977; some of them
can send the stock market down, and, in a sense, they
are going to be with us for a long, long time to come.

But it is true that "the truth shall make and keep you
free." Here is the beginning of that national maturity that
always was predicted for the American people once Pluto,
Uranus and Neptune lined up in Libra, Scorpio and Sagittarius and permitted an overview of American history.

There will be a total eclipse of the Sun on October
12th. It will take place in the second half of Libra, where
it will give greater clarity to the matter of gender equality,
the struggle of women for complete liberation, and the

institution of marriage itself. The mistakes that we have been making in trying to legislate greater equality will come to the fore. Sadly, the struggle for greater equality of men perhaps always ends in greater inequality. This certainly is true in Soviet Russia and other Communist countries, where equality of genders, races and religions was the original idea. Equality of the various groupings of people—peasants, the military, government employees, workers in the factories—was the ideal, but there is enormous inequality between all of these classes in Russia today. Now, in late 1977, you will see that the struggle to award greater equality to women generally will result in some new types of discrimination against men. The struggle to award greater equality to blacks and to Spanish-speaking minorities will result in new forms of discrimination against nonblack, non-Spanish-speaking minorities.

Naturally, all of these trends will have enormous impact upon the economy of the second half of 1977 and they will be prevalent over the October-December interval. In any economic forecast, you, the reader, are expected to do some of the work yourself. Publishing space doesn't permit mentioning all the various ways in which the big trends of 1977 can actually touch your purse, but if you think about them you will quickly be able to tie them up with what you are observing in the economy, in the stock market, in the way you must stretch your dollar and meet the costs of food, housing, clothing, etc.

Certainly, you can tie up what the fight for women's equality, the development of new birth-control methods and the popularity of abortion as a form of birth control have done to the market that used to produce baby food, high chairs, cribs, maternity gowns, toys and, ultimately, elementary schools, etc., for children. Certainly, you can see what the fight to give women equality and to get women into jobs that pay well, and the resulting development of the two-paycheck way of life in American society have done to the matter of inflation. These are good democratic gains, but they don't come without a price. In evaluating the economic trends related to the big trends in the US national horoscope over 1977, keep in mind that old Spanish proverb that said, "Take what you want, said God; 'take it and pay for it . . .' "

You develop machinery that does the job better than the people who used to do the job could possibly perform. But that means people coming back again to the job market, looking for jobs. You permit people to moonlight. That means that some people have two jobs whereas other people who should have those "second" jobs have no job at all. What we believe, what we do, what we aim for in our life styles all—all—has due impact upon the economy we experience, and this truth was never more evident than during the second half of 1977.

Do you want clean air? Then you may have to close plants that employ many people. Or you may have to impose an antipollution budget on industries that might result in their moving overseas. Antipollutionists almost wrecked the Alaskan oil pipeline. They almost kicked nuclear reactors and plants out of the state of California. In the new maturity that is falling upon the American people, they are going to have to answer some pretty cogent questions.

More and more, the type of economy in this country will be a matter of *your* own doing.

With Uranus in the US sixth house, so recently vacated by Neptune, the job picture is going to change radically. People educated for one type of work will shift into another. As old jobs pass in the wake of automation, new jobs will be born. Many younger people will find their way into the Ralph Nader type of watchdogging job. Others can find their way into greater utilization of data processing and information retrieval. Still others can find their way into the new emphasis on keeping our national parks, streets, places of recreation cleaner and more widely used. There will be greater emphasis on giving more education in elementary and high schools to fewer children. Ultimately, the lower birth rate will mean fewer workers and may possibly result in the importation of people from strongly underprivileged nations to do the "dirty" work—Orientals and Latin Americans taking precedence here over Europeans and Africans. Uranus will be in pertinent degrees of Scorpio, where it awakens the population to the nefarious practices of labor unions; you can thus expect some pretty strong legislation to be developed over the last three months of 1977. The unemployment rate in October can be pretty well stabilized around six percent.

There will be parallel moves within industry over the October-December period to streamline and get rid of do-nothing, oversalaried, so-called "executives." The aim is increased efficiency at lower costs and this can be more than the goal during November and December. It can be an actual gain.

The price of gold and of land will largely have leveled off by the close of 1977.

Greater amounts of federal monies are going to American colleges, including private colleges and those which were once religiously oriented. But the school population of the United States will become more and more stable.

In mid-November, Saturn makes its Virgo ingress and can be somewhat depressing on farming for the time being. There is a great slowing down of national effort from mid-December until the close of the year. Jupiter will be retrograde in Cancer at the month's beginning. Mars will assume apparent retrograde movement in Leo on December 13th. Mercury at the same time will assume apparent retrograde movement in Capricorn, the zone of the Washington administration. Saturn will commence its period of retrogression in Virgo on the 11th.

The second half of December offers a good pause in which the stock market may make adjustments in over-inflated prices. It offers everybody a good opportunity to absorb the momentous economic changes of 1977, with its problems at the beginning of the year and the momentous climb of the gross national product over the second half.

There will be no boom at year's end, but a great deal of confidence in the workings of the system itself and in the economy, as an improved year is about to break on the horizon.

Commodity Futures Trading 1977

Dale Richardson

Commodity futures trading is big business. It is a market-place that now trades more than 500 billion dollars a year worth of commodities contracts, more than double the yearly business of the nation's stock exchanges. Compared to that, our wealthiest families, like the Rockefellers, the DuPonts, the Mellons, the Kennedys, and those giants of Texas—Murchison, Richardson and Hunt—seem like poor relations. Sooner or later you may be exposed to some salesman who wants you to "take a flyer" in this or that commodity, due to this or that "looming shortage." I note particularly the "commodities options rackets" of 1972.

The Commodities Options Rackets

Since commodities are very risky business, some bright salesmen got the brilliant brainstorm to "sell options." For a fixed sum of money you could contract to buy or sell—either one: if the price rose, you could pocket the difference; if it dropped, you could exercise your option to sell at the contract price and buy back at the cheaper price. The most you could lose was your option deposit.

The joker in the deck: in the event these prove very profitable for some client, who is going to pay? For the system to work at all, the broker would have to buy/sell an equivalent contract to offset the client's contract.

That would mean he would have to know the market, and most brokers are not that smart. What was the solution for most of them? Bankruptcy, which in these cases usually was a legal term for a swindle. One lady called me saying she had been "led" to an options firm ("led" in the sense of being "divinely guided"). She didn't want to bother with losses on the ordinary exchange. "My husband left me some money. You'll never get rich by putting it in the bank at six percent interest or collecting rents on an apartment house." I did not say much then, but some weeks later, called her. She was in tears. No, she didn't get any money. "I would have done beautifully if the firm hadn't gone bankrupt."

The Gold Bust

Gold and silver were other booms "full of sound and fury," but signifying very little. Sales were helped enormously by such scare books as Harry Browne's *How You Can Profit from the Coming Devaluation* and *You Can Profit from a Monetary Crisis.* Silver and wheat both peaked out—and have not reached these highs since—when the grand trine of Saturn, Jupiter and Uranus ended in February of 1974. That was apparently, for the time being at least, the peak of the inflationary psychology. Since then, many commodities reached a more realistic level. That did not keep shortages from developing in individual commodities, like sugar in 1974 or pork bellies in 1975. But under the squares of Saturn to Pluto, and Saturn to Uranus in 1974, 1975 and 1976, recession was felt and prices dropped, at least in farm produce.

I have felt, and said so, that gold is a commodity like anything else. It is *not* "the world's last hope." The world situation being what it is, it certainly will not be gold that saves us, if anything does. The Europeans were legally able to buy gold. By the time Americans could, the

Europeans were in a selling mood. "Let the suckers have it!" And the boom collapsed, triggered by Mars transiting over a Neptune-Jupiter square. Mars punctured the bubble scheme.

Aspects and Attitudes
More Important than Rulerships

Simplistic astrologers read some statement in a book, such as "Leo rules gold." Ergo, the obvious conclusion is that when Saturn gets into Leo, gold will drop. One guy who hadn't made it in the stock brokerage business and went into astrology, hoping to make a quick buck on the astrological bandwagon, said that very thing.

Another lady who was with me on a TV show said, "When gold was thirty-five dollars an ounce, I advised my clients to buy it and sell it when it reached one-hundred ninety-five dollars an ounce. It went a little higher, and they were a bit ungrateful." What I did not point out, in the interests of harmony on the TV show, was that *U.S. citizens could not own gold at thirty-five dollars an ounce.* It had reached 200 dollars an ounce in Paris before U.S. citizens could legally own it. When the mad stampede to own gold did not develop, gold eroded down to 165 dollars an ounce before stabilizing. She must have had a lot of Canadian or European clients.

I had written in an article, "Does Gold Rule Our Economic Future?" (*Horoscope Magazine*, August, 1975), that the price of gold is psychological, not economic (or "real" as some would put it), and that *it is the aspects of the transiting planets to each other,* which bring the rises and falls in psychological estimation of its worth, that determine price. With bearish aspects forming, we thought that, if gold broke the 165-dollar level, it could go down to 129 dollars an ounce. It did. It reached a peak under Mars conjunct Neptune (Neptune balloons prices, especially if a bubble scheme is afoot which is stimulated by Mars), but then Mars went on to square Jupiter: the bubble popped. The subsequent low was reached after Labor-Day weekend, 1975, when the Sun from Virgo squared Neptune in Sagittarius, and Mars from Gemini opposed it. Far from being inflationary, these aspects to Neptune were balloon-busters. *Both times when we have had lows in gold so far, Saturn has been in Cancer.* Both times, we have had adverse aspects to Neptune. So you see, we are not really dealing with gold at all on this level; *we are dealing with the collapse of an inflated price that was not real in the first place.*

An interesting point is Mr. Browne's stars. We could not get his horoscope, but his book says he was born in 1933. Even that tells us a lot. Neptune was in Virgo all year. Jupiter was there until September 10th, and Mars until July 6th, retrograding back and forth. You have the possibility there of vastly inflated ideas—which may not come due anyway. When we got the gold-price drops, Neptune in Sagittarius was being triggered adversely by minor planets in unfavorable relation to Virgo, probably afflicting Browne's horoscope. It would be embarrassing to write a book like *The Coming Profit in Gold*, and then find the price melting.

That is not to say that gold won't go up. It should go up on the bull aspects as well as go down on the bear aspects. The point is that gold fluctuates. It is *not*, financially, "the last exit from Dunkirk." With prosperity again perhaps appearing, with continuing fears of inflation, some gold promoters might dust off their gear and start promoting again. One enterprising genius who had gone bankrupt in the options racket and was convicted of fraud was back at it again in 1975 selling something called "gold extract." Still, "there's a sucker born every minute," to quote P. T. Barnum. Each new spring seems to bring some new swindle scheme. I do not want you to be that sucker.

Your Personal Horoscope and the Market

There are all sorts of books written on financial and economic subjects these days. Doubtless you have run across some of these books. The one that got me started on commodities was Morton Shulman's *Anyone Can Make a Million*. In it is a chapter on commodities where he mentions the potential of a very small investment's running into a fortune. Now, I believe most of you are versed enough in astrology to know that *your own horoscope determines this*. Unless your horoscope indicates substantial wealth, you aren't going to make it trading commodities or anything else. Further, unless you have a favorable fifth house (speculation) and ninth house (long-range planning) and eighth house (the flow of money toward you, as in profits from commodities or profits from self-employment), then it is doubtful that you will get very far trading commodities. Without such favorable indications, you would be far better off in a profession or business or even a salaried position, where someone else takes the risks.

But even with favorable indications, timing is all important, and the great mistake of many astrologers is that they forget timing. Despite a splendiferously aspected Jupiter and Venus in the fifth house, when these come under affliction by the transiting planets, you usually either make the wrong moves or listen to bad advice. Therefore, the idea that "Oh, I have a wonderful fifth house, I would do well at it," is one that should be approached with the utmost caution. Astrology students, please note (and this warning includes the professionals as well, most of whom were of no help at all in figuring out what little we know about commodities): planetary aspect assets in a horoscope do *not* cancel out the aspect liabilities. Usually the different aspects refer to different situations. "A little knowledge is a dangerous thing." "Pride goeth before a fall." Both these maxims became very familiar in my search for "the key to Fort Knox."

Caveat Emptor

When we did perhaps find it, we also found that there were far more fascinating things to do than sit and watch the "bellies" go up and down on the Chicago Mercantile Exchange price board. Yes, we did that: we sat and recorded *every price change* in bellies and eggs—and sometimes wheat and corn—for months on end.

According to trend-line theory, "Prices tend to move in trends, and the same old patterns repeat and repeat." However, the commodities market, far from being an "Anyone-Can-Make-a-Million" situation, to adapt a book title of Mr. Shulman's, is closer to "Fleecing the Lambs," to apply a title of Christopher Elias'. His contention is that the traders must buy at wholesale (market bottoms) and sell at retail (market tops). Who makes up the difference? The public. As a rule, you have a "selling climax" at bottoms, where the public has decided to buy before things get higher—and that's usually the top of the market. The major bull markets, far from being a Roaring Gravy Train, often turn out to resemble more the rainbow with its proverbial pot of gold, the rainbow which evaporates when you get to what should have been its foot. Be especially cautious about news items coming over the radio, TV, or in the newspapers, because by the time something receives wide media coverage, the "smart money" has bought long ago, and is now ready to sell—and the public is a willing buyer. So you have this continual battle between the public and the professionals, which the public usually loses.

The Buyer Is The Last To Know

Therefore, if some very attractive, very persuasive

salesman threatens to sell you some "Gold in Golconda,"
in the form of potatoes ("Europe is dry, Britain is driest
since 1780"), or coffee ("A freeze hit Brazil; it will take
two or three years to restore normal production") or live
hogs or pork bellies ("We have the shortest hog crop in
forty years; them things are gonna be selling like gold!"),
then run, *run*, RUN for the nearest escape route. These
are examples of conditions that all prevailed in 1975 and
1976.

BUT by the time *you* know about them, it's too late.
Further, you can get killed financially in the price fluctuations. The stock market and commodities futures markets
are peculiarly attractive to bright, young men fresh out of
college wanting to make a great deal of money. The money is there; getting it is another question. The usual procedure is to set up shop, get a set of clients and start trading. Since most brokers do not know any more than the
novice trader, the result is that all too often the client
loses his money, the broker loses his client, and has to go
"hustle" some new clients. My rather blunt terminology
was derived from watching these operations for about
eight years.

Being Your Own Broker
vs.
Selecting One

You have to decide, first of all, *who is going to run the
account.* You are better off becoming your own analyst,
buttressed by your own charting, reading, and so on. If
you can't do that, *select a knowledgeable broker.* A man
once told me he usually selected the youngest broker in
the office because he would do just exactly as he was told.
The man, however, knew what he was doing. If you don't,
the best bet is an older broker who has "been through the
mill," the ups and downs of markets. Always, of course,
the final decision is up to you. It is your money, and you

have to approve "suggested trades." Therefore, a seasoned broker is more likely to come up with more good trades than bad ones, but the young brokers rely on "the mighty resources of our research department."

You Can't Trade "Fundamentals"

Research departments may be able to tell you stocks on hand, present demand, and present world crop conditions, but not *future* demands, weather conditions, purchasing power, or consumer resistances; nor, additionally, which government may poke its nose in and apply some new regulation—particularly important in international commodities like cocoa, sugar, silver, gold and coffee. The Arabs demonstrated this tactic very amply with oil. Facts such as Russia is buying, or bellies went up three cents in Chicago, or it rained in Kansas are "fundamentals." *You can't, in my opinion, over the long term, trade "fundamentals."* They rule in the *end*, at contract settlement. In the meantime, the "technical approach" applies.

For example, the "fundamental" reflects what the thing is *really* worth (and who knows that?) as opposed to the sum total of what all traders *think* it's worth, or will be at time of delivery, the time of the expiring contract. *Price is made by the sum total of opinions of those trading.* This fluctuates.

For example, the May, 1976, Maine potato contract was trading in the eight-to-nine dollar range in the summer of 1975. Then an adverse government crop estimate came out, and it was limit-up every day for several days in a row. Everybody thought there would be a great shortage of potatoes. The following crop estimate a month later revealed more than expected, and potatoes were limit-down every day for a number of days. That contract went to $19 per cwt., dropped back to near $14, went to $17 or $18, down to $11, then back to $15, and finally closed out at $8.70. The final day of trading saw potatoes open at $10, go to $10.70, drop to $8, finally closing at $8.70. All this time the "technical" approach did show tops and bottoms and gave buy and sell signals. Many of them, in the face of the subsequent government reports, were not usable, because to be caught by surprise in this contract proved lethal financially.

All commodities have a "limit." That is, the Board of Governors sets a figure beyond which price may not fluctuate. A sudden factor that changes the picture may result in several days of limit moves—with no trading. Potatoes were fifty points. A lower estimate resulted in all buyers, no sellers. Therefore, the market opened fifty points higher bid, and did that each day until the price reached a level attracting sellers. If you were "short," there was no way to cover that short until somebody was willing to sell.

Planetary Pressures on Commodities Trading

It is in these price fluctuations during the life of the contract that money is made or lost. You can buy ("go long") a contract almost any time or sell ("go short") at almost any time. *However,* unless you are in the business, and take delivery at the expiration date of the commodity, or deliver the commodity itself (farmers, processors, etc.) against the contract, *each contract you buy has to be sold, and each contract you sell (short) has to be bought back and "covered"* before the expiration date of that contract.

Therefore, as you note, you are not dealing in wheat, pork bellies or any other physical commodity; *you are dealing in contracts.* It is not a question at all, consequently, of the Sun's ruling gold, Venus' ruling copper, or the Moon's ruling silver. We are dealing with buying and selling contracts (Mercury), money (Venus), optimism (Jupiter), pessimism or reality (Saturn), and the activities (Mars) and the surprises that come into the market, especially government reports (Uranus), baloonment and delusion (Neptune), and the activities of the giant trusts (Pluto).

All these planets work. The idea that Uranus, Neptune and Pluto are merely transcendental planets, working only on our "psyche," has always seemed a little silly to me. After all, our ideas are translated into acts *in* the ordinary workaday world of time and space.

Now, what are "commodity futures?" *They are contracts to buy or sell a given quantity of a specified grade product at a given date.* Usually they cover one carload of pork bellies, wheat, corn, etc. Things like platinum or gold are contracted in ounces. Your broker can give you all this information. For practical purposes, you don't worry about that. All you are concerned about is the margin requirement, the down payment you put up to buy or sell the contract. This varies, usually running five to ten percent of the value of the contract. You have tremendous leverage, and that is perhaps the prime asset of commodity futures. For a comparatively small sum, you control a large sum of money. When a commodity gets violent, as sugar did in the fall of 1974, going limit-up every day from 42¢ to 64¢, turning around and dropping limit every day back to 46¢, the Board of Governors raises the margin—in this case to $20,000 a contract. You are better off avoiding violent markets.

Contracts have a delivery date, geared to the peak production/consumption months of the different commodities. Pork bellies have February, March, May, July and August delivery months. Shell eggs have a contract every month, with usually September and December most heavily traded. *Stay out of the current month on eggs*; you can get a delivery notice and you may have to take delivery. That's a peculiarity of the egg contract which may be changed. Other than that, usually the nearest month is the most-traded month, and that's where the psychology is; therefore, that's where planetary pressures would work the best. You don't usually have to worry about having a carload of wheat dumped on your lawn, because (a) you'd have to put up a lot more money, and (b) your broker would be screaming and tearing his hair for you to dispose of the contract.

You have to go to a brokerage house and open an account before you can trade. *Be sure to choose one that is solvent.* It does you no good to make a profit if the brokerage firm can't pay up. And in the past, some wheeler-dealer brokers have put firms into near-bankruptcy. Firms like E. F. Hutton may require around 3,000 dollars, whereas some commodities-only firm may take an account of 1,000 dollars or less. *Don't risk money you can't afford to lose.* That's true of any business venture, but especially in commodities. If you can't sleep nights, get out.

There is the *possibility* of making a fortune. There is also the possibility of losing your shirt. "If you're so smart, why aren't you rich?" Some people are analysts and some people are speculators. The two don't always go together.

Before you take a position, are planning, *you are operating on an intellectual wavelength;* after you take that position, *you are operating on an emotional wavelength.* The two are not the same thing at all. The problem in achieving success is *not* a shortage of knowledge—we are drowned in that. The problem for all of us is our psychological hangups. There may be no answer to that.

Trend-line Theory

Nobody can possibly know all the factors influencing any market; therefore, *the only reliable indicator is price.* Varying price fluctuations create patterns or pictures, and these, over the years, repeat themselves. I cannot here more than touch on this. I recommend that you pick up a book on charting, like *Modern Commodity Futures Trading* by Gerald Gold, published by Commodity Research Bureau, New York.

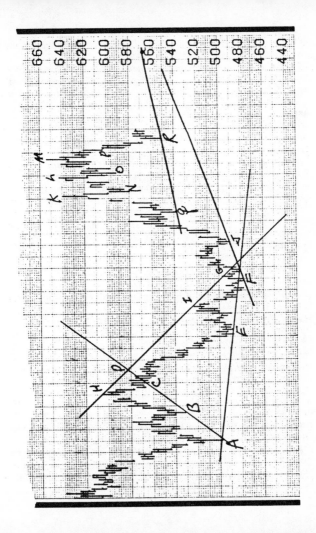

The accompanying chart is published by Commodity Perspective, 141 W. Jackson Blvd., Rm 2440, Board of Trade Bldg., Chicago, Ill. 60604 and is reprinted with their permission. They provide a chart service. Contact them for details.

This chart is for November, 1975, soybeans. However, a chart is a chart is a chart—and the same rules apply to any of them. At times some charts may be choppier than others. A *trend* is formed any time you have *two successive tops or bottoms.* It may be extremely short-lived; we often get a trend reversal in the volatile pork bellies and eggs every other day. Here the patterns involve weeks. Rising bottoms, of course, indicate an uptrend; declining tops indicate a downtrend. Often you have flat tops or bottoms, and this is a "trading range"—which is better avoided.

Using Trend Lines To Place "Stop-loss Orders"

You absolutely need a "stop-loss order" of some sort. Where it is placed is a matter of judgment. Setting it too close can knock out your position; placing it too far away results in larger losses. For the long term, buying close to A (see chart) with a stop below that could have retained your gain clear to C. The price decline at B did not go below A, and formed a rather stable trend line. When it broke on the downside at C, you should have been out of the market; or you could have gone short at C, with a buy-stop at D.

The "natural position" in commodities is "short," because the only thing that makes commodities go up is shortage. Rising prices stimulate production and price declines follow. "Shorting" is selling a contract in the hopes that it will decline in price and you can buy back for less than you sold for, thus liquidating the contract.

A bottom was formed at E, with a subsequent rise and decline to F. F is not a sell signal, because violation of the line A-E-F was not decisive, exhibiting "no follow-through." G is a buy signal, since it broke the trend line H-D-I on the upside, with a stop below F. The rise from J's bottom allows a new trend line F-J. L could be a sell signal, because it didn't go higher than K. When it did at M, it could be a buy signal, but with a stop should be placed just below K or L because the signal could be misleading—which it was. Often (not always) we get very choppy action at tops. It is "toppy action." Unless you had sold at M, very definitely you should be out of the market when a line drawn from N-O-P broke. Any doubts about a bear market should have been removed with the breaking of the line Q-R.

Brokers can argue that all charting does is show past action. *True, but past action repeats.* Not only that, charting is the most sacred cow in the business. Whether justified or not, it has more followers than anything else, and can even create its own price movements.

Weather scares can be very important. The line from J to M reflects dry weather in the corn belt; that from M to R, an "overbought condition." The May, 1976, wheat contract was run up from about $3.28 a bushel to $4.01 because of news of the new dust bowl. It then declined to $3.25. The point is, prices fluctuate. Whether you are a speculator, a farmer or housewife, you *may* be able to take advantage of these fluctuations.

Other Uses for Trend Lines

Market traders can save on their grocery bills by noting price trends. When sugar began to skyrocket on the futures market, sugar could be bought far more cheaply than later. The same was true of grains in 1973, or coffee in 1976. That is not "hoarding"; it is "taking sensible precautions," as you do when you buy apples in fall, at cheap harvest prices, to last through the winter, or buy fruit to can in the summer when it is cheaper.

Farmers can use these trends in marketing crops. The 1972 Russian wheat deal is a case in point. The grain sale was very secretive, but the futures prices were rising. The same was true in 1975, when prices were rising, and another Russian sale was in the offing. We do, of course, have to export. Our productive capacity is far in excess of domestic needs. If you had soybeans on hand, it would have been wise to sell them, or part of them, when the trend broke at N-O-P, because a break in so heavy a top would mean that the party was over.

The frozen pork-belly contract deserves special mention. The "old crop" ends in August; the new crop begins in February. You cannot carry bellies from August to February like wheat; they are perishable. Bellies are the slabs from which bacon is made. After August, futures can rise above cash, and usually do. The day of reckoning comes in the July and August contracts. *Futures have to decline two to three cents below cash bellies if they are to be got out of cold storage and processed*; otherwise processors buy fresh bellies instead of frozen ones.

We have had more success forecasting the pork-belly market than any of the others, followed by shell eggs, the grains and gold. *Planetary aspects indicate pressures, not absolutes.* Government reports, if a surprise, are powerful enough to overcome any aspect. So is the weather. What you have to do is use planetary indications as an idea *when* a decline or rise might be taking place. Then play that against your good chart pattern. It is not so simple as selling at the good aspects and buying after the bad ones are finished. Commodities trading is perhaps the most sophisticated system of investment in the world. You can get nowhere bucking the trend. The hope lies in the little fish figuring out which way the whale is going—and following the whale.

Monthly Indications

And now, let us look at monthly indications. They are expressed as bullish (rising) and bearish (dropping). I am not attempting to give you all the indicators; they are not available this far in advance. Also, these indicators are presented for observation only; we cannot possibly guarantee results or accuracy in the future equal to that in the past. If you are trading, however, some idea of *when* a trend change, or price drop or rise *might* occur may be of some help.

First, some general observations. Trends for dates falling on weekends or holidays usually operate the day before or day after. You have to establish the trend. Bull dates in a bear tread produce, as a rule, upswings, and then the downtrend resumes. Bear dates in a bull trend usually work as dips, and the uptrend resumes. Dates that are both bullish and bearish, having both bull and bear aspects, are usually trading ranges or whipsaw markets. Aspects give a bullish or bearish tone to the market, sometimes swinging the whole board. We don't pretend to know anything about sugar, cocoa, cotton, etc. Our aspects work mainly on bellies, eggs, live hogs and grains, but they *may* work on the others. Use your charts. If one thing may be stronger than others, it is noted.

January. The 2nd is bullish (grains); the 4th and 7th, bearish (gold, bellies), with the possibility that storms may knock out communications lines. The 9th is bullish (meats, eggs, wheat; cattle are excepted as not working according to our indicators, though they might). The 11th is bullish, and so is the 14th (bellies, wheat). The 15th should be bullish. It should bearish around the 18th, 19th; bullish on the 24th, bearish and cold on the 27th. The 28th will be mixed: some markets are bullish, some bearish.

February. The 1st is bearish (bellies, eggs), followed by a rise on the 2nd through the 3rd. Meats and wheat are very active on the 11th. A bearish tone is possible on the 14th, especially in bellies, gold, silver. Expect a bullish 16th, a bearish 17th and 18th (bellies, eggs), also storms and cold weather. The 20th is very mixed: some markets are down, some up; a drop is followed by a rise. This rise is short-lived; the 23rd is adverse: sharp drops in bellies, and business and economic news can be bad. The bearish aspect of Saturn square Uranus operates as a broad, general undertone for some weeks. The 26th is bearish (grains) but there may be some buying in bellies on the 27th.

March. Expect a bullish 1st (wheat, bellies), a bearish 6th and 11th (gold, bellies). There may be manipulation; the 8th may be bullish (bellies). Expect a bearish 15th, a bullish 16th. The 23rd is bullish for some markets, bearish in bellies and wheat. The 24th is bearish. There might be a rise on the 26th, again on the 30th (potatoes, silver, gold, eggs).

April. Expect storms and a bearish 1st; a rise in bellies on the 2nd; general optimism (short-lived) on the 5th. The balloon is punctured by the 9th—as is the gold market. Expect a cold, stormy, bearish 10th and 11th, perhaps some rally on the 17th. A major bearish aspect is exact on the 22nd, and retriggered on the 30th. There could be earthquakes, tornadoes, a late freeze—none is good for crop production. *Question: Is the bearishness in crop destruction, or is it in price?* Watch trend lines!

May. The 1st is bearish (bellies); the 5th and 7th bullish. Broad supportive aspects *may* be forming— exact in the last half of month. Expect a bearish 11th and 12th, a bullish 17th, a bearish 22nd, a bearish trend which may continue until a bearish 27th and late freezes. The 30th is likely to be bearish.

June. Expect a bullish 1st and 2nd. Whipsaw markets (Jupiter sextile Saturn but opposed Neptune) dominate half of June. Expect bearish bellies and wheat on the 14th and 16th; a bullish 20th. Saturn trines Neptune in the last half of the month, but eggs, gold, and silver will be bearish on the 20th, 21st and 25th. This may be a short-term bottom; expect bullish bellies and wheat on the 28th and 29th.

July. Expect a bearish 1st (bellies) and 3rd; a bullish 6th (meats); a bearish 14th; a bullish 16th; a bearish 17th and 19th. There may be cool weather and freezing in susceptible areas—maybe Brazil. Expect a bullish 24th, a bearish 30th—again freezing.

August. Expect a bullish 1st and 3rd; a bearish, bubble-popping 5th and 6th (gold, wheat, bellies); same for 8th; a rally in bellies on the 9th. It may be cool, bearish on the 12th; bullish on the 23rd (grains) and 31st (bellies).

September. Very mixed. The 3rd and 4th will be bullish, with little manipulation. The market will be bullish in grains on the 4th, bearish in bellies; bullish the 7th to 8th; mixed the 17th (bullish in bellies, bearish in eggs; a runup followed by selloff). Expect a bullish 19th (bellies), a bearish 23rd; a bullish 26th (grains) and 30th (bellies).

October. Expect a bearish 3rd (manipulation) but a bullish 6th and 7th; a bullish 10th, 11th, and 12th (meats, wheat); a mixed 20th and 21st, with both bullish and bearish indicators. The 25th and 28th are bullish, but there may be a selloff in bellies on the 28th.

November. Bullish 4th (bellies), bearish 8th, possible early storms. Expect a bullish 14th, a bearish 15th, a bullish 19th and 20th (bellies); a bearish 22nd, plus storms.

December. Expect a bullish 1st (eggs and silver); a bullish 2nd (meats); a bearish 4th (eggs and grains); a bullish 7th, 8th, 12th, and 16th; a bullish 21st.

For further, more specifically tailored commodities information, see my Astrological Research Foundation Market Letter. It covers minor aspects, plus other indicators not available at this writing. Dates given in it may even be contradictory to these shown here. If interested, write me in care of the publisher. It may help those already trading improve results.

I hope this has been somewhat enlightening on what the commodities markets are all about. The big firms won't tell you. They are in the business of buying and selling contracts or stocks. They do not train their salesmen, euphemistically known as account executives, as much as they should in market techniques. They concentrate instead on "getting the business." Unless the salesman does his homework, it's the customer who "gets the business." One office manager was pouring religiously through *Winning Through Intimidation*. More to the point might have been a study of trend lines. May you have Jupiter trines in 1977.

DONALD BRADLEY's
Solar and Lunar Returns

Learn how to get a more personalized view of your coming year—one tailored to the particular time and place of your birth.

Donald Bradley's *Solar and Lunar Returns* uses the sidereal system as the basis of chart construction—a technique that many claim results in more accurate forecasting.

Farm
and Garden

Using Your
Farm and
Garden Section

The "Farm and Garden" section has been expanded considerably this year. There is a greater focus on gardening for the city-dweller, to supplement *The Moon Sign Book*'s traditional emphasis on farming. The guide to organic gardening, the articles on companion planting and astronutrition, and the essay by Lynne Dusenberry on the reverence for place fundamental to gardening—all new this year—aid the city-dweller in his search to anchor his roots in more congenial soil.

The whole of *The Moon Sign Book* is predicated on, and directed toward the realization of, the ideal of living one's life in harmony with Nature. The grandeur of celestial mechanics is translated into the humble routine of daily life. It is in the activities described in this section, however, that this ideal can be most intensely realized for most readers. Farming and gardening by the Moon involve more than following certain celestial cycles; they require one's intimate participation, the mingling of one's labor and love, with the life processes of Nature herself.

For this reason, this section is introduced by Lynne Dusenberry's "In My Garden," which dramatizes the awe and reverence for Nature that alone sanctify man's attempt to husband her resources.

The next two articles, "A Brief Guide to Organic Gardening" and "Try Companion Planting," describe some of the gardening techniques that derive from this reverence. They show *how* to garden in harmony with Nature. The article which follows them, "Gardening by the Moon," shows *when* to undertake various gardening activities. Based on the "Moon Tables" and "Daily Activities" sections, it gives the rules for astrological timing necessary to productive gardening.

There follows an article on the planetary rulerships of plants, which supplements the preceding article on timing by allowing you to factor in lunar aspects as well as the Moon's position and phase in determining the best time to do something.

The "Planting Guide" which follows gives you a concise listing of the best periods to plant a host of vegetables, fruits, herbs, trees and shrubs. If you have a question about a specific item, this is where to look. "Best Planting Dates," the next feature, provides you with a comprehensive gardening program, laid out day by day, for the entire year. This is where to look for the best date to perform a certain activity and for planning your schedule.

Other features include this year's winners in the gardening contest, a listing of the best dates for breeding animals and setting eggs and for destroying unwanted plant and animal life. Also included are two features on health: a listing of the herbs useful in remedying a wide variety of ailments and a discussion of growing sprouts to harness the Sun's energies in months when its light is insufficient for growing vegetables and fruits.

♈♉♊♋ **THE 1977 ASTROLOGICAL CALENDAR** ♌♍♎

Companion to the *Moon Sign Book* with lunar sign and phase changes, planetary motion and daily planetary aspects—plus a table of keywords describing their effects. You can't have one without the other. Order your calendar today! The *1977 Astrological Calendar*, only $2.00. See page *vi*.

In My Garden
Lynne   Dusenberry

The Site

*Do not move the rock or anything placed in its
place by God. Not a leaf from a tree not a bird from
its nest not a spider's silver thread. These things
will fall soon enough in their time. The earth has
roots, and the roots belong to the soil. If you cut
a hole in the soil you have damaged the earth.
You must therefore be certain it is necessary.*

—FROM THE TAOS PUEBLO[1]

Standing in the space of land that will be the garden, I
observe the surroundings. From the beginning of the earth
this space has been here in balance and relationship with
all the other spaces around it. In the east is a steep side
hill, sloping down to the nearly level garden spot. In the
south the length of the canyon reaches for the river.
Toward the west are the willow and aspens who cherish
and conceal the nearness of the creek. And in the north
the junipers and fir make a forest cover for the small
creatures of the mountain. Above is the sky of sun and
rain; below is the fertile earth.

For many years the creatures and beings of this place
have known this spot and lived here. The sun has seen
it and called forth the grasses and wildflowers; the ants
and birds have felt the spring here. The stones and brush

have worked together to hold the soil. In geological time, it is a brief moment that the hand of the white man has been felt in this garden, but the evidence is obvious: a few broken glass bits, some tin cans. And now I, standing with a spade. Standing here placed in my place by God, I contemplate the surroundings, and the surroundings contemplate me.

> *O mountain and birds, O grains of earth and tiny insects, O grasses and flowers and brush, O forests and hills and each being of this place, I am a small human who finds myself here in this space, and I wish to change this place. May I dig here and make a garden? I shall plant seed that will make tame plants that you have not seen in this place before. It is to eat that I shall do this, for the growing things of this place are bitter and strange to my mouth; they cannot sustain my life. I have been put here to live my life and to learn the earth. Teach me then, spirits and beings of this place, for you have lived here a long time and know how things grow here. Have pity on my ignorance, and protect me from mistakes, that from this garden I may derive long life and the strength and wisdom of this place. In return I shall learn to know and respect you, and will caretake this hole I am cutting in the soil.*

As the digging goes forward, there are many things to observe and learn. The garden space is worked over many times. First, the soil is broken; the ground cover is loosened from its ancient place. Then the clumps of sod are broken up with a second spading. A few days later when the exposed clods have dried in the sun, the entire patch is gone over by rake and by hand. The dirt is shaken free; the dying plants are put in a pile to begin

to become compost. Now the patch is raw exposed soil.
I touch the earth, sifting the dirt through my fingers.
I feel the texture and ask the earth what it needs to be a
richer and more fertile spot. It likes the idea of being
fed and soon fills my intuitive understanding with an
awareness of its needs. Constantly I state my ignorance;
my gardening experience is small and I must ask this
particular patch for information on how I may tend
it correctly. I also have a comprehensive gardening book,
but am involved in trying to apply that information to
a particular place, with its own peculiar needs. The only
way I can fulfill the needs of this garden is if the garden
itself can direct me. So always I seek, with respect, to
understand its needs and to know what will fill those
needs.

In a fruitful sign of the Moon, at the time of the dark-
ening of its light, I apply organic material and dig it into
the topsoil. A final raking completes the preparations;
the garden sleeps through the New Moon.

The Planting

I have made a footprint, a sacred one.

*I have made a footprint, through it the blades
push upward.*

*I have made a footprint, through it the blades
radiate.*

*I have made a footprint, over it the blades float
in the wind.*

*I have made a footprint, over it the ears lean toward
one another.*

*I have made a footprint, over it I bend the stalk
to pluck the ears.*

*I have made a footprint, over it the blossoms
lie gray.*

*I have made a footprint, smoke arises from my
house.*

> *I have made a footprint, there is cheer in my house.*
> *I have made a footprint, I live in the light of day.*
> —FROM THE OSAGE[2]

In my relationship to my garden, the space and the projected crops are viewed as a whole. Thought and research determine what shall be planted and in what part of the space, which kind of plant shall grow next to which other ones. After this the furrows can be made, and planting begins when the Moon is right. The seeds lie in my palm, little and dry, hiding secrets of life. They shall grow into living things and will in turn become part of my life. I hold a running conversational monologue as the seeds are tucked away into the incubator, the womb of Mother Earth.

> *Little seeds you must be brave and do not fear the dark. I want you to love and trust me for I will try to do whatever you need to grow strong and healthy. This is a severe climate we have here, so you might have to be very hardy. I am a human being. I will bring you water; I will serve your life. But you must know me and tell me what to do, for I do not know you yet. Feel the Sun pouring into the Earth, calling you forth to green and life. Drink the water I shall bring, or perhaps together we can call the Thunder Beings from the Western Sky. Grow with joy, poke up your heads soon and look around. Look for me, learn me as I learn you, for there will come a day when I will ask you to Give Away to me. In that day, I hope you will have grown to love me; I shall take your love and life and change it into my life, and in that way you will always be with me. Little seeds you must be brave and do not fear the dark for soon you will be dancing in the Sun and I shall love you . . . .*

As I tread the rows, packing the soil above the newly sown seed, I think of the wisdom of the Native American People, who advise their children, "Walk in balance." I try to make the treading a dance in balance, to share the balance with the Earth whose natural course I have changed in this spot, to share the balance with the seeds whose life I seek to promote. For myself, I dance so that my contact with the forces of life, my deliberate involvement with growth and earth and may here balance me and teach me of the mysteries of the Greater Harmony.

The Care

Truly in the east
The white bean
And the great corn-plant
Are tied with the white lightning.
Listen! rain approaches!
The voice of the bluebird is heard.
Truly in the east
The white bean
And the great squash
are tied with the rainbow.
Listen! rain approaches!
The voice of the bluebird is heard.

—FROM THE NAVAHO[3]

The seeds dream of life and the Sun. On days when the Moon is in nurturing and watery signs, I bring water to them; on the earthy days, I lay a mulch of straw over their beds. I sing to them—mindless little lullabies, ditties made up on the spot just for them. The words come from what I see around me, the birds or clouds, the wind, or just my mood of the moment in relation to the garden. Whenever I am in the garden, the intent and focus of my mind is firmly upon the invisible seeds, their safety, warmth and nourishment.

Then the exciting days come when the little friends appear! The double leaves poking out, peering at the Sun and at me. *Hello, hello! How good to see you. You are so small and good and brave. Look at you there! And oh! There's another kind, look at you! Are you all right? You will have to be very strong and healthy, you know...*

The maintenance work in the garden is a time of open-hearted peace and giving. Healthy plants are the best protection against pests and disease; care and love are the best protection of health. The blooming green of the garden does attract certain insects, ones I would rather not have in that space. I have agreed to promote Life here. A poison spray would contradict the agreement. So I recognize the forces of Life, respectfully, aloud:

> *Now you eaters and nibblers who have come to this garden! I can understand why you are here. All this green must look pretty tasty to you as you are coming by! So drop in and have a taste—I won't begrudge you a bite. But please, these things are growing for my life-needs, so don't take it all. Have a treat, then move along in your natural way; let me eat my garden . . .*

By honoring everything's right to life, I gain a perfect garden: no worms in the broccoli, no holes in the cabbage . . .

The Vision of Caring

Summer days bring the magic of the ripening friendships, the movement of growth and life before my very eyes. In the evening light, I enjoy going into the garden and closing the gate (the plants there feel more secure and private with the garden gate shut). Going to the very center of the garden space, I sit on the earth and close my eyes. I feel my body sitting on the earth, and I find

my center of balance. My heartbeat and the pulse of the
Earth are one; my heartbeat and the rhythm of life in
the plants are one. Together my garden and I drift into
a waking dream . . . The Vision Spirits come and carry
us away, carry us far away.

*We float above the planet. Eons roll backwards to
our Sight, and we see a world of plants in the age
before human beings; great and noble forest nations,
meadows of fern and flowers, seas of grasses. Days
and nights shift before our Eyes. The plant world
sleeps at the dark of the Moon. The waxing light
then adds its glow to the Sun of the days and the
plants grow. At the time of the Full Moon all things
respond to the constant light. The relationship of
Earth and Moon is made clear before us as a dance
of two companions. A network of interaction; an
inevitability of influence impresses itself upon our
consciousness. From the understanding of the
Earth-Moon exchange, we see the flow of relationship of all things of the planet: the cloud patterns
following the air currents, the water flowing from
the clouds to the seas, the animals appearing from
the fruit of the forests and existing within the paths
and byways of the plant kingdom.*

*From our position above the Sky, we see the
emergence of the first human beings, the Old Ones.
We watch. With great respect, the Wise Ones of
these People relate to the ancient of days. They
speak of the plants and call them by their Names.
The plant nations are honored by this recognition
of their age-old dominion. They respond; they reach
out to the People and watch over them. The People
are fed and protected by the vast reaches of forest
and grassland. We see the People honoring and loving their benefactors. The Wise Ones of the plants*

teach the Wise Ones of the Peoples how to use the
plant friends and relatives; for food, for medicine,
for magic. And the plant nations also teach the
People how to talk and pray to the spirits of Life, to
strengthen the Life Force and to cause it to respond. At last a chain of Caretakers is spread over
the face of the planet. Every area is protected and
cared for by the loving, respectful activities of those
among the tribes who understand the need, those
who know that without the good friendship and
health of the plant nation, the life of the People
would be extinguished. Thus the great purpose of
Human Beings as Caretakers of the Life Force is
established and perpetuated.

The Caretaking becomes so well performed that
the life of the People becomes easy and a time of
plenty is visited upon them. The centuries are whirling forward very fast now to our Vision. In the time
of plenty there is also a great forgetting among the
People. The number of Wise Ones decreases, and the
People forget to care for the Spirit of Life. A time
of danger comes, for without Caretakers the earth
garden begins to sprout strange growths and configurations.

The Spirit of Life whispers in the remaining forests and grasslands. A stiff wind of authority and
purpose blows from the mountains into the popu-
lous valleys. Through the suburbs and the cities the
Wind of the Life Force moves, and before it are
driven certain people. They are driven from their
comfortable homes; they are driven from universi-
ties and civilized employment. The details of their
experience are many and varied, but the Force behind them is the same: the Wind of Change, the
purposeful, inexorable Current of Life. We see the
Wind blowing Care and Insight into the hearts of

*these Ones, we see the great plant nations teaching
the People again, we see the beginning of Spheres of
Care reaching across continents.*

Suddenly without warning, the feeling of falling
through darkness engulfs us. With a jolt we are back in
the garden. I feel tears on my cheeks. When I open my
eyes, I see that the Vision of Caring has called the Thun-
derbirds to my garden and to the natural garden of the
surrounding hills. As the first raindrops fall upon the
receptive earth, I scurry to the cabin, small and power-
less in the wake of the Winds of Purpose.

The Harvest
*What is there for me when I have finished planting?
What is there for me at the end of the row I must
hoe?
What is there for me when the harvest is over?
Better corn.
That is all.*

               –FROM THE TAOS PUEBLO[4]

Now the garden is an oasis of green in the early fall
landscape. The soft green June grasses have bleached to
gold, but within the garden fence the lushness goes on.
My friends are full-grown. Already during the weeks of
ripening I have picked among them for my meals. So
when I come to the harvest, the ones still growing there
can see that their brothers and sisters have become my
body, are living still through me. They can perceive that
this harvesting is not death for them, merely a change
of form. And so I pick, talking and singing to them as
I proceed, keeping the flow of the friendship. I call
the Ones outside the fence to witness: the trees and
others who have watched the entire process, and thereby
involve the wildness, the primitive Life Force.

A Thanksgiving feast provides an opportunity to review the events of the garden and to honor the powerful forces which operate there. I do not *grow* my garden; I am merely the Caretaker of it. In return it cares for me by giving away its life into my life. It teaches me the secrets of the Greater Harmony in which each One has a Place; it teaches me to care for the Life Force in the ways of the Old Ones; it teaches me my Place. For all these things, my heart sings.

The Great Wheel turns. As the soft snow clouds float high over my head, I turn the soil in the garden spot. The summer's mulch is buried to rot into food for next year; the evidences of this year's rows and plantings disappear. Once again the patch becomes raw, exposed, a hole cut in the soil. I renew my promise to take responsibility for what I have done here, so that this spot and its environs may be cared for in the ancient way.

The garden sleeps under the snows of Winterman. In February the first robin and the first seed catalog announce the return of spring. The circle is complete.

> *In beauty it is begun.*
> *In beauty it is begun.*
> *In peace it is finished.*
> *In peace it shall never end.*
>
> —FROM THE TAOS PUEBLO[5]

FOOTNOTES

1. Nancy and Myron Wood, *Hollering Sun* (New York: Simon and Schuster, 1972).

2. Francis La Flesch, "The Osage Tribe, Part I," *36th Annual Report of American Ethnology* (Washington, D.C., 1921): 37-597.

3. Washington Matthews, "Songs of Sequence of the Navahoes," *Journal of American Folklore* 7 (1894): 185-94.

4. *Hollering Sun.*

5. *Ibid.*

A Brief Guide to Organic Gardening

Here is a brief guide to some of the major steps in growing a good vegetable garden. The guide follows the course of the planting year and stresses primarily organic techniques as those most compatible with working according to the cycles of nature. This is primarily a guide to *how* to set up your garden, but it will make frequent reference to the astrology of *when* to do this or that. Throughout, the emphasis will be on methods allowing the home gardener maximum use of his limited space.

Composting

Composting should be begun as soon as possible, for compost is the basis of the rich, friable soil necessary to high-yield gardening. In composting, you use natural wastes—such as leaves, trimmings, last year's dead vegetation, and garbage—and accelerate the recycling process of nature, supplementing the material with additional nutrients. Compost heaps are best started in Cancer, Scorpio and Pisces when the Moon is in its fourth quarter.

A Basic Method. Wrap small-mesh wire fencing around three or four four-foot stakes stuck about a foot into the ground. On top of each four- to six-inch layer of material, sprinkle agricultural lime, a layer of garden soil, and on top of that a layer of manure, followed, if necessary, by another soil to keep down the smell. Leave a depression in the center to catch rain; water the pile occasionally if rain is light. Turn the pile over every four to six weeks so that the material on the edges becomes mixed with the active central core. In three to six months, when it is dark and crumbly, the compost will be ready to use.

A Fast Method. In a large garbage can or large dark-colored plastic bag, put a two-inch layer of soil or peat moss; add waste kitchen materials and, occasionally, garden wastes; when full, close and set out in full sunlight for about three weeks, after which the compost will be ready to use.

Some Tips on Composting. Keep particle size small to speed decomposition. If heat production is low, add nitrogen in the form of fresh manure or blood meal to accelerate bacterial action. A pile must be of the right height to maintain its proper heat: too low, and it will lose heat; too high, and it will become compressed, shutting off the air supply to the bacteria. Maintain a moisture content of about forty to sixty percent; the pile should be about as wet as a squeezed-out sponge.

If you don't have the facilities for making compost, rotted manure is an adequate substitute.

Situating the Garden

The garden should be placed in an area that receives *a minimum of six hours of direct sunlight* every day. If you live on a shaded lot and such area is at a premium, you can reserve your sunlit areas for just the sun-loving vegetables such as tomatoes, corn, cucumbers and melons, placing shade-tolerant vegetables such as lettuce and pumpkins elsewhere. You can also plant in tubs and on stakes and trellises, taking advantage of what little sunlit area you have.

The area should be well drained; water should not stand on the surface long. Making a clayey soil into a loamy one (as described under "Soil Preparation") will remedy mild drainage problems, but avoid low, swampy spots or a depression at the base of a hill.

Keep your bed at least twenty feet from shallow-rooted trees like elms, maples and poplars, for their roots will compete for water and nutrients. Generally, the roots of a tree feed in an area whose radius is equal to the tree's widest reaching branch; plants do poorly in this area.

If space is scarce, it may be helpful to keep in mind that the garden doesn't have to be in one place only. Vegetables can be planted with flowers, on trellises affixed to walls and fences, in pots on patios, and in various mini-gardens tucked in your yard's nooks and crannies.

Soil Preparation

If the soil is prepared in the fall, planting can begin immediately in the spring; also the soil has a chance to assimilate, before planting begins, the nutrients added to it. The best time to cultivate is when the Moon is in a barren sign (Aries, Gemini, Leo, Virgo, Aquarius) and decreasing, preferably in the fourth quarter, when sprouting weed seeds are best killed.

In preparing the soil, you should be concerned with four points: soil type, nutrients, pH and soil structure. The objective is to create a super-fertile, well-textured soil that will support many vegetables in a small space.

Soil Type. There are three kinds of soils: sandy, clayey and loamy. The best soil is the loamy type, which has enough sand to allow for proper aeration of the roots and proper drainage, unlike the clayey type, which compacts and retains excessive moisture. The loamy type also has enouch clay to retain sufficient moisture between rainfalls, unlike sandy soils; and it has enough decomposing organic matter, called *humus*, to nourish plant growth. The ideal mix is about one-third sand, one-third clay and one-third humus, or compost. These should be thoroughly

mixed, as per the instructions under "Soil Structure."

Nutrients. Once the soil is of the right type, you should supplement it with the three major nutrients: nitrogen, phosphorus and potassium. Ideally, these nutrients should come from *organic* materials, such as compost, manure, bone meal, wood ash (or a substitute) and fish emulsion. Compost is the main source of these nutrients, but even to a well-balanced soil you should add:

- **Animal manures**—a good source of nitrogen; best used in rotted form, not fresh, which is more easily absorbed by the plant. Hen, horse, sheep and rabbit manures are highest in nitrogen.
- **Bone meal**—twenty to twenty-five percent phosphorus. Substitutes are rock phosphate and superphosphate.
- **Wood ash**—contains seven to eight percent potassium and can be obtained from your fireplace. Substitutes are green sand and granite dust, which can be purchased at many nurseries.
- **Fish emulsion**—a good source of nitrogen.

Other nutrient supplements are blood meal and Milorganite, both heavy in nitrogen. The proportions in which these supplements should be added to the soil are covered under "Soil Structure."

pH. If you follow the method under "Soil Structure," pH will automatically be taken care of, except where the soil is extremely alkaline (salt marshes) or acidic (peat bogs). The ideal soil pH for vegetables is 6.5 to 7—a reading that is neutral or slightly acid. To test soil, send a sample to the state agricultural department or purchase a soil-testing kit. If it is acidic, less than 6.5 on the pH scale, add dolomitic limestone at five pounds per 100 square feet. If it is alkaline, over 7, add large amounts of organic matter in the early spring.

Soil Structure. In addition to well-balanced, fertile soil, you want soil that is properly layered and textured to promote efficient aeration and water conduction. The basic objective is to get the soil coarse below and fine-textured above. While French-Intensive methods of soil cultivation take more time than other methods, they are worth the extra effort because of the time later saved in cultivation and weeding. A simple and a more complex method are outlined below. For further information, see Duane Newcomb's excellent book, *The Postage Stamp Garden Book* (Los Angeles: J.P. Tarcher, Inc., 1975), on which the following account is based.

The General Intensive Method

- Rototill your bed at least one foot deep.
- If you have clayey soil, turn sand and compost into your soil until it consists of one-third compost, one-third sand and one-third original soil. For sandy soils, turn compost into your bed until you have one-third to one-half compost, the rest original soil.
- Level the bed with a rake.
- Over the entire bed spread a two-inch layer of rotted manure, a sprinkling of bone meal (four pounds for fifty square feet), and a small dose of wood ash (three pounds for fifty square feet). With a rake, turn this into just the top portion of the soil, and then rake the topsoil to a light texture.

A Modified French-Intensive Method

- For clayey soils, cover the entire bed six to eight inches with a mixture of one-half compost and one-half sand; for sandy soils, cover with four to five inches of pure compost.
- Along one side of the bed dig a trench one spade wide and deep (see next page for figure). Put the excavated topsoil, along with the compost-sand mix,

aside where you can get it later. Loosen the subsoil
in the trench you've just dug one spade-depth more
(for a total of about eighteen to twenty inches
deep); the subsoil should be loose but not too fine.

- Remove one spade-depth of topsoil, plus compost-
sand mixture, from the strip of bed directly beside
the first trench, and fill in the original trench,
making sure that you mix well the topsoil and compost-sand mixture. The object is to grade the soil
from the loose subsoil to the finely textured topsoil.

- You now have a new trench beside the one that you
just filled; dig that trench down one spade-depth
more to loosen the subsoil. Dig a new trench beside
it, placing the excavated topsoil and compost-sand
mixture in the trench where you have just loosened
the subsoil. Then loosen the subsoil in the new
trench and continue the process.

- Fill in the last trench with what you excavated from
the first.

- Let the soil stand for a few days so that the air can
get into it; then rake the topsoil to a fine texture.

- Over the entire surface spread two inches of rotted
manure, a small amount of bone meal (four pounds
per fifty square feet), and a small amount of wood

1. Put a layer of compost over the garden; remove topsoil-compost
to one spade's depth in the first trench, and reserve in a pile.
2. Loosen the subsoil in the first trench by cultivating it another
spade's depth. 3. Dig a second trench one spade deep beside the
first, and place excavated topsoil-compost into the first trench,

ash (three pounds per fifty square feet). Work these materials into the top five to six inches of the soil.

There is also the Expert French-Intensive Method, which involves adding the nutrients at precise levels, on the assumption that root growth will speed up if the soil is structured to encourage that growth. For information on this, see Newcomb's *The Postage Stamp Garden Book.*

Whatever method you use, earthworms (the gray pink ones: *Helodrilus caliginosus* and *Helodrilus trapezoides*) will assist in keeping the soil well-textured for air and water conduction and in fertilizing it with their castings.

Planning Your Garden

Planning should begin early enough to allow you to purchase seed catalogues, buy your seeds, start your seedlings if you are going to transplant, and prepare the soil if you have not already done so in the fall. January is not too early. Here follows a listing of points to consider, based on *The Time-Life Encyclopedia of Gardening: Vegetables and Fruits* (New York: Time-Life Books, 1972).

Plant Vegetables That Taste Notably Better Fresh Than Bought: tomatoes, asparagus, sweet corn, peas, beans,

mixing it well. 4. Repeat step 2 for the second trench: spade the subsoil. 5. Repeat step 3 for the second trench: fill it with well-mixed topsoil-compost excavated from the third trench. 6. Continue the process the full width of the garden, filling the last trench with the topsoil-compost reserved from the first.

young onions, carrots, lettuce and summer squash. Winter squash and mature potatoes and onions, on the other hand, lose little when purchased at the supermarket.

Choose Varieties That Will Grow Well in Your Climate. Consult your garden-store proprietor, state agricultural extension agent or state agricultural college.

Know Your Local Frost Dates. You can get the average first and last killing-frost dates from your local weather bureau or county agent but note that these dates are affected by altitude, proximity to bodies of water, etc. (see "When To Plant").

Plant Cool-Weather Crops Early or Late in the Year. Many crops, especially those of the cabbage family, can be planted as early as six weeks before the last frost date and will grow until the ground freezes. Spinach and many kinds of peas and lettuce do well only when it is cool, so one crop can be planted in early spring and another in the fall.

Plant Warm-Weather Crops When Temperatures Remain Above the Required Level. Melons, tomatoes, eggplants, sweet potatoes, etc., will do well only when planted in warmer weather (see "When To Plant"). These can be started earlier or bought as transplants to get a head start.

Make Successive Plantings To Distribute the Harvest Over a Longer Period. Unleess you want to harvest all at once for canning purposes, it is best to plant root and leafy vegetables and corn at seven- to ten-day intervals until midsummer or to mix earlier and later maturing varieties of vegetables like tomatoes and cabbage.

Know Each Vegetable's Average Time to Maturity. This is listed in seed catalogues and on seed packets.

Start Successive Planting in a Nursery Bed To Save Garden Space. Crops which can be grown as second crops, like lettuce, cabbage, broccoli and cauliflower, can be grown for two or three weeks before the first crop is ready for harvest and then transplanted.

Grow More Plants in a Limtied Space Through Interplanting. Smaller, fast-maturing crops can be grown between larger, slow-maturing ones and harvested before the larger plant needs its full space. Lettuce can be planted between cabbages (which require one and one-half to two feet between them) and harvested before the slower-growing cabbage overshadows it. Spinach can be planted between rows of tomatoes, snap beans between rows of parsnips.

Locate Perennial Vegetables Out of the Way so that they will not be disturbed by cultivation.

Place Tall-Growing Vegetables So That They Will Not Shade Low-Growing Ones. Corn, pole beans, tomatoes or cucumbers trained on stakes should be set at the north side of the garden.

You Don't Have To Plant in Rows. Maximum use of space can be achieved if you thin out your plants so that they just touch upon maturity; this procedure will have a mulching effect, and keep down weed growth and retain soil moisture (see "Planting").

Use the Air Space Above Your Garden. Train tomatoes cucumbers and other vines and trailing plants up trellises, fences, poles, etc.

Don't Limit Yourself to Vegetables. Herbs and flowers such as marigolds brighten a garden and benefit garden health.

Plan Successive Plantings To Maintain Soil Fertility. Rotate crops so that heavy feeders are followed by light feeders. Light feeders are beets, carrots, onions, radishes, rutabagas and turnips. Heavy feeders are broccoli, Brussels sprouts, cabbage, cauliflower, corn, cucumber, eggplant, kale, lettuce, melons, mustard greens, New Zealand spinach, okra, peppers, spinach, squash, Swiss chard, and tomatoes. If a heavy feeder must follow a heavy feeder, then add some source of nutrients, such as fish emulsion.

By planting legumes such as beans and peas, you can rotate crops to *restore* lost nitrogen to the soil.

When Interplanting, Recognize Plant Affinities. Plants that like each other: members of the cabbage family (broccoli, Brussel sprouts, cauliflower, cabbage) and smelly herbs, onions; carrots and peas; corn and legumes, vine crops; radishes and peas, pole beans, nasturtiums, leaf lettuce; spinach and cabbage; tomatoes and asparagus, parsley, cabbage, mustard greens; turnips and rutabagas. Plants that don't get along: members of the onion family and peas, beans; beets and pole beans; dill and carrots, tomatoes.

Interplant To Control Pests. Folk wisdom has it that chives repel insects; garlic controls blight and repels aphids, mosquito larvae, some caterpillars, and sucking bugs; leek repels the carrot fly; marigolds kill nematodes and the tomato whitefly; mint repels ants and cabbage-worm butterflies; nasturiums repel squash bugs; radishes repel the striped cucumber beetle; rosemary repels the carrot fly; sage protects against the cabbage butterfly; tomatoes planted near cabbage repel the cabbage butterfly.

These are some of the points to consider when planning your garden. The more thought you give early in the year to planning, the more your garden will take care of itself later in the season. On page 423 is a list of seed companies you can write to for catalogues, and on the following pages appear a table of average harvests and a recommended planting schedule which will assist you in planing, plus a sample garden plan illustrating some of the planning principles outlined above. For further information on harvests and planting schedules, send seventy-five cents for the fifty-page bulletin entitled, "Growing Vegetables in the Home Garden," put out by the U.S. Government Printing Office, Washington, D.C. 20402, and ask for Home and Garden Bulletin No. 202. For a variety of

Average Harvests

Crop	Seed for 25 ft. row	Growing Period (to medium size)	Edible period (weeks)	Est. Yield per 25 foot row
Asparagus	12 plants	2-3 years	4-5	12-15 lb.
Beans, bush	2 oz.	50-70 days	4-5	2-3 pk.
Beans, bush lima	2 oz.	60-90	3-4	20-30 lb.
Beans, pole	1 oz.	60-90	6-8	3-4 pk.
Beets	¼ oz.	55-100	4-6	40-50 lb.
Broccoli	¼ pkt.	80-120	8-10	10-15 heads
Brussels sprouts	¼ pkt.	70-110	6-8	10-15 qt.
Cabbage	¼ pkt.	75-130	4-6	20-40 lb.
Cabbage, Chinese	¼ pkt.	70-85	4-6	12-15 heads
Carrots	1 pkt.	65-85	6-8	25-30 lb.
Cauliflower	¼ pkt.	65-90	1-2	8-12 heads
Celery	1 pkt.	100-140	6-8	40-50 plants
Chard, Swiss	1 pkt.	55-70	until fall	35-40 lb.
Corn, sweet	1 pkt.	65-100	1-2	30-50 ears
Cucumbers	1 pkt.	60-100	4-6	40-50 fruits
Eggplant	¼ pkt.	110-150	until fall	12-25 fruits
Endive	1 pkt.	80-100	3-4	12-15 plants
Kale	¼-1 pkt.	70-100	until fall	30-40 lb.
Kohlrabi	1 pkt.	55-75	2-3	25-40 lb.
Lettuce, leaf	1 pkt.	40-50	2-3	10-12 lb.
Lettuce, head	¼ pkt.	75-100	2-3	10-15 heads
Muskmelons	1 pkt.	90-120	3-4	20-30 fruits
Onions (seed)	½ pkt.	110-140	4-8	1-2 pk.
Onions (sets)	¼ lb.	50-100	4-8	2-3 pk.
Parsley	1 pkt.	90-120	until fall	10-12 lb.
Parsnips	1 pkt.	100-150	fall	30-50 lb.
Peas, early	¼ lb.	50-70	1-2	5-7 lb.
Peas, late	¼ lb.	70-100	1-2	5-7 lb.
Peppers	¼ pkt.	100-140	until fall	40-50 fruits
Potatoes (early)	2-3 lb.	80-110	. . .	30-40 lb.
Potatoes (late)	2-3 lb.	110-140	. . .	30-40 lb.
Pumpkins	1 pkt.	90-120	until fall	12-20 fruits
Radishes	1 pkt.	30-65	1-2	150-300
Rutabagas	1 pkt.	95-110	fall	25-35 lb.
Salsify	1 pkt.	130-150	fall	30-40 lb.
Spinach	1 pkt.	40-60	1-3	10-12 lb.
Spinach, N.Z.	1 pkt.	70	until fall	20-30 lb.
Squash, summer	1 pkt.	60-80	until fall	30-40 fruits
Squash, winter	1 pkt.	100-140	fall	15-20 fruits
Tomatoes	¼ pkt.	100-150	6-12	1½-2 bu.
Turnips	1 pkt.	50-70	1-3	30-40 lb.
Watermelons	1 pkt.	90-130	3-4	10-15 fruits

Recommended Planting Schedule

Vegetable	Start seeds indoors	Plant seeds or transplant	Inches between rows	Inches betw'n plants	Seeding depth (inches)	Amount to order per 100 feet of row
Asparagus	...	Ap 15-May 1	36-48	18-24	6 (plants)	60 plants
Beans, Snap (bush)	...	May 15-Jl 1	18-24	3-4	1½	2 pounds
Beans, Snap (pole)	...	May 15-Jl 1	36	36	1½	2 pounds
Beans, Dry Shell	...	May 15	18-24	3-4	1½	2 pounds
Beans, Lima	...	May 20-Je 10	18-24	4-6	1½	1 pound
Beets	...	Ap 15-Jl 1	18-24	2-4	1	1 ounce
Broccoli	Mar 1-15	Ap 15/Je 1	24-30	24	¼*	1 pkt, 30 plants
Brussels Sprouts	Mar 1-15	Ap 15/Je 1	24-30	24	¼*	1 pkt, 30 plants
Cabbage, Early	Mar 1-15	Ap 15/Je 1	24-30	18	¼*	1 pkt, 40 plants
Cabbage, Late	Ap 15-May 1	Ap 15-May 1	24-30	24	¼**	1 pkt, 60 plants
Cabbage, Chinese	...	Je 1 Jl 1	18-24	12-18	½	1 pkt
Carrots	...	Ap 15-Je 15	18-24	2-3	½	1 pkt
Cauliflower	Mar 1-15	Ap 15/Je 1	24-30	18-24	¼*	1 oz
Celery	Feb 15-Mar 1	May 15	18-24	6-8	1/8*	1 pkt, 30 plants
Chard, Swiss	...	May 1	18-24	6-8	1	1 pkt, 100 plants
Cucumbers	...	May 15-Je 1	48-60	48-60	1-2	½ oz
Eggplant	Mar 15-Ap 1	Je 1	24-30	24	¼*	1 pkt, 12 plants
Endive	...	Ap 15	18-24	8-12	½	1 pkt
Horseradish	...	Ap 15-May 1	24-30	12-18	6 (roots)	20 plants
Kale	...	Ap 15-Jl 15	18-24	12-18	½	1 pkt
Kohlrabi	...	Ap 15-Je 1/ Aug 1-15	18-24	6-8	½	1 pkt
Lettuce, Leaf	...	Ap 15-Je 1/ Aug 1-15	18-24	4-8	½	½ oz

Lettuce, Head	Mar 1-15	Ap 15-May 1	18-24	12	¼*	1 pkt, 25 plants
Muskmelon	...	May 20-Je 1	60-72	60-72	1-2	½ oz
Onion, Seeds	...	Ap 15	18-24	2	1	1 oz
Onion, Transplants	Feb 1-15	Ap 15	18-24	2-3	½*	1 oz
Onion, Sets	...	Ap 15	18-24	2-3	1-2	6 pounds
Onion, Winter	...	Aug 1-15	18-24	1	4	1 oz
Parsley	...	Ap 15-May 1	18-24	4-6	¼	1 pkt
Parsnips	...	May 1-15	18-24	3-4	½	½ oz
Peas	...	Ap 15-May 1	18-24	2	2-3	5 pounds
Pepper	Mar 15-Ap 1	Je 1	18-24	18-24	¼*	1 pkt, 20 plants
Potatoes, Irish	...	Ap 15-Je 1	24-30	12-18	4-6	1½ bushels
Potatoes, Sweet	Ap 15 (roots)	Je 1	36-48	18-24		150 plants
Pumpkin	...	May 20-Je 1	72-96	72-96	1-2	½ oz
Radishes	...	Ap 15-Je 1/ Aug 1-15	18-24	1-2	1	1 oz
Rhubarb	...	Ap 15-May 1	36-48	36-48		12 plants
Rutabaga	...	May 15-Je 15	18-24	6-8	½	½ oz
Salsify	...	Ap 15-May 1	18-24	2-3	½-1	¼ oz
Spinach	...	Ap 15/Aug 1-15	18-24	3-4	1	2 oz
Spinach, New Zealand	...	May 1	30-36	12-18	1	1 pkt
Squash, Summer	...	May 20-Je 1	36-48	36-48	1-2	½ oz
Squash, Winter	...	May 20-Je 1	72-96	72-96	1-2	1 oz
Sweet Corn	...	May 10-Jl 1	30-36	30-36	1-2	1½ pounds
Tomatoes	Ap 1-15	Je 1	36-48	36-48	¼*	1 pkt, 60 plants
Turnips	...	Ap 15/Aug	18-24	3-4	½	1 pkt
Watermelons	...	May 20-Je 1	60-72	60-72	1-2	1 oz

*--INDOORS; **--SEEDBED.

The dates in this table are based on an average last frost date falling somewhere between May 1 and May 15. For areas where the last frost date is earlier or later, you will have to make adjustments.

		10'		

WIRE FENCE — WIRE FENCE

SAVORY | LETTUCE harvested before BEANS grow, intercropped with RADISHES / ZUCCHINI or other bush SQUASH
(right top) | TOMATOES inter-croppedwithRADISHES, LETTUCE, and ONIONS / early BEETS for greens followed by CUCUMBERS on supports | **CHIVES**

BASIL | ¹ bibb ¹ loose- ¹ head ² ² leaf ² — LETTUCE – LETTUCE — ³ ³ ³ / NEW ZEALAND SPINACH or SWISS CHARD
(center N/S axis) | N / BROCCOLI followed by summer SQUASH in air / S / PEPPERS intercropped with RADISHES, LETTUCE, or ONIONS | **MINT / GARLIC**

THYME | 1 2 / C A R R O T S / 3 / RADISHES
 | 1 2 3 / BEETS / 1 2 3 / GREEN or BULB ONIONS | **MARJORAM**

MARIGOLDS | MARIGOLDS

12'

Reprinted from Duane Newcomb's *The Postage Stamp Garden Book*. Illustrates some basic gardening principles. Tall, slow-growing vine plants rise on the north, and are interplanted with fast-growing, cool-weather crops. Areas for carrots, beets, onions, and lettuce are sectioned to allow for plantings 7-10 days apart, for continuous harvests. Cucumbers are trained in air. Companion plants border the garden.

useful garden plans, get a copy of Duane Newcomb's *The Postage Stamp Garden Book.*

Seed Companies

- Burpee Seed Co., Philadelphia, Pa. 19132
- Burgess Seed Co., Galesburg, Mich. 49053
- Farmers Seed & Nursery Co., Faribault, Minn. 55021
- Harris Seed Co., Rochester, N.Y. 14624
- Northrup King and Co., Minneapolis, Minn. 55413
- Geo. W. Park Seed Co., Inc., Greenwood, S.C. 29646
- Stokes Seeds Inc., Box 548, Buffalo, N.Y. 14240
- Otis S. Twilley Seed Co., Salisbury, Md. 21801

When To Plant

In general, sow during the waxing phases of the Moon. See "Gardening by the Moon" for more specific instructions regarding various kinds of vegetables. Ideal astrological times, of course, must be reconciled with prevailing weather conditions.

Cool-Season Crops are those that will tolerate day temperatures of fifty-five to seventy degrees. Those that are tolerant of some frost: asparagus, beets, broccoli, Brussels sprouts, cabbage, kale, mustard greens, New Zealand spinach, onions, radishes, spinach, turnips and rutabagas. Cool-season crops intolerant of frost at maturity: carrots, cauliflower, endive, lettuce, peas, rhubarb and Swiss chard.

Warm-Season Crops are those requiring sixty-five- to eighty-degree temperatures day and night. Readily damaged by frost, this group includes beans, corn, cucumbers, eggplant, melons, okra, pepper, squash and tomatoes.

A frost map, readily found in most gardening books, or a call to the weather bureau or county agent will tell you the last frost date in your area. This date can be used as a guide to planting vegetables, when coupled with the following information.

In the South, Southwest and California, plant these vegetables from fall to early spring; in all other areas, plant them two to four weeks before the last killing frost in spring: broccoli, Brussels sprouts, kale, lettuce, mustard greens, peas, onions, radishes, rutabagas and turnips.

Plant the following vegetables on approximately the last frost date: beets, cabbage, carrots, cauliflower, Swiss chard.

Plant the following vegetables after the ground has warmed up: beans, corn, cucumbers, eggplant, melons, okra, peppers, squash and tomatoes.

Since frost dates are average dates and don't take into account whether you live in a valley or near a large body of water, a surer guide to when to plant is the following: when spring bulbs begin to blossom, plant beets, carrots, leaf lettuce, onions, peas, radishes and spinach. When

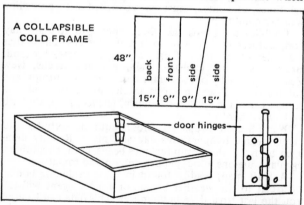

A COLLAPSIBLE COLD FRAME

48"

back 15" front 9" side 9" side 15"

door hinges

plum and cherry blossoms appear, plant head lettuce. When apple, quince and strawberry blossoms appear, plant everything else: cucumbers, squash, tomatoes, etc. Using the Moon and the signs of nature itself, you can't go wrong on your timing.

Planting

Starting Ahead of Time. Slow-growing plants such as tomatoes, eggplants, peppers cabbages and the many vine crops can be started early and set out in the garden when the weather is warm enough, or they can be purchased from a nursery and transplanted. If you grow them indoors, you can purchase necessary equipment from seed companies such as George W. Park Seed Company, Inc., Greenwood, South Carolina 29646. To grow them outdoors, you will need a cold frame.

Making a Cold Frame. Take half of a 4 x 8 sheet of ½-inch exterior-grade plywood and saw it into four pieces as indicated in the accompanying diagram. Assemble the

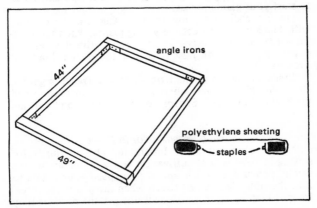

pieces with removable-pin hinges so that the frame can be taken apart each year for storage. Treat against rot with a preservative stain containing copper naphthenate (preparations containing creosote, mercury compounds and pentachlorophenol are toxic to plants). For the cover, fasten lengths of 1¼-by-3-inch lumber with angle irons. Paint and wrap with four- to six-mil clear polythylene sheeting, fastened underneath the frame by heavy staples. Hinge cover to base with removable-pin hinges. Hooks and eyes in front will hold the cover closed in cold and windy weather. The cold frame should be positioned with its higher side to the north so that it gets the full benefit of the Sun.

To Make a Hot Frame, lay lead-covered electric heating cables (available at your garden store or through seed catalogues) four inches below soil or sand in the bottom of the cold frame, and cover with hardware cloth to prevent damage to the cable from gardening implements. The heat will cause earlier germination of seeds and will allow you to start your plants earlier.

On especially cold nights the frame can be covered with blankets to protect the young plants. When temperatures are between sixty-five and seventy-five degrees, the cover must be kept raised so that the plants don't get overheated.

Transplanting of plants from your cold frame or garden store should be done when the Moon is increasing and preferably in Cancer, Scorpio or Pisces. Evening hours are best.

Sowing Broadside or in Rows

Nature casts her seeds broadside. The argument for sowing in rows is that cultivation and weeding are easier. But if you use a mulch and if you space your plants so that the outer leaves just touch when the plants are three-fourths mature, then weeds will not get the sunlight they need to grow and the soil will not become dried out and compacted; furthermore, the yield of a given space will be increased. The table which follows gives the space, in inches, that should be left between plants.

Spacing Between Plants

Asparagus	12	Melons,	
Beans, bush	4	(trained in air)	24
Beans, pole	10	Mustard greens	4
Beets	2	New Zealand	
Broccoli	15	spinach	8
Brussels		Okra	15
sprouts	16	Onions	2-3
Cabbage	12	Peas	
Carrots	1	(trained in air)	2
Cauliflower	30	Peppers	14
Corn	8	Radishes	1
Cucumbers		Rhubarb	12-36
(trained in air)	4	Rutabagas	6
Eggplant	25	Spinach	6
Kale	16	Squash, bush	18
Lettuce,		Swiss chard	4
butterhead	4-5	Tomatoes	
Lettuce, head	10	(trained in air)	18
Lettuce, leaf	4-5	Turnips	6

Watering

Using a mulch and planting close together will cut down on the need for watering because the soil will be assisted in retaining moisture. Water in a moist sign: Cancer, Scorpio, Pisces or Libra.

While waiting for seeds to germinate, keep the soil constantly damp but never soggy. Young, growing vegetables do best when they receive an inch of water each week.

Water mature plants well, to a depth of about two feet, once a week. Depth can be checked with a quarter-inch-diameter rod which will easily penetrate the moist soil but stop when it reaches the dryer layers. Plants that are alternately starved for and saturated with water will not do well.

If you water from above rather than through furrow irrigation, make sure that the leaves have a chance to dry before nightfall ; otherwise they will be susceptible to disease.

Weeding

Weeding is best done when the Moon is in the fourth quarter, although the third is also effective. Weeding can be minimized through mulching and through planting your vegetables so that the leaves just touch when the plants are three-fourths mature.

Fertilizing

Fertilizing is best done when the Moon is in a fruitful sign (Cancer, Scorpio, Pisces). If a chemical fertilizer is used, select a time when the Moon is increasing; organic fertilizers should be used when the Moon is waning. Careful preparation of compost and soil minimizes the need for additional fertilization. If crops are rotated so that light feeders follow heavy ones, and so that the soil is replenished naturally through the periodic planting of legumes such as peas and beans which restore nitrogen to the soil, the need for midseason fertilization is further minimized. For the heavy feeders such as tomatoes, however, you may have to add fish emulsion or some other fertilizer at midseason. If your garden soil is in generally good shape, the application of compost to just the places where plants will grow, rather than to the whole garden, may be just the boost they need to get them through the season.

Pest Control

Pests are best destroyed when both the Sun and Moon are in barren signs (Leo, Aries, Virgo, Aquarius, Gemini and Sagittarius) and the Moon is decreasing, fourth quarter preferred. Keeping the garden well-managed is one way to control pests or at least to maintain a balanced pest population so that they will control each other. Crop rotation; use of viable, dated, disease-resistant seed; good drainage; keeping out of the garden when the leaves are wet; and keeping the garden free of dead vegetation — all these methods will help to control pests.

Physically removing the trespassers or hosing down the garden with a soap-and-water spray are other non-drastic control measures. Companion-planting, discussed earlier in this article (under "Planning Your Garden") and elsewhere in the Farm and Garden Section ("Try Companion Planting"), is an additional non-drastic method of pest control.

Another way of using nature to do your policing for you is the purchase of insects which prey on garden pests. Lacewing flies feed on aphids; ladybugs eat aphids, thrips, tree-lice and the eggs and larvae of many other plant-destroying insects; young praying mantises go after aphids, flies and other small insects, while the adults destroy great numbers of beetles, caterpillars, grasshoppers and other damaging garden pests; and trichogramma wasps feed on the larvae of the cabbage worm. Many of these predator insects may be purchased from W. Atlee Burpee Company, P.O. Box 6929, Philadelphia, Pennsylvania 19132.

If these natural methods fail you, you still have one other recourse before turning to chemical sprays: organic sprays. Ryania may be used to control corn borers, cranberry fruitworm, coddling moth, Oriental fruit moth, Cotton-boll worm and other insects. Rotenone is also effective against many insects. Pyrethrum may be combined with rotenone for a very effective spray. Good

botantically based sprays can be made from the leaves of
companion plants such as mint, rosemary and radishes
which are supposed to repel certain insects. A useful
spray is made from a mash of garlic and hot peppers
soaked in water overnight and then supplemented with
soap to enable it to adhere better to the leaves. Milk
sprays comprised of one pound of skim milk mixed with
a gallon of water have been found to work well on tomato
plants.

Harvesting

Harvesting must be done at the right time to get full
flavor and nutritional value from your vegetables. Harvest
root crops during the decrease of the Moon (third and
fourth quarters) and in the dry signs (Aries, Leo Sagittarius, Gemini, and Aquarius). If you are harvesting root
crops for seed, do so at the Full Moon.

For further specific information, see "Gardening by
the Moon" in this section and "Astrological Encyclopedia" in the Daily Activities section. In addition, the
following books are highly recommended:

Planetary Planting by Louise Riotte. A Guide to Organic Gardening by the Signs of the Zodiac. New York:
Simon and Schuster, 1975.
The Postage Stamp Gardening Book by Duane Newcomb. How to Grow All the Food You Can Eat in
Very Little Space. Los Angeles California: J.P. Tarcher, Inc., 1975.
*The Time-Life Encyclopedia of Gardening: Vegetables
and Fruits.* New York: Time, Inc. 1972.

Additional information may be obtained by writing to the
Superintendent of Documents, Government Printing
Office, Washington, D.C. 20250, for these publications:

"List of Available Publications of the USDA," Bulletin No. 11 (45 cents).

"Minigardens for Vegetables," H&G Bulletin No. 163 (15 cents).

"Growing Vegetables in the Home Garden," H&G Bulletin No. 202 (75 cents).

Write directly to the Publications Division, U.S. Department of Agriculture, Washington, D.C. 20250 for the following publication:

"Suburban and Farm Vegetable Gardens," Bulletin No. G9 (free).

Try Companion Planting

Louise Riotte

Just what is companion planting? Briefly, it is placing plants in close proximity so they may help each other grow, or repel their enemies, which may be insects or even other plants. It may also be succession planting; for instance, corn, which needs nitrogen, may follow a crop of early peas, which restore nitrogen to the soil by drawing it out of the air. Because of its high saponin content, spinach is useful as a pre-crop and does especially well planted with strawberries. The solanine in tomatoes will protect asparagus against asparagus beetles. In turn a chemical derived from asparagus juice has been found effective when used on tomato plants as a killer of nematodes.

Nature's Order

Diversification is needed in the process of building a farm or a garden, just as in the growth of an organism. This means using a variety of different crops and also crop rotation. Fortunately a variety of produce is just what the home gardener wants.

Nature abhors idle ground. If given her way she will always have roots hanging into the topsoil to prevent erosion. And she almost never leaves wide, unplanted, unmulched areas between growing plants. Furthermore, her plants, in most instances, grow very closely together.

And she is totally realistic in the matter of checks and balances. Instead of isolating particular kinds or varieties, she often places them "shoulder to shoulder" with each other. Thus they become—in her plan—a source of needed shade, a climbing support, or a provider of mulch and soil-conditioning food. They may even repel other plants, preventing a sturdy, too-aggressive species from completely taking over.

Planting Thickly

And Nature, unlike we who make gardens, also avoids planting in long, straight rows, preferring to broadcast her seeds. Granting that we cannot entirely go her way—order and cultivation being necessary if the garden is not to become a complete weed patch—we can still learn a great deal.

Once upon a time I planted radishes one by one, a few inches apart in a long, narrow row. Now I make my radish row (as well as my carrot and beet row), about a foot wide, broadcast the seeds in this space, and do very little thinning. I find that the plants shade each other—something very important in my hot, dry climate—and the crisp, moist radishes will produce well into summer.

I plant a single row of onions and then plant a staggered row on each side. When they are large enough for table use, I pull every other one, leaving wider spaces between those intended to be used at maturity for dry onions.

Interplanting for Increased Production

In my cold frame I keep a succession of lettuce plants coming up to use for transplants between broccoli, cauliflower or cabbage. As the brassicas grow and need more room, the lettuce is pulled. It is crisp and sweet right into hot weather because it has grown in the shade of the larger plants. With this type of planning, it is possible to get nearly twice as much production from a given garden area.

Let Your Plants Do Your Fertilizing!
Succession Planting and Soil Restoration

Something else to consider is ways to get the most mileage out of compost or fertilizer. Not all vegetable plants have the same requirements in this respect. First we have the heavy feeders such as broccoli, Brussels sprouts, cabbage, cauliflower, celeriac, celery, chard, cucumber, endive, kohlrabi, leek, lettuce, spinach, squash, sweet corn and tomato. Plant these in soil newly fertilized with well-decomposed manure or other organic matter.

You will still have vigorous plants if, without additional fertilizing, you follow the heavy feeders with beets, carrots, radishes, rutabagas and turnips, which also thrive on finely pulverized raw rocks and compost. These are the light feeders.

Legumes, the third of your chain of succession plantings, include broad and lima beans, bush and pole beans, peas and soybeans. These are the improvers of the soil for they collect nitrogen on their roots and restore it into the earth.

Companion Plants as "Helpers"

In your garden, companion plants may act as supports. Grow cucumbers with sunflowers. The cucumbers will climb upward and at the same time benefit the sunflowers by providing a living mulch to keep their roots cool and the soil from drying out.

Farmers have been planting squash with corn for a long, long time—or pumpkins with corn. This is of particular assistance to corn in areas where raccoons need to be discouraged. Many believe that the coons will not come into the corn rows because they like to be able to stand up and look around while they eat, and the big leaves make this impossible.

Two-Level Gardening

Other types of companion planting include "two-level" gardening. This means planting together vegetables which occupy different soil strata. You can plant asparagus with parsley and tomatoes, beets with kohlrabi, beets with onion, garlic with tomatoes, carrots with peas, leeks with vine plants, strawberries with bush beans and many other combinations. Never, however, plant together those that will compete for the same space and light, or those whose root excretions react unfavorably on each other such as dill and carrots, or onions with beans.

Harvesting in Succession

Nature has a way of anticipating when it is time for a particular crop to emerge or mature, and the environment has been readied for the next one. And, like nature, we can learn to anticipate the needs of plants in the maturing phase.

Plant beets, for instance, about thirty inches apart between rows, in the plot reserved for late potatoes. Beets can be counted on to grow well during the wet, cool days of early spring. Along about June plant late potatoes down the center of the beet rows. Potatoes grow quickly in warm weather and in a few weeks they will be producing sufficient shade to enable the beets to produce large, succulent roots in spite of high daytime temperatures which would ordinarily make them fibrous and "woody." This interplanting will also give your potatoes more time to mature before the cool days of fall.

Don't be too eager to cut down your cornstalks. Starting a fall garden in hot, dry midsummer isn't easy, so take another lesson from Nature who starts hers in the cool shade of tall sunflowers. Let your stalks remain standing and cultivate down the middle of each row, cutting the corn roots to make later removal easy. In the tilled area you can plant turnips, cabbage, late peas, collards, beans, rutabagas, and some types of lettuce. I find that, given a little moisture, the seeds will sprout quickly in the shade. When the little plants become well-established and the Sun less warm, it is time to pull the cornstalks and give the new plants more light. You can even get further use from the stalks by laying them down and using them for mulch. Walking on them to harvest the late crops will break them down and they can be tilled under later on.

These are only a few of literally hundreds of ways that companion planting can be of tremendous value to the gardener. In my book *Secrets of Companion Planting for Successful Gardening* I have enumerated all these ways in detail.

Gardening
by the Moon

Marylee Satren

*To everything there is a season, and a time to every
purpose under heaven:*
*A time to be born, and a time to die; a time to
plant, and a time to pluck up that which is planted;*

This popular Bible verse has long been quoted to prove
the validity of timing events to coincide with the planetary cycles. Actually, man has always been aware of the
existence of natural cycles in the activities of plants, animals, and other natural phenomenon such as the tides,
and has striven to take advantage of these cycles.

The Sun's cycles are perhaps the most visible—the seasons being so dramatic. But the Moon is also responsible
for natural cycles affecting many animals, but plants in
particular. Of course its affects on sea life have long been
known: the running of the grunion takes place shortly
after the Full Moon; a species of seaweed, Dictyota, syn-
chronizes its reproductive cycles to the phases of the
Moon; the sea urchins in the Red Sea (where tides are virtually nonexistent, by the way) also reproduce according
to the lunar cycles.

Oysters, too, open and shut according to the Moon's
rhythms. When kept alive in a salt water tank far from the

ocean, oysters will time their activities to the tides which would take place in that locality if the ocean were there!

Many scientific experiments have been done proving the effects of the Moon on plants, as well. Results show that the germination rates and oxygen respiration patterns of plants are affected by lunar phases. Many scientific theories have been advanced to explain this phenomenon: magnetism, gravitational fields, light variations, and humidity—none of them wholly satisfactory.

We are not concerned here with trying to explain why the Moon has such an important affect on living organisms, only with stating that a variety of scientific and subjective experience has proven over and over again that *the positions of the planetary bodies, especially the Sun and Moon, coincide with the natural cycles of all living things.*

If we accept this statement, the next step is to try to find out specifically what these effects are, so that we can use them to our own advantage, and live more harmoniously with the natural rhythms.

Here we are usually forced to fall back on astrological tradition. The bulk of the information we have on lunar gardening, therefore, has gradually accumulated through centuries of subjective experimentation, and is laced with superstition and metaphor. However, it is important to note that whenever controlled scientific experiments have been performed they usually substantiate this folklore. The true scientist is open-minded about the traditional wisdom. Where experimental results seem to contradict tradition, it is usually shown to be caused by a difference in the system of recording the Moon's position, and when this difference is compensated for, the principles of astrology are upheld.

It is most important that only Llewellyn's *Moon Sign Book* and *Astro-Calendar* be used to time your gardening activities; they are calculated correctly for this purpose, using the geocentric system. Most almanacs and calendars show the Moon's signs heliocentrically, and thus incorrectly for Moon planting.

We heartily encourage our readers to undertake their own controlled experiments in this field and to let us know the results, so that we may add to our body of knowledge about gardening by the moon.

The Practice of Lunar Gardening

Following is a summary of the general principles of lunar gardening. This includes an outline of what activities to undertake during each lunar phase and zodiacal sign. This is followed by the *Planting Guide* showing the best phase and sign in which to plant many specific plants, and when to undertake such related activities as fertilization and cultivation. The *Best Planting Dates* tables, further on in this section, are calculated for this year's lunar cycles, and indicate specific dates for specific activities.

However, we want to stress that an important factor in successful lunar gardening, as in all other activities, is one which only you can provide—common sense. Obviously if there is three feet of snow on the ground in your area when we recommend planting flowers, the correct lunar position cannot compensate for weather conditions. Weather, season, temperature, and your own schedule must also affect your gardening activities.

Another important factor affecting the outcome of your garden is your "vibes," or green thumb. If you enjoy what you are doing, if you identify with your work, and visualize the results, those results are more apt to be successful, in gardening as in all other activities.

Many people claim that not only do they achieve larger produce by gardening by the Moon, but that their fruits and vegetables are more flavorful and more nutritious. We tend to think so. These general principles have been practiced for so long—literally thousands of years—all over the world, that this alone is enough to recommend them.

The *Foxfire Book* (Anchor Books, Doubleday and Co., Inc., Garden City, New York, 1972), a composite of information about homesteading skills based on interviews with old-timers in Appalachia, has a chapter on lunar gardening. Most of the oral tradition recorded in the *Foxfire Book* is consistent with the principles the *Moon Sign Book* has been advocating since it was first published in 1906. Some of their advice:

> Corn planted in Leo will have a hard, round stalk and small ears.
>
> Root flower cuttings, limbs, vines, and set out flower bushes and trees in December and January when the signs are in the knees [Capricorn] and feet [Pisces].
>
> Never transplant in the heart [Leo] or head [Aries] as both these signs are "Death Signs."
>
> If you want a large vine and stalk with little fruit, plant in Virgo—"bloom days."
>
> Don't plant potatoes in the feet [Pisces]. If you do, they will develop little nubs like toes all over the main potato.

Planting by the Moon's Phase

During the *increasing light* (from New Moon to Full Moon), plant annuals that produce their yield above the ground. An annual is a plant that completes its entire life cycle within one growing season, and has to be seeded anew each year.

During the *decreasing light* (from Full Moon to New Moon), plant biennials, perennials, bulb and root plants. Biennials include crops that are planted one season to winter over and produce crops the next, such as winter wheat. Perennials, and bulb and root plants include all plants that grow from the same root year after year.

A simple, though less accurate, rule is to plant crops that produce above ground during the increase of the

Moon, and to plant crops that produce below ground during the decrease of the Moon. This is the source of the old adage, "plant potatoes during the dark of the Moon."

You can further increase your accuracy by paying attention to which of the four quarters the Moon is in. The times of these phase changes appear in the *Moon Tables* in the front of the *Moon Sign Book,* and are recorded on the *Astro-Calendar* pages.

First Quarter (increasing from New Moon to about half-full): Plant annuals producing their yield above ground, which are generally of the leafy kind that produce their seed outside the fruit. Also cereals and grain. Examples of such plants are asparagus, cabbage, celery, endive, spinach, etc. As an apparent exception to the rule, we find that cucumber seems to do best in the First Quarter rather than in the Second, even though the seeds are inside the fruit.

Second Quarter (increasing from about half-full to Full Moon): Plant annuals producing their yield above ground, which are generally of the viney kind that produce their seed inside the fruit. Examples include beans, peas, peppers, squash, tomatoes, etc. Also cereals and grains, again.

These are not hard and fast divisions. If you can't plant during the First Quarter, you will be safe to plant during the Second, and vice versa. And there are many plants that seem to do almost equally well planted in either quarter, such as watermelon, garlic, hay—and as indicated, the cereals and grains.

Third Quarter (decreasing from Full Moon to about half-full): Plant biennials, perennials, and bulb and root plants, including crops planted in one season to winter over and produce their crops the next season. Also, trees, shrubs, berries, onion sets, potatoes, rhubarb, winter wheat, grapes, etc.

Fourth Quarter (decreasing from about half-full to

New Moon): Best for cultivation, pulling weeds and destroying pests of all kinds, turning sod, etc. Especially
when the Moon is in one of the barren signs (see below).

Planting by the Moon's Signs

We must also consider the Moon's signs in our gardening, and in the planting dates tables the Moon's phase and
sign are both considered. In each of the twelve zodiacal
signs the Moon reflects the special characteristics associated with that sign, and your activities should be
coordinated to take benefit from *these* natural cycles,
also. What follows are some general rules for using the
Moon's signs in gardening.

Moon in Aries: Barren and dry; fiery and masculine;
used for destroying noxious growth, pests, etc., and for
cultivating, plowing, and tilling.

Moon in Taurus: Productive and moist; earthy and
feminine; used for planting many crops, more particularly
potatoes and root crops, and when hardiness is important.
Also for lettuce, cabbage, and similar leafy vegetables.

Moon in Gemini: Barren and dry; airy and masculine;
used for destroying noxious growths, weeds and pests,
and for cultivation.

Moon in Cancer: Very fruitful and moist; watery and
feminine. This is the most productive sign; used exten-
sively for planting and irrigation.

Moon in Leo: Barren and dry; fiery and masculine.
This is the most barren sign; used only for killing weeds
and other noxious growths, and for cultivation.

Moon in Virgo: Barren and moist; earthy and feminine. Considered good for cultivation and destroying weeds
and pests.

Moon in Libra: Semi-fruitful and moist; airy and
masculine; used for planting many crops, producing good
pulp growth and roots. It is a very good sign for flowers

and vines. Also used for seeding hay, corn fodder, and other livestock feed.

Moon in Scorpio: Very fruitful and moist; watery and feminine. Very nearly as productive as Cancer and used for the same purposes. Especially good for vine growth, and for sturdiness.

Moon in Sagittarius: Considered barren and dry, but often used for onions, seeding for hay, etc. Fiery and masculine, it is also used for cultivation.

Moon in Capricorn: Productive and a little more dry than Taurus; earthy and feminine. Used for potatoes, tubers and root crops.

Moon in Aquarius: Barren and dry; airy and masculine; used for cultivation, and also for destroying noxious growths, weeds, and pests.

Moon in Pisces: Very fruitful and moist; watery and feminine. Used along with the other water signs, Cancer and Scorpio, but especially good for root growth.

To summarize: we will use Cancer, Scorpio, and Pisces for planting whenever possible, unless the nature of the plant itself points to another sign. Taurus and Capricorn are next in the order of preference, especially for root crops; and then Libra, Sagittarius, and Aquarius, in that order. *Don't forget to combine the Moon signs with the Moon phases in selecting your planting dates.*

Other Gardening Activities

As we have already indicated, there are many activities which benefit from using the Moon's guidance to natural timing. The following is a condensed dictionary of what to do when:

Cultivating: Cultivate and turn sod when the Moon is in a barren sign (Aries, Gemini, Leo, Virgo, Aquarius) and decreasing—Fourth Quarter preferred.

Fertilizing: Fertilize when the Moon is in a fruitful sign

(Cancer, Scorpio, Pisces) and use Taurus or Capricorn if necessary. If you are using a chemical fertilizer, then apply during the increase, First or Second Quarter. If you are using an organic fertilizer, apply during the decrease Third or Fourth Quarters.

Harvesting: Harvest root crops for food during the Third or Fourth Quarters, and in a dry sign (Aries, Leo, Sagittarius, Gemini, Aquarius). Harvest root crops intended for seed at the Full Moon. Harvest grain which is to be stored or used for seed just after the Full Moon, but avoid the watery signs. Harvest fruit in the decrease of the Moon and in dry signs.

Irrigation: Irrigate when the Moon is in a water sign: Cancer, Scorpio, Pisces.

Lawn Mowing: Mow in the First and Second Quarters to increase growth, and in the Third or Fourth Quarters to decrease growth.

Mushrooms: These are best gathered at the Full Moon.

Pruning: Prune during the decrease; Third Quarter and Scorpio are best to retard branch growth and make better fruit.

Spraying: Spray, weed, and otherwise destroy pests and noxious growths during the Fourth Quarter and when the Moon is in a barren sign.

Planetary Rulerships of Plants

Here are some general guidelines for using the influence of the various planets in timing your gardening activities. These should be used in addition to the lunar information given previously.

Sun-loving plants should be set out while the Sun is in the sky, and shade-loving plants, after it has set. Delicate plants that prefer the Sun should be set out during the period of the waning Sun—in the late afternoon hours when the Sun is yet visible, but not powerful enough to damage them. Sun-loving plants started from seed should be placed in the ground in the early morning hours, during the period of the increasing Sun.

When the "Lunar Aspectarian" tables show a trine, sextile or conjunction between Mars and the Moon (the Mars column is marked with a T, Sx, or C), it is the best time to plant biennials. A trine, sextile, or conjunction between Jupiter and the Moon is best for transplanting perennials. For dividing, pruning, and trimming perennials, both Jupiter and Saturn should be marked T, Sx, or C, if possible.

In starting the plant from seed, or in any respect in which the activities of the plant take place primarily beneath the surface of the soil (bulb growth, rooting of cuttings—activities ruled by Pluto) a glance at the "Lunar Aspectarian" tables under the column for Pluto should

help you start these plants right. Pluto should be marked
T, Sx, or C. A good Pluto aspect during the correct Moon
phase will do wonders for the effectiveness of fertilization, tilling, plowing or drainage projects.

Planetary Rulers

It is sometimes necessary to know the planetary ruler
of a plant—particularly medicinal herbs and magical plants
used in religious ceremonies. It may also be helpful, if you
want to invoke a certain feeling in your garden, to cultivate plants ruled by the planet or sign consistent with
your purpose. The following information is meant to
supplement, not replace, the principles of lunar gardening
already given.

Annual plants are ruled by the Sun, for they follow the
cycle of the Sun in growth and reproduction. Biennial
plants are ruled by Mars, for they follow a two-year cycle
in growth, the first year producing a sturdy plant, the
second year a full bloom or crop. Perennials are ruled by
expansive Jupiter, not following a twelve-year cycle, but
requiring much more time for development of the plant
before bloom and fruition, and developing to greater size
than annuals or biennials. Root crops are ruled by Pluto,
which rules the underground.

Astrological tradition also assigns specific rulerships to
plants, as indicated in the table on the following pages.

Astrological Rulership of Plants

EDIBLE PLANTS

Artichoke: Venus
Asparagus: Venus, Jupiter
Barley: Saturn
Beans: Venus
Beets: Saturn
   White beets: Jupiter
Blackberry: Scorpio, Mars
Cabbage: Moon
Capers: Mars
Chickory: Sagittarius, Jupiter, Sun
Chickpea: Venus
Coffee: Neptune
Corn: Sun
Cress: Mars
   Watercress: Moon
Cucumber: Moon
Endive: Virgo, Mercury, Jupiter
Garlic: Aries, Mars
Gooseberry: Venus
Grape: Sun
Horseradish: Scorpio, Mars
Leeks: Scorpio, Mars
   Houseleeks: Jupiter
Lettuce: Cancer, Moon
Mushrooms: Neptune
Mustard: Aries, Mars, Sun
Onion: Saturn, Mars
Pepper: Aries, Mars
Pineapple: Mars
Pumpkin: Moon
Rhubarb: Mars

Rice: Sun
Rye: Venus, Saturn
Strawberry: Venus
Tomato: Jupiter
Wheat: Venus

HERBS

Agrimony: Sagittarius, Jupiter
Aniseed: Jupiter
Basil: Mars
Belladona: Saturn
Borage: Jupiter
Caraway: Gemini, Mercury
Catmint: Libra, Venus, Mars
Chamomile: Sun
Chervil: Jupiter
Cinnamon: Jupiter
Coltsfoot: Taurus, Venus
Comfrey: Cancer, Moon, Capricorn, Saturn
Dandelion: Sagittarius, Jupiter
Deadly Nightshade: Taurus, Venus
Fennel: Virgo, Mercury, Aquarius, Saturn
Ginseng: Jupiter
Goldenrod: Taurus, Venus
Hemlock: Capricorn, Saturn
Hops: Aries, Mars
Horehound: Scorpio, Mars
Licorice: Virgo, Mercury
Marijuana: Saturn
Medicinal herbs in general: Virgo
Mistletoe: Leo, Sun
Motherwort: Venus
Mullein: Virgo, Gemini, Mercury, Saturn
Nettles: Aries, Mars

Parsley: Gemini, Mercury, Venus
Pennyroyal: Libra, Venus
Plantain: Taurus, Venus, Mars, Saturn
Rosemary: Sun
Sage: Aries, Mars, Taurus, Venus, Jupiter
Sarsaparilla: Scorpio, Mars
Slippery Elm: Capricorn, Saturn
Tansy: Taurus, Venus
Thistle: Aries, Scorpio, Mars, Saturn
Thyme: Taurus, Libra, Venus, Capricorn,
    Saturn
Valerian: Aquarius, Saturn, Mars
Vervain: Libra, Taurus, Venus
Witchhazel: Mars
Wormwood: Scorpio, Mars
Yarrow: Venus

ORNAMENTAL PLANTS

Buttercup: Aquarius, Uranus, Saturn
Columbine: Venus, Mars
Daisy: Venus
    English Daisy: Mars
Ferns: Gemini, Mercury
    Maidenhair fern: Libra, Taurus, Venus
Geranium: Mars, Moon
Gladiola: Gemini, Mercury
Honeysuckle: Aries, Mars, Cancer, Moon
Iris: Jupiter, Moon
Irish Moss: Pisces
Ivy: Saturn
Juniper: Sun, Mars
Lilies—
    Lily of the Valley: Gemini, Mercury
    Meadow lily: Moon

Waterlily: Cancer, Moon
Marigold: Leo, Sun
Myrtle: Mars
Orchid: Venus
Pansy: Saturn
Peony: Moon
Pinks: Jupiter
Poppy: Venus, Saturn, Moon
   Opium poppy: Neptune
Roses—
   Damask rose: Venus
   Red rose: Jupiter
   White rose: Libra, Taurus, Venus, Moon
Sunflower: Sun
Violets: Libra, Venus, Cancer, Moon
   Waterviolets: Moon

TREES

Alder: Venus
Almond: Sun
Apple: Venus
Apricot: Jupiter
Ash: Sun
Aspen: Saturn
Bay: Aries, Mars, Sun
Beech: Saturn
Birch: Venus
Boxwood: Mars
Cherry: Venus
Chestnut: Venus, Jupiter
Citrus fruit in general: Sun
Fig: Jupiter
Hawthorne: Mars
Holly: Saturn

Laurel: Sun
Lemon: Sun
Lime: Jupiter
Maple: Jupiter
Oak: Sagittarius, Jupiter
   English Oak: Saturn
Olive: Sun
Orange: Sun
Peach: Venus
Pear: Venus
Pine: Mars
Plum: Venus
Poplar: Saturn
Quince: Capricorn, Saturn
Walnut: Leo, Sun
Willow: Moon

OTHER PLANTS

Cocaine: Neptune
Flax: Gemini, Mercury
Indigo: Venus
Lichin: Neptune, Jupiter
Linseed: Gemini, Mercury
Myrrh: Jupiter
Rushes: Saturn
Sponges: Neptune
Tobacco: Mars

Planting Guide

Plant	Phase	Sign
Annuals	1st or 2nd	
Apple trees	2nd or 3rd	Sagittarius
Asparagus	1st	Cancer, Scorpio, Pisces,
Asters	1st or 2nd	Virgo
Barley	1st or 2nd	Cancer, Scorpio, Pisces, Libra Capricorn
Beans	2nd	Cancer, Scorpio, Pisces, Libra, Taurus
Beech trees	3rd	Capricorn
Beets	3rd	Cancer, Scorpio, Pisces, Libra, Capricorn
Berries	2nd	Cancer, Scorpio, Pisces
Biennials	3rd or 4th	
Broccoli	1st	Cancer, Scorpio, Pisces, Libra
Brussel Sprouts	1st	Cancer, Scorpio, Pisces, Libra
Buckwheat	1st or 2nd	Capricorn
Bulbs	3rd	Cancer, Scorpio, Pisces
Bulbs for seed	2nd or 3rd	
Cabbage	1st	Cancer, Scorpio, Pisces, Libra Taurus,
Cantaloupes	1st or 2nd	Cancer, Scorpio, Pisces, Libra
Carrots	3rd	Cancer, Scorpio, Pisces, Libra
Cauliflower	1st	Cancer, Scorpio, Pisces, Libra
Celery	1st	Cancer, Scorpio, Pisces
Cereals	1st or 2nd	Cancer, Scorpio, Pisces, Libra
Chard	1st or 2nd	Cancer, Scorpio, Pisces, Libra
Chicory	2nd or 3rd	Cancer, Scorpio, Pisces, Sagittarius
Chrysanthemums	1st or 2nd	Virgo
Clover	1st or 2nd	Cancer, Scorpio, Pisces
Corn	1st	Cancer, Scorpio, Pisces

Corn for fodder	1st or 2nd	Libra
Coryopsis	2nd or 3rd	Libra
Cosmos	2nd or 3rd	Libra
Cress	1st	Cancer, Scorpio, Pisces
Crocus	1st or 2nd	Virgo
Cucumbers	1st	Cancer, Scorpio, Pisces
Daffodils	1st or 2nd	Libra, Virgo
Dahlias	1st or 2nd	Libra, Virgo
Deciduous trees	2nd or 3rd	Cancer, Scorpio, Pisces
Egg plant	2nd	Cancer, Scorpio, Pisces, Libra
Endive	1st	Cancer, Scorpio, Pisces, Libra, Virgo, Gemini, Sagittarius
Flowers for beauty	1st	Libra
for abundance	1st	Cancer, Pisces, Virgo
for sturdiness	1st	Scorpio
for hardiness	1st	Taurus
Garlic	1st or 2nd	Scorpio, Sagittarius
Gladiolas	1st or 2nd	Libra, Virgo
Golden glow	2nd or 3rd	Libra
Gourds	1st or 2nd	Cancer, Scorpio, Pisces, Libra
Hay	1st or 2nd	Cancer, Scorpio, Pisces, Libra, Taurus, Sagittarius
Honeysuckle	1st or 2nd	Scorpio, Virgo
Hops	1st or 2nd	Scorpio, Libra
Horse radish	1st or 2nd	Cancer, Scorpio, Pisces
Iris	1st or 2nd	Cancer, Virgo
Kohlrabi	1st	Cancer, Scorpio, Pisces, Libra
Leeks	2nd or 3rd	Sagittarius
Lettuce	1st	Cancer, Scorpio, Pisces, Libra, Taurus
Lilies	1st or 2nd	Cancer, Scorpio, Pisces
Maple trees	2nd or 3rd	Sagittarius
Melons	2nd	Cancer, Scorpio, Pisces

Moon vine	1st or 2nd	Virgo
Morning glory	1st or 2nd	Cancer, Scorpio, Pisces, Virgo
Oak trees	2nd or 3rd	Sagittarius
Oats	1st or 2nd	Cancer, Scorpio, Pisces, Libra
Onion seeds	2nd	Scorpio, Sagittarius
Onion sets	3rd or 4th	Libra, Taurus, Pisces
Pansies	1st or 2nd	Cancer, Scorpio, Pisces
Parsley	1st	Cancer, Scorpio, Pisces, Libra
Parsnips	3rd	Cancer, Scorpio, Pisces, Libra
Peach trees	2nd or 3rd	Taurus, Libra
Peanuts	3rd	Cancer, Scorpio, Pisces
Pear trees	2nd or 3rd	Taurus, Libra
Peas	2nd	Cancer, Scorpio, Pisces, Libra
Peonies	1st or 2nd	Virgo
Peppers	2nd	Scorpio, Sagittarius
Perennials	3rd	
Petunias	1st or 2nd	Libra, Virgo
Plum trees	2nd or 3rd	Taurus, Libra
Pole beans	1st or 2nd	Scorpio
Poppies	1st or 2nd	Virgo
Portulacca	1st or 2nd	Virgo
Potatoes	3rd	Cancer, Scorpio, Taurus, Libra, Capricorn, Sagittarius
Privet	1st or 2nd	Taurus, Libra
Pumpkins	2nd	Cancer, Scorpio, Pisces, Libra
Quinces	1st or 2nd	Capricorn
Radishes	3rd	Libra, Taurus, Pisces, Sagittarius, Capricorn
Rhubarb	3rd	Aries
Rice	1st or 2nd	Scorpio
Roses	1st or 2nd	Cancer
Rutabagas	3rd	Cancer, Scorpio, Pisces, Taurus
Saffron	1st or 2nd	Cancer, Scorpio, Pisces

Sage	3rd	Cancer, Scorpio, Pisces
Salsify	1st or 2nd	Cancer, Scorpio, Pisces
Spinach	1st	Cancer, Scorpio, Pisces
Squash	2nd	Cancer, Scorpio, Pisces, Libra
Strawberries	3rd	Cancer, Scorpio, Pisces
String beans	1st or 2nd	Taurus
Sun flowers	2nd, 3rd, 4th	Libra
Sweet peas	1st or 2nd	Cancer, Scorpio, Pisces
Tomatoes	2nd	Cancer, Scorpio, Pisces
Trumpet vines	1st or 2nd	Cancer, Scorpio, Pisces
Tubers for seed	3rd	Cancer, Scorpio, Pisces, Libra
Tulips	1st or 2nd	Libra, Virgo
Turnips	3rd	Cancer, Scorpio, Pisces, Taurus, Capricorn, Libra
Valerian	1st or 2nd	Virgo, Gemini
Watermelons	1st or 2nd	Cancer, Scorpio, Pisces, Libra
Wheat	1st or 2nd	Cancer, Scorpio, Pisces, Libra

Miscellaneous

Compost heap, start	4th	Cancer, Scorpio, Pisces
Crabs, gather	Full Moon	time when plentiful
Cultivate	4th	Virgo, Leo, Gemini
Fall planting	3rd	
Fertilizing		
chemical	1st or 2nd	Cancer, Scorpio, Pisces
organic	3rd or 4th	Cancer, Scorpio, Pisces
Grafting	1st or 2nd	Cancer, Scorpio, Pisces
Harvesting fruit and root crops	3rd or 4th	Aries, Leo, Sagittarius, Gemini, Aquarius
Mowing lawn		
to increase growth	1st or 2nd	Cancer, Scorpio, Pisces
to retard growth	3rd or 4th	Leo, Virgo, Gemini
Mushrooms, pick	Full Moon	time when plentiful

Important Gardening Dates
Central Standard Time

Dates

Dec 30, 0:45 am — Jan 1, 1:47 pm
Taurus 2nd quarter

Jan 4, 1:10 am — Jan 5, 6:51 am
Cancer 2nd quarter

Jan 5, 6:51 am
Full Moon Cancer

Jan 5, 6:51 am — Jan 6, 10:33 pm
Cancer 3rd quarter

Jan 6, 10:33 pm — Jan 8, 5:54 pm
Leo 3rd quarter

Jan 8, 5:54 pm — Jan 10, 11:15 pm
Virgo 3rd quarter

Jan 13, 2:47 am — Jan 15, 3:39 am
Scorpio 4th quarter

Jan 15, 3:39 am — Jan 17, 6:40 am
Sagittarius 4th quarter

Jan 21, 1:42 pm — Jan 23, 9:27 pm
Pisces 1st quarter

What To Do

Plant annuals for hardiness; trim to increase growth

Plant annuals, grains; irrigate; fertilize (chemical); trim to increase growth

Gather mushrooms; harvest root crops for seed

Plant biennials, perennials, bulbs and roots; irrigate; fertilize (organic)

Harvest root crops and fruit; trim to retard growth

Cultivate; destroy weeds and pests; trim to retard growth

Irrigate; fertilize (organic); trim to retard growth

Harvest; cultivate; destroy weeds and pests; trim to retard growth

Plant leafy annuals, grains; irrigate; fertilize (chemical); trim to stimulate growth

Jan 26, 11:12 pm — Jan 28, 9:32 pm Taurus 2nd quarter	Plant annuals for hardiness; trim to increase growth
Jan 31, 9:18 am — Feb 2, 6:23 pm Cancer 2nd quarter	Plant annuals, grains; irrigate; fertilize (chemical); trim to increase growth
Feb 3, 10:35 pm Full Moon Leo	Gather mushrooms; harvest root crops for seed
Feb 3, 10:35 pm — Feb 5, 0:32 am Leo 3rd quarter	Harvest root crops and fruit; trim to retard growth
Feb 5, 0:32 am — Feb 7, 5:10 am Virgo 3rd quarter	Cultivate; destroy weeds and pests; trim to retard growth
Feb 9, 9:03 am — Feb 10, 10:09 pm Scorpio 3rd quarter	Plant biennials, perennials, bulbs and roots; prune; irrigate
Feb 11, 11:45 am — Feb 13, 2:34 pm Sagittarius 4th quarter	Harvest; cultivate; destroy weeds and pests; trim to retard growth
Feb 15, 5:59 pm — Feb 17, 10:08 pm Aquarius 4th quarter	Harvest; cultivate; destroy weeds and pests; trim to retard growth
Feb 17, 10:52 pm — Feb 20, 6:35 am Pisces 1st quarter	Plant leafy annuals, grains; irrigate; fertilize (chemical); trim to stimulate growth
Feb 22, 5:00 pm — Feb 25, 5:36 am Taurus 1st quarter	Plant annuals for hardiness; trim to increase growth
Feb 27, 5:59 pm — Mar 2, 3:23 am Cancer 2nd quarter	Plant annuals, grains; irrigate; fertilize (chemical); trim to increase growth
Mar 5, 11:33 am Full Moon Virgo	Gather mushrooms; harvest root crops for seed

Mar 8, 2:46 pm — Mar 10, 4:48 pm Scorpio 3rd quarter	Plant biennials, perennials, bulbs and roots; irrigate; fertilize (organic); prune
Mar 10, 4:48 pm — Mar 12, 5:37 am Sagittarius 3rd quarter	Harvest roots and fruits; trim to retard growth
Mar 15, 0:26 am — Mar 17, 6:23 am Aquarius 4th quarter	Harvest; cultivate; destroy weeds and pests; trim to retard growth
Mar 17, 6:23 am — Mar 19, 1:09 pm Pisces 4th quarter	Irrigate; fertilize (organic)
Mar 22, 1:06 am — Mar 24, 1:30 pm Taurus 1st quarter	Plant annuals for hardiness; trim to increase growth
Mar 27, 2:00 am — Mar 29, 12:43 pm Cancer 1st and 2nd quarters	Plant annuals, grains; irrigate; fertilize (chemical); trim to stimulate growth
Apr 2, 10:37 pm — Apr 3, 10:19 pm Libra 2nd quarter	Plant annuals for beauty; trim to increase growth
Apr 3, 10:19 pm Full Moon Libra	Gather mushrooms; harvest root crops for seed
Apr 4, 11:26 pm — Apr 7, 0:20 am Scorpio 3rd quarter	Plant biennials, perennials, bulbs and roots; prune; irrigate; fertilize (organic)
Apr 7, 0:20 am — Apr 9, 1:52 am Sagittarius 3rd quarter	Harvest roots and fruits; trim to retard growth
Apr 9, 1:52 am — Apr 10, 1:17 pm Capricorn 3rd quarter	Plant potatoes and tubers
Apr 11, 5:49 am — Apr 13, 12:25 pm Aquarius 4th quarter	Harvest; cultivate; destroy weeds and pests; trim to retard growth

Apr 13, 12:25 pm — Apr 15, 9:33 pm Pisces 4th quarter	Irrigate; fertilize (organic)
Apr 15, 9:33 pm — Apr 18, 5:12 am Aries 4th quarter	Harvest; cultivate; destroy weeds and pests; trim to retard growth
Apr 18, 8:23 am — Apr 20, 8:39 pm Taurus 1st quarter	Plant annuals for hardiness; trim to increase growth
Apr 23, 9:26 am — Apr 25, 8:59 pm Cancer 1st quarter	Plant leafy annuals, grains; irrigate; fertilize (chemical); trim to stimulate growth
Apr 30, 9:09 am — May 2, 10:00 am Libra 2nd quarter	Plant annuals for beauty; trim to increase growth
May 2, 10:00 am — May 3, 6:49 am Scorpio 2nd quarter	Plant annuals, grains; irrigate; fertilize (chemical); trim to stimulate growth
May 3, 6:49 am Full Moon Scorpio	Gather mushrooms; harvest root crops for seed
May 3, 6:49 am — May 4, 9:46 am Scorpio 3rd quarter	
May 4, 9:46 am — May 6, 9:47 am Sagittarius 3rd quarter	Plant biennials, perennials, bulbs and roots; prune; irrigate; fertilize (organic) Harvest roots and fruits; trim to retard growth
May 6, 9:47 am — May 8, 12:16 pm Capricorn 3rd quarter	Plant potatoes and tubers
May 8, 12:16 pm — May 9, 10:10 pm Aquarius 3rd quarter	Harvest roots; cultivate; trim to retard growth
May 9, 10:10 pm — May 10, 5:48 pm Aquarius 4th quarter	Harvest; cultivate; destroy weeds and pests; trim to retard growth

May 10, 5:48 pm – May 13, 3:06 am Pisces 4th quarter	Irrigate; fertilize (organic)
May 13, 3:06 am – May 15, 2:36 pm Aries 4th quarter	Harvest; cultivate; destroy weeds and pests; trim to retard growth
May 20, 3:29 pm – May 23, 3:16 am Cancer 1st quarter	Plant leafy annuals, grains; irrigate; fertilize (chem- ical); trim to stimulate growth
May 27, 6:31 pm – May 29, 8:36 pm Libra 2nd quarter	Plant annuals for beauty; trim to increase growth
May 29, 8:36 pm – May 31, 8:32 pm Scorpio 2nd quarter	Plant annuals, grains; irrigate; fertilize (chemical); trim to stimulate growth
June 1, 2:15 pm Full Moon Sagittarius	Gather mushrooms; harvest root crops for seed
June 1, 2:15 pm – June 2, 7:57 pm Sagittarius 3rd quarter	Harvest roots and fruits; trim to retard growth
June 2, 7:57 pm – June 4, 8:56 pm Capricorn 3rd quarter	Plant potatoes and tubers
June 4, 8:56 pm – June 7, 0:53 am Aquarius 3rd quarter	Harvest roots; cultivate; trim to retard growth
June 7, 0:53 am – June 8, 9:09 am Pisces 3rd quarter	Plant biennials, perennials, bulbs and roots; irri- gate; fertilize (organic)
June 8, 9:09 am – June 9, 8:55 am Pisces 4th quarter	Irrigate; fertilize (organic)
June 9, 8:55 am – June 11, 8:21 pm Aries 4th quarter	Harvest; cultivate; destroy weeds and pests; trim to retard growth

June 14, 9:02 am — June 16, 12:28 pm
   Gemini 4th quarter

June 16, 9:32 pm — June 19, 8:57 am
   Cancer 1st quarter

June 24, 1:52 am — June 26, 5:40 am
   Libra 1st and 2nd quarters

June 26, 5:40 am — June 28, 7:07 am
   Scorpio 2nd quarter

June 30, 9:33 pm
   Full Moon Capricorn

June 30, 9:33 pm — July 2, 7:10 am
   Capricorn 3rd quarter

July 2, 7:10 am — July 4, 9:53 am
   Aquarius 3rd quarter

July 4, 9:53 am — July 6, 4:19 pm
   Pisces 4th quarter

July 6, 4:19 pm — July 7, 10:41 pm
   Aries 3rd quarter

July 7, 10:41 pm — July 9, 2:40 am
   Aries 4th quarter

July 11, 3:34 pm — July 14, 4:00 am
   Gemini 4th quarter

July 14, 4:00 am — July 16, 2:43 am
   Cancer 4th quarter

Harvest; cultivate; destroy weeds and pests; trim to retard growth

Plant leafy annuals, grains; irrigate; fertilize (chemical); trim to stimulate growth

Plant flowers and annuals for beauty; trim to increase growth

Plant annuals, grains; irrigate; fertilize (chemical); trim to stimulate growth

Gather mushrooms; harvest root crops for seed

Plant potatoes and tubers

Harvest roots; cultivate; trim to retard growth

Plant biennials, perennials, bulbs and roots; irrigate; fertilize (organic)

Harvest roots and fruits; trim to retard growth

Harvest; cultivate; destroy weeds and pests; trim to retard growth

Harvest; cultivate; destroy weeds and pests; trim to retard growth

Irrigate; fertilize (organic)

July 21, 7:05 am — July 23, 12:18 pm
Libra 1st quarter
Plant flowers and annuals for beauty; trim to increase growth

July 23, 12:18 pm — July 25, 3:07 pm
Scorpio 1st and 2nd quarters
Plant annuals, grains; irrigate; fertilize (chemical); trim to stimulate growth

July 27, 4:17 pm — July 29, 5:36 pm
Capricorn 2nd quarter
Plant annuals; trim to stimulate growth

July 30, 5:32 am
Full Moon Aquarius
Gather mushrooms; harvest root crops for seed

July 30, 5:32 am — July 31, 7:53 pm
Aquarius 3rd quarter
Harvest roots; cultivate; trim to retard growth

July 31, 7:53 pm — Aug 3, 1:04 am
Pisces 3rd quarter
Plant biennials, perennials, bulbs and roots; irrigate; fertilize (organic)

Aug 3, 1:04 am — Aug 5, 10:21 am
Aries 3rd quarter
Harvest roots and fruits; trim to retard growth

Aug 5, 10:21 am — Aug 6, 2:42 pm
Taurus 3rd quarter
Plant potatoes and tubers

Aug 7, 10:32 pm — Aug 10, 11:15 am
Gemini 4th quarter
Harvest; cultivate; destroy weeds and pests; trim to retard growth

Aug 10, 11:15 am — Aug 12, 10:15 pm
Cancer 4th quarter
Irrigate; fertilize (organic)

Aug 12, 10:15 pm — Aug 14, 3:46 pm
Leo 4th quarter
Harvest; cultivate; destroy weeds and pests; trim to retard growth

Aug 17, 12:38 pm — Aug 19, 5:25 pm
Libra 1st quarter
Plant flowers and annuals for beauty; trim to increase growth

Aug 19, 5:25 pm — Aug 21, 7:05 pm
Scorpio 1st quarter
Plant leafy annuals, grains; irrigate; fertilize (chemical); trim to stimulate growth

Aug 23, 11:18 pm — Aug 26, 1:59 am
Capricorn 2nd quarter
Plant annuals; trim to increase growth

Aug 28, 2:52 pm
Full Moon Pisces
Gather mushrooms; harvest root crops for seed

Aug 28, 2:52 pm — Aug 30, 10:35 am
Pisces 3rd quarter
Plant biennials, perennials, bulbs and roots; irrigate; fertilize (organic)

Aug 30, 10:35 am — Sept 1, 6:47 pm
Aries 3rd quarter
Harvest roots and fruits; trim to retard growth

Sept 1, 6:47 pm — Sept 4, 6:24 am
Taurus 3rd quarter
Plant potatoes and root crops

Sept 4, 6:24 am — Sept 6, 7:08 pm
Gemini 3rd and 4th quarters
Harvest; cultivate; destroy weeds and pests; trim to retard growth

Sept 6, 7:08 pm — Sept 9, 6:35 am
Cancer 4th quarter
Irrigate; fertilize (organic)

Sept 9, 6:35 am — Sept 11, 2:55 pm
Leo 4th quarter
Harvest; cultivate; destroy weeds and pests; trim to retard growth

Sept 11, 2:55 pm — Sept 13, 3:46 am
Virgo 4th quarter
Cultivate; destroy weeds and pests; trim to retard growth

Sept 13, 8:16 pm — Sept 15, 11:43 pm
Libra 1st quarter
Plant flowers and annuals for beauty; trim to increase growth

Sept 15, 11:43 pm — Sept 18, 2:11 am
Scorpio 1st quarter
Plant leafy annuals, grains; irrigate; fertilize (chemical); trim to stimulate growth

Sept 20, 5:00 am — Sept 22, 8:15 am
Capricorn 2nd quarter

Plant annuals; trim to increase growth

Sept 24, 12:52 pm — Sept 26, 7:01 pm
Pisces 2nd quarter

Plant annuals, grains; irrigate; fertilize (chemical); trim to stimulate growth

Sept 27, 2:53 am
Full Moon Aries

Gather mushrooms; harvest root crops for seed

Sept 27, 2:53 am — Sept 29, 3:23 am
Aries 3rd quarter

Harvest roots and fruits; trim to retard growth

Sept 29, 3:23 am — Oct 1, 2:20 pm
Taurus 3rd quarter

Plant potatoes and root crops

Oct 1, 2:20 pm — Oct 4, 2:58 am
Gemini 3rd quarter

Harvest roots; cultivate; destroy weeds and pests; trim to retard growth

Oct 4, 2:58 am — Oct 5, 3:23 am
Cancer 3rd quarter

Plant biennials, perennials, bulbs and roots; irrigate; fertilize (organic)

Oct 5, 3:23 am — Oct 6, 3:07 pm
Cancer 4th quarter

Irrigate; fertilize (organic)

Oct 6, 3:07 pm — Oct 9, 0:28 am
Leo 4th quarter

Harvest; cultivate; destroy weeds and pests; trim to retard growth

Oct 9, 0:28 am — Oct 11, 6:00 am
Virgo 4th quarter

Cultivate; destroy weeds and pests; trim to retard growth

Oct 13, 8:09 am — Oct 15, 9:36 am
Scorpio 1st quarter

Plant leafy annuals, grains; irrigate; fertilize (chemical); trim to stimulate growth

Oct 17, 10:50 am — Oct 19, 1:35 pm
Capricorn 1st and 2nd quarters

Plant annuals; trim to stimulate growth

Oct 21, 6:43 pm — Oct 24, 1:41 am
Pisces 2nd quarter

Plant annuals, grains; irrigate; fertilize (chemical); trim to stimulate growth

Oct 26, 5:43 pm
Full Moon Taurus

Gather mushrooms; harvest root crops for seed

Oct 26, 10:44 am — Oct 28, 9:48 pm
Taurus 3rd quarter

Plant potatoes and root crops

Oct 28, 9:48 pm — Oct 31, 10:19 am
Gemini 3rd quarter

Harvest roots; cultivate; destroy weeds and pests; trim to retard growth

Oct 31, 10:19 am — Nov 2, 11:12 pm
Cancer 3rd quarter

Plant biennials, perennials, bulbs and roots; irrigate; fertilize (organic)

Nov 2, 11:12 pm — Nov 3, 10:00 pm
Leo 3rd quarter

Harvest root crops and fruit; trim to retard growth

Nov 3, 10:00 pm — Nov 5, 9:30 am
Leo 4th quarter

Harvest; cultivate; destroy weeds and pests; trim to retard growth

Nov 5, 9:30 am — Nov 7, 4:06 pm
Virgo 4th quarter

Cultivate; destroy weeds and pests; trim to retard growth

Nov 9, 6:38 pm — Nov 11, 1:32 am
Scorpio 4th quarter

Irrigate; fertilize (organic); trim to retard growth

Nov 13, 7:02 pm — Nov 15, 8:30 pm
Capricorn 1st quarter

Plant annuals; trim to stimulate growth

Nov 18, 0:10 am — Nov 20, 7:32 am
Pisces 2nd quarter

Plant annuals, grains; irrigate; fertilize (chemical); trim to stimulate growth

Nov 22, 5:08 pm — Nov 25, 4:38 am
Taurus 2nd quarter

Plant annuals for hardiness; trim to increase growth

Nov 25, 11:37 am Full Moon Gemini	Gather mushrooms, harvest root crops for seed
Nov 25, 11:37 am – Nov 27, 5:05 pm Gemini 3rd quarter	Harvest roots; cultivate; destroy weeds and pests; trim to retard growth
Nov 27, 5:05 pm – Nov 30, 5:37 am Cancer 3rd quarter	Plant biennials, perennials, bulbs and roots; irrigate; fertilize (organic)
Nov 30, 5:37 am – Dec 2, 5:14 pm Leo 3rd quarter	Harvest root crops and fruits; trim to retard growth
Dec 2, 5:14 pm – Dec 5, 1:19 am Virgo 3rd and 4th quarters	Cultivate; destroy weeds and pests; trim to retard growth
Dec 7, 5:29 am – Dec 9, 6:10 am Scorpio 4th quarter	Irrigate; fertilize (organic); trim to retard growth
Dec 9, 6:10 am – Dec 10, 12:01 pm Sagittarius 4th quarter	Harvest; cultivate; destroy weeds and pests; trim to retard growth
Dec 11, 5:41 am – Dec 13, 5:31 am Capricorn 1st quarter	Plant annuals; trim to stimulate growth
Dec 15, 7:55 am – Dec 17, 1:40 pm Pisces 1st and 2nd quarters	Plant annuals, grains; irrigate; fertilize (chemical); trim to stimulate growth
Dec 19, 10:56 pm – Dec 22, 10:53 am Taurus 2nd quarter	Plant annuals for hardiness; trim to increase growth
Dec 24, 11:33 am – Dec 26, 7:13 am Cancer 2nd quarter	Plant annuals, grains, irrigate; fertilize (chemical); trim to stimulate growth
Dec 26, 7:13 am Full Moon Cancer	Gather mushrooms; harvest root crops for seed

Dec 26, 7:13 am — Dec 27, 11:51 am
Cancer 3rd quarter

Dec 27, 11:51 am — Dec 29, 11:25 pm
Leo 3rd quarter

Dec 29, 11:25 pm — Jan 1, 8:43 am
Virgo 3rd quarter

Plant biennials, perennials, bulbs and roots; irrigate; fertilize (organic)

Harvest root crops and fruit; trim to retard growth

Cultivate; destroy weeds and pests; trim to retard growth

Best Dates for Destroying Unwanted Plant and Animal Life

Central Standard Time

Dates		Moon's Sign	Moon's Phase
Jan 6, 10:33 pm	—	Jan 8, 5:54 pm	Leo	3rd quarter
Jan 8, 5:54 pm	—	Jan 10, 11:15 pm	Virgo	3rd quarter
Jan 15, 3:39 am	—	Jan 17, 6:40 am	Sagittarius	4th quarter
Feb 3, 10:35 pm	—	Feb 5, 0:32 am	Leo	3rd quarter
Feb 5, 0:32 am	—	Feb 7, 5:10 am	Virgo	3rd quarter
Feb 11, 11:45 am	—	Feb 13, 2:34 pm	Sagittarius	4th quarter
Feb 15, 5:59 pm	—	Feb 17, 10:08 pm	Aquarius	4th quarter
March 5, 11:33 am	—	March 6, 12:48 pm	Virgo	3rd quarter
March 10, 4:48 pm	—	March 12, 7:47 pm	Sagittarius	3rd and 4th quarters
March 15, 0:26 am	—	March 17, 6:23 am	Aquarius	4th quarter
April 7, 0:20 am	—	April 9, 1:52 am	Sagittarius	3rd quarter
April 11, 5:49 am	—	April 13, 12:25 pm	Aquarius	4th quarter
April 15, 9:33 pm	—	April 18, 5:12 am	Aries	4th quarter
May 4, 9:46 am	—	May 6, 9:47 am	Sagittarius	3rd quarter
May 8, 12:16 pm	—	May 10, 5:48 pm	Aquarius	3rd and 4th quarters
May 13, 3:06 am	—	May 15, 2:36 pm	Aries	4th quarter
June 1, 2:15 pm	—	June 2, 7:57 pm	Sagittarius	3rd quarter
June 4, 8:56 pm	—	June 7, 0:53 am	Aquarius	3rd quarter
June 9, 8:55 pm	—	June 11, 8:21 pm	Aries	4th quarter
June 14, 9:02 am	—	June 16, 12:38 pm	Gemini	4th quarter

July 2, 7:10 am	—	July 4, 9:53 am	Aquarius	3rd quarter
July 6, 4:19 pm	—	July 9, 2:40 pm	Aries	3rd and 4th quarters
July 11, 3:34 pm	—	July 14, 4:00 pm	Gemini	4th quarter
July 30, 5:32 am	—	July 31, 7:53 pm	Aquarius	3rd quarter
Aug 3, 1:04 am	—	Aug 5, 10:21 am	Aries	3rd quarter
Aug 7, 10:32 pm	—	Aug 10, 11:15 am	Gemini	4th quarter
Aug 12, 10:15 pm	—	Aug 14, 3:46 pm	Leo	4th quarter
Aug 30, 10:35 am	—	Sept 1, 6:47 pm	Aries	3rd quarter
Sept 4, 6:24 am	—	Sept 6, 7:08 pm	Gemini	3rd and 4th quarters
Sept 9, 6:35 am	—	Sept 11, 2:55 pm	Leo	4th quarter
Sept 11, 2:55 pm	—	Sept 13, 3:46 am	Virgo	4th quarter
Sept 27, 2:53 am	—	Sept 29, 3:23 am	Aries	3rd quarter
Oct 1, 2:20 pm	—	Oct 4, 2:58 am	Gemini	3rd quarter
Oct 6, 3:07 pm	—	Oct 9, 0:28 am	Leo	4th quarter
Oct 9, 0:28 am	—	Oct 11, 6:00 am	Virgo	4th quarter
Oct 28, 9:48 pm	—	Oct 31, 10:19 am	Gemini	3rd quarter
Nov 2, 11:12 pm	—	Nov 5, 9:30 am	Leo	3rd and 4th quarters
Nov 5, 9:30 am	—	Nov 7, 4:06 pm	Virgo	4th quarter
Nov 25, 11:37 am	—	Nov 27, 5:05 pm	Gemini	3rd quarter
Nov 30, 5:37 am	—	Dec 2, 5:14 pm	Leo	3rd quarter
Dec 2, 5:14 pm	—	Dec 5, 1:19 am	Virgo	3rd and 4th quarters
Dec 9, 6:10 am	—	Dec 10, 12:01 pm	Sagittarius	4th quarter
Dec 27, 11:51 am	—	Dec 29, 11:25 pm	Leo	3rd quarter
Dec 29, 11:25 pm	—	Jan 1, 8:43 am	Virgo	4th quarter

Breeding Animals and Setting Eggs by the Moon

Eggs should be set, or animals mated so that the young will be born when the Moon is increasing in a fruitful sign. The fruitful signs are the feminine Water Signs of Cancer, Scorpio, and Pisces. Cancer is considered the most fruitful of all the signs. Young born during the fruitful signs are generally more healthy, mature faster, and make good breeding stock. Those born during the semi-fruitful signs, the Earth Signs of Taurus and Capricorn, will generally still mature fast, but will produce leaner meat, while the sign of Libra yields beautiful, graceful animals, for showing and racing.

To determine the best date to mate animals, or set eggs, subtract the number of days given for incubation or gestation from the fruitful dates given in the following tables. Gestation is the time between impregnation and birth of the young. In egg-laying animals, this is the incubation time. Cats and dogs are mated sixty-three days previous to the desired birth date, as shown. Chicken eggs are set twenty-one days previous.

Gestation and Incubation Figures

Animal	No. of Young	Gestation
Elephant	1	600 days
Giraffe	1	420 days
Camel	1	395 days
Ass	1	365 days
Seal	1	350 days
Horse	1	346 days
Cow	1	283 days
Monkey	1	164 days
Goat	1 to 2	151 days
Sheep	1 to 2	150 days
Pig	10	112 days
Lion	2 to 4	110 days
Chinchilla	2	110 days
Fox	5 to 8	63 days
Dog	6 to 8	63 days
Cat	4 to 6	63 days
Guinea Pig	2 to 6	62 days
Ferret	6 to 9	40 days
Rabbit	4 to 8	30 days
Rat	10	22 days
Mouse	10	22 days
Opossum	18	11 days

Domestic Fowl	No. of Eggs	Incubation
Turkey	12 to 15	26 to 30 days
Guinea	15 to 18	25 to 26 days
Pea Hen	10	28 to 30 days
Duck	9 to 12	25 to 32 days
Geese	15 to 18	27 to 33 days
Hen	12 to 15	19 to 24 days
Pigeon	2	16 to 20 days
Canaries	3 to 4	13 to 14 days

Best Dates for Setting Chicken Eggs
Central Standard Time

Dates to be Born	Moon's Sign and Phase	Set Chicken Eggs
Dec 30, 0:45 am—Jan 1, 1:47 pm	Taurus 2nd quarter	Dec 9—Dec 11
Jan 4, 1:10 am—Jan 5, 6:51 am	Cancer 2nd quarter	Dec 14—Dec 15
Jan 21, 1:42 pm—Jan 23, 9:27 pm	Pisces 1st quarter	Dec 31—Jan 2
Jan 26, 8:51 am—Jan 28, 9:32 pm	Taurus 1st and 2nd quarters	Jan 5—Jan 7
Jan 31, 9:18 am—Feb 2, 6:23 pm	Cancer 2nd quarter	Jan 10—Jan 12
Feb 17, 10:52 pm—Feb 20, 6:35 am	Pisces 1st quarter	Jan 27—Jan 30
Feb 22, 5:00 pm—Feb 25, 5:36 am	Taurus 1st quarter	Feb 1—Feb 4
Feb 27, 5:59 pm—March 2, 3:23 am	Cancer 2nd quarter	Feb 6—Feb 9
March 22, 1:06 am—March 24, 1:30 pm	Taurus 1st quarter	March 1—March 3
March 27, 2:00 am—March 29, 12:43 pm	Cancer 1st and 2nd quarters	March 6—March 8
April 2, 10:37 pm—April 3, 10:19 pm	Libra 2nd quarter	March 12—March 13
April 18, 8:23 am—April 20, 8:39 pm	Taurus 1st quarter	March 28—March 30
April 23, 9:26 am—April 25, 8:59 pm	Cancer 1st quarter	April 2—April 4
April 30, 9:09 am—May 2, 10:00 am	Libra 2nd quarter	April 9—April 11
May 2, 10:00 am—May 3, 6:49 am	Scorpio 2nd quarter	April 11—Arpil 12
May 20, 3:29 pm—May 23, 3:16 am	Cancer 1st quarter	April 29—May 2
May 27, 6:31 pm—May 29, 8:36 pm	Libra 2nd quarter	May 6—May 8
May 29, 8:36 pm—May 31, 8:37 pm	Scorpio 2nd quarter	May 8—May 10

June 16, 9:32 pm—June 19, 8:57 am	Cancer 1st quarter	May 26—May 29
June 24, 1:52 am—June 26, 5:40 am	Libra 1st and 2nd quarters	June 3—June 5
June 26, 5:40 am—June 28, 7:07 am	Scorpio 2nd quarter	June 5—June 7
July 21, 7:05 am—July 23, 12:18 pm	Libra 1st quarter	June 30—July 2
July 23, 12:18 pm—July 25, 3:07 pm	Scorpio 1st and 2nd quarters	July 2—July 4
Aug 17, 12:38 pm—Aug 19, 5:25 pm	Libra 1st quarter	July 27—July 29
Aug 19, 5:25 pm—Aug 21, 8:46 pm	Scorpio 1st and 2nd quarters	July 29—July 31
Aug 23, 11:18 pm—Aug 26, 1:59 am	Capricorn 2nd quarter	Aug 2—Aug 5
Sept 13, 3:46 am—Sept 15, 11:43 pm	Libra 1st quarter	Aug 23—Aug 25
Sept 15, 11:43 pm—Sept 18, 2:11 am	Scorpio 1st quarter	Aug 25—Aug 28
Sept 24, 12:52 pm—Sept 26, 7:01 pm	Pisces 2nd quarter	Sept 3—Sept 5
Oct 13, 8:09 am—Oct 15, 9:36 am	Scorpio 1st quarter	Sept 22—Sept 24
Oct 17, 10:50 am—Oct 19, 1:35 pm	Capricorn 1st and 2nd quarters	Sept 26—Sept 28
Oct 21, 6:43 pm—Oct 24, 1:41 am	Pisces 2nd quarter	Sept 30—Oct 3
Nov 13, 7:02 pm—Nov 15, 8:30 pm	Capricorn 1st quarter	Oct 23—Oct 25
Nov 18, 0:10 am—Nov 20, 7:32 am	Pisces 2nd quarter	Oct 28—Oct 30
Nov 22, 5:08 pm—Nov 25, 4:38 am	Taurus 2nd quarter	Nov 1—Nov 4
Dec 11, 5:41 am—Dec 13, 5:31 am	Capricorn 1st quarter	Nov 20—Nov 22
Dec 15, 7:55 am—Dec 17, 1:40 pm	Pisces 1st and 2nd quarters	Nov 24—Nov 26
Dec 19, 10:56 pm—Dec 22, 10:53 am	Taurus 2nd quarter	Nov 28—Dec 1
Dec 24, 11:33 pm—Dec 26, 7:13 am	Cancer 2nd quarter	Dec 3—Dec 5

Important Information

Dry Measures

Bushel

One bushel is the equivalent of a cube measuring 12.9074" (about 13") on a side. It contains 32 quarts, 4 pecks, or 1.244 cubic feet. *Metric equivalent: 35.238 liters.*

Cord

A cord of wood is a pile 4' wide, 4' high, and 8' long, and containing 128 cubic feet. *Metric equivalent: 3.584 cubic meters.*

To find the contents of a pile of wood in cords: multiply the length, width and thickness (in feet) together and divide by 128.

Land Measures

Rod

One rod equals 5.50 yards, or 16.5 feet. *Metric equivalent: 5.029 meters.*

One square rod equals 30.25 square yards. *Metric equivalent: 25.293 square meters.*

Acre

One acre is a square measuring 208.71 feet on a side (about 2/3 of a football field). It contains 43,560 square feet, 4,840 square yards, or 160 square rods. *Metric equivalent: 4,047 square meters or 0.407 hectares.*

To find the number of acres in a field: multiply the length and the breadth (in yards) together and divide by 4,840.

Section

One section equals one square mile, or 640 acres. *Metric equivalent: 2.59 square kilometers.*

Mile

One mile equals 5,280 feet, 1,760 yards, or 320 rods. *Metric equivalent: 1.609 kilometers.*

One square mile equals one section, 640 acres, or 102,400 square rods. *Metric equivalent: 2.590 square kilometers.*

Township

One township is a square measuring six miles on a side. It contains 36 sections. *Metric equivalent: 93.24 square kilometers.*

Liquid Measures

Gallon

A gallon is a cube measuring 6.135792 inches on a side. It contains 4 quarts, 8 pints, or 128 ounces. *Metric equivalent: 3.785 liters.*

One gallon of water weighs about 8.31 pounds. There are 7.48 gallons in a cubic foot.

To find the number of gallons in a cistern: for a square or rectangular cistern, multiply the height, length, and width (in feet) together and multiply the result by 7.48; for a round cistern, multiply 3.1416, the square of the radius, and the height (in feet) together and multiply the result by 7.48.

Barrel

One barrel equals 31.5 gallons, 126 quarts, or 252 pints. *Metric equivalent: 119.228 liters.*

Cooking and Baking

Can sizes

Buffet	8 oz	1 cup
No ½ flat (Tuna)	8 oz	1 cup
No 1 Picnic	10½-12 oz	1¼ cups
No 300	14-16 oz	1¾ cups
No 303	16-17 oz	2 cups
No 2	1 lb 4 oz	2½ cups
No 2½	1 lb 13 oz	3½ cups
Cond Evap Milk	15 oz	1 1/3 cups
Tall Evap Milk	14½ oz	1 2/3 cups
Short Evap Milk	6 oz	2/3 cup

Eggs

1 lg chicken egg	2 oz	5 to a cup
1 med chicken egg	1.75 oz	6 to a cup
1 sm chicken egg	1.5 oz	7 to a cup
1 bantam egg	2/3 oz	
1 duck egg	3 oz	
1 goose egg	8-10 oz	
Dried eggs	2½ tbsp + 2½ tbsp water = 1 whole egg	

Weights

1 lb whole apples	3 cups pared, sliced
1 lb butter	2 cups
1 lb cheese	5 cups grated
1 lb cottage cheese	2 cups
1 oz chocolate	4 tbsp grated
1 lb cocoa	4 cups
1 lb cornmeal	3 cups
1 lb whole wheat flour	3¾-4 cups

1 lb white four	4 cups
1 lb honey	1¼ cups
1 lb macaroni	4 cups dry
1 lb nuts in shell	about 2 cups shelled
1 lb rolled oats	4¾ cups
1 lb raisins	2¾ cups seedless; 3¼ cups seeded
1 lb long grain rice	2½ cups
1 lb granulated sugar	2 cups
1 lb packed brown sugar	2¼ cups

Astro-Nutrition by Sun Power

Louise Riotte

*Harness the fantastic power of the Sun
and make it work for you all year long!*

The power of the Sun is so immense that it staggers the imagination, emitting as it does in one second more energy than man has used in all the time since civilization began.

Nevertheless, every year the season arrives when solar energy lessens. This does not occur because of the regular alteration of Earth's distance from the Sun but because the angle of the Earth's axis changes. During the summer the northern part of the Earth's axis is tilted toward the Sun, even though the Earth is approaching aphelion, the point furthest from it.

At this time the Sun's rays fall for long hours from high in the sky. But during the winter, after the time of harvest has come and gone in the northern hemisphere, the angle of the axis changes. Then the northern part of the earth is aimed away from the Sun so that the rays fall for short hours and hit the earth obliquely because the Sun is so low in the sky. For the southern hemisphere this process is the same but of course the seasons are reversed.

The foods that you eat at different times of year are directly influenced by the angle at which the Sun's rays hit the Earth. In summer you will have a great variety of fresh produce available for cooking because the Sun is high in the sky. But later in the year, in fall and winter when the tilt begins to angle away from the Sun, the kind and quality of fresh produce changes whether you grow it in your own garden or buy it at the supermarket.

Tomatoes will no longer ripen will in the cooler air, but winter squash, turnips, cauliflower, Brussels sprouts, parsnips, potatoes and lettuce are crisp and fresh. These are all delicious vegetables but are not quite as high in vitamins A and C as the bright yellow, orange and red vegetables which you could grow outdoors during the summer. Finally, as the days grow colder, there comes a time when only a very few fresh vegetables may still be grown outdoors.

Then is the time to begin thinking about sprouts of all kinds to add to your family's menu. Sprouts are so sweet-tasting and crunchy as well as highly nutritious that growing them makes a lot of sense. Besides it's fun.

Just what are sprouts anyway? They are seeds of grains or legumes that have germinated and by so doing have converted their fats and starches into vitamins, sugars and proteins. Some rather extravagant claims have been made, such as saying that two ounces of sprouted soybeans contain as much vitamin C as six cups of orange juice. This seems a bit far-fetched to me but in actual fact they do contain some of this precious vitamin along with some of the B vitamins and traces of such minerals as calcium, iron and magnesium. And if you grow them yourself, they will be fresher and tastier.

You don't have to settle for just soy beans. Almost any viable seed can be sprouted under the right conditions. However, some are more palatable than others, have more varied uses and will add a sparkle to your menu because of their different tastes and textures.

Sprouting seeds is not a new idea. It is time-honored and practical, the earliest recorded mention being in China around 2939 B.C. Of the many varieties, Mung beans, an old Chinese favorite, is one of the easiest to sprout.

But there are many others such as wheat "berries" or seeds, the small but very prolific alfalfa, dry peas, corn, barley, sunflower seeds, radishes, mustard, lentils, fenugreek, and the new grain called "triticale" which originated at the International Wheat and Maize Center in Mexico. Beans such as garbanzo, lima, red kidney, pinto, great northern, white or fava will also sprout well.

Sprouts are highly nutritious, natural additives to your diet, but they are not miracle foods; use them for flavor, nutrition and texture just as you would other vegetables.

A seed consists of the embryo and the endosperm, which is stored carbohydrates, oils and protein. Before sprouting, it is full of fats and starches but under correct conditions of germination—and harvesting at the right time—these fats and starches are changed, becoming more digestible, less fattening and more nutritious than they were before. Because the starch in the sprouts is converted into sugar, the sprouts are quickly and easily assimilated by the body, helping us produce the quick energy we all need.

Water for Sprouting

The water used for sprouting your seeds should be the purest possible. Avoid fluoridated water which will not grow good sprouts. If your city water is treated with chemicals, there is still a way. Catch rain water and store it. In the spring when I make my pickles, I save all the glass or plastic jugs that vinegar comes in, wash and sun them for later use as storage vessels. In the winter you can use clean, melted snow. Snow is one of nature's best fertilizers, containing not only nitrogen but phosphorus and other minerals. It also contains forty percent less heavy water, or deuterium oxide, than normal water. Deuterium is a heavy isotope of hydrogen. Combined with water it does not form H_2O, the water molecule, but D_2O instead. According to Russian scientists, heavy water slows down some of the chemical and biological processes of growing plants; they seem to grow faster when the heavy water molecules are removed.

Where Will You Grow Your Seeds?

Having decided upon the seeds you want to grow and made sure, insofar as possible, that your water is pure, you will need a place to put your trays. You must give some thought to this because where you live will make a difference. If yours is a hot, dry climate, the sprouts will need extra humidity. Kitchen shelves, providing there is good air circulation, may be just the thing.

In a humid, colder climate good air circulation is very important because sprouts may produce a feathery white mold without it. Sprouts should receive at least some natural daylight for good color and health; and they should be kept from temperatures above eighty degrees. If a window is not practical, try using an open counter away from the stove or sink where the tray will not be in the way.

What Will You Use For Containers?

There are commercial containers on the market and you may prefer one of these, such as a type of jar with a screened lid which must be tilted so that too much water will not accumulate.

On the other hand, you can start out by using a number of household items. Plastic lids from coffee cans, perforated with an ice pick and then placed on a dish, may be used, or those white styrofoam trays used for prepackaged grocery items can be punched full of holes and then placed with a pan or plate underneath to catch the drainage.

Seeds to be sprouted should be moist but should not be allowed to sit in water. A seed will start to grow under almost any condition; in fact it is said that the early Christians planted lentil seeds down in the dark catacombs on Ash Wednesday which would attain a height of six inches by Maundy Thursday. Nevertheless, a "sprout garden" cannot be neglected. Sprouts definitely do need rinsing three or four times a day. But if you work out a regular schedule, sprouts will produce fresh food for you every day.

If you don't like the idea of the tray method, try putting your seeds into wide-mouth fruit jars. For this way you will also need two pieces of screening, which may be aluminum, plastic or nylon, to fit over the jar openings and wire rings to hold the screen in place.

To Prepare Your Seeds

Wash your seeds in a strainer and, if you are using beans, pick them over to remove any that are broken. Place them in a jar or bowl and cover them with water, being sure that there is at least twice as much water as seeds. With large seeds such as beans you may need three or four times as much as you would with small seeds like alfalfa.

Cover the jar or bowl and let your seeds soak overnight. For your first venture don't use too many seeds. You will be surprised at how they expand as they grow. Try, for instance, one-fourth cup of Mung beans, which are very strong, dependable growers, and find out how quickly you will use these up. You may want more or less next time.

After soaking your seeds, you will find the following morning that they have increased in size amazingly.

Now is the time to rinse them off and place them on your lids or trays. Keep them shaded the first few days but make sure that air circulation is adequate. When they are growing well, permit more light to enter by partially removing the lid.

At this stage all that is necessary is sprinkling a little water on the seeds a couple of times each day, but never let them sit in water; and never let the seeds be packed too tightly, but rather see to it that they are spread in a loose layer. Rot will be encouraged if there are too many.

Depending on various factors, your seeds should be ready to eat in from three to five days. Eat them when they are from one to three inches long. When they are ready to use, they should be rinsed carefully in clean water, letting the water run off. Place them—dry—in a bowl in the refrigerator.

Timing Sprouts Astrologically for Growth

Timing your little indoor "sprout garden" is just as important as observing correct timing in the one you plant outdoors. Planning a little timetable can be very useful. You should consider first the tilt of the earth's axis. Check on the Sun signs which coincide with the short days in your area; under these enter the signs which coincide with the long days. Though sprouts will grow all the year around, they will be ready one or even two days sooner when the Sun is in the long-day signs.

Now that you have grouped your Sun signs make your table a little more specific. Allow a space for each month in which you plan to grow sprouts, and show here the days of the lunar phases. As with outdoor plants, sprouts will grow with a waning Moon but will grow faster as the Moon waxes. You may expect them to grow fastest of all just after the New Moon.

Now, besides these lunar phases, enter the days when

the Moon is passing through the three water signs of
Cancer, Scorpio and Pisces, which are the most fertile
for plant growth. Sprouts may be considered as "annuals" and you can use any other growing advice which
applies to these.

Other monthly aspects may be useful for noting on
your timetable. Aspects, including parallels of declination, between the Sun and the Moon are useful to note
because they show days of speeded-up growth or of
special delay. Atmospheric moisture is often indicated
in aspects which include Mercury, Jupiter and Saturn,
and important ones such as the conjunctions may be
entered. These last are not absolutely necessary and may
be omitted if you wish; however, they are helpful, even
though the information for timing is included in the
solar and lunar information.

None of this is difficult once you have worked out
your timetable, and you will be far more successful if
you pay attention to timing.

As mentioned previously, I feel that sprouts grow better and are far healthier when they receive light. However,
the direct light of the Sun is very strong and powerful;
I have greater success with indirect sunlight. I live in a
climate which does not have very many cold days even in
winter. If you live farther north, you may find direct
winter sunlight to be just right.

A Word About Seeds

To sprout well, seeds must be fresh and viable. They
should be untreated with chemicals. Such seeds are
carried by most health-food stores or they may be purchased mail-order from one of the large natural-food
sources. Having bought good seeds, store them carefully.
Keep them dry in air-tight jars and many of them will
retain their viability for a long time.

How Will You Use Your Sprouts?

Just about the most simple way to use your sprouts, and the one that comes first to mind, is using them in salads, an addition particularly welcome at a time of year when fresh salad ingredients are a bit scarce.

But, delicious as sprouts are in salads, you may find your family will soon tire of them if they are used too often in this way. They may be incorporated so well and so easily into other foods that there is no need to serve them always the same way. They can become a real asset to your most creative cooking.

Mung beans, for instance, can be combined with meat and other vegetables in chowders, in sea-food dishes and in delicious omelets. They add a different texture and taste to rice dishes and are fine to combine with other foods for stuffings. They are good even in baked foods such as biscuits.

Sprouted lentils are so delectable and crisp when eaten raw that they add wonderfully to the pleasure of eating sandwiches. Cooked with tomatoes or in an egg-plant dish, they lend a sweet and nutty flavor. However, they really come into their own when cooked with onions, herbs and a bit of meat and made into soup. Or roll them into a meat loaf for a different taste and texture. If you have access to mushrooms, these also combine well with lentil sprouts.

Soybeans, which contain up to forty percent protein and are full of vitamin B, will stretch the nutritional value of any dish which includes them. The green edible bushy soybean is an ambitious sprouter. Try roasting and grinding some of the sprouts and use them as a substitute for peanut butter in cupcakes, cookies or muffins.

Alfalfa is not just forage for cattle. It is thirty-five percent protein and when sprouted contains vitamins D, E, K and C as well as such minerals as phosphorus, iron and silicon. You can add a lot of nourishment to breads, cakes and even cheese. Dried sprouts (which have been placed in a 300-degree oven for about forty-five minutes) may be used in many recipes calling for nuts. Alfalfa is a blood-builder, and is also good for teeth and bones. It is a splendid milk-producer for nursing mothers.

Wheat is one of our most important crops—a valuable source of vitamins, nicotinic acid, B_6, pantothenic acid and E. Containing little fat, it is a good source of protein. Wheat sprouts are sweet and crunchy. They may be used as toppings for fruit pies or, dried and ground, incorporated into cake or cookie batters.

Triticale is a plant we are just beginning to discover the wonders of; when sprouted, it doubles in protein. It is an exciting new seed to add to our list of "sprouters" and is a natural additive to such breakfast fare as muffins, breads and waffles. Treat it as you would wheat, grinding, blending or drying before adding to other ingredients.

Radishes are one of the quickest and easiest seeds to sprout in the garden, yet it does not occur to many that they may also be used as "sprouting material" indoors. Radish sprouts give a tangy, peppery flavor to salads and other foods; they are especially good in sandwiches. Containing vitamins B_1 and C, they are good for teeth, gums, nerves, hair and nails.

Mustard seeds should not be left out just because they are so tiny. There's a lot of strength there as well as flavor, for the mustard seed, when sprouted, is strong and spicy. Treat it with respect; it is an excellent tonic, being a good source of vitamin A. Used a bit sparingly with other greens, it will add a lot of character.

Barley has its own special properties, being one of our best body-builders. It has long been considered a remedy for ailments of kidneys and bladder; it is blood-cooling and tonic and contains the vitamins B_1 and B_2. Try sprouting some occasionally for a special taste treat.

The sunflower, that sun-worshiping plant, produces one of our very best sprouts, containing as they do the vitamins B_1, A, D and F. Sunflower sprouts are good body-building food and are helpful in countering weak eyes, arthritis and other problems such as tooth decay and dryness of the skin.

Corn. The list of seeds that can be sprouted could go on and on, almost endlessly, but I'm going to stop with corn, that great vegetable which we have from the American Indian. Corn is highly nutritious, containing the vitamins B_1, C, A and B_2, in that order of importance. It is one of the great body-builders and makes an excellent addition in the form of sprouts to many everyday dishes, adding both flavor and nutritional value.

If you would like detailed recipes for sprouts, there is an excellent book, *The Sprouter's Cookbook For Fast Kitchen Crops*, by Marjorie Page Blanchard. It is published by Garden Way Publishing Company, Charlotte, Vermont 05445.

Herbs for Health

Vicki Zastrow

Herbal healing predates recorded history. Its methods, handed down from generation to generation, were the basics for the witch lore of the past, and they supplied, as well, the first medical advances in the treatment of most human disease.

In a modern society with countless synthetic drugs, the question may be asked: Why use herbs? After witnessing the side effects of medicines artificially prepared, people today are turning again to the valuable remedial properties of herbs and fruit and vegetable juices. Nature's cures are the herbs and their seeds that have grown naturally for centuries all over the earth. For every disease that afflicts man there is a natural remedy—an herb.

Unnecessary advertising in our society has turned people's heads toward the quick acting pain relieving drugs of science that eliminate the body's symptoms and warning signals, but do not eradicate the cause of the disease. Herbs are food for the human body and mind. They contain the vitamins and minerals necessary to the balance of the body's systems, as do the other natural foods we eat (vegetables, fruits, grains, etc.)

The purpose of a remedy is to help the body cure itself. When certain organic minerals and vitamins necessary for balance are lacking in our diet, disease results. Therefore, the body must be supplied with the essential elements it needs to rebuild the areas weakened or damaged by disease.

Natural herbs have an advantage over modern drugs. As they are grown, herbs contain an organic combination of substances in the proportions needed by the human body. In their natural form the body can easily convert them into healing remedies. Further, because of these elements, herbs can be used effectively as an aid to the body in preventing as well as healing disease.

How to Prepare Herbal Remedies

Infusions are made as is regular tea, by pouring 1 pint boiling water over ½ ounce of herb flowers or leaves and steeping for a few minutes. Honey is sometimes added for sweetening.

Decoctions are made of the hard parts of the herb—the stems, roots, bark, seeds—and they have to boil for some time to extract their full value.

To make a **fomentation** dip a cloth or heavy towel into a decoction or an infusion. Wring out the extra moisture and apply externally to the affected area.

For **salves**, take 8 parts vaseline or lard to 2 parts herbal, stir, and mix well while hot. Use when cool.

To make a **poultice**, put the herbs loosely in a flannel bag large enough to cover the area. Pour boiling water over the bag and then wring out the extra moisture inside a towel. Use the poultice as hot as possible. It is good for nerve pains, painful joints and muscles, and promotes restful sleep when applied to the abdomen.

Listed here are some common complaints and the herbal remedies used for them all over the world.

Backache

Exercise is important: lie on floor on back with legs up—cycle! Teas of nettle, rosinweed.

Bites, insect

Apply eucalyptus oil, thyme oil or distilled witch hazel extract.

Boils and Blisters

Poultice of lobelia and slippery elm; hops; skunk cabbage; solomon's seal; for blisters use onion juice plus salt.

Burns

Poultice of comfrey; mustard; yarrow (excellent). Particularly good salves are made from elderberry blossom, golden seal, or red clover. You may also use wheat germ oil.

Colds

Teas of balsam; catnip (plus hot foot bath); elderberry and peppermint; golden seal; mullein; rosemary; sarsaparilla. A hot foot bath for 20 minutes plus epsom salts. For quick recovery take 2t. honey and 2t. cider vinegar in a glass of water; or eat raw or cooked onions.

Constipation

Teas of blue flag and cascara sagrada are the best known remedies; also red clover.

Corns

Tie lemon slices over the corn overnight. Apply thuja fluid extract morning and night; or tie a cloth soaked in turpentine around them overnight.

Dandruff

After your hair is rinsed massage well into the scalp: oils of rosemary and eucalyptus; a tea made of willow leaves and bark. A very successful remedy is a tea made of 1 oz. rosemary steeped in a pint of boiling water. (Be sure to let the water cool before you use it!)

Diarrhea

Raw apples and bananas (children also); teas of crowfoot (best); peppermint; red raspberry; slippery elm (most useful).

Eczema
Make an ointment of apple cider vinegar or boric acid instead of soap and water. Internally, you can take lecithin daily, or spikenard, valerian, plantain.

Eyes, black or sore
Use arnica in water if the skin isn't broken, or witch hazel in water if it is broken. A poultice made of scraped raw potato is also effective.

Fevers
Teas of chamomile (most effective); sweet cicely; yarrow (said to relieve fever in 24 hours if taken every 30 minutes); catnip; elderberry; peppermint and honey. Also sponge patient with common baking soda water. Spearmint tea for children.

Frostbite
Paint the area with Friar's Balsam and rub olive oil gently onto same place after a few minutes.

Gums, tender
Try a mixture of orris root, myrrh, and borax.

Headache
Most important is to lie down and rest where there is quiet and fresh air. Also: hot teas of peppermint (most popular); catnip; spearmint; chamomile; a very hot foot bath for 5—10 minutes with 1T. mustard; hot water with lemon juice; onion plus honey.

Hiccoughs
Most popular and effective are: the juice of half an orange; swallowing very hot or very cold water; sipping peppermint tea; pineapple juice; a very hot foot bath; a mouthful of cold water taken, held in mouth, the middle fingers of each hand placed in both ears, the water swallowed, and the fingers removed after a moment.

Insomnia
Teas of chamomile; catnip; hops (or pillow stuffed with under head); lady's slipper (highly recommended); eating raw onions; a very hot foot bath before bed; rose leaves with mint heated as compress.

Irritations, skin
Take citrus fruits; teas of balsam root; yarrow or red clover blossoms and chickweed internally.

Pains, Menstrual
Teas of pennyroyal (best); black cohosh (depressed feelings); chamomile; catnip; sweet cicely.

Sores, Cuts, Wounds
Poultice of grated raw carrot; comfrey; dandelion; juniper; red clover; sweet cicely; skunk cabbage; yarrow and yerba mansa (best); cod-liver oil (stops infection); elderberry blossom salve; and grindelia decoction.

Stomach ache
A glass of milk taken 2 hours after each meal; for gas—caraway and sweet cicely teas; teas of sage (most useful); golden seal; chamomile; marigold leaves (highly recommended); mint; peppermint; slippery elm; valerian; yarrow; and dandelion.

Sunburn
Make an ointment of glycerine, witch hazel, and sunflower seed oil.

Sunstroke
Put your feet in a hot mustard foot bath and apply hot or cold cloths to the forehead and back of neck.

Swellings, Sprains
Poultices of chamomile and hops; caraway and hyssop (black and blue marks); juniper; mullein plus pennyroyal;

sweet cicely; skunk cabbage; solomon's seal; yarrow; yerba mansa. You may also use a comfrey fomentation.

Toothache

The most liked remedy is the poultice: juniper; willow; and hops plus coarse salt. Herbs directly put into a cavity are: yarrow; raw cow parsnip; grindelia; sweet cicely (pain reducer). Chewed herbs are: tobacco (best); yarrow; yerba mansa; blue flag. Hops tea is given for baby teething.

Travel sickness

Sips of a cup of hot water every ten or fifteen minutes help; take only a light meal before starting a trip; ingest lemon juice plus salt every few minutes at the first signs of illness.

Varicose veins

Lie on your back and elevate your legs to relieve the pressure. Try bathing your legs with white oak bark. Sea salt baths are also effective. Overnight, apply cloths soaked in distilled witch hazel extract and cover with a dry towel until morning. Stroke your legs upward toward your hips whenever possible. Teas made of golden seal, myrrh, tansy or bran, taken internally, help strengthen the veins.

Care of the Hair
Baldness

Try massaging oils of clove and eucalyptus into your scalp; or, after washing, rinse your hair with marsh mallow tea. You might also drink sarsaparilla tea and eat more wheat germ, carrots, apples, bananas, tomatoes, strawberries, lettuce, cantaloupe and dried peas.

Grey hair

To darken, use a rinse made from a handful of stinging nettle boiled in a quart of water; or use an ounce of chamomile or sage boiled in a quart of water for twenty minutes.

Growth

To encourage growth ingest wheat germ, cod-liver oil or lecithin daily.

Texture

To brighten and improve the texture of your hair, use rinses of plantain and shepherd's purse; any mixture of peppergrass; marsh mallow; mullein; nettle; sage or burdock. Chamomile rinses are good for blondes.

Beauty Treatments for Skin
Aging

Apply leaves and roots of comfrey.

Dry

The oldest known moisturizers are glycerine and honey; next to these are lecithin, lanolin, natural menthol, and oils of quince, avocado, apricot kernal, almond, sesame and wheat germ.

To soften your complexion, smooth mashed papaya on your face and rest with your feet up, then rinse.

Bath oils: Hang a bag of meadow sweet, or a bag of rosemary, lavender, or comfrey in the bath. Or combine a pint of vegetable oil, a small amount of liquid shampoo and a few drops of perfume and add 2T. to your bath.

Dry hands

You can make a good hand lotion of glycerine and benzoin; or ½ oz. each of glycerine and rosewater and ¼ oz. of witch hazel, mixed and shaken well. If your hands are chapped after having been in water, rub dampened table salt on them and rinse.

Oily

Make an astringent of honey and glycerine; cucumber slices on the face daily; or witch hazel on a cloth over the eyes and rest for 15 minutes.

Texture

The skin is one of the ways the body breathes, so try a cold friction bath in the morning to open the pores and improve skin texture. Wet your hands and body and slap yourself for a few moments. Dry yourself well and massage your skin tenderly with almond oil until it's all absorbed.

Wrinkles

Make a lotion of benzoin, glycerine and honey plus a few drops of cologne. Or try warm olive oil massaged into the forehead. Barley water plus a few drops of balm of gilead also works.

Other Beauty Aids
Breath

Improve your breath by chewing anise seed, orris root, angelica root, cardamon seed or nutmeg; or by drinking chamomile tea.

Eyes

For dark circles and faded eyes, try eating more blueberries, tomatoes, avocados, eggplant, and sunflower seeds.

Teeth

To whiten teeth, an old English recipe suggests a mixture of honey and vegetable charcoal.

HEALING HERBS

Sports and Recreation

Moon Tables
and
Recreation

Everyone is affected by their lunar cycle, as described in the Moon Tables section of the *Moon Sign Book*. Your lunar high occurs when the Moon is in your Sun Sign, and your lunar low occurs when the Moon is in the sign opposite your Sun Sign. The handy *Favorable and Unfavorable Dates* tables in the Astrological Encyclopedia section give the lunar highs and lows for each Sun Sign every day of the year.

This lunar cycle influences all your activities: your physical strength, mental alterness, and manual dexterity are all affected. Bowling scores, for example, have been found to be significantly higher when bowlers were at their lunar cycle highs than when they were at their lows.

Astrological Rulership

By combining the *Favorable and Unfavorable Dates* tables and the "Lunar Aspectarian" tables with the information given below in the list of astrological rulerships of leisure-time activities, you can choose the best time for a variety of activities.

The best time to perform an activity is when its ruling planet is in favorable aspect to the Moon or when the Moon is in its ruling sign—that is, when its ruling planet is trine, sextile, or conjunct the Moon, marked with a T, Sx, or C, in the "Lunar Aspectarian," or when its ruling sign is marked *Favorable* in the *Favorable and Unfavorable Dates* tables.

For example, go bicycling when Uranus or Mercury are marked with a T, Sx, or C, or when Gemini is marked with an *F*. Ice skating is enjoyed more when Neptune is trine, sextile, or conjunct the Moon, and films are more rewarding when Neptune or Uranus is marked T, Sx, or C or when Leo or Aquarius is marked *F*.

ARTS

Acting, actors Neptune, Pisces, Sun, Leo
Art in General Venus, Libra
  Art dealers, stores Taurus, Venus
  Art museums Venus
Ballet Neptune, Venus
Ceramics Saturn
Craftsmen Mercury
Dancing, dancers Venus, Taurus, Neptune, Pisces
Drama Venus, Neptune
Embroidery, embroiderers Venus
Etchings Mars
Films, filmmaking Neptune, Leo, Uranus, Aquarius
Handicrafts Venus
Literature, literary ability Mercury, Gemini
Music, musicians Venus, Libra, Taurus, Neptune
Paintings, painters Venus, Libra
Photography, photographers Neptune, Pisces, Uranus, Aquarius
Printing, printers Mercury, Gemini
Symphonies Venus
Theaters Sun, Leo, Venus

HUNTING AND PETS

Animals in general Mercury, Jupiter, Virgo, Pisces
  Game animals Sagittarius
  Animal training, trainers Mercury, Virgo

Cats   Leo, Sun, Virgo, Venus
Dogs   Mercury, Virgo
Firearms   Uranus, Mars
Fishing, fish   Neptune, Pisces, Moon, Cancer
  Pet birds   Mercury, Venus
  Birds of prey   Mars
  Game birds   Uranus, Sagittarius
Horses, trainers, riders   Jupiter, Sagittarius
Hunting, hunters
  Hunters   Jupiter, Sagittarius
  Hunting grounds   Libra
  Game preserves   Aries, Leo

SPORTS

Archery, archers   Jupiter, Sagittarius
Ball games in general   Venus
  Baseball   Mars
  Football   Mars
Bicycling, bicyclists   Uranus, Mercury, Gemini
Boxing matches, boxers   Mars
Bullfights   Mars
Calisthenics   Mars, Neptune
Deep-sea diving, divers   Neptune, Pisces
Horseracing   Jupiter, Sagittarius
Jogging   Mercury, Gemini
Polo   Uranus, Jupiter, Venus, Saturn
Racing   (other than horse)   Sun, Uranus
Running, runners   Mercury, Gemini
Shooting, shooters   Mars
Skating, skaters
  Ice skating   Neptune
  Roller skating   Mercury
Sports, sporting events in general   Sun, Leo
  Competitive sports in general   Mars
  Sporting equipment   Jupiter, Sagittarius
  Sports organizations   Jupiter, Mars

Swimming, swimmers   Neptune, Pisces, Moon, Cancer
Tennis, courts, players   Mercury, Venus, Uranus, Mars
Wrestling, wrestlers   Mars

TRAVEL
Air travel, airplanes   Mercury, Sagittarius, Uranus
Automobile travel, automobiles   Mercury, Gemini
Boating, boats   Moon, Cancer, Neptune
Camping, campers   Leo
Exploration, explorers   Uranus, Aquarius, Jupiter,
   Sagittarius
Helicopters   Uranus
Highways   Uranus, Gemini
Hotels   Cancer, Venus
Motorcycle travel, motorcycles   Uranus, Aquarius
Parks, playgrounds   Sun, Leo
Picnics   Venus, Leo
Restaurants   Moon, Cancer, Virgo, Jupiter
Rail travel, railroads   Uranus, Mercury, Gemini
Travelers in general   Mercury, Gemini
   Long journeys   Jupiter, Sagittarius
   Short journeys   Mercury, Gemini
Vacations, holidays   Venus, Neptune
Yachting, yachts   Neptune, Moon

OTHER ENTERTAINMENTS
Acrobatics, acrobats   Mars, Aries
Amusements in general   Venus, Leo
Autographs   Mercury
Barbeques   Moon, Mars
Casinos   Venus, Sun, Jupiter
Chess   Mercury, Mars
Circuses   Sun, Leo, Venus
Collections, collectors   Moon, Cancer
Festivals   Venus
Gambling   Sun, Leo, Jupiter

Gardening, gardens   Capricorn, Saturn, Cancer, Venus
   Virgo
Parades   Jupiter, Venus
Parties   Venus, Leo
Receptions   Venus
Showboats   Leo, Sun
Social clubs   Venus, Leo
Sunbathing   Sun
Taverns   Moon, Cancer

Hunting and Fishing

It is possible in some hunting activities to be more specific as to correct astrological timing. A combination of folklore, tradition, and astrological research has resulted in the following rules:

Hunting Birds by Trap or Dogs: Moon in Gemini, Libra, or Aquarius, and trine, sextile, or conjunct Mercury and Venus, and not square or opposite Saturn or Mars.

Hunting Birds by Gun or Hawk: Moon in Aries, not square or opposite Mars.

Fishing: See the following *Best Fishing and Hunting Dates* tables and when the Moon is not square or opposite Saturn or Mars.

Teaching Dogs to Hunt: Begin with Moon in Aquarius, and trine, sextile, or conjunct Mars and Jupiter.

Buying Falcons and Hawks: Moon in Gemini, Libra or Aquarius.

Teaching Hawks and Falcons: Begin with Moon in Aquarius, and trine, sextile, or conjunct Mars.

Buying Pigeons: Moon trine, sextile, or conjunct Venus.

Flying Pigeons: Moon trine, sextile, or conjunct Jupiter or Venus, and not square or opposite Mars or Saturn.

Training Dogs or Taming Small Animals: Moon increasing (First or Second Quarter) and trine, sextile, or conjunct Jupiter or Venus.

Best Hunting and Fishing Dates
Central Standard Time

Dates		Moon's Sign	Moon's Phase
Jan 4, 1:10 am	—	Cancer	2nd and 3rd quarters
Jan 5, 6:51 am		Cancer	Full Moon
Jan 13, 2:47 am	—	Scorpio	4th quarter
Jan 15, 3:39 am		Scorpio	
Jan 21, 1:42 pm	—	Pisces	1st quarter
Jan 23, 9:27 pm		Pisces	
Jan 31, 9:18 am	—	Cancer	2nd quarter
Feb 2, 6:23 pm		Cancer	
Feb 3, 10:35 pm		Leo	Full Moon
Feb 9, 9:03 am	—	Scorpio	3rd and 4th quarters
Feb 11, 11:45 am		Scorpio	
Feb 17, 10:52 pm	—	Pisces	1st quarter
Feb 20, 6:35 am		Pisces	
Feb 27, 5:59 pm	—	Cancer	2nd quarter
March 2, 3:23 am		Cancer	
March 5, 11:33 am		Virgo	Full Moon
March 8, 2:46 pm	—	Scorpio	3rd quarter
March 10, 4:48 pm		Scorpio	
March 17, 6:23 am	—	Pisces	4th and 1st quarters
March 19, 2:42 pm		Pisces	
March 27, 2:00 am	—	Cancer	1st and 2nd quarters
March 29, 12:43 pm		Cancer	
April 3, 10:19 pm		Libra	Full Moon
April 4, 11:26 pm	—	Scorpio	3rd quarter
April 7, 0:20 am		Scorpio	
April 13, 12:25 pm	—	Pisces	4th quarter
April 15, 9:33 pm		Pisces	

Dates		Moon's Sign	Moon's Phase
April 23, 9:26 am	April 25, 8:59 pm	Cancer	1st quarter
May 2, 10:00 am	May 4, 9:46 am	Scorpio	2nd and 3rd quarters
May 3, 6:49 am		Scorpio	Full Moon
May 10, 5:48 pm	May 13, 3:06 am	Pisces	4th quarter
May 20, 3:29 pm	May 23, 3:16 am	Cancer	1st quarter
May 29, 8:36 pm	May 31, 8:32 pm	Scorpio	2nd quarter
June 1, 2:15 pm		Sagittarius	Full Moon
June 7, 0:53 am	June 9, 8:55 am	Pisces	3rd and 4th quarters
June 16, 9:32 am	June 19, 8:57 am	Cancer	1st quarter
June 26, 5:40 am	June 28, 7:07 am	Scorpio	2nd quarter
June 30, 9:33 pm		Capricorn	Full Moon
July 4, 9:53 am	July 6, 4:19 pm	Pisces	3rd quarter
July 14, 4:00 am	July 16, 2:55 pm	Cancer	4th and 1st quarters
July 23, 12:18 pm	July 25, 3:07 pm	Scorpio	1st and 2nd quarters
July 30, 5:32 am		Aquarius	Full Moon
July 31, 7:53 pm	Aug 3, 1:04 am	Pisces	3rd quarter
Aug 10, 11:15 am	Aug 12, 10:15 pm	Cancer	4th quarter
Aug 19, 5:25 pm	Aug 21, 8:46 pm	Scorpio	1st quarter
Aug 28, 5:20 am	Aug 30, 10:35 am	Pisces	2nd and 3rd quarters
Aug 28, 2:52 pm		Pisces	Full Moon

Dates		Moon's Sign	Moon's Phase
Sept 6, 7:08 pm	—		
Sept 15, 11:43 am			
Sept 24, 12:52 pm			
Sept 27, 2:53 am			
	Sept 9, 6:35 am	Cancer	4th quarter
	Sept 18, 2:11 am	Scorpio	1st quarter
	Sept 26, 7:01 pm	Pisces	2nd quarter
		Aries	Full Moon
Oct 4, 2:58 am	—		
Oct 13, 8:09 am			
Oct 21, 6:43 pm			
Oct 26, 5:43 am			
Oct 31, 10:19 am	—		
	Oct 6, 3:07 pm	Cancer	3rd and 4th quarters
	Oct 15, 9:36 am	Scorpio	1st quarter
	Oct 24, 1:41 am	Pisces	2nd quarter
		Taurus	Full Moon
		Cancer	3rd quarter
Nov 9, 6:38 pm	—		
Nov 18, 0:10 am			
Nov 25, 11:37 am			
Nov 27, 5:05 pm	—		
	Nov 2, 11:12 pm	Cancer	4th and 1st quarters
	Nov 11, 7:16 pm	Scorpio	2nd quarter
	Nov 20, 7:32 am	Pisces	Full Moon
	Nov 30, 5:37 am	Gemini	3rd quarter
Dec 7, 5:29 am	—		
Dec 15, 7:55 am			
Dec 24, 11:33 pm			
Dec 26, 7:13 am			
	Dec 9, 6:10 am	Cancer	4th quarter
	Dec 17, 1:40 pm	Scorpio	1st and 2nd quarters
	Dec 27, 11:51 am	Pisces	2nd and 3rd quarters
		Cancer	Full Moon

BUILD A TAPE LIBRARY

*Learn more easily
through the personal touch
of the human voice.*

Color Magic
by Helen Peterson
Use color as a psychic focus for healing, protection, transmutation of negative energies, love or strength. Color correspondences are discussed, as well as invocations of the guardians of the seven rays.
No. 923   **$6.95**

**ESP Induction Through
Forms of Self-Hypnosis,
I & II**
By Richard Miller
Based on five years of research at the University of California; includes definition and examples of hypnosis, psionic fields and PSI energy formation.
No. 981   2 tapes, $6.95 ea.

**The Coming Great
Purification**
by Brad Steiger
How to prepare for the Great Cleansing which all the ancient prophecies declare is at hand.
No. 918   **$6.95**

**Reincarnation, Karma
and Astrology**
by Roy Eugene Davis
The "Cycle of Necessity" explained; how to neutralize karmic patterns; our place in the cosmic scheme.
No. 922   **$6.95**

The Aquarian Dispensation
by Marcia Moore
The significance of astrology in the Age of Aquarius, including an exploration of ways in which a reconciliation between faith and reason can be accomplished through the development of a purified form of astrology.
No. 944   **$6.95**

**Working the 31st Path
Working the 32nd Path**
by Carl L. Weschcke
Instructions, relaxation help, and guidance through the Paths, based on the Aurum Solis technique as given in *The Magical Philosophy*. Voice: Carl L. Weschcke, O.S.V.
No. 900   **$6.95**

*All tapes are prefix No. 3-87542. Use prefix and
suffix when ordering from Gnostic-Aquarian Booksales. See order form on last page.*

Picking Winners

Marylee Satren

Forecasting the winners of sporting events has long held fascination for astrologers, psychics, and the general public. Many schemes have been proposed, some based on numerology, others based on the ouija board, dream analysis, and astrology, all with varying results. Among the most successful forecasters: Llewellyn George, who consistently chose the correct winner of the Rose Bowl Game, and Sydney Omarr, who as a young astrologer in Philadelphia picked 25 fights in a row correctly.

Though we make no claims or guarantees for any predictive method, we give here three of the most popular astrological methods of choosing the winner of competitions.

One note, however—certain types of competitions seem immune to ordinary methods of prediction. These are contests where preparation rather than luck decides the outcome. These include information quizzes, certain card games, and chess games.

The Lunar Cycle Method

This method, first developed by Carl Payne Toby, works best when several opponents are competing as individuals, as in foot races, boxing matches, swimming meets, tennis games, and so forth.

It is based on the principle that when the transiting

Moon is in a person's Sun Sign he is at the height of his lunar cycle and his judgment, dexterity, and strength are at their highest. When the Moon is in the opposite sign from his natal Sun, he is at his lunar-cycle low. It is therefore likely that a person at the peak of his lunar cycle will do better than an otherwise equal opponent at his lunar-cycle low.

So, with the knowledge of the competitor's Sun Sign (taken from his birth date), and the position of the Moon at the time of the event (available from the **Moon Tables** in the *Moon Sign Book*) we can predict a likely winner.

The Astrological Hunch Method

This method consists of equal parts astrological symbolism, sympathetic magic, and intuition. It is best suited to horse racing and has been perfected by Sydney Omarr, as explained in detail in Jess Stearn's *A Time for Astrology*.

It is first necessary to know the Moon's Sign (see the **Moon Tables**) and the Ascendant. This is easily calculated if the time of sunrise is known. At dawn the Rising Sign is the same as the Sun's Sign, and it advances one sign every two hours.

If, for example, a race takes place at noon on March 14, the Moon will be in Aries, the Sun in Pisces, and the Ascendant in Gemini. (The Ascendant is in Pisces at dawn, around 6 am, changes to Aries at 8 am, to Taurus at 10 am, and enters Gemini at noon.) We would then study the racing form for names of horses and jockeys that tie in with the Aries Moon and Gemini Ascendant. Examples might be horses named Man o' War (Aries rules war) or Secretariat (Gemini rules clerical work), or jockeys named Grant (a famous soldier) or Castor (one of the Gemini twins).

Here follows a general list of the types of names ruled by the planets:

The Sun (ruler of Leo): short names; names derived from nature or royalty.

The Moon (ruler of Cancer): family names of the rural variety, suggesting simplicity, domesticity, or collectivism.

Mercury (ruler of Gemini and Virgo): common, conventional names.

Venus (ruler of Taurus and Libra): long names; names that are euphonious and musical, or ornate names pleasant to the ears or suggestive of glamor.

Mars (ruler of Aries): short names; names that are concise, blunt, militant; names that are popular among fiction writers as typical names of heroes.

Jupiter (ruler of Sagittarius): short names; royal or biblical names.

Saturn (ruler of Capricorn): long names; names suggestive of dignity, tradition, or history.

Uranus (ruler of Aquarius): unusual, startling names, either ultramodern or archaic.

Neptune (ruler of Pisces): names which lend a note of mystery to the imagination.

Pluto (ruler of Scorpio): names associated with the underworld or politics.

Horary Astrology Method

This is the traditional Horary Astrology method of contest analysis, as described by Llewellyn George ir. *The A to Z Horoscope Maker and Delineator,* somewhat simplified for our *Moon Sign Book* readers. It involves the basic astrological skills—the ability to draw up charts, knowledge of the essential natures of the signs, planets, and houses.

Basically, a chart is erected for the time and place of the competition to be analyzed: post time at the races, kick-off at the stadium, the beginning of the first round of the match, etc. The chart is then interpreted according to the rules of contest analysis.

In this explanation we refer to the "home team" as the team playing in its own stadium, the champion, or title defender. The "visiting team" refers to the opponent, the challenger, the "away team." Thus, the twelve houses are allotted as follows:

The First House or Ascendant: the home team.
The Seventh House or Descendant: the visiting team.

These are the teams' own houses.

The Second House: the home team's fans and odds.
The Eighth House: the visiting team's fans and odds.

These houses show the support and assets (traditional Second-House rulership—the Eighth House being the second from the visiting team's own house) of the teams and the box office intake which in some instances determines the odds.

The Third House: the home team's coach or captain.
The Ninth House: the visiting team's coach or captain.

These houses indicate the person through whom the progress of the event is directed by means of pep talks, messages, and signals (traditional Third-House rulership).

The Fourth House: the visiting team's score.
The Tenth House: the home team's score.

The Tenth House naturally indicates scoring, inasmuch as points are credits and honors, while the ultimate score mirrors the comparative achievement. (The Fourth House is the tenth from the visiting team's own house.)

The Fifth House: the home team's game.
The Eleventh House: the visiting team's game.

These houses show the actual operations, the performance of the teams in action, and the morale or fitness of the players. (The Fifth House traditionally rules sporting events and contests; the Eleventh is the fifth from the visiting team's own house.)

The Sixth House: the visiting team's penalties.
The Twelfth House: the home team's penalties.

These houses indicate the obstacles confronting the

teams from the very outset and throughout the event, and so are taken to represent the disadvantages, setbacks, and penalties suffered. A truly clean game has a minimum of Twelfth-House overtones; there are few fouls and errors in such instances. (The Sixth House is the twelfth from the visiting team's own house.)

In addition to the traditional interpretations of the planets—the Sun representing the native; the Moon, public opinion; Mars, physical strength; Jupiter, luck, and so forth—we must analyze the chart for vitality, alertness and the psychological index of the immediate temperament of the contestants, whether they are optimistic or pessimistic. In this manner, the Sun, Moon and Mars represent vitality; Mercury and Uranus represent alertness; and Venus, Jupiter, Saturn, and Neptune represent the psychological index.

The chart is then carefully analyzed for the six important circumstances indicating gain or loss of both teams. The team with the greatest number of favorable indices is slated to win.

The home team will win if:

- The home team's planet is in the Midheaven, unafflicted and direct.
- The Moon applies favorably to the home team or adversely to the visiting team.
- The Moon separates favorably from the visiting team or adversely from the home team.
- The Sun applies favorably to the home team or adversely to the visiting team.
- The Sun separates favorably from the visiting team or adversely from the home team.
- The Fifth House is better and stronger than the Eleventh House.

Conversely, the visiting team will win if:

- The visiting team's planet is in the Midheaven, unafflicted and direct.
- The Moon applies favorably to the visiting team or adversely to the home team.
- The Moon separates favorably from the home team or adversely from the visiting team.
- The Sun applies favorably to the visiting team or adversely to the home team.
- The Sun separates favorably from the home team or adversely to the visiting team.
- The Eleventh House is better and stronger than the Fifth House.

Other Factors

The houses have further significance in that they describe the stages of the game. In football, for example, the first four houses describe the home team's performance and trends during the four successive quarters of the game, while the Seventh through Tenth Houses suggest the circumstances experienced by the visiting team.

Therefore, the four quarters in official football bring the game to the Fifth and Eleventh House cusps, while the nine innings in baseball bring both clubs to the Tenth and Fourth House cusps, etc.

Do not rely too heavily on the importance of the slower-moving planets (Jupiter, Saturn, Uranus, Neptune, and Pluto), especially in connection with periodically recurring events, such as a season's regular schedule. Their house positions will be repeated too often during a season's series. Their aspects involving rapidly moving planets, however—particularly the Moon—are all important.

Annual events, such as holiday games which are played at the same time every year, will have the same planetary rulers with similar house cusps and placement of the Sun and slow-moving planets. Greater weight should be attached to the Moon and transient planets in this case, too.

We wish our readers luck in trying any of the above predictive methods, and would like to hear about the outcome of their predictions.

Ask the Oracle

The Magical

Philosophy

Thousands of persons have been misled: it is a *lie* to say that the West is "materialistic" and that only the East has produced a spiritual science!

East is East and West is West. To some certain degree of truth, the West has its own spiritual destiny, and the East its own. Wisdom and Knowledge are universals, but none of us has a complete vision, and each of us has his own karmic pattern to fulfill—and it is not being fulfilled for Westerners who unquestioningly adopt Eastern methods: retreating from the challenge unique to this land and this moment in time!

Yoga vs. Magick

Many tenets of the Ancient Wisdom are held jointly by the Eastern and Western sages, but some aspects of methodology are specific to each. Yoga (broadly defined as the "way of return") is more suited to the Eastern-born person (although Hatha Yoga must be acknowledged as the most efficient method of physical exercises suitable for the modern urban dweller), while Magick (broadly defined as the "Path of Glory") is more suited to the Western-born person.

The West is not materialistic! Rather, the Western Esoteric Tradition accepts as intrinsic the responsibility of the individual person towards the Natural World, and sees

Man and Nature in a partnership within which Man has certain special evolutionary roles to fulfill on *behalf* of Nature!

Through Magick, Man works with FORM: he works as a transFORMer on the Astral Plane to affect substance. He alters the *inner* form through which the FORCES of Nature manifest themselves.

Western Culture

The Western Tradition, Magick, is consistent with the achievements of Western Culture: the discoveries of science and the training of the rational mind. The Eastern Tradition, Yoga, is consistent with the achievements of Eastern Culture. Both Traditions have their disciplines and training methods—in which there are many similarities, but also many important differences. In both Traditions the trained mind is used to contact and direct currents of energies—but the Western methods work with these currents at the higher Astral level, while the Eastern methods work primarily at the physical level.

Awareness of the Inner Rhythm. Because the Western Initiate is working on the Astral Plane, he is aware—must be aware—of the great tides of energy that ebb and flow in the Natural World. He learns to work in conscious attunement to the rhythms of Nature and Cosmos. For him, the Earth is alive and beloved: it is Church and Bride.

In both Traditions, the psychic centres of the subtle bodies must be awakened, but the Western methods utilize more psychological techniques, while the Eastern methods employ more of a physical "forcing" of the gates, dependent upon the extremes of body purification and physical training.

The World Around

The Western Magical Tradition is based upon knowledge of the "inner circuitry" of the world, and the manipulation of energies by working the switches and altering resistances to effect changes in the physical world. The Eastern Yogic Tradition is based upon a marvelous and intimate knowledge of the body itself, and depends more on changes in the physical world to affect the subtle bodies. It is thus that the great yogis can demonstrate control over the physical body and still ignore the world around them. The accomplished magician would rather reach into the higher dimensions and effect transformations in the world around him than to be able to walk on hot coals or alter his heartbeat at will.

The Planetary Crisis. Western Man, in ignorance of these inner dimensions, has already had great affect upon the physical world about him: bringing the planet to the brink of disaster! And time is running out; changes must be made now, or the point of no return may soon be passed. And it is for this reason that we say that Western Man must work with knowledge of these inner dimensions to reverse the tragic crisis of our times. It is our dharma!

At the same time, the Easterner must work with his special knowledge to restore health to the *social* body, and we must learn from the Eastern Tradition as the Easterner must learn from the Western. But while we may learn from the Eastern Tradition, we must *work* the Western!

The Magical Philosophy

The western Tradition is ancient, but it is also modern and has advanced just as has our science and technology. In THE MAGICAL PHILOSOPHY it is presented as a restatement of the Ancient Wisdom in today's terminology with modern understanding of the techniques involved.

Magick is seen as a system of spiritual growth based upon real knowledge of the psyche itself. It is based on an understanding of the Universe and Man's place therein that restores to the individual personal worth and responsibility and the basis for intelligent cooperation with the Forces of the Natural World.

A Valid Magical Order. THE MAGICAL PHILOSOPHY is a curriculum of study and exercise in a system effective in the development of true magical power and understanding suited to the intellect formed in Western Culture. THE MAGICAL PHILOSOPHY is not a remnant drawn from the archives of a deceased occult order . . . rather it is a living and vital, and complete, study and development program of a valid working Magical Order.

THE MAGICAL PHILOSOPHY series of books—really study manuals—eventually allows the student access to participation with study groups, and opens the opportunity for contact with the initiatory order. Nothing in these books *requires* participation in group programs—in fact, the material presented in these books provides a complete system of individual study as well as all that is necessary to develop and independent magical order.

THREE COMPLETE, AND INDEPENDENT, BOOKS IN *THE MAGICAL PHILOSOPHY* SERIES ARE NOW AVAILABLE.

I. ROBE AND RING: Philosophy of the Magical Art.

The purpose of life in this world, as defined in the language of Western Occultism, is to discover one's True Will and to do it. Those who follow exoteric forms of religion, would say in their corresponding terms, that every individual should find his true vocation and fill it. If God is envisaged as an external Supreme Being who calls (Latin, *vocare*) his summons to mankind, this assessment of the purpose of human life is a valid one; but when Deity is contemplated as the Divine Spark within, and the "call" is understood not as an outward but as an inward motivation, then the true Vocation in turn becomes recognized as the True Will. The pursuit of it, then, is not at all a question of pleasure or of vanity; it is the one supremely serious and sacred task.

The philosophic basis and history of the Western Mystery Tradition is seen as culminating in the emergence of magical principles in modern psychology and the relevance of psychology to modern magick. Through study and practical exercise, the Aspirant gains understanding of the Work of the Mind and development of the Higher Faculties, working always in balance of the inner nature and harmony with Nature and growing awareness of the spiritual energy which underlies the physical universe.

Full 6" x 9", clothbound, illustrated with color plates
Order No. 1-87542-176-8 $10.00

II. THE APPAREL OF HIGH MAGICK: Symbolism in the Magical Art.

The power of ritual to make contact with the hidden levels of the mind is very subtle, yet very simple. No matter how deeply the subconscious mind may be buried beneath inhibitions, rationalizations or, frequently, beneath loads of ephemeral rubbish, one line of communication must remain open: that is, through the sympathetic nervous system, upon which we all depend to look after our digestion and our breathing, and even to keep the heart beating while we sleep.

Symbolism in the *mystical apparel* in which ritual is clothed.

In this volume are presented the basic symbol systems of Western Occultism culminating in the one comprehensive system of the Tree of Life in which all are related into a single whole. Planets and Zodiacal Signs, Mineral, Plant and Animal Kingdoms, Calendar, Mathematics and man-designed Cities and Temples—all are used as vehicles for the projection of human concepts of perfection.

Full 6" x 9", clothbound, illustrated with color plates
Order No. 1-87542-177   *$10.00*

III. THE SWORD AND THE SERPENT—Cosmo-Dynamics

Movement is life; ast least in the world of magical ritual it is so, and shows itself to be so in many modes. The sacred dance proclaims it, from the cosmic rapture of the dedicated dervish or shaman to the intricate spring courtship dance of the Maypole, which likewise had its cosmic dedication. The rhythm of the Ephesian krotalon or of the timbrel proclaims it, urging the steps of Maenads dancing for Cybele or for Dionysus, of *ibaou* dancing for Hathor. With gesture and circumambulation, with vibration of voice and battery and bell, of color and of fragrance, the magician sets in motion the subtle waves of the physical and astral levels within the temple; here too the local has reference to the cosmic, the actions stir up a current which unites within its impulses the related levels of being.

From cover to cover, this book is replete with information on the essential Qabalah, as taught for practical magical use by a long-established but progressive school of the Western Mysteries. The traditional structures and dynamics are fortified with a fresh, valid and vigorous approach, which enriches the presentation of the Correspondences, the Magical Tides, and the vital secrets here set forth for the control of the Astral Light.

6" x 9", clothbound, illustrated with color plates
Order No. 1-87542-178   *$10.00*

Please use Order Form on last page.

Classifieds

Classified Ad Specifications

Classified ads are set in 8-point Univers type with the first two words set in all caps at no extra charge. When placing an ad, be sure to specify the standard heading under which the ad is to be run.

Standard Headings:

ASTROLOGY
BOOKS AND MAGAZINES
GRAPHOLOGY
HEALTH
HERBS
MISCELLANEOUS
MONEY-MAKING

NURSERY STOCK AND SEEDS
OCCULT
OF INTEREST TO WOMEN
PERSONALS
PSYCHIC AND
 PARAPSYCHOLOGY
RELIGIOUS AND SPIRITUAL
WITCHCRAFT

Classified Ad Rates and Terms

$.75 per word; minimum charge, $7.50.
Boxing, $3.00.   Special Bold headline, $2.50.

Every letter or combination of letters and numbers separated by a space is considered a chargeable word. Post office box and number are counted as two words. City, state and zip code are counted as two words. Please count your words carefully.

Payment is required with order except to recognized advertising agencies. 15% agency commission. 2% discount on net for payment in 10 days, net 30. No discounts on classified ads. Checking copies will be sent when the publication is issued.

Classifed Ad Deadline

The closing date for advertising is July 15th, the year preceeding the date of issue. Therefore, all ads for the 1978 *Moon Sign Book* must be received by July 15, 1977. Cancellations must be received in writing before the deadline. For more information, send for a free copy of our rate card.

Astrology

ASTROLOGY CATALOGUE. World's largest book selection, 25¢. ASI, Dept L, 127 Madison Avenue, NYC 10016.

HOROSCOPE: CHART plus 10-page report. Send birth information, $7.00: Michael Wood, 56 South Russell, Boston, Mass. 02104.

ORIENTAL (Zodiac) HOROSCOPE Booklet. Based on Astrology and Astronomy dating back at least 5,000 years. Your year of Birth Horoscope will be found under one of 12 given Animal Signs, also your 3 Lucky Numbers, Best Suited Animal Sign Mate, much more. $1.50 FALCON, Box 331-M, HIALEAH, FLORIDA 33011.

ASTROLOGY AND Numerology. Books and Supplies, Oils, Incense, Charms. Free catalog. 16177 Wisconsin, Detroit, Mich. 48221.

**PERSONAL HORO-
SCOPES**

Natal-life analysis—$30. Year's forecast—$35.00. Marriage comparison—$25.00. Vocational analysis—$15.00. Send birth data—Robert Raymond Shanks, Box 15065, San Diego, California 92115.

ASTROLOGICAL CATALOG—Never before has there been a jam-packed catalog like this. Items such as books, supplies, gifts, crystal balls, pyramid supplies, biomate and biorhythm kits, watches, towels. Do *all* your shopping in one place. For your copy, send name, address and $1.00 to L&S Enterprises, 6 Foley Drive, Framingham, Mass. 01701.

Books & Magazines

"CHROMOTHERAPY" LEARN the occult principles of healing through color. Send $4.00 for *Family Health Protector*, Dinshah P. Ghadiall. Very rare—long out of print. Includes esoteric philosophy, nutrition and more. Free book list of many other works for the seeker of truth. F. J.

Cardamone, 93 Clinton Place, Staten Island, NY 10302.

MYSTIC MIND: book by mystic on soul evolution. Learn truth about yourself. $4.95 (Calif. residents 6% tax) 50¢ postage to: Arkus Publications. 8312 Yorkshire, Anaheim, CA 92804.

WORLD'S MOST outspoken publication, natural health, healing, organic gardening. Free copy. Provoker Press, St. Catharines 142, Ontario, L2R 7C9.

JESUS, BUDDHA, Occult—book catalog. The Metta Company, #115; Box 932; Moorhead, MN 56560.

RARE BOOKFINDER: Vantreuren, 1950 Post, #108-MSB, San Francisco, CA 94115. Send wants.

NATURE'S ANSWER against cancer, heart attack, arthritis, diabetes, cataract. Free Information, Provoker Press, St. Catharines 242, Ontario, L2R 7C9.

OCCULT CATALOG. Leslie, 10359 Livernois, Detroit, MI 48204. Send 25 cents.

MODERN INTRODUCTION To Astrology, $2. "Best Beginning Book," ASI, Dept L, 127 Madison Avenue NYC 10016.

GNOSTICA—America's most respected Occult journal. One year subscription (6 issues), $5.00. *Gnostica,* Box 3383 -MSB, St. Paul, MN 55165.

LUCKY OR NOT?

EVER NOTICE how some people you know have more friends, better jobs, happier marriages or perpetual good health? Certainly you have. But have you wondered why others with the same intelligence fail at one thing or another? Is it good looks, Luck or even Fate? No! It's simply that successful people have developed the Art of Self Mastery. They are in control of their problems and opportunities. To learn more about how to put your problems in perspective and lead the rewarding life you deserve, send for a FREE BOOK, telling how we can help. No obligation. Just write The Mayans, Box 2710, Dept. MS-7, San Antonio, Texas 78299.

Farm & Garden

ORGANIC FERTILIZER, Garden Plants. Perkins Crosslake Garden Center and Nursery, Crosslake, Minnesota 56442. Phone: 218/ 692-3805.

"PET-SNAKE"

Bird-away fruit, vegetable protection device. Thousand organic items. Vita Green, Box 878 MS, Vista, CA 92083.

Graphology

PRIVATE 'I'

In the English-speaking world the capital letter "I", expressing the ego, constitutes the most important letter of the alphabet for graphologists. In her book *You and Your Private 'I'*, Jane N. Green has given the most thorough insight into this uniquely meaningful letter with many well-illustrated case histories and an overview of gestalt graphology. Find out for yourself what your Private "I" reveals. $5.35 postpaid in U.S. from Gnostica Book Store, Dept. MSBC, 213 E. 4th St., St. Paul, MN 55101.

Health

ACUPUNCTURE, BIOFEEDBACK. Herbs. Massage. Yoga, etc. Book catalogue, 25¢ ASI, Dept L, 127 Madison Avenue, NYC 10016.

CURED CANCER, Proof. $25.00 for treatment. Ailene Espinoza, 5033 Dovecote Dr., Nashville, Tenn. 37220.

AT ANY AGE, youthfully smooth skin, the cleanest, clearest ever, using Natura—ancient Egyptian Herbal Earth & Moisturizer. Proven results or return for refund. $10 postpaid. Richard Allan, Box 322-M, Banning, CA 92220.

"LEISURE METAPHYSICAL" exercise for a better, healthier, younger you. Complete, $1.00. Internal Exercise Company, Box 596, Jamestown, NY 14701.

NASAL-CLEAR, Enjoy Prompt Nasal Breathing, Congestion Relief in Head Colds, Allergies, Hay Fever, Sinus, Rhinitas. Also relieves Headache, Neuralgia Pain as well as Snoring. Simply apply NEW Liquified MENTHOL NASAL-CLEAR to Nostrils. Stop taking Harmful Drugs, Pills, Capsules, Drops. Large 2 oz. Bottle, $3.50. FALCON, Box 331-M, HIALEAH, FLORIDA 33011.

Herbs

IF YOU seek Success, Security, and Prestige you should become a Master Herbologist. Now is the time. Write: Emerson College of Herbology, Ltd. 815 Bancroft, Pointe Claire, Quebec, Canada H9R 4L6.

HERBAL APHRODISIAC. African Yohimbe, 100 tablets, $7.95. Smoking Blend, 2 oz., $2.95. Revealing Catalog, $1.00. Herbal Holding Company, Box 5854-MS, Sherman Oaks, CA 91413.

HERBS FOR HEALTH! Korean Ginseng, Fo-ti-seng, Golden Seal, 60 caps, $5.00. Gota Kola, Hawthorn Berries, Comfrey; 60 caps, $3.50. Siberian Ginseng Extract, 2 oz.-45 day supply, $9.95. Catalog, 10¢. GOLDEN GATE HERBS, INC.—MSB, 140 Market Street, San Rafael, CA 94901.

"PET-SNAKE" Bird-away fruit, vegetable protection device. Thousand organic items. Vita Green, Box 878 MS, Vista, CA 92083.

HERBOLOGIST, ASTROLOGER, Psychic Counsellor, Dr. Nicky Marchese, Box 326, Hamilton, Ontario, Canada L8N 3C8.

ZODIAC SALTS (cell salts), set of 12, $7.90 PPD with descriptions. Free Information. Beyer, 3815 Pittsburgh, MS, Chicago, IL 60634.

HEALING HERBS of the Zodiac. Simple guidance to

health problems of the Birth Signs and to the herbs that restore health. Illustrated book *Healing Herbs of the Zodiac* only $1.40 postpaid in U.S. from Gnostica Book Store, Dept MSBC, 213 E. 4th St., St. Paul, MN 55101.

PYRAMID SPROUTERS, iso-tonics, sun teas, cell salts, non-meat menus, other unique, simple aids/info for a health-ier, happier you. Send S.A.S.E. Healthy Self Center, Box 42R, 204 West 20th Street, New York City, 10011.

Misc

"BACKWOODS JOURNAL"—Paradox 7, N.Y. 12858. Un-usual Nature Quarterly—$3.00/Year. Sample 75¢.

"SECRETS OF the Spirit World!" Only 70¢ postpaid. METHODS, Box 1202M, San Carlos, CA 94070.

FREE! OCCULT-WITCH-CRAFT-SPIRITUAL catalog. 100 pages illustrated—jewelry, books, herbs, supplies. 25¢ handling. Treasure House, Box 2506-F, North Hollywood, California 91602.

RARE GENUINE Crystal Balls cut from gem quartz crystal. For brochure write: Ron Bodoh—Gem Cutter, 417 Twelfth Street, Box 36, Men-omonie, WI 54751.

EVERYONE NEEDS help solv-ing problems. Protecting fami-lies' health/safety/property!! 70 exclusive home remedy solutions. Saves time! work!

money! Info. SASE. Hurry!
Specialities, 4252MS Fremont,
Seattle, 98103.

MAGIC TRICKS

Free Trick and Magic Catalog,
50¢. Magic & Fun, Box
1936-AB, NY, NY 10017.

HORSEPLAYERS! STOP
gambling on chance! Use "The
Law of Cycles" by Solastro
and prove as one buyer has
that "it is the most successful
system I have used to date."
Free details from E.M.S.
Latimer, Post Box 396, Rex-
dale, Ontario, Canada.

LUCKY STONE

Inyan Waken-Stone Indians
talked to—Received An-
swers. Instructions. $5—
Check or MO: Rock Lady,
Box 291, Dept M7, Stream-
wood, Illinois 60103.

Money· Making

UNIQUE MAILING Program.
20 Sales Brings $200. Details.
E. Kribbs, Dept. MO, 1320
Delia, Akron, OH 44320.

BE LOVED, Happy, Prosper-

ous! "Success Package," $2.25.
Financial-MB, Rt 1, Box 387-
A, Northport, Alabama 35476.

EXCLUSIVE WORKSHOP
sparetime moneymaker!! Using free waste shipping cartons. Hurry! Plans/sample
product only $5.00. Work-
shop, 4252MS Fremont,
Seattle, WA 98103.

CASH IN ON ASTROLOGY
BOOM. Everyone interested.
Sell our Astrological Calendar,
$2, Moon Sign Book, $2.95,
complete 12 volume Principles
& Practice of Astrology with
Study Guide, $60. Details:
Aquarian Age Book Distribu-
tors, P.O. Box 3383-MSB,
St. Paul, MN 55165.

YOUR BIG OPPORTUNITY!!
Make Workshop pay $5.00/
hour. Using free waste shipping cartons! Exclusive plan/
sample product only $5.00.
Hurry!! Sutton's, 4252-MS
Fremont, Seattle, 98103.

CONTEST MILLIONS! Get
your share! "Winformation"
Subscription, $7.50. Box
21069MB, St. Petersburg,
Florida, 33742.

NOW YOU CAN EARN $300-
$700 MONTHLY while having
the fun of Raising Rabbits and
Other Laboratory Animals for
us. We supply a complete line

of Equipment, Breeders and easy to follow Instructions. Financing Arrangements are possible. For further details send 25¢ to: Laboratory Animals, Inc. MB, County Line Road, Pentwater, Michigan 49449.

Occult

$1.00 PER QUESTION. Send three or more questions, birthdate, hair color, stamped envelope. O. Barrett, 2585 Aqueduct Road, Schenectady, New York 12309.

PYRAMIDOLOGY: For an extensive list of hard to find pyramid-related books and products, send 25¢ to Cheops Pyramid Co., 8143-L Big Bend, St. Louis, MO 63119.

QUEST—a quarterly journal of the Western Magical Tradition mailed direct from Britain. Send $1 for sample copy to Quest, P. O. Box 6567, Charlottesville, VA 22906.

"SEX IS, directly or indirectly, the most powerful weapon in the armoury of the Magician." So said Aleister Crowley. Learn why in *A Manual of Sex Magick,* $5.40 postpaid in U.S. from Gnostica Book Store, Dept. MSBC, 213 E. 4th St., St. Paul, MN 55101.

BIORHYTHM. Not a cheap computer printout. Graphically charted in three colors, information booklet. For personal, 1-year chart send $7.50 and birthdate. BioRhythm Profiles, Dept. MSB, 1541 Queen, Ft. Worth, TX 76103. Satisfaction Guaranteed.

BE A CERTIFIED TAROT MASTER! International Grand Lodge offers private training, secret spreads. Tarot International, Box 32545, Carbondale, IL 62901.

GIFTED SEER (Genesis I:14) prepares your personalized Master Reading, plus effective guidance on THREE QUESTIONS. Penetrating analysis, usable information. Only $5.00 for invaluable counsel. State full names, complete birthdates. Talisman (regularly $5.00) included FREE! Glenn Williams, Box 821, Cape Girardeau, Missouri 63701.

WHAT SCIENCE Knows of the Spiritual World—*The Great Known.* Here is a book with a message for Individuals seeking demonstrated information concerning Life beyond physical death—Spiritual Planes, Occupations and Customs, Spiritual Governments, Spiritual Education, Reincarnation, etc. PBK $3.25 ppd. Information Brochure $.25. School of Natural Science, 25355 Spanish Ranch Road, Los Gatos, CA 95030. The Great School of Natural Science, a tax-exempt organization, admits students of any race, color, national or ethnic origin.

Of Interest to Women

Psychic

An Experiment

Learn the details of an experiment now being conducted by the Planning Group on the Astral Plane directed at nothing less than accelerating human evolution. Received in automatic writing from a Being intimately involved in that Experiment, *The Jupiter Experiment* shows you just how much and in what ways the immortals on the Astral Plane are involved with our life here on earth. *The Jupiter Experiment*, $2.35. Order No. 1-87542-498 from Gnostic-Aquarian Booksales, Box 3383-MSBC, St. Paul, MN 55165.

EARTH CHANGE NEWS, Physical and Spiritual Guidance. Sample Newsletter Free. Future Foundation, Box 26, Steinauer, Nebr. 68441.

"PSYCHIC READER"—
Send 3 questions, birthdate, $10.00. 'ROZE,' 510 Pacesetter Parkway, Riverdale, IL 60627.

TOOL FOR CONSCIOUS EVOLUTION

SPECTRUM SUITE— unique music and color experience that Resonates, Elevates, Attunes your chakras and energy fields. Excellent for Meditation, Relaxation, Yoga—alone or in group. Available from: Spectrum Research Institute, 231 Emerson, Palo Alto, CA 94301 (Dept. LMS). $15 includes stereo LP or cassette, special Color Transparency Wheel, LP alone: $9.95. Quantity discounts available.

PSYCHIC DEVELOPMENT— proven methods work. Magnet, Healing, Kundalini, Astral Projection, Psychic Photography, Mirror, Mantras, etc. You can have ESP powers! Dr. Crawford's complete, illustrated book, *Methods of Psychic Development,* $3.35 postpaid in U.S. from Gnostica Book Store, Dept. MSBC, 213 E. 4th St., St. Paul, MN 55101.

Personals

ESPecially yours: psychometry reading from your signature, $5.00. For problem-discussion, personality-pointers, three questions, add birthdate. 35 years experience. Rev. Mabel Hazell, Box 1005, Dept. M, South San Francisco, CA 94080.

PSORIASIS SUFFERERS: Discouraged? Write for free important information that is helping thousands. PIXACOL, Box 29277-MS, Parma, Ohio 44129.

DATES GALORE! Meet singles anywhere. Call DATE-LINE, toll-free: (800) 451-3245.

BUTTERFLIES: EXTINCT? Save them! Donations: Nonprofit Butterfly Zoo, Box 7306-MB, St. Petersburg, Florida 33734.

SEX ENERGY is the creative energy of all geniuses. There has never been, and never will be, a great leader lacking in the driving force of sex. But sex energy must be transmuted from mere desire into mental and spiritual power through sex magick principles. *A Manual of Sex Magick,* $5.40 postpaid in U.S. from Gnostica Book Store, Dept. MSBC, 213 E. 4th St., St. Paul, MN 55101.

LUCK, LOVE from God's hand for all. Business and prayer for healing. Send $37.50. Henderson, 603 East 71st Street, Chicago, 60619.

INSTANT MEMORY . . . New Way to Remember! No memorization, no word associations, no keywords. Release your Photographic memory instantly. Nothing is forgotten! Discover "controlled" intuition, ESP, confidence, self-mastery. Immediate results! Send for free information. Institute of Advanced Thinking, Box 845-MS2 Via Lapaz, Pacific Palisades, California 90272.

Religious & Spiritual

FREE "New World" Catalogue! Send stamped, addressed envelope: SAGE(L),

Box 938, Humboldt, Saskatchewan, Canada.

BIBLE EXPLAINS ghosts. A. Candle, Box 2325, Lehigh Valley, Penna. 18001.

MAN, KNOW THYSELF

In this New Age, men and women may receive the Ancient Wisdom Teachings that reveal the Way to gain their freedom in the Universal Mind of God. The Holy Order of MANS Discipleship Movement offers a correspondence course in the teachings of the Master Jesus and the great Teachers of mankind, with personal and spiritual guidance by a class master. For further information: Holy Order of MANS Discipleship Movement, P. O. Box 308-M, Cheyenne, Wyoming, 82001.

LEGAL ORDINATION: Established Church + Tax Advantages. Donation, $10.00. Oneness-Aum Temple, Box 20169, St. Petersburg, Florida 33742.

PRAY for everyday needs. Send birthday, picture, $10.50. We will send prayer sheet for your need. Frank Henderson, 603 East 71st Street, Chicago, IL 60619.

TROUBLED, MISFORTUNED, HEXED?

Try the Legendary Powers of the Unknown ... $3.00 Contribution Appreciated. Witch Adonia L, P. O. Box 1119, Gretna, LA 70053. Catalog, $1.50.

The Great Work—This book presents those basic principles underlying individual evolution in accordance with natural and moral law. Nature evolves man/woman and he/she in turn may become an intelligent co-operator, controller and master of natural forces, through "living the life and knowing the law". PBK, $3.25 ppd. Information brochure, $.25. School of Natural Science, 25335 Spanish Ranch Road, Los Gatos, CA 93030. The Great School of Natural Science, a tax-exempt organization, admits students of any race, color, national or ethnic origin.

 Gnostic-Aquarian Booksales
Box 3383-MSB
St. Paul, MN 55165

I have enclosed a check or money order for $ _____.
Please send me the following:

Author	Title	Price

Be sure to include 25 cents plus 15 cents per item postage except on subscriptions and the entire Tyl series. Allow 30 days for delivery. Complaints will be promptly adjusted if addressed to C. T. Blough c/o Llewellyn Publications.

Name _____

Address _____

City, State, Zip _____

Minnesota residents add 4% sales tax.
No cash or C.O.D.'s please.

Llewellyn's
Moon Sign Book
and
Daily Planetary Guide

1977

Standard Book Number: 87542-445-7
Llewellyn Publications, Saint Paul, Minnesota 55165

Copyright © 1976 by Llewellyn Publications
All rights reserved

First Published 1906. 72nd annual edition 1977
Printed in the United States of America